D1096091

Thank you for picking up *Haikyu!!* volume 23! The Rio Summer Olympics started while I was working on the cover illustration for this volume. Lounging around and watching Olympic volleyball with a beer and some edamame was the best. Heck, it would've been the best even without the beer and edamame! Congrats to the Brazil men's team for winning the gold medal!

HARUICHI FURUDATE began his manga career when he was 25 years old with the one-shot *Ousama Kid* (King Kid), which won an honorable mention for the 14th Jump Treasure Newcomer Manga Prize. His first series, *Kiben Gakuha, Yotsuya Sensei no Kaidan* (Philosophy School, Yotsuya Sensei's Ghost Stories), was serialized in Weekly Shonen Jump in 2010. In 2012, he began serializing *Haikyu!!* in Weekly Shonen Jump, where it became his most popular work to date.

HAIKYU!!

VOLUME 23
SHONEN JUMP Manga Edition

Story and Art by
HARUICHI FURUDATE

Translation  ADRIENNE BECK
Touch-Up Art & Lettering ❷ ERIKA TERRIQUEZ
Design ❸ JULIAN [JR] ROBINSON
Editor ❹ MARLENE FIRST

HAIKYU!! © 2012 by Haruichi Furudate
All rights reserved.
First published in Japan in 2012 by SHUEISHA Inc., Tokyo.
English translation rights arranged by SHUEISHA Inc.

Printed in the U.S.A.

Published by VIZ Media, LLC
P.O. Box 77010
San Francisco, CA 94107

10 9 8 7 6 5 4 3 2 1
First printing, May 2018

www.shonenjump.com

www.viz.com

HAIKYU!!

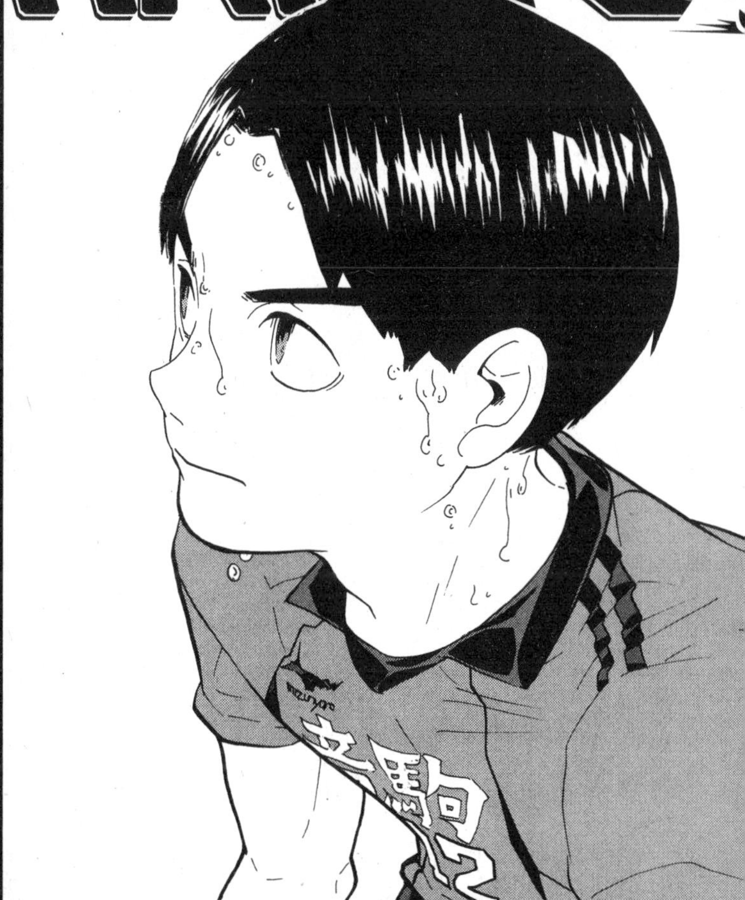

HARUICHI
FURUDATE

THE BALL'S PATH

23

Karasuno High School Volleyball Club

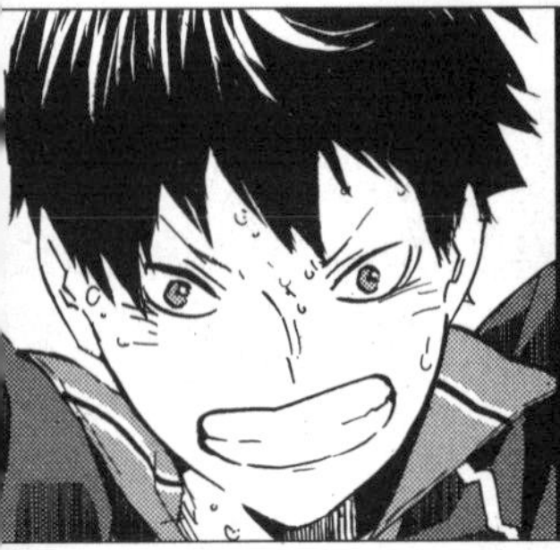

TOBIO KAGEYAMA

1ST YEAR / SETTER

His instincts and athletic talent are so good that he's like a "king" who rules the court. Demanding and egocentric.

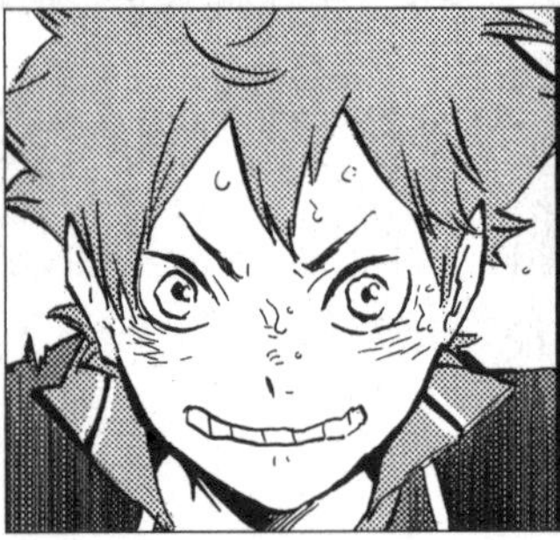

SHOYO HINATA

1ST YEAR / MIDDLE BLOCKER

Even though he doesn't have the best body type for volleyball, he is super athletic. Gets nervous easily.

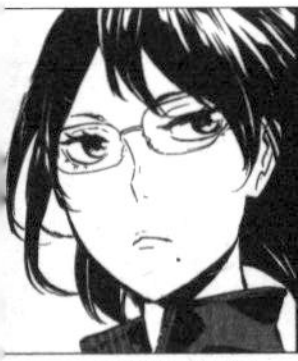

KIYOKO SHIMIZU

3RD YEAR
MANAGER

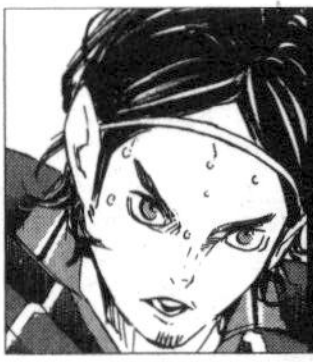

ASAHI AZUMANE

3RD YEAR
WING SPIKER

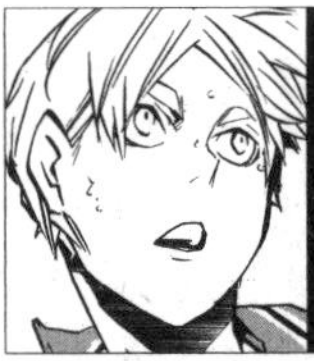

KOUSHI SUGAWARA

3RD YEAR (VICE CAPTAIN)
SETTER

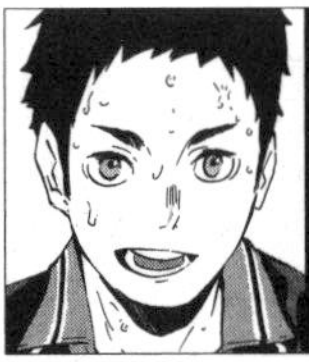

DAICHI SAWAMURA

3RD YEAR (CAPTAIN)
WING SPIKER

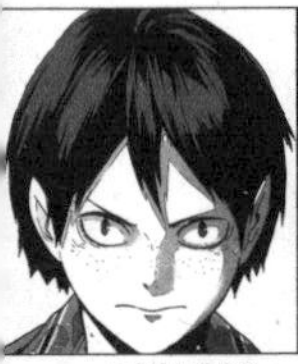

TADASHI YAMAGUCHI

1ST YEAR
MIDDLE BLOCKER

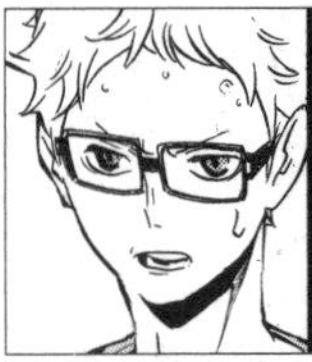

KEI TSUKISHIMA

1ST YEAR
MIDDLE BLOCKER

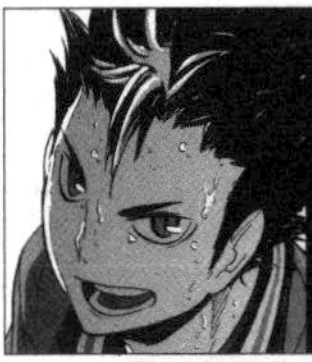

YU NISHINOYA

2ND YEAR
LIBERO

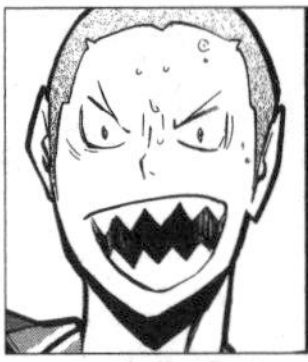

RYUNOSUKE TANAKA

2ND YEAR
WING SPIKER

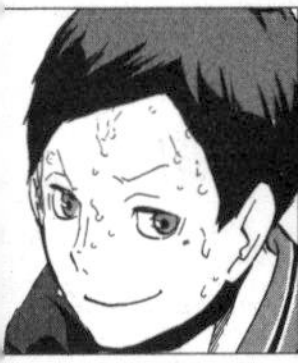

CHIKARA ENNOSHITA

2ND YEAR
WING SPIKER

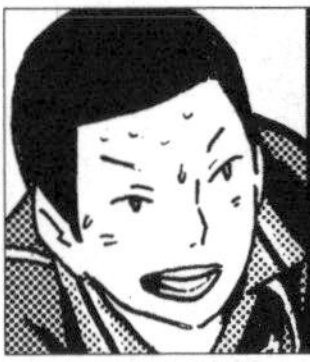

KAZUHITO NARITA

2ND YEAR
MIDDLE BLOCKER

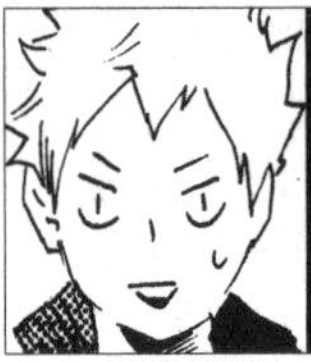

HISASHI KINOSHITA

2ND YEAR
WING SPIKER

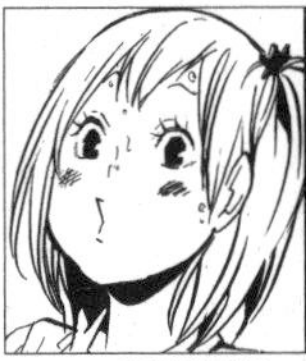

HITOKA YACHI

1ST YEAR
MANAGER

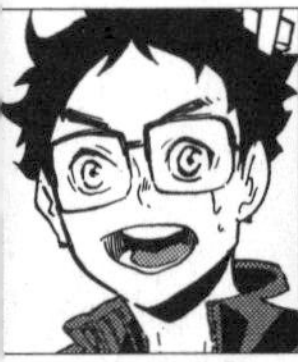

ITTETSU TAKEDA

ADVISER

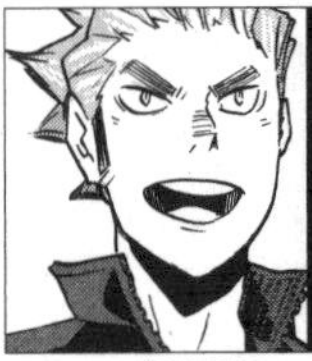

KEISHIN UKAI

COACH

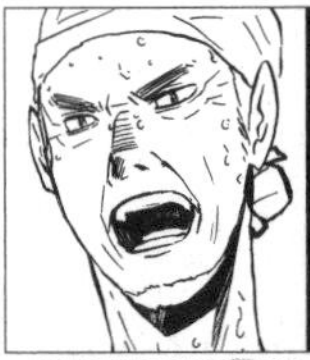

IKKEI UKAI

FORMER HEAD COACH

CHARACTERS

TOKYO PREFECTURE SPRING TOURNAMENT QUALIFIER TOURNAMENT ARC

Nekoma Team

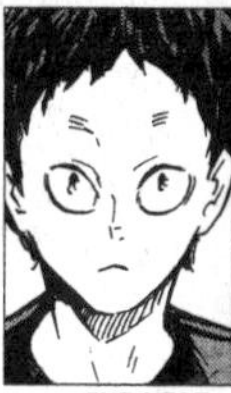
SHOHEI FUKUNAGA
2ND YEAR
WING SPIKER

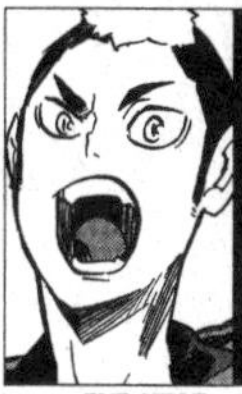
TAKETORA YAMAMOTO
2ND YEAR
WING SPIKER

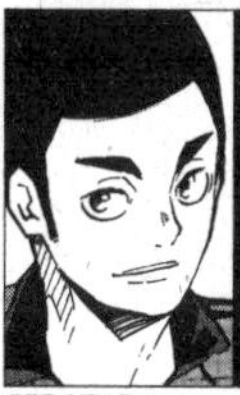
NOBUYUKI KAI
3RD YEAR (VICE CAPTAIN)
WING SPIKER

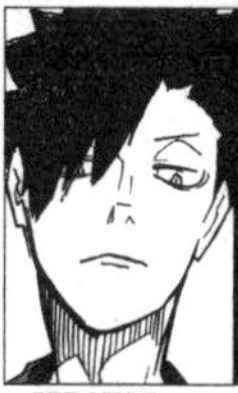
TETSURO KUROO
3RD YEAR (CAPTAIN)
MIDDLE BLOCKER

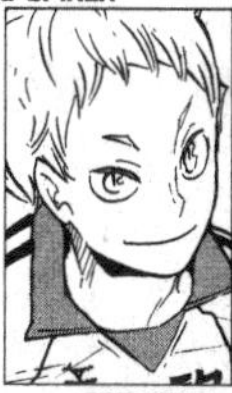
MORISUKE YAKU
3RD YEAR
LIBERO

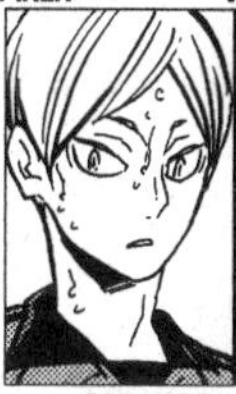
LEV HAIBA
1ST YEAR
MIDDLE BLOCKER

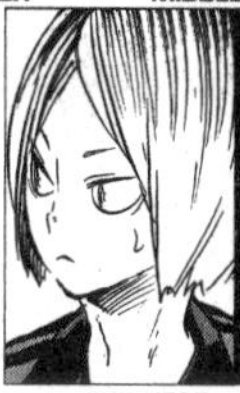
KENMA KOZUME
2ND YEAR
SETTER

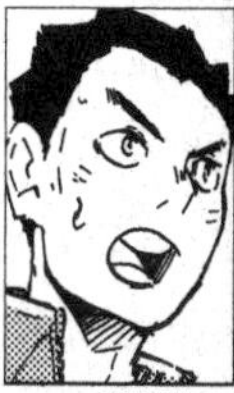
MANABU NAOI
COACH

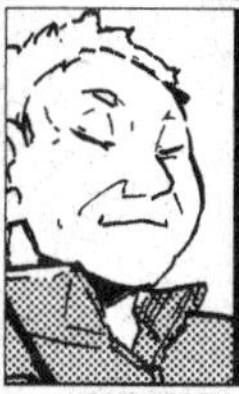
YASAFUMI NEKOMATA
HEAD COACH

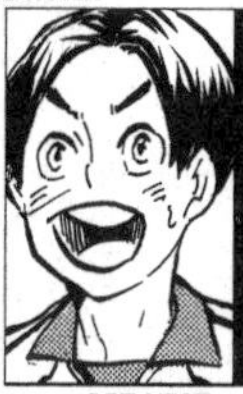
YUKI SHIBAYAMA
1ST YEAR
LIBERO

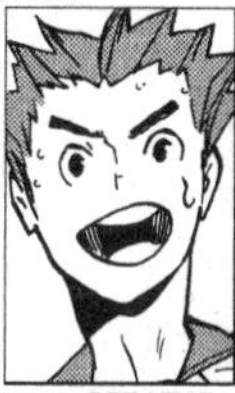
SOU INUOKA
1ST YEAR
MIDDLE BLOCKER

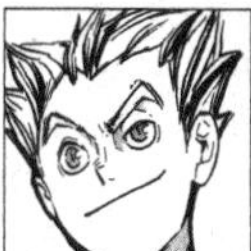
Fukurodani Academy Volleyball Club
KOTARO BOKUTO
3RD YEAR (CAPTAIN)
WING SPIKER

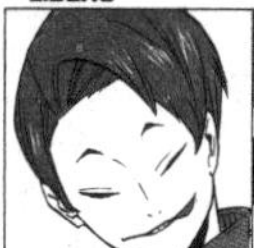
Nohebi Academy Volleyball Club
SUGURU DAISHO
3RD YEAR (CAPTAIN)
WING SPIKER

Ever since he saw the legendary player known as "the Little Giant" compete at the national volleyball finals, Shoyo Hinata has been aiming to be the best volleyball player ever! He decides to join the volleyball club at his middle school and gets to play in an official tournament during his third year. His team is crushed by a team led by volleyball prodigy Tobio Kageyama, also known as "the King of the Court." Swearing revenge on Kageyama, Hinata graduates middle school and enters Karasuno High School, the school where the Little Giant played. However, upon joining the club, he finds out that Kageyama is there too! The two of them bicker constantly, but they bring out the best in each other's talents and become a powerful combo. After a long and bitterly fought game, Karasuno finally defeats Shiratorizawa and wins the Miyagi Prefecture Qualifiers! Meanwhile, Fukurodani beats Nekoma in the Tokyo Area Qualifiers, earning them a spot in the finals and the Spring Tournament. Now Nekoma's only hope is to win the third-place match and snag the last open slot as the venue sponsor representative They're up against Nohebi Academy, a devious team that turns the atmosphere of the whole stadium to their advantage and goads their opponents into imploding. To make things worse, Nekoma's libero and defensive ace, Yaku, gets injured...!!

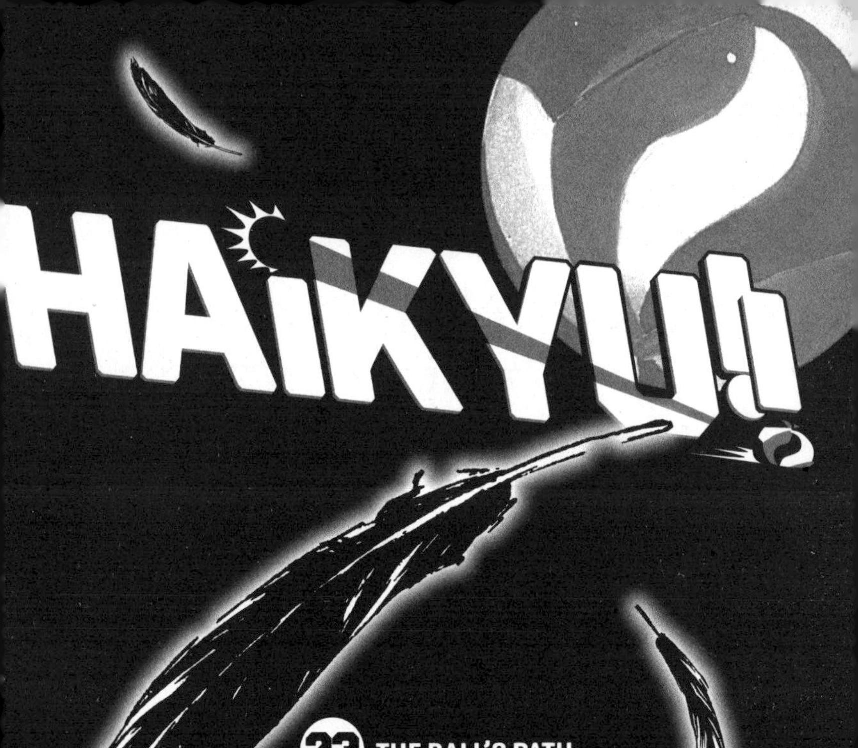
HAIKYU!!

23 THE BALL'S PATH

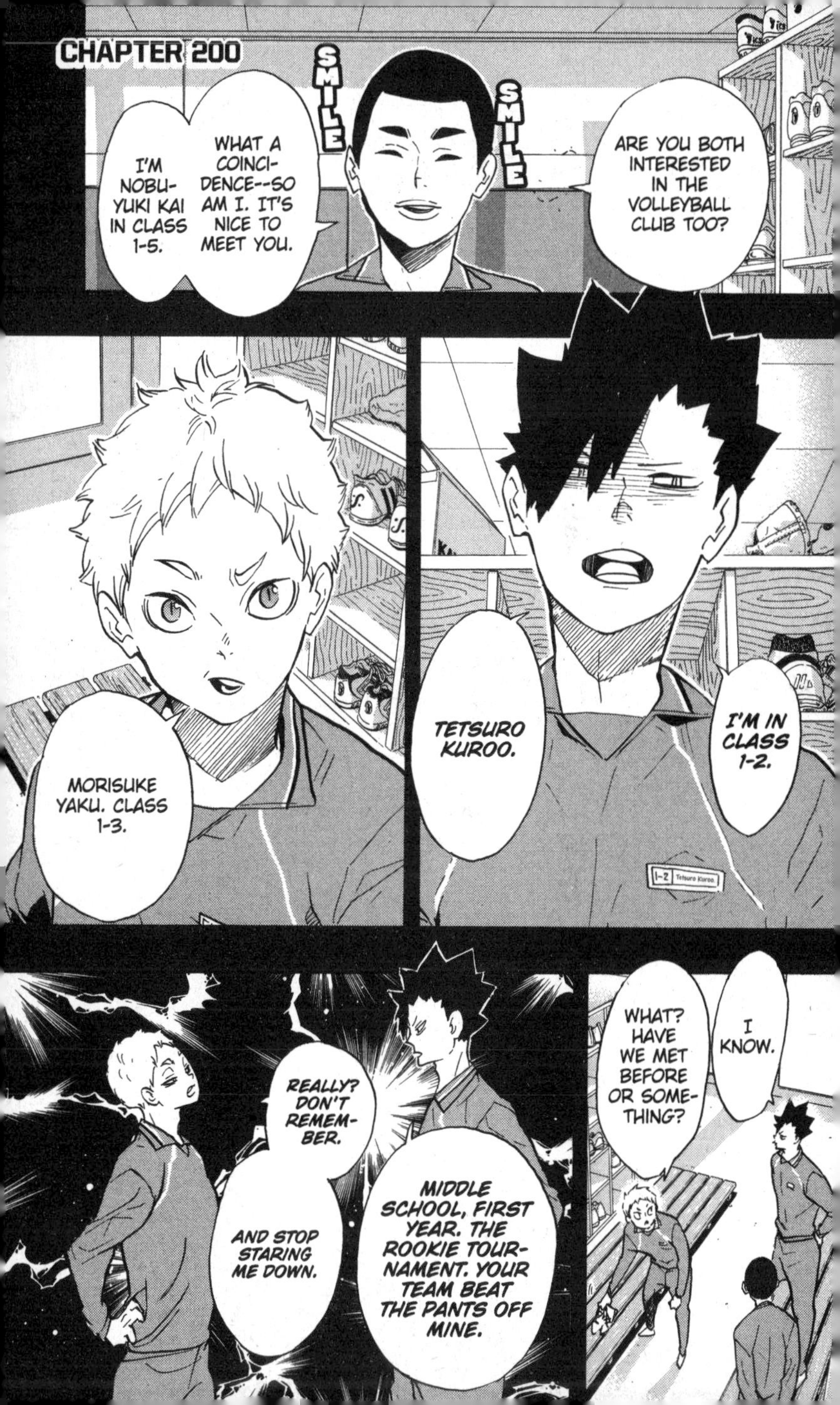
CHAPTER 200
ARE YOU BOTH INTERESTED IN THE VOLLEYBALL CLUB TOO?
SMILE
SMILE
WHAT A COINCIDENCE--SO AM I. IT'S NICE TO MEET YOU.
I'M NOBUYUKI KAI IN CLASS 1-5.
I'M IN CLASS 1-2.
TETSURO KUROO.
1-2 Tetsuro Kuroo
MORISUKE YAKU. CLASS 1-3.
I KNOW.
WHAT? HAVE WE MET BEFORE OR SOMETHING?
MIDDLE SCHOOL, FIRST YEAR. THE ROOKIE TOURNAMENT. YOUR TEAM BEAT THE PANTS OFF MINE.
REALLY? DON'T REMEMBER.
AND STOP STARING ME DOWN.

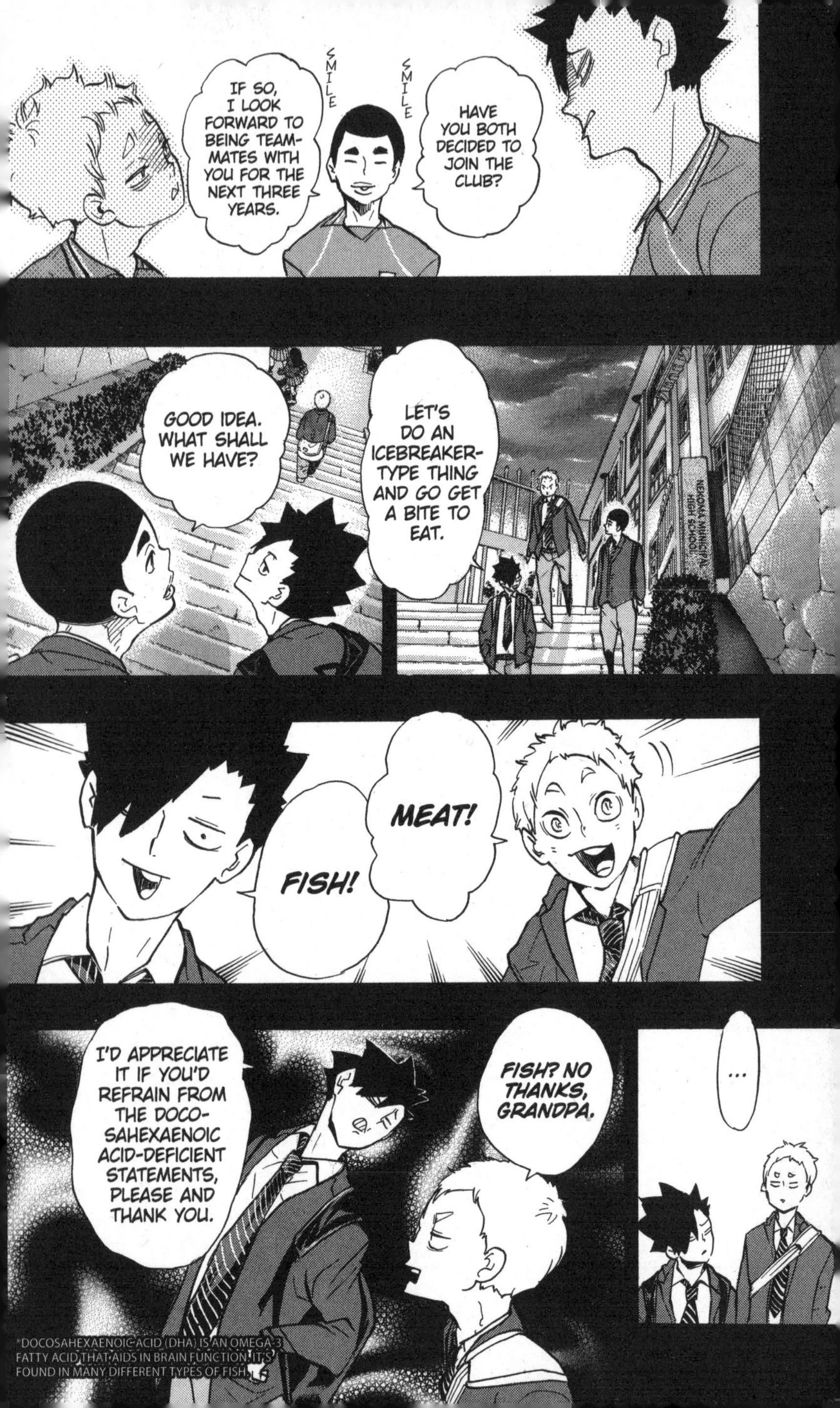
HAVE YOU BOTH DECIDED TO JOIN THE CLUB?
SMILE
SMILE
IF SO, I LOOK FORWARD TO BEING TEAM-MATES WITH YOU FOR THE NEXT THREE YEARS.
NEKOMA MUNICIPAL HIGH SCHOOL
LET'S DO AN ICEBREAKER-TYPE THING AND GO GET A BITE TO EAT.
GOOD IDEA. WHAT SHALL WE HAVE?
MEAT!
FISH!
...
FISH? NO THANKS, GRANDPA.
I'D APPRECIATE IT IF YOU'D REFRAIN FROM THE DOCO-SAHEXAENOIC ACID-DEFICIENT STATEMENTS, PLEASE AND THANK YOU.

*DOCOSAHEXAENOIC ACID (DHA) IS AN OMEGA-3 FATTY ACID THAT AIDS IN BRAIN FUNCTION. IT'S FOUND IN MANY DIFFERENT TYPES OF FISH.

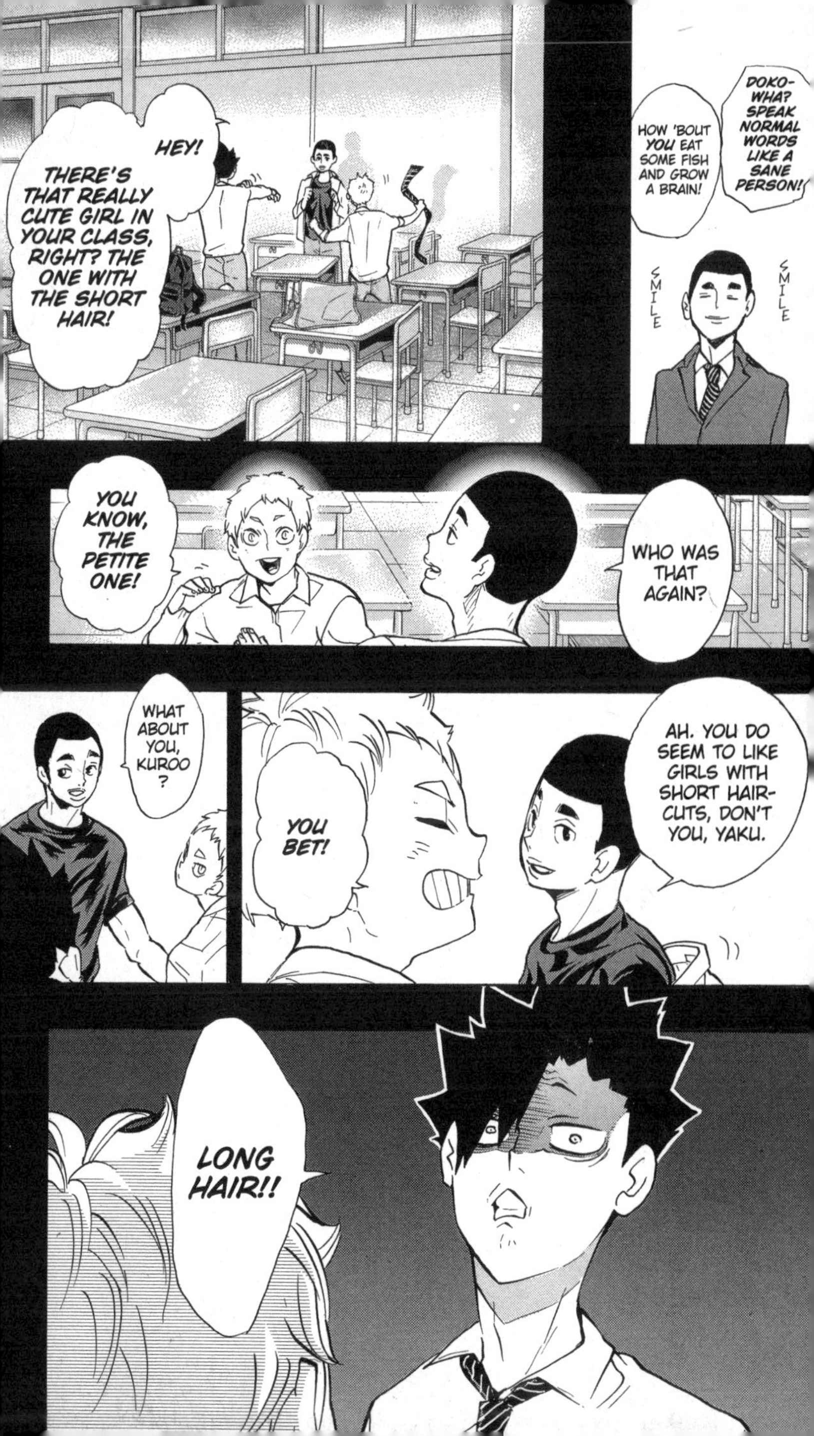
DOKO-WHA? SPEAK NORMAL WORDS LIKE A SANE PERSON!
HOW 'BOUT YOU EAT SOME FISH AND GROW A BRAIN!
SMILE
SMILE
HEY!
THERE'S THAT REALLY CUTE GIRL IN YOUR CLASS, RIGHT? THE ONE WITH THE SHORT HAIR!
WHO WAS THAT AGAIN?
YOU KNOW, THE PETITE ONE!
AH. YOU DO SEEM TO LIKE GIRLS WITH SHORT HAIR-CUTS, DON'T YOU, YAKU.
YOU BET!
WHAT ABOUT YOU, KUROO?
LONG HAIR!!

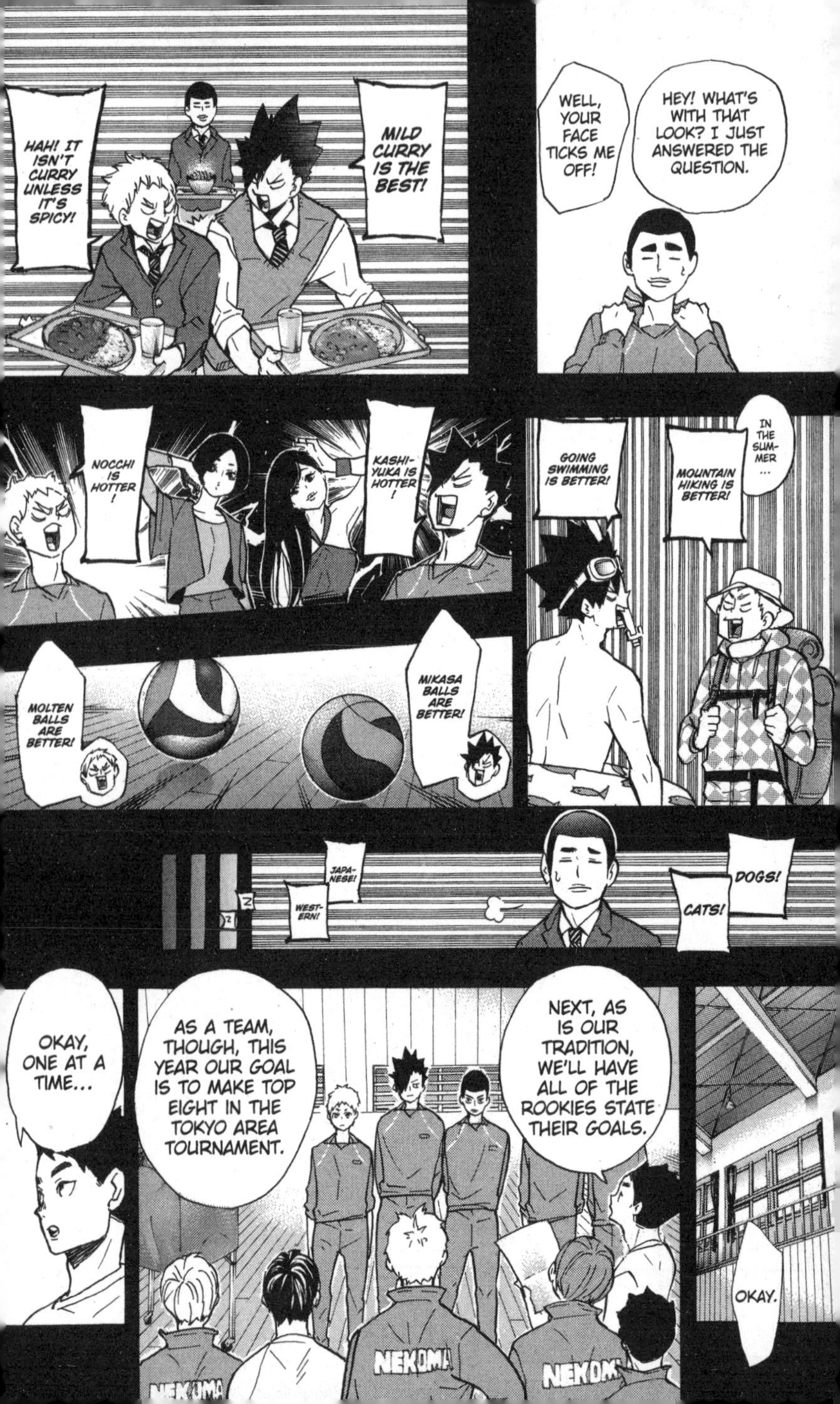
HEY! WHAT'S WITH THAT LOOK? I JUST ANSWERED THE QUESTION.
WELL, YOUR FACE TICKS ME OFF!
MILD CURRY IS THE BEST!
HAH! IT ISN'T CURRY UNLESS IT'S SPICY!
IN THE SUMMER...
MOUNTAIN HIKING IS BETTER!
GOING SWIMMING IS BETTER!
KASHIYUKA IS HOTTER!
NOCCHI IS HOTTER!
MIKASA BALLS ARE BETTER!
MOLTEN BALLS ARE BETTER!
DOGS!
CATS!
JAPANESE!
WESTERN!
Z
Z
OKAY.
NEXT, AS IS OUR TRADITION, WE'LL HAVE ALL OF THE ROOKIES STATE THEIR GOALS.
AS A TEAM, THOUGH, THIS YEAR OUR GOAL IS TO MAKE TOP EIGHT IN THE TOKYO AREA TOURNAMENT.
OKAY, ONE AT A TIME...
NEKOMA
NEKOMA
NEKOMA

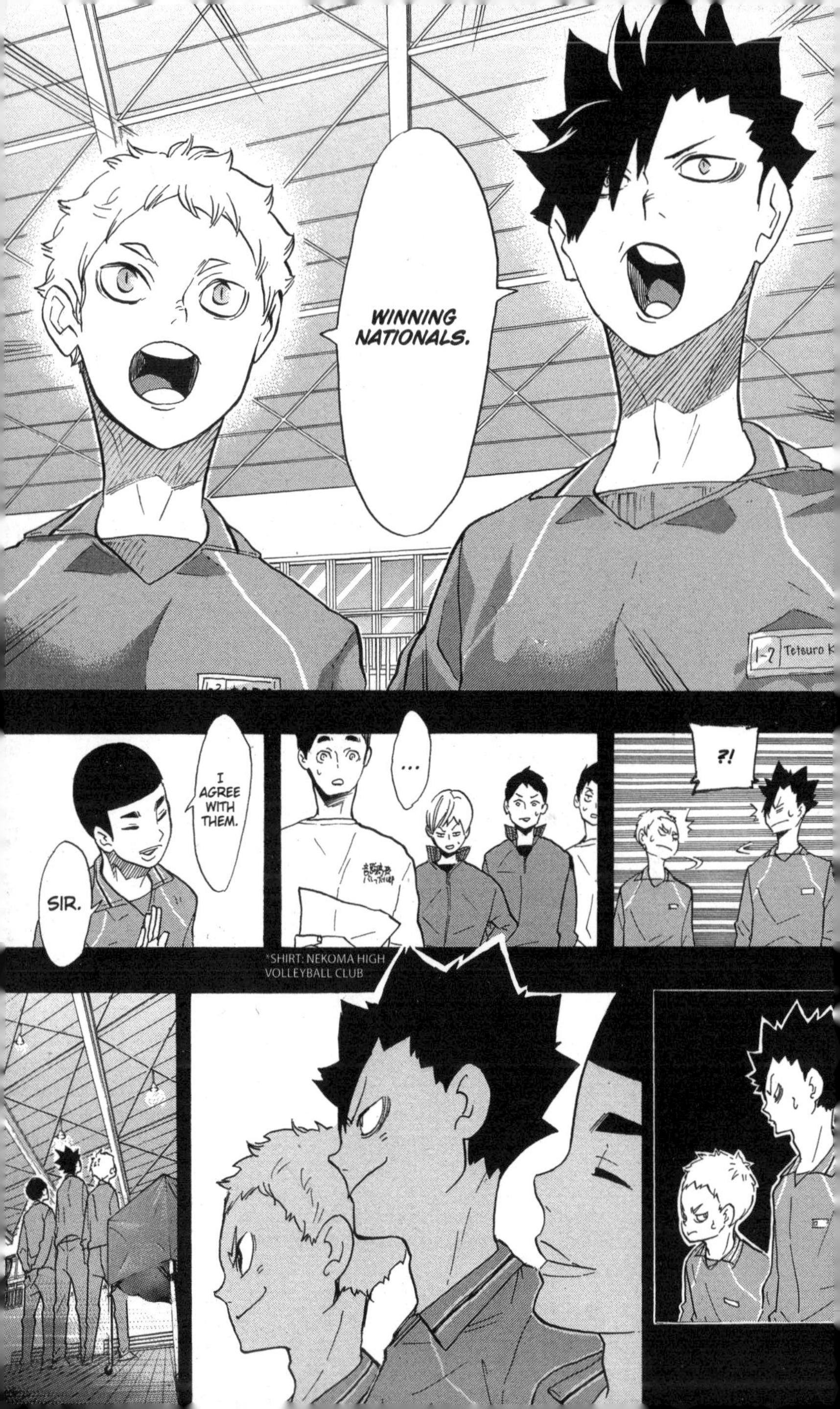
WINNING NATIONALS.
1-2 Tetsuro K
?!
...
I AGREE WITH THEM.
SIR.
*SHIRT: NEKOMA HIGH VOLLEYBALL CLUB

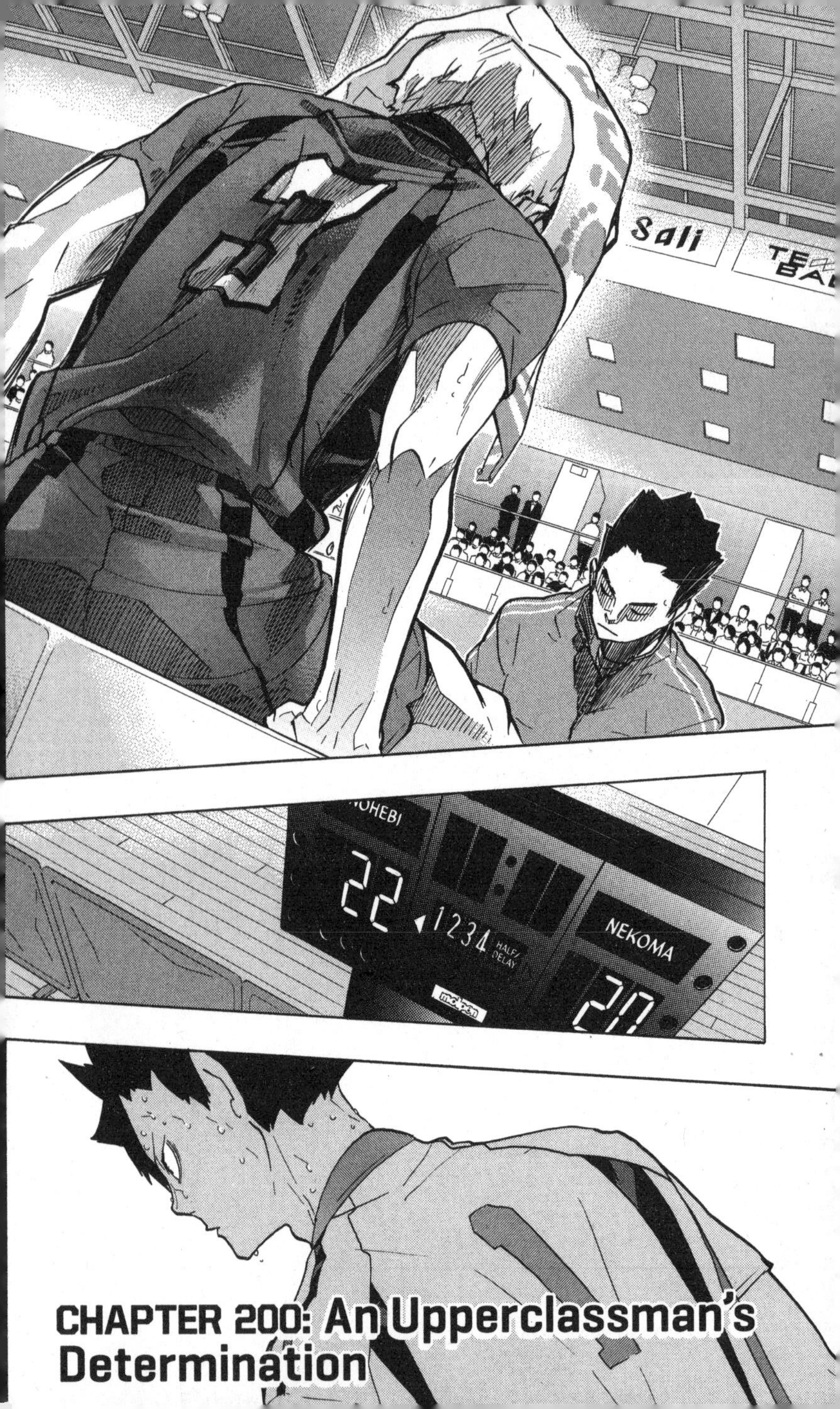
Sali
22
1234 HALF/DELAY
NEKOMA
20
CHAPTER 200: An Upperclassman's Determination

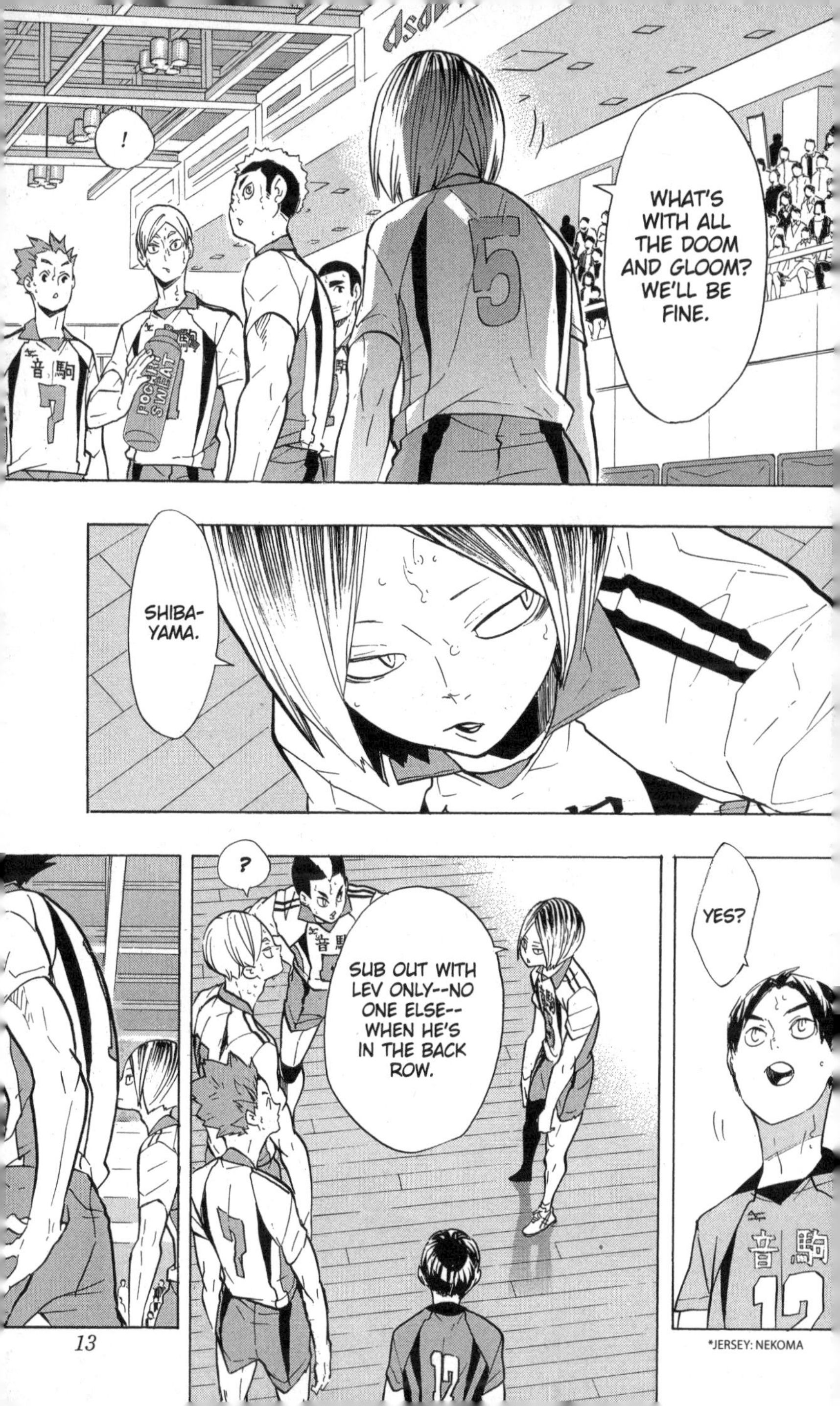

WHAT'S WITH ALL THE DOOM AND GLOOM? WE'LL BE FINE.
!
SHIBA-YAMA.
YES?
SUB OUT WITH LEV ONLY--NO ONE ELSE--WHEN HE'S IN THE BACK ROW.
?

*JERSEY: NEKOMA

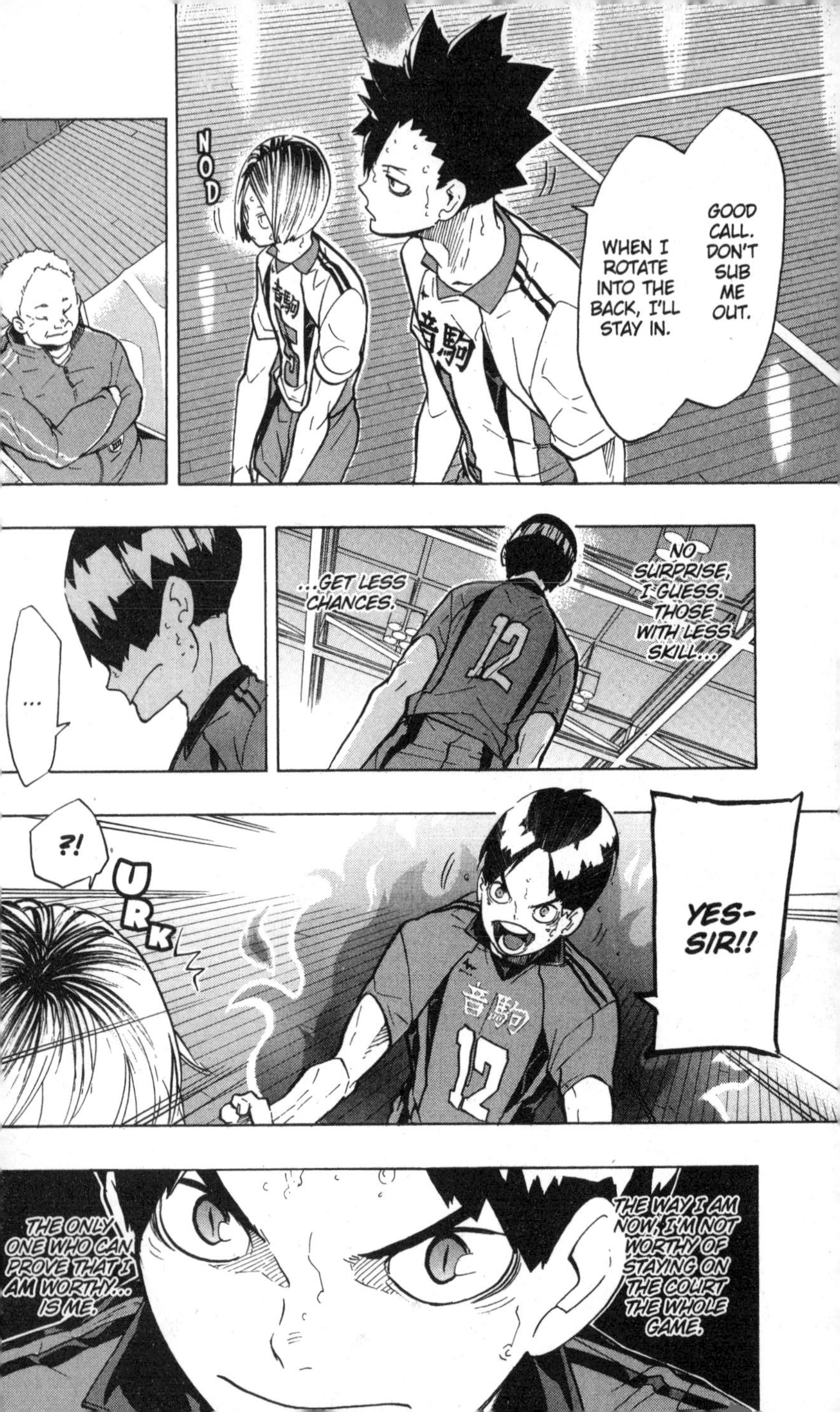
GOOD CALL. DON'T SUB ME OUT.
WHEN I ROTATE INTO THE BACK, I'LL STAY IN.
NOD
NO SURPRISE, I GUESS. THOSE WITH LESS SKILL...
...GET LESS CHANCES.
...
YES-SIR!!
URK
?!
THE WAY I AM NOW, I'M NOT WORTHY OF STAYING ON THE COURT THE WHOLE GAME.
THE ONLY ONE WHO CAN PROVE THAT I AM WORTHY... IS ME.

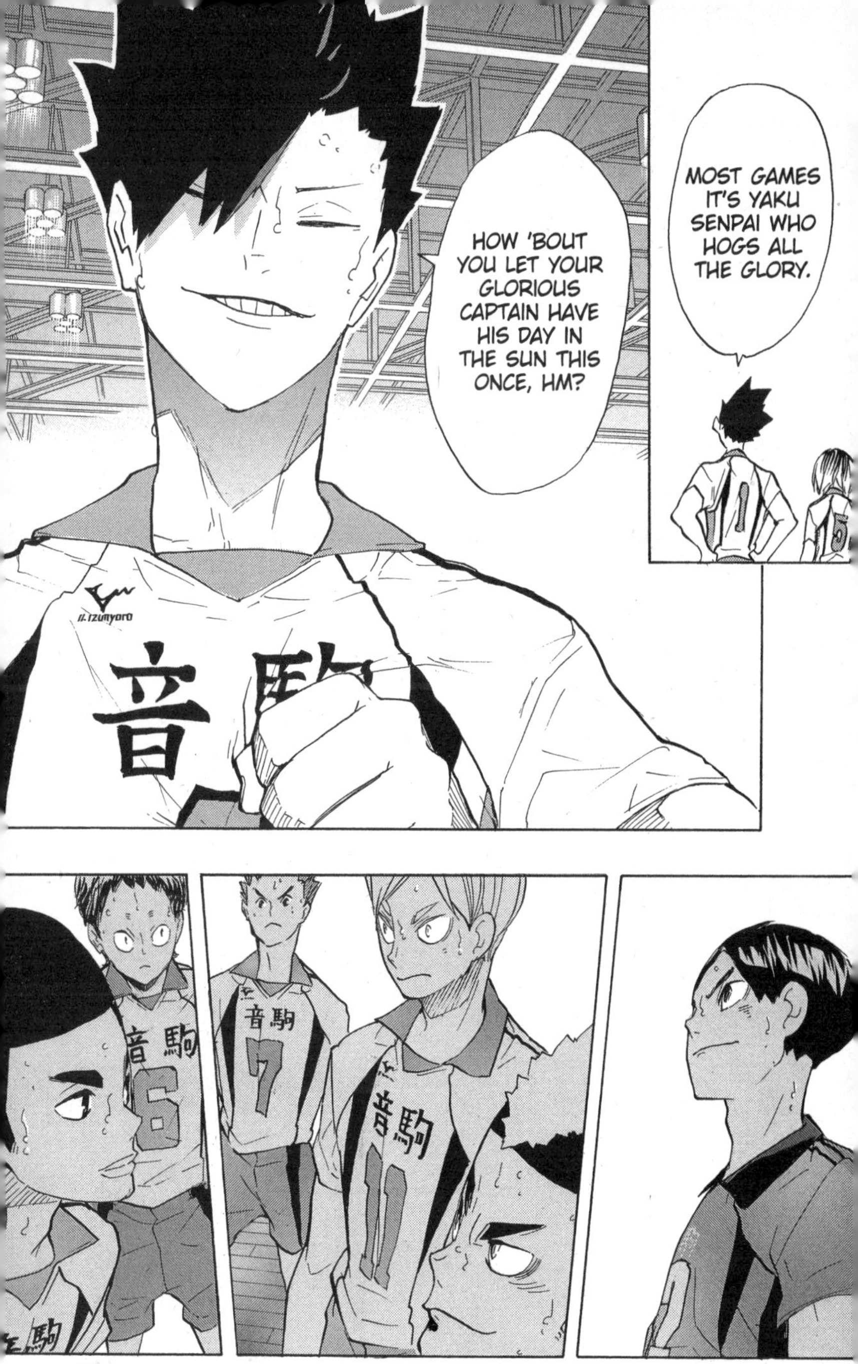
MOST GAMES IT'S YAKU SENPAI WHO HOGS ALL THE GLORY.
HOW 'BOUT YOU LET YOUR GLORIOUS CAPTAIN HAVE HIS DAY IN THE SUN THIS ONCE, HM?

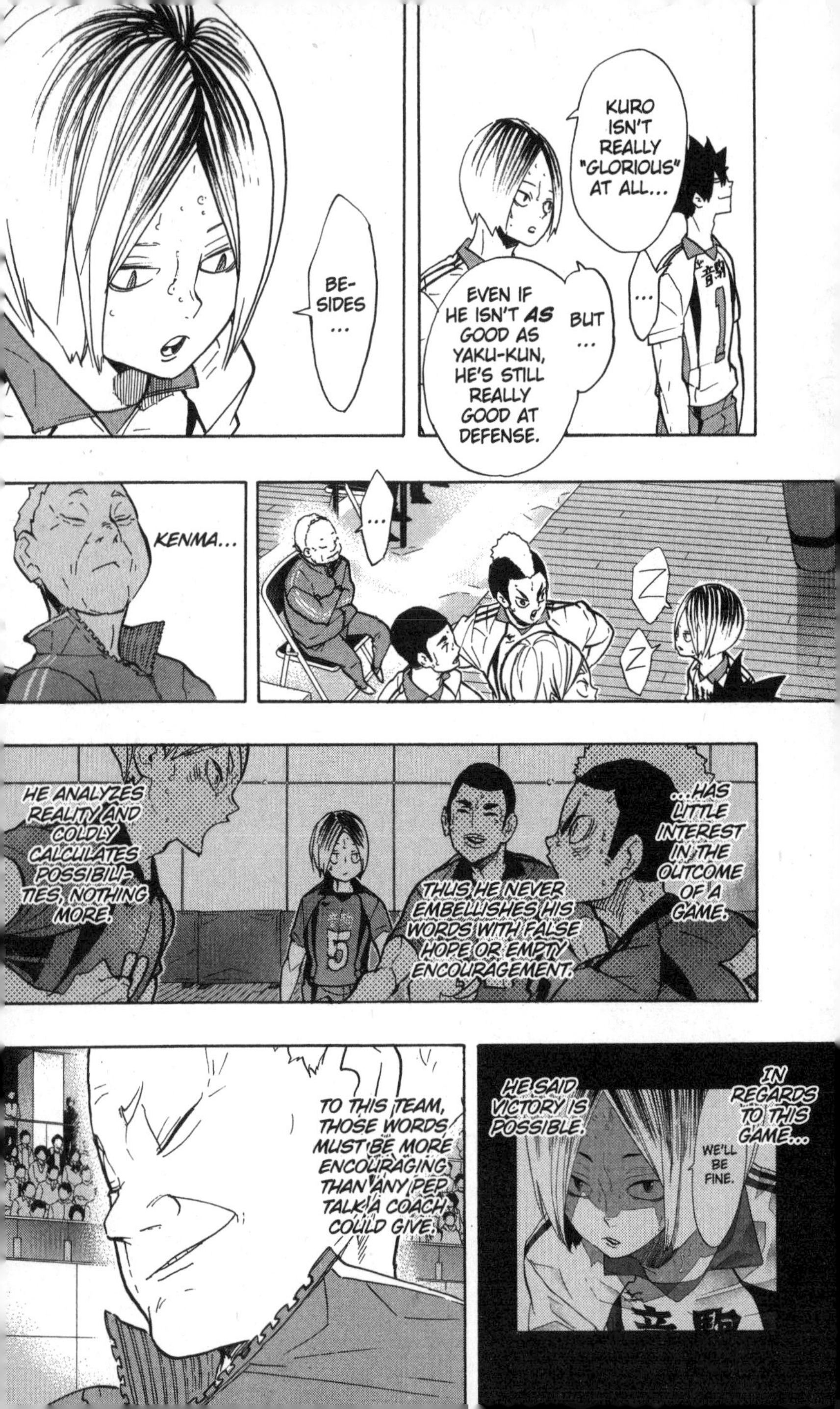
KURO ISN'T REALLY "GLORIOUS" AT ALL...
...
BUT ...
EVEN IF HE ISN'T AS GOOD AS YAKU-KUN, HE'S STILL REALLY GOOD AT DEFENSE.
BE-SIDES ...
...
Z
Z
KENMA...
...HAS LITTLE INTEREST IN THE OUTCOME OF A GAME.
HE ANALYZES REALITY AND COLDLY CALCULATES POSSIBILI-TIES, NOTHING MORE.
THUS HE NEVER EMBELLISHES HIS WORDS WITH FALSE HOPE OR EMPTY ENCOURAGEMENT.
IN REGARDS TO THIS GAME...
HE SAID VICTORY IS POSSIBLE.
WE'LL BE FINE.
TO THIS TEAM, THOSE WORDS MUST BE MORE ENCOURAGING THAN ANY PEP TALK A COACH COULD GIVE.

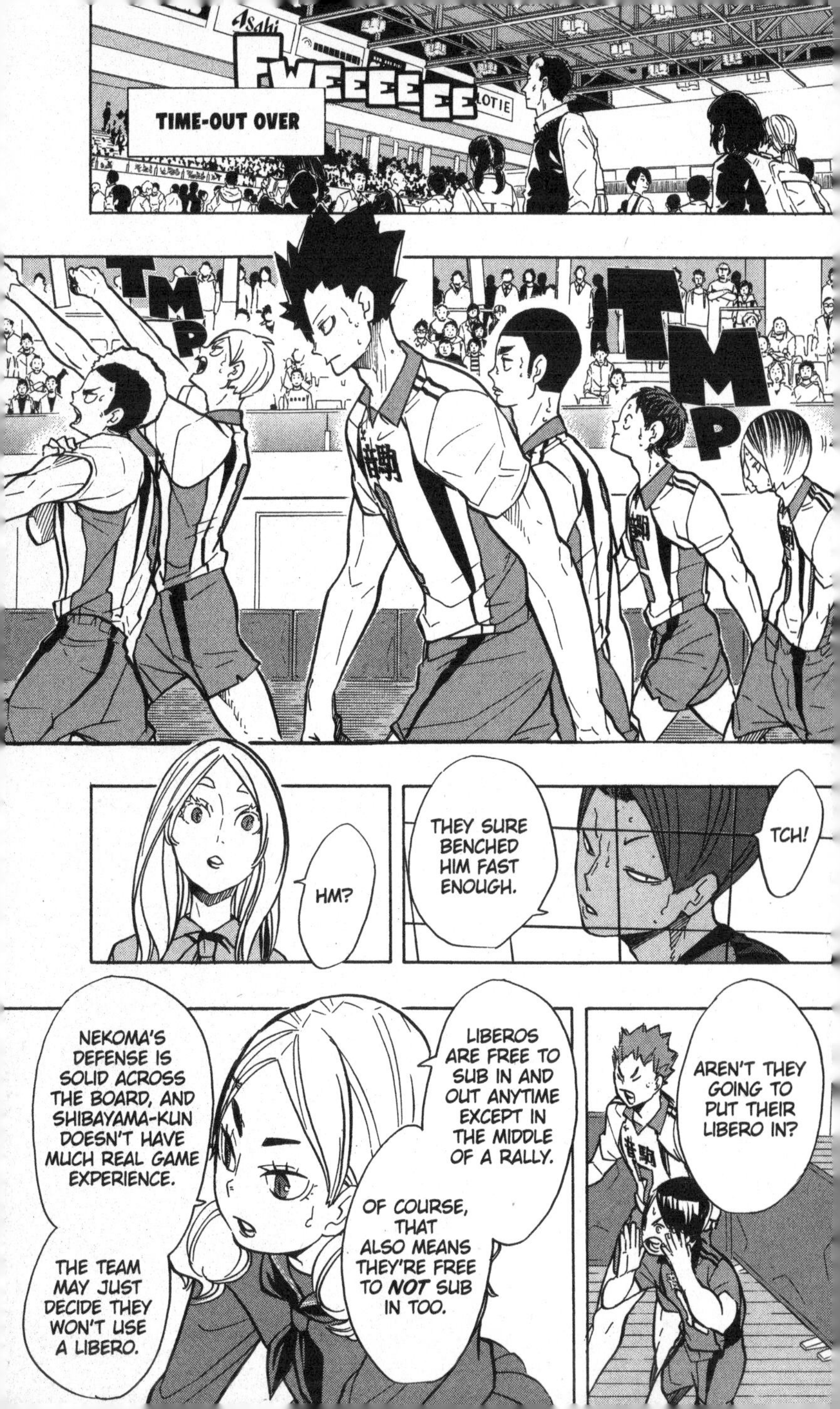
FWEEEEEE
TIME-OUT OVER
TMP
TMP
TCH!
THEY SURE BENCHED HIM FAST ENOUGH.
HM?
AREN'T THEY GOING TO PUT THEIR LIBERO IN?
LIBEROS ARE FREE TO SUB IN AND OUT ANYTIME EXCEPT IN THE MIDDLE OF A RALLY.
NEKOMA'S DEFENSE IS SOLID ACROSS THE BOARD, AND SHIBAYAMA-KUN DOESN'T HAVE MUCH REAL GAME EXPERIENCE.
OF COURSE, THAT ALSO MEANS THEY'RE FREE TO ***NOT*** SUB IN TOO.
THE TEAM MAY JUST DECIDE THEY WON'T USE A LIBERO.

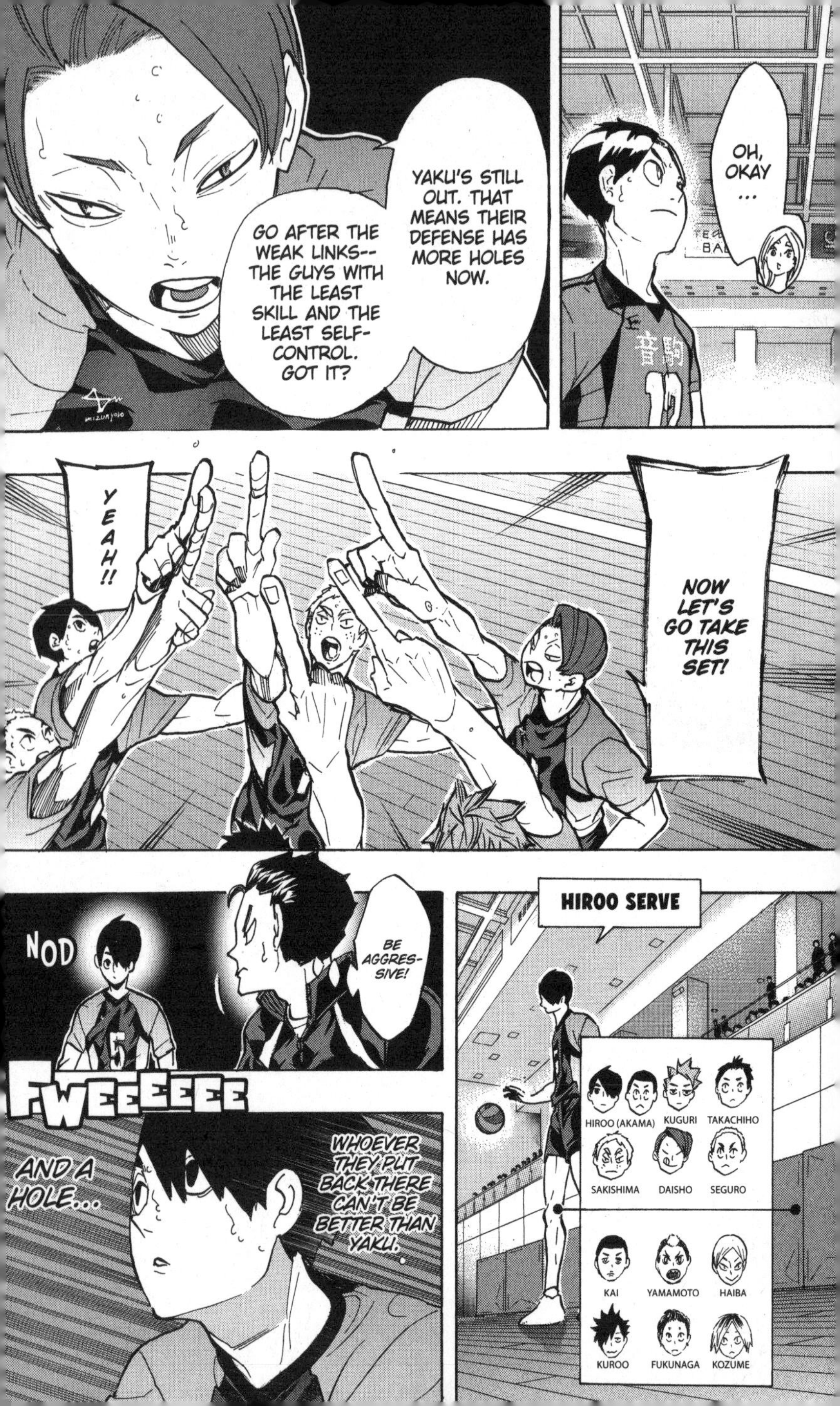
OH, OKAY ...
YAKU'S STILL OUT. THAT MEANS THEIR DEFENSE HAS MORE HOLES NOW.
GO AFTER THE WEAK LINKS--THE GUYS WITH THE LEAST SKILL AND THE LEAST SELF-CONTROL. GOT IT?
NOW LET'S GO TAKE THIS SET!
YEAH!!
HIROO SERVE
HIROO (AKAMA)
KUGURI
TAKACHIHO
SAKISHIMA
DAISHO
SEGURO
KAI
YAMAMOTO
HAIBA
KUROO
FUKUNAGA
KOZUME
BE AGGRES-SIVE!
NOD
FWEEEEEE
WHOEVER THEY PUT BACK THERE CAN'T BE BETTER THAN YAKU.
AND A HOLE...

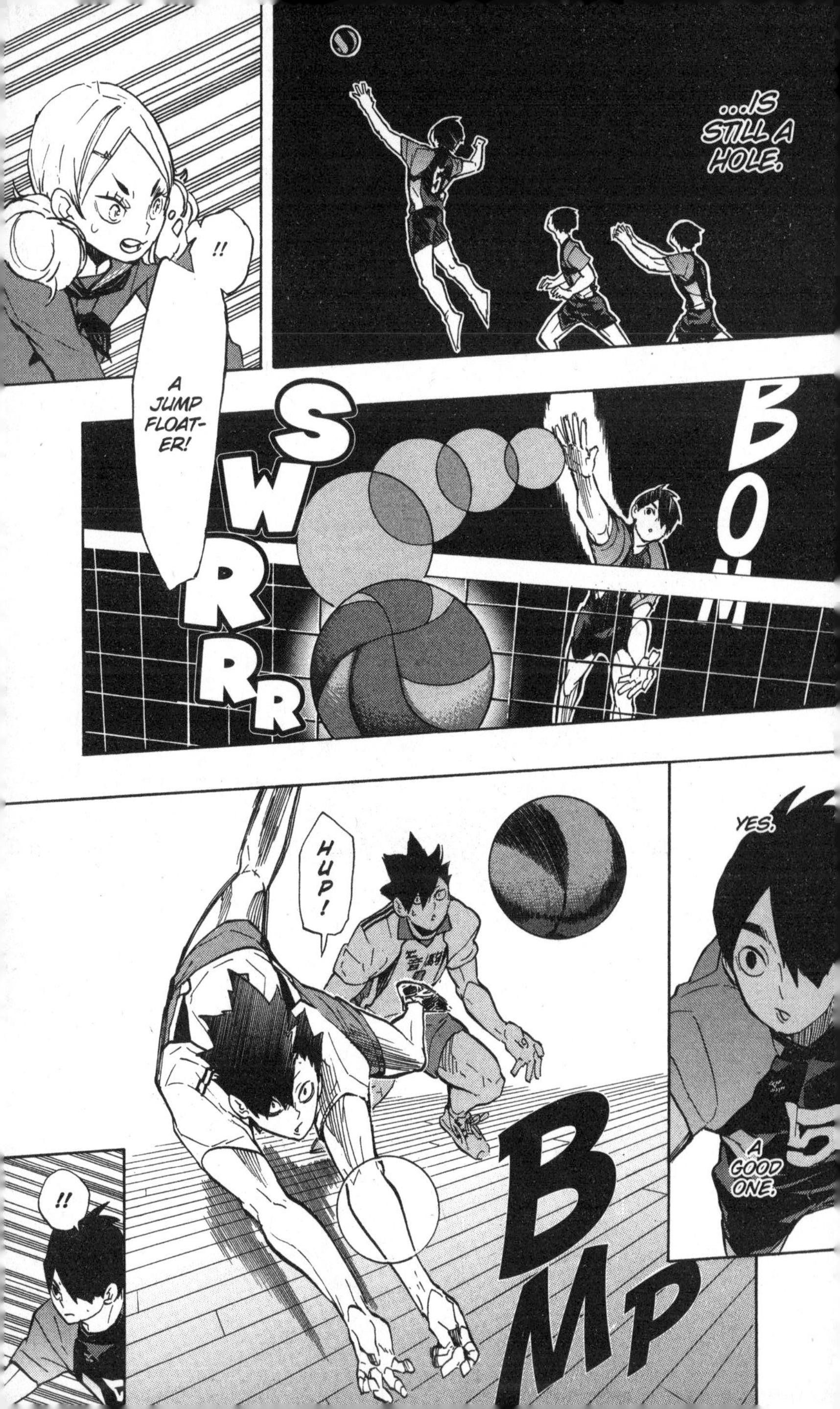
...IS STILL A HOLE.
!!
A JUMP FLOATER!
BOOM
SWRRR
YES.
A GOOD ONE.
HUP!
BMP
!!

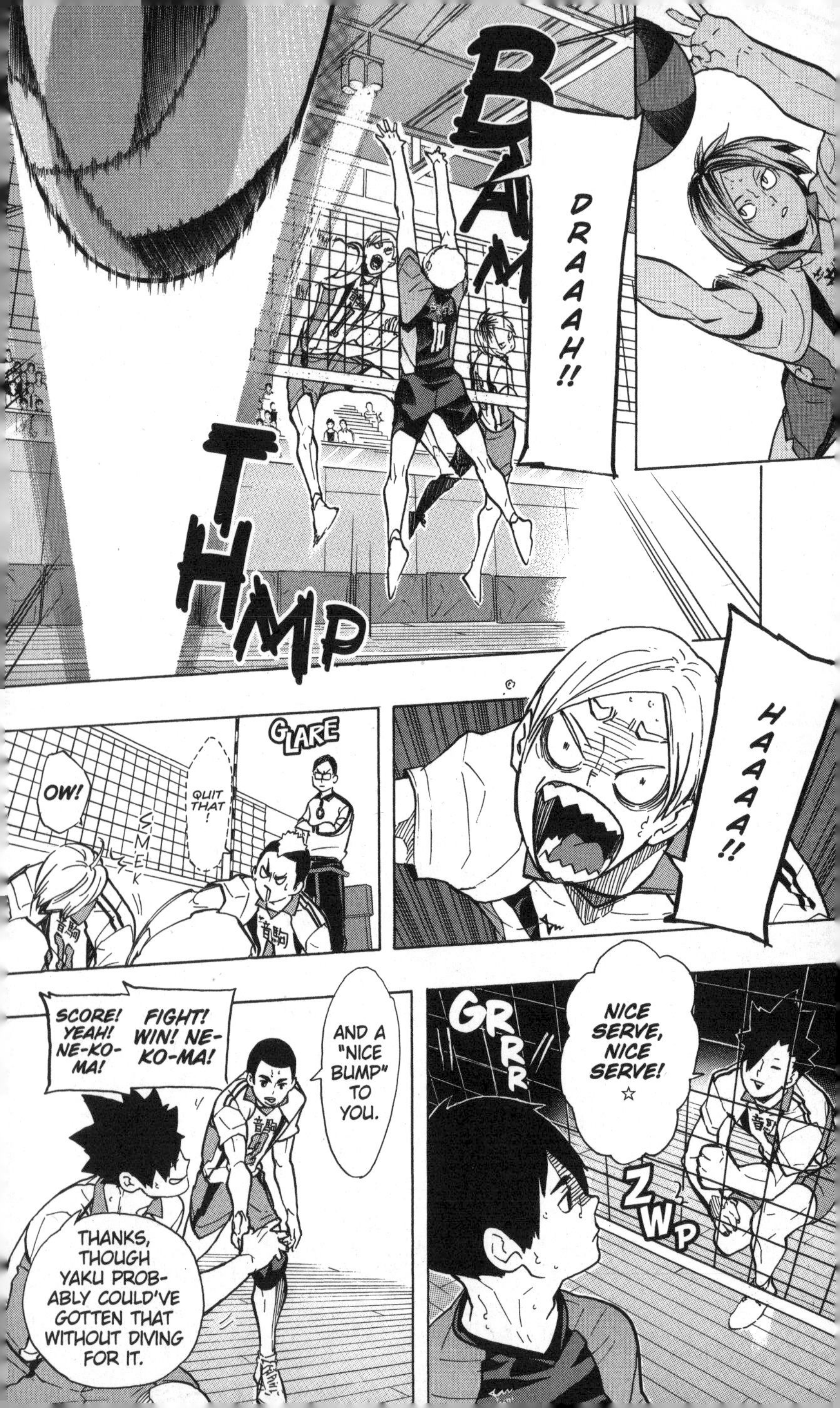
DRAAAAH!!
BAM
THMP
HAAAAA!!
GLARE
QUIT THAT!
OW!
SMEK
NICE SERVE, NICE SERVE! ☆
GRRR
ZWP
AND A "NICE BUMP" TO YOU.
FIGHT! WIN! NE-KO-MA!
SCORE! YEAH! NE-KO-MA!
THANKS, THOUGH YAKU PROBABLY COULD'VE GOTTEN THAT WITHOUT DIVING FOR IT.

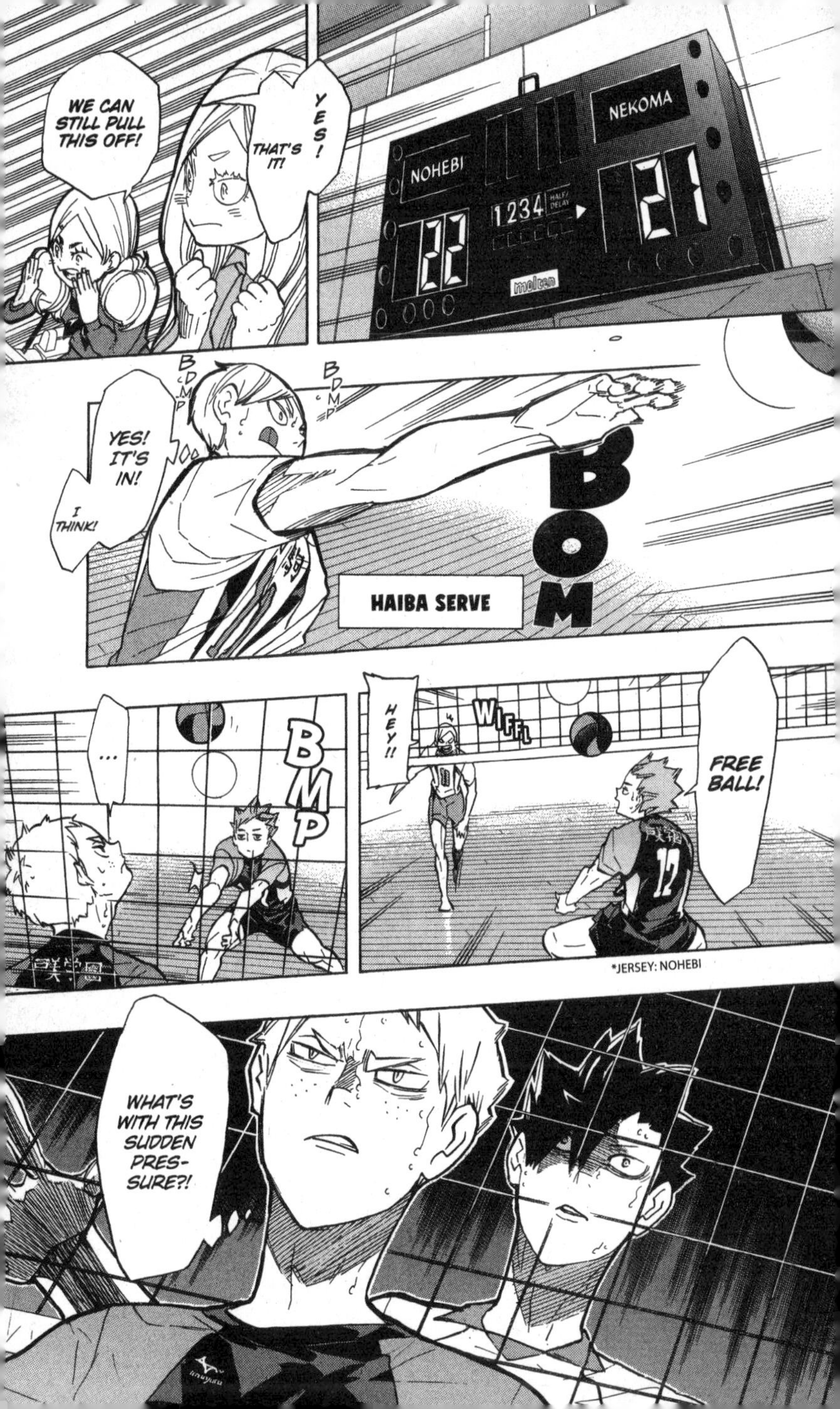

NEKOMA
21
NOHEBI
22
1234
HALF/DELAY
molten
YES!
THAT'S IT!
WE CAN STILL PULL THIS OFF!
BDMP
BDMP
BOM
HAIBA SERVE
YES! IT'S IN!
I THINK!
FREE BALL!
WIFFL
HEY!!
*JERSEY: NOHEBI
BMP
...
WHAT'S WITH THIS SUDDEN PRES-SURE?!

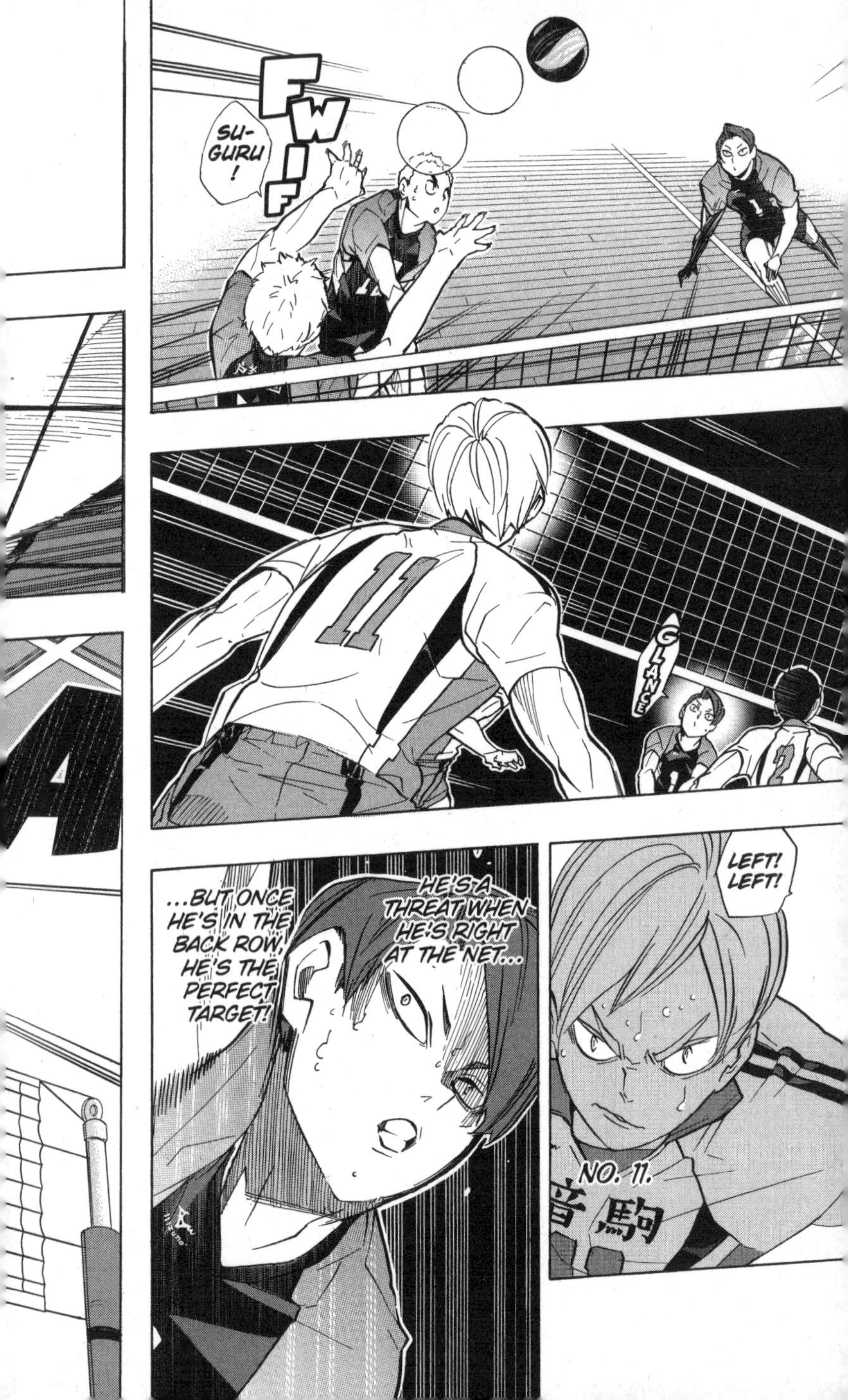
SU-GURU!
FWIF
GLANCE
LEFT! LEFT!
NO. 11.
音駒
HE'S A THREAT WHEN HE'S RIGHT AT THE NET...
...BUT ONCE HE'S IN THE BACK ROW, HE'S THE PERFECT TARGET!

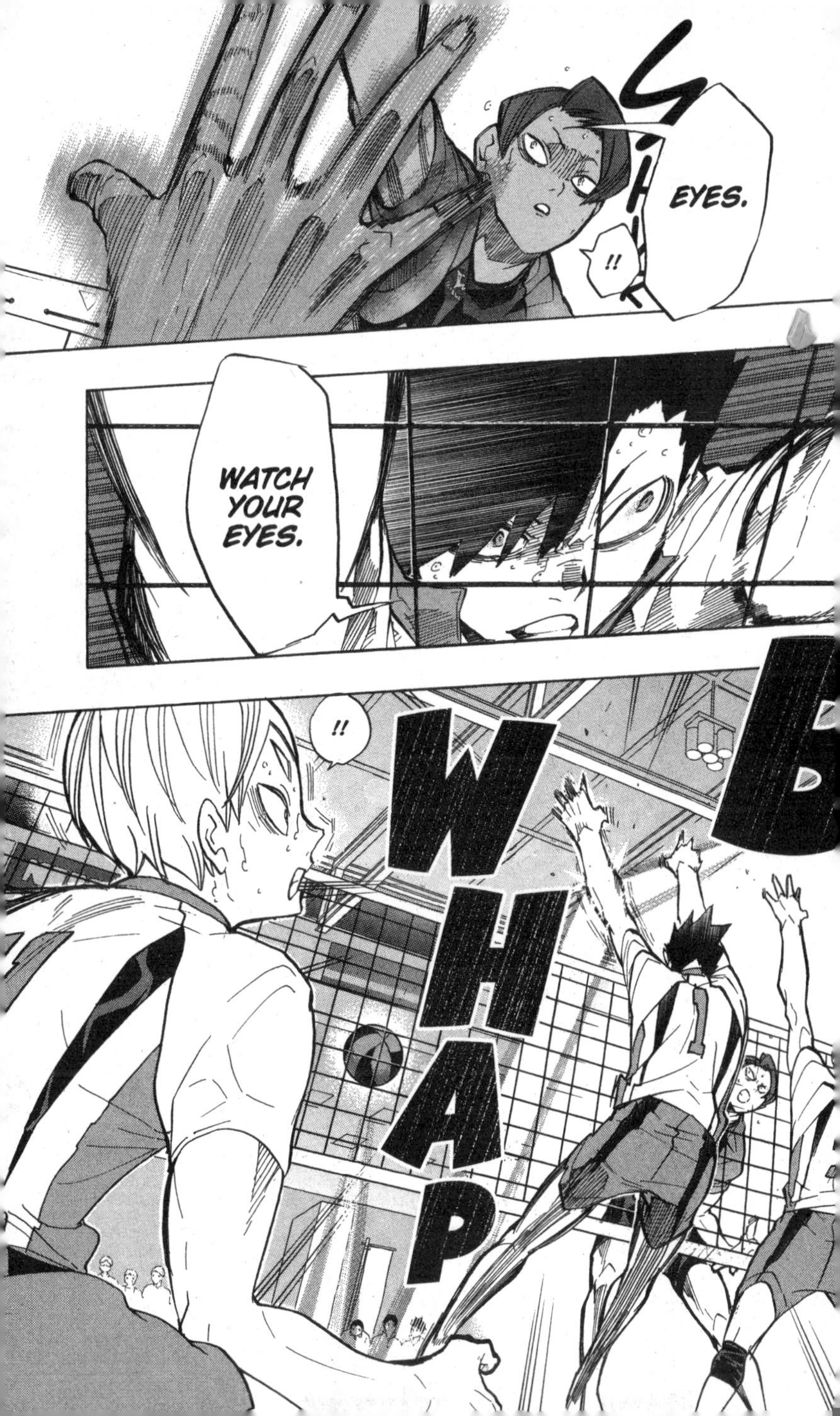
EYES.
!!
WATCH YOUR EYES.
WHAP
!!

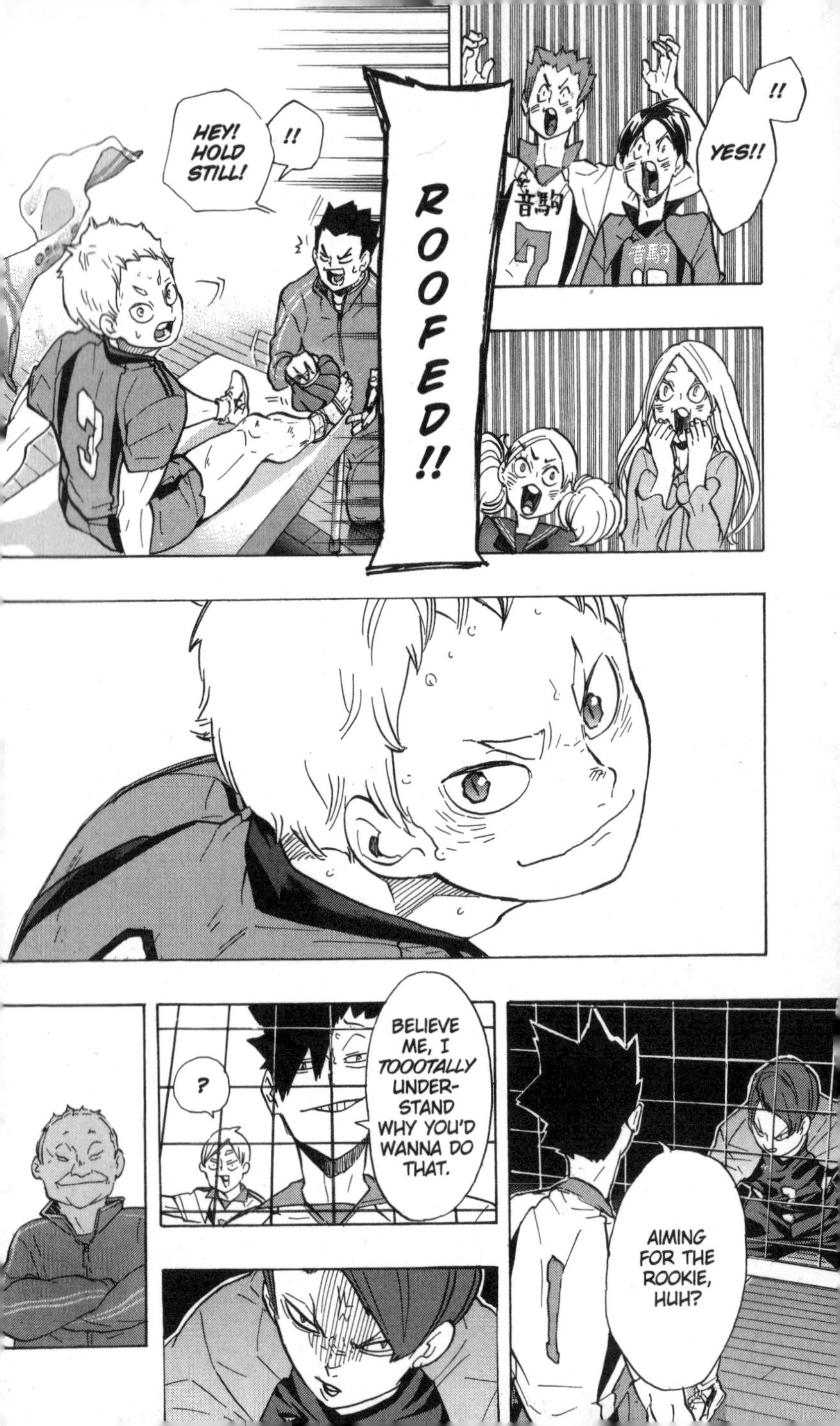
!!
YES!!
ROOOFED!!
!!
HEY! HOLD STILL!
AIMING FOR THE ROOKIE, HUH?
BELIEVE ME, I *TOOOTALLY* UNDER-STAND WHY YOU'D WANNA DO THAT.
?

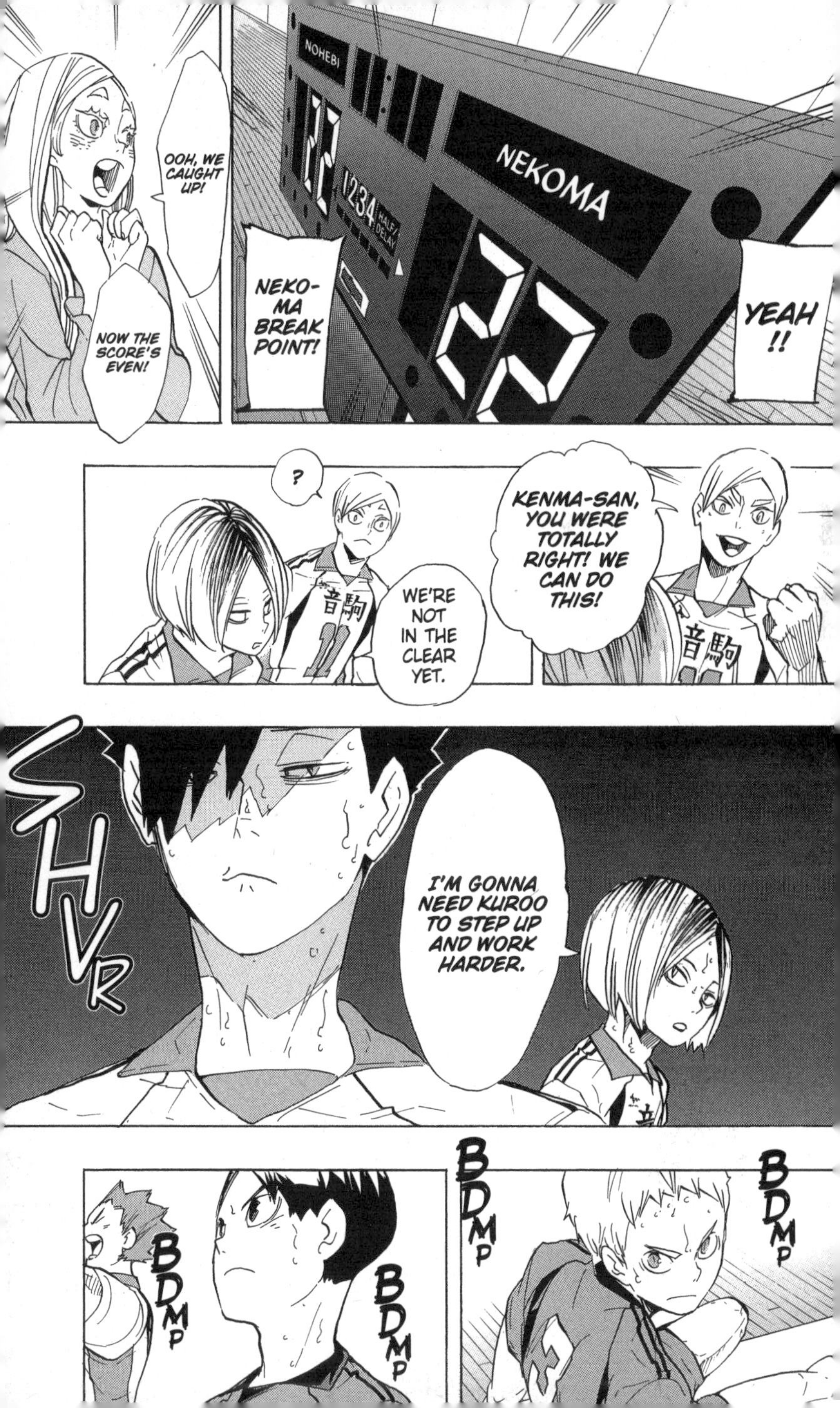
NOHEBI
NEKOMA
YEAH !!
NEKO-MA BREAK POINT!
OOH, WE CAUGHT UP!
NOW THE SCORE'S EVEN!
KENMA-SAN, YOU WERE TOTALLY RIGHT! WE CAN DO THIS!
音駒
?
WE'RE NOT IN THE CLEAR YET.
音駒
SHVR
I'M GONNA NEED KUROO TO STEP UP AND WORK HARDER.
BDMP
BDMP
BDMP
BDMP

KOJI HIROO

NOHEBI ACADEMY
CLASS 3-6

POSITION:
MIDDLE BLOCKER

HEIGHT: 6'1"

WEIGHT: 156 LBS.
(AS OF NOVEMBER, 3RD YEAR
OF HIGH SCHOOL)

ABILITY PARAMETERS
(5-POINT SCALE)

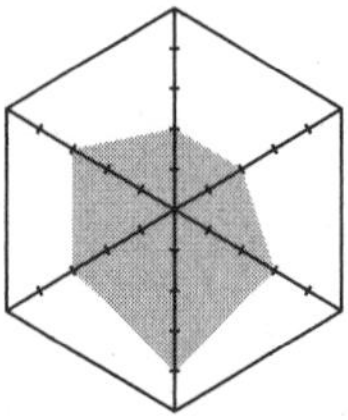

POWER
(2)
JUMPING
(2)
STAMINA
(3)
INTELLIGENCE
(4)
TECHNIQUE
(3)
SPEED
(3)

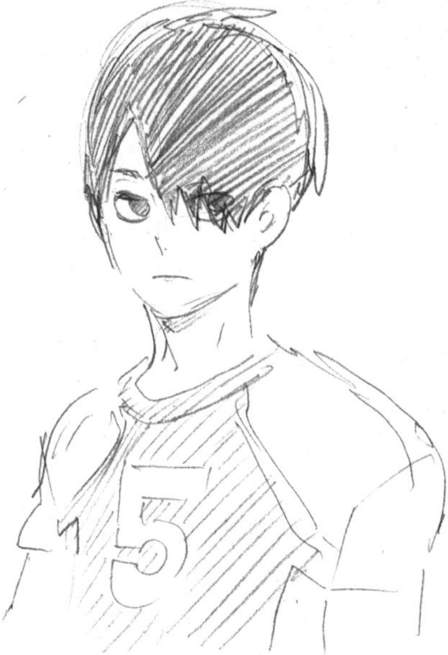

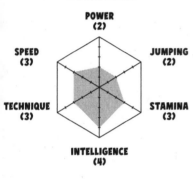

AKIHIKO SEGURO

NOHEBI ACADEMY
CLASS 2-1

POSITION:
MIDDLE BLOCKER

HEIGHT: 6'2"

WEIGHT: 166 LBS.
(AS OF NOVEMBER, 2ND YEAR
OF HIGH SCHOOL)

ABILITY PARAMETERS
(5-POINT SCALE)

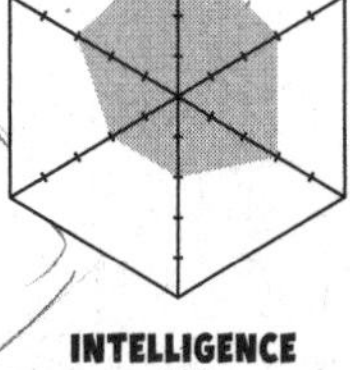

POWER
(4)
JUMPING
(3)
STAMINA
(3)
INTELLIGENCE
(2)
TECHNIQUE
(2)
SPEED
(3)

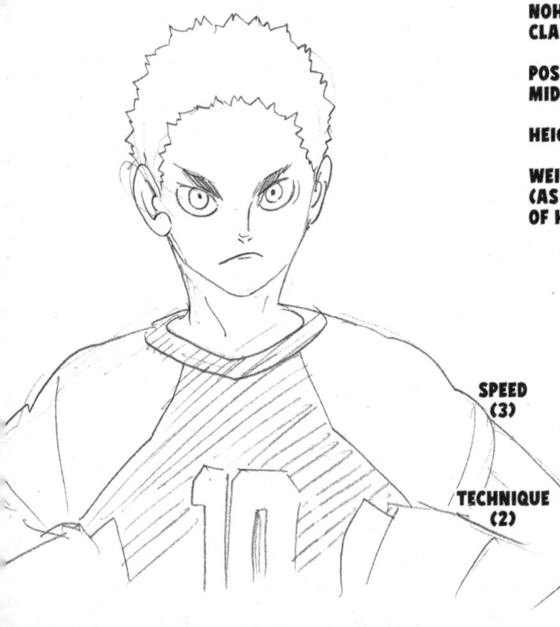

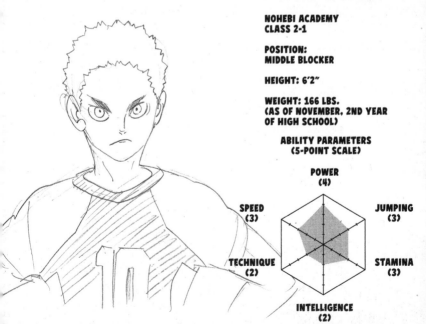

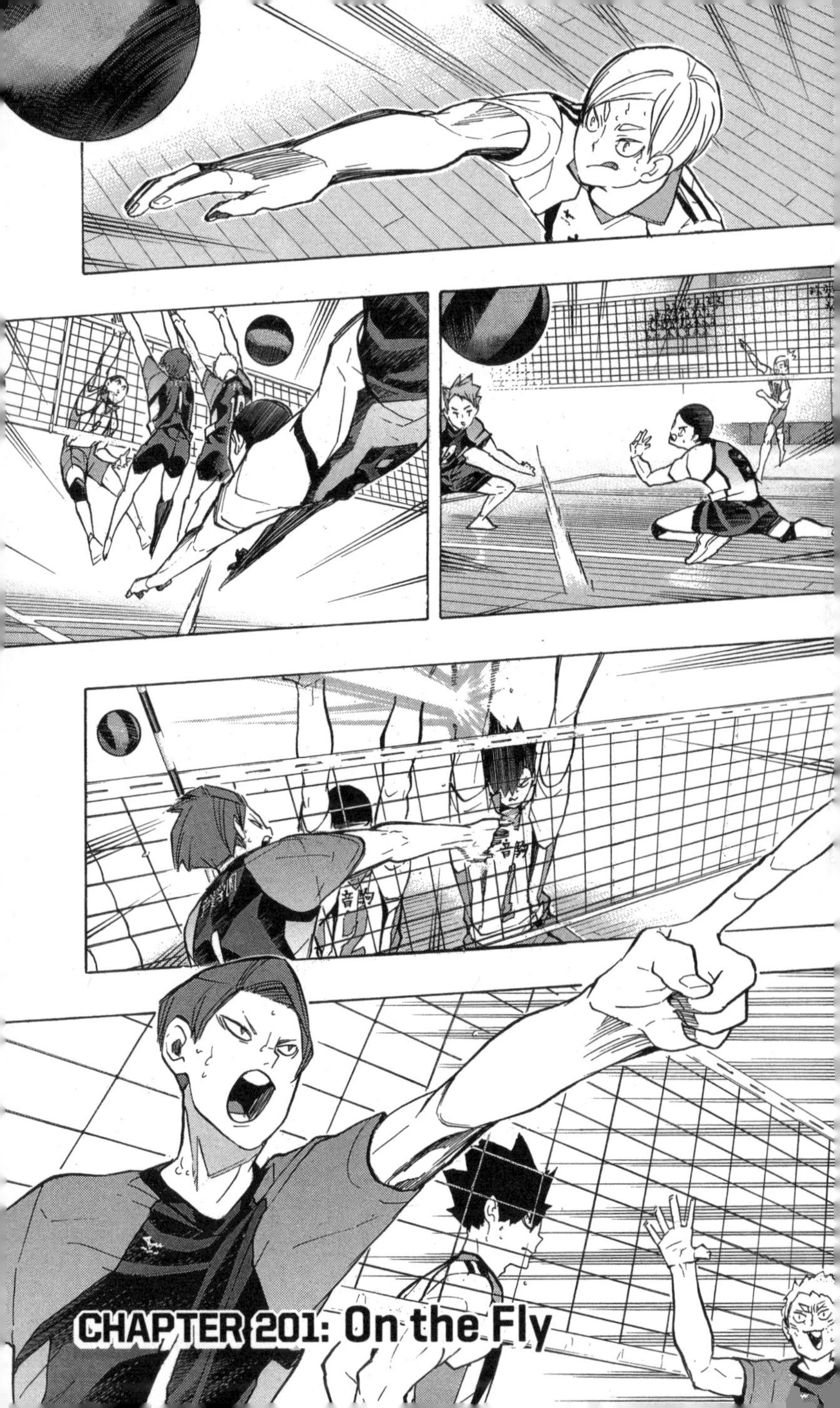
CHAPTER 201: On the Fly

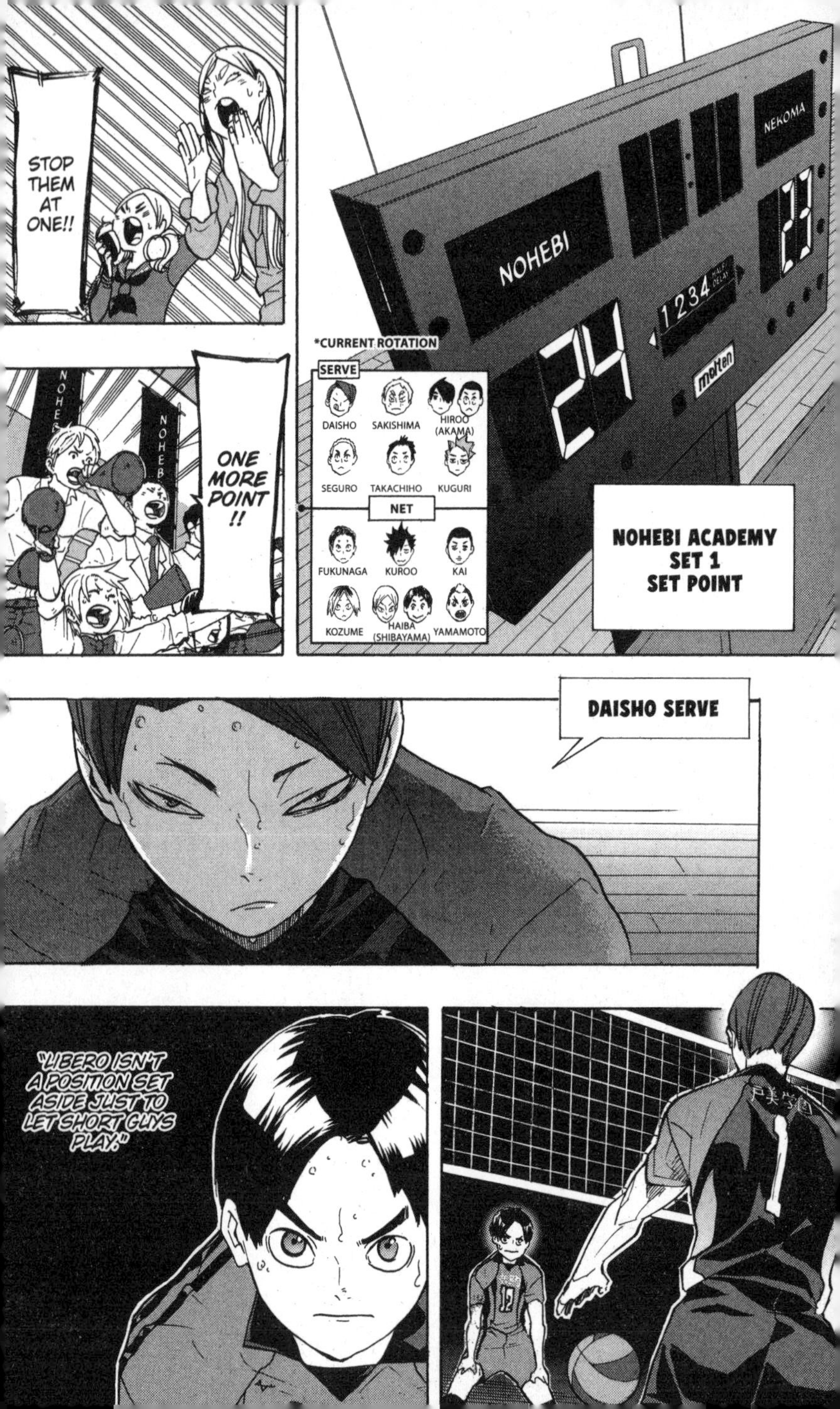
NEKOMA
NOHEBI
24
23
1234
molten
*CURRENT ROTATION
SERVE
DAISHO
SAKISHIMA
HIROO (AKAMA)
SEGURO
TAKACHIHO
KUGURI
NET
FUKUNAGA
KUROO
KAI
KOZUME
HAIBA (SHIBAYAMA)
YAMAMOTO
NOHEBI ACADEMY SET 1 SET POINT
STOP THEM AT ONE!!
NOHEBI
ONE MORE POINT!!
DAISHO SERVE
"LIBERO ISN'T A POSITION SET ASIDE JUST TO LET SHORT GUYS PLAY."

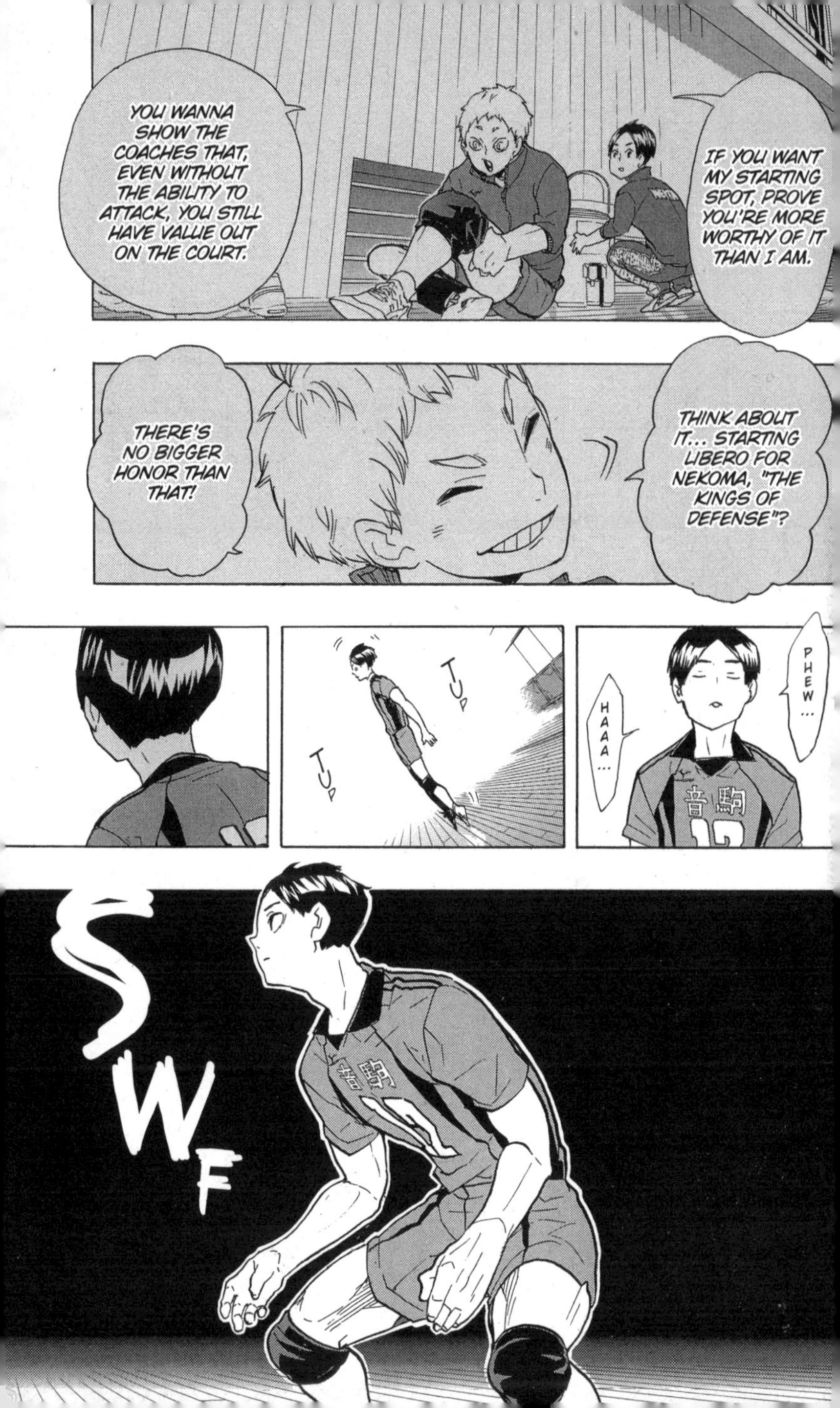
IF YOU WANT MY STARTING SPOT, PROVE YOU'RE MORE WORTHY OF IT THAN I AM.
YOU WANNA SHOW THE COACHES THAT, EVEN WITHOUT THE ABILITY TO ATTACK, YOU STILL HAVE VALUE OUT ON THE COURT.
THINK ABOUT IT... STARTING LIBERO FOR NEKOMA, "THE KINGS OF DEFENSE"?
THERE'S NO BIGGER HONOR THAN THAT!
PHEW...
HAAA...
TUP
TUP
SWF

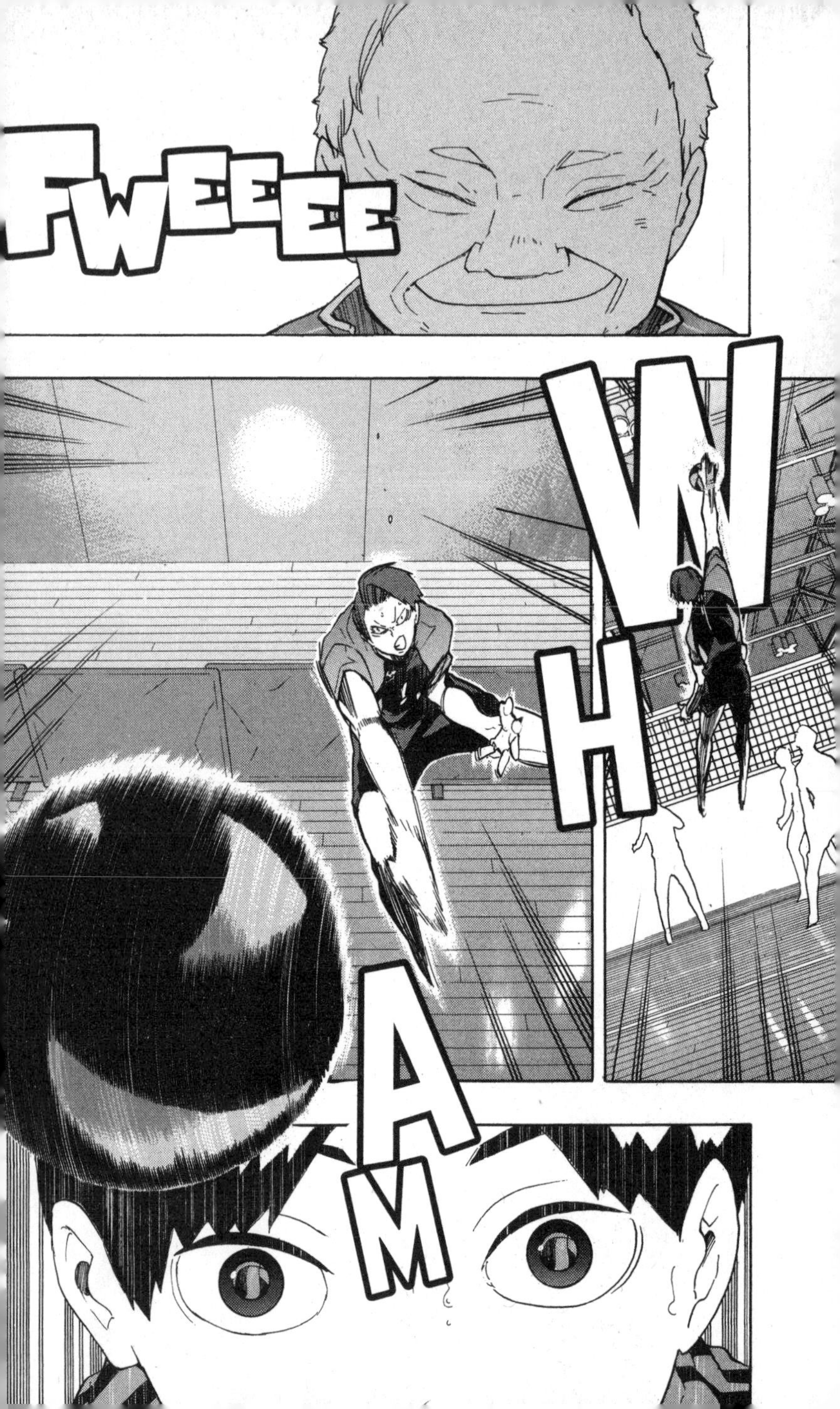
FWEEEE
WHAM

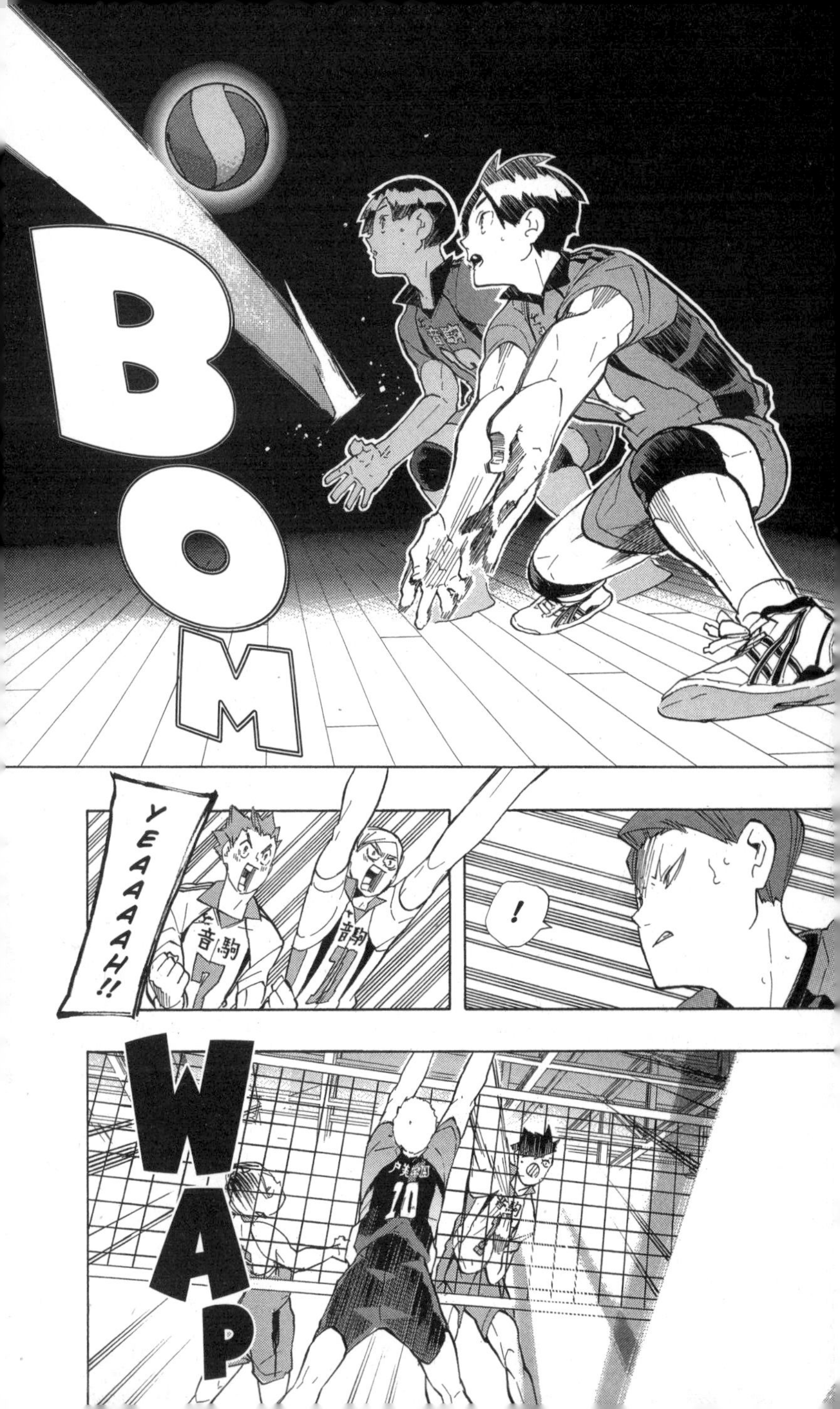
BOOM
!
YEAAAAAH!!
WAP

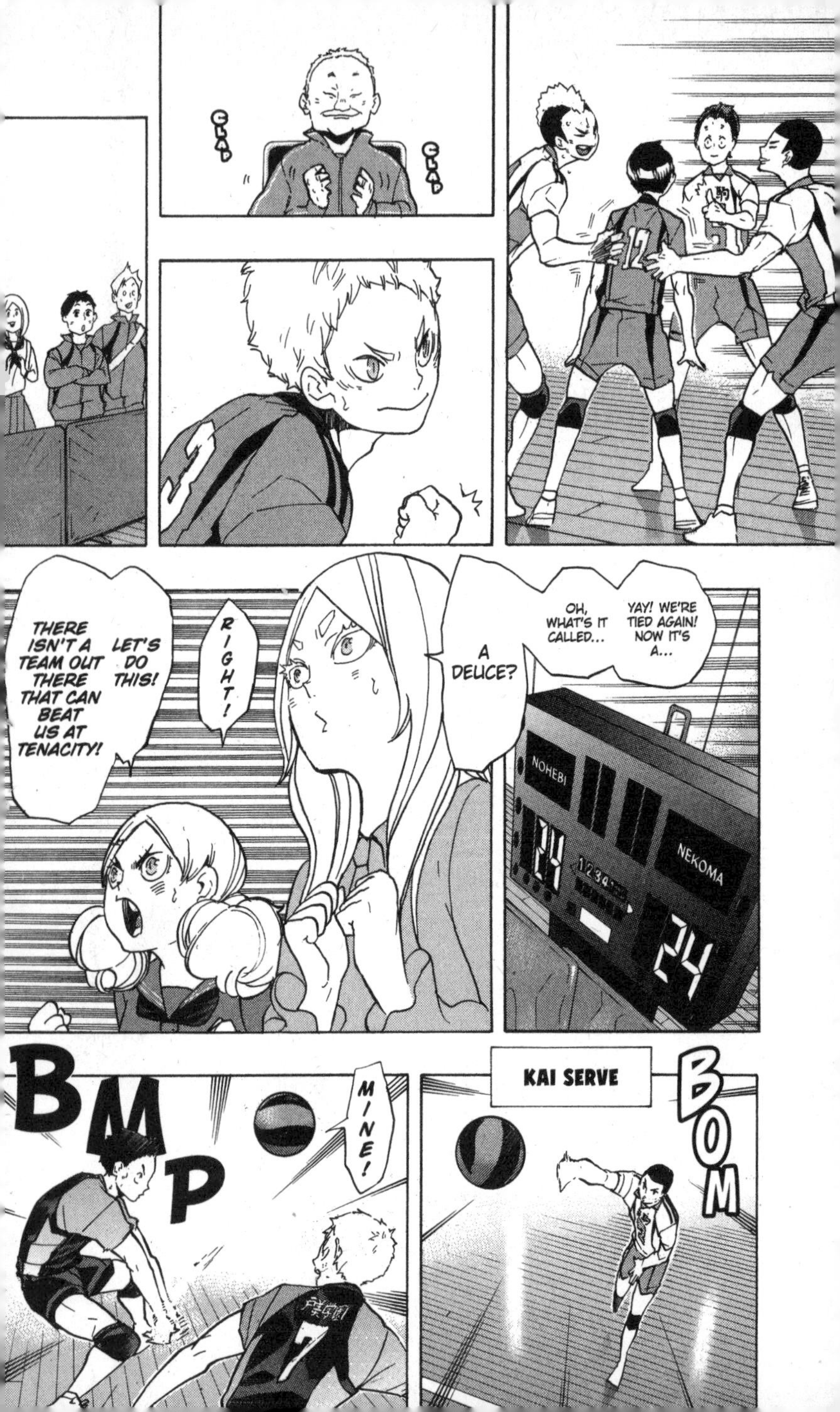
CLAP
CLAP
YAY! WE'RE TIED AGAIN! NOW IT'S A...
OH, WHAT'S IT CALLED...
A DEUCE?
NOHEBI
24
NEKOMA
24
RIGHT!
LET'S DO THIS!
THERE ISN'T A TEAM OUT THERE THAT CAN BEAT US AT TENACITY!
KAI SERVE
BOM
MINE!
BMP

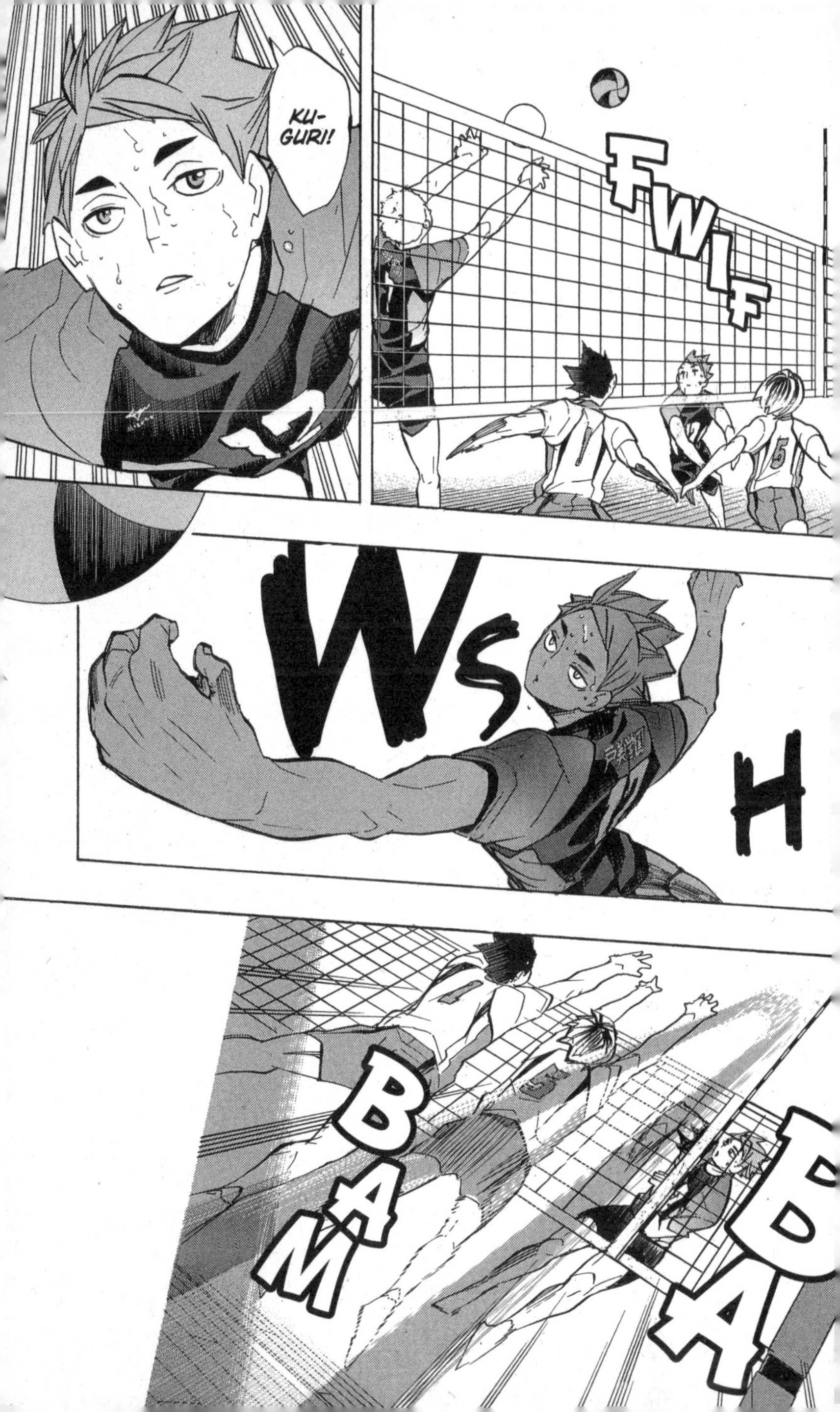

FWIF
KU-GURI!
WSH
BAM

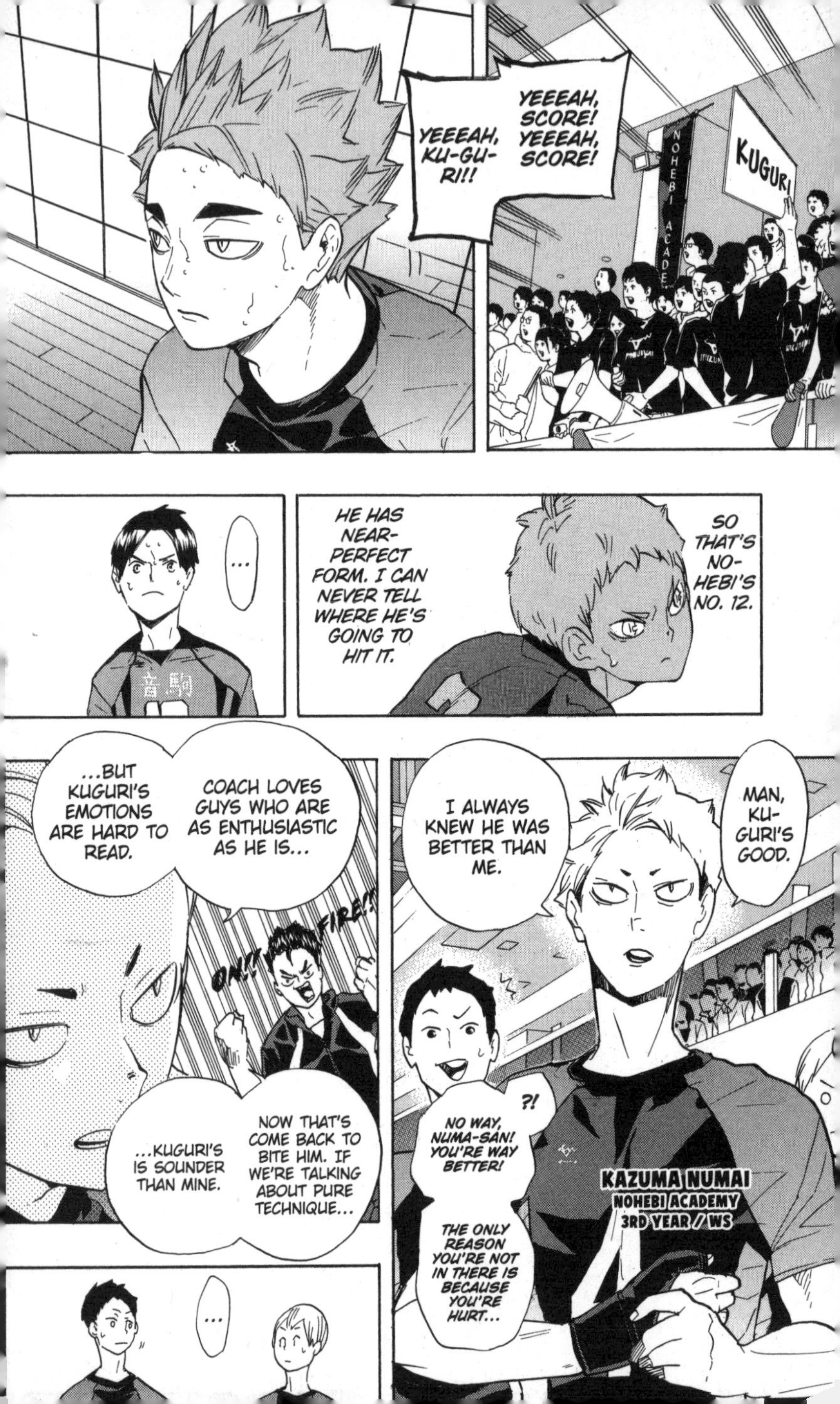
YEEEAH, SCORE! YEEEAH, SCORE!
YEEEAH, KU-GURI!!
KUGURI
NOHEBI ACADE
SO THAT'S NO-HEBI'S NO. 12.
HE HAS NEAR-PERFECT FORM. I CAN NEVER TELL WHERE HE'S GOING TO HIT IT.
...
MAN, KU-GURI'S GOOD.
I ALWAYS KNEW HE WAS BETTER THAN ME.
?!
NO WAY, NUMA-SAN! YOU'RE WAY BETTER!
THE ONLY REASON YOU'RE NOT IN THERE IS BECAUSE YOU'RE HURT...
KAZUMA NUMAI
NOHEBI ACADEMY
3RD YEAR / WS
COACH LOVES GUYS WHO ARE AS ENTHUSIASTIC AS HE IS...
...BUT KUGURI'S EMOTIONS ARE HARD TO READ.
ON!! FIRE!!
NOW THAT'S COME BACK TO BITE HIM. IF WE'RE TALKING ABOUT PURE TECHNIQUE...
...KUGURI'S IS SOUNDER THAN MINE.
...

NOHEBI	NEKOMA
25	25

YEAH! GREAT SHOT!

TUMP

FUKU-NAGA!

THAT'S WHERE YOU'RE SUPPOSED TO SAY "NO IT ISN'T!"

!!

DAM-MIT...

THIS ISN'T GONNA BE THE END OF THE ROAD FOR US.

SCORE! YEAH! NE-KO-MA!

FIGHT! WIN! NE-KO-MA!

GRAB IT NO MATTER WHAT IT TAKES!!

GRAB OUR TICKET TO NATONALS, GUYS!!

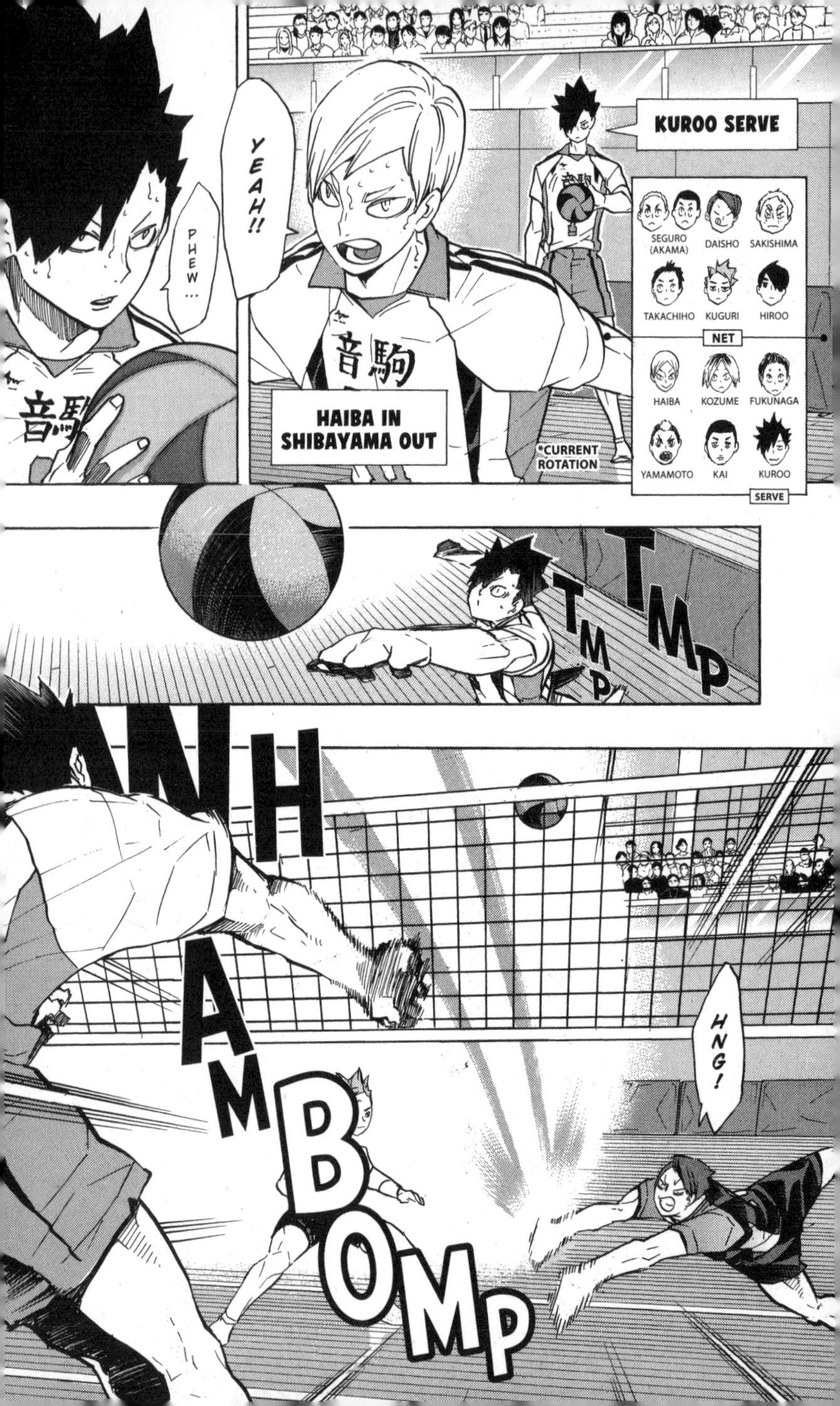
YEAH!!
KUROO SERVE
HAIBA IN SHIBAYAMA OUT
SEGURO (AKAMA)
DAISHO
SAKISHIMA
TAKACHIHO
KUGURI
HIROO
NET
HAIBA
KOZUME
FUKUNAGA
YAMAMOTO
KAI
KUROO
SERVE
*CURRENT ROTATION
PHEW...
TMP
TMP
HAM
BOMP
HNG!

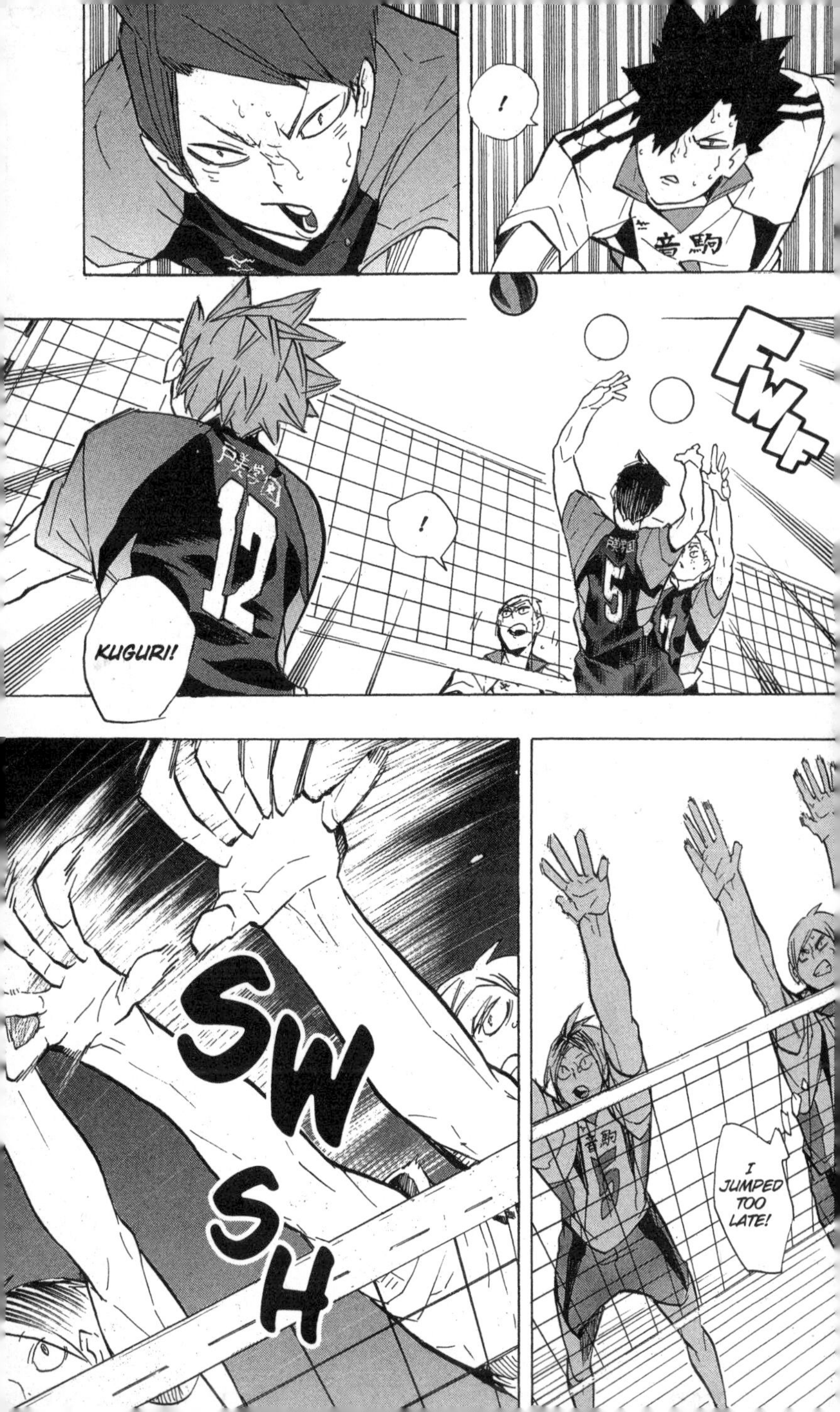
!
FWIF
!
KUGURI!
I JUMPED TOO LATE!
SW
S
H

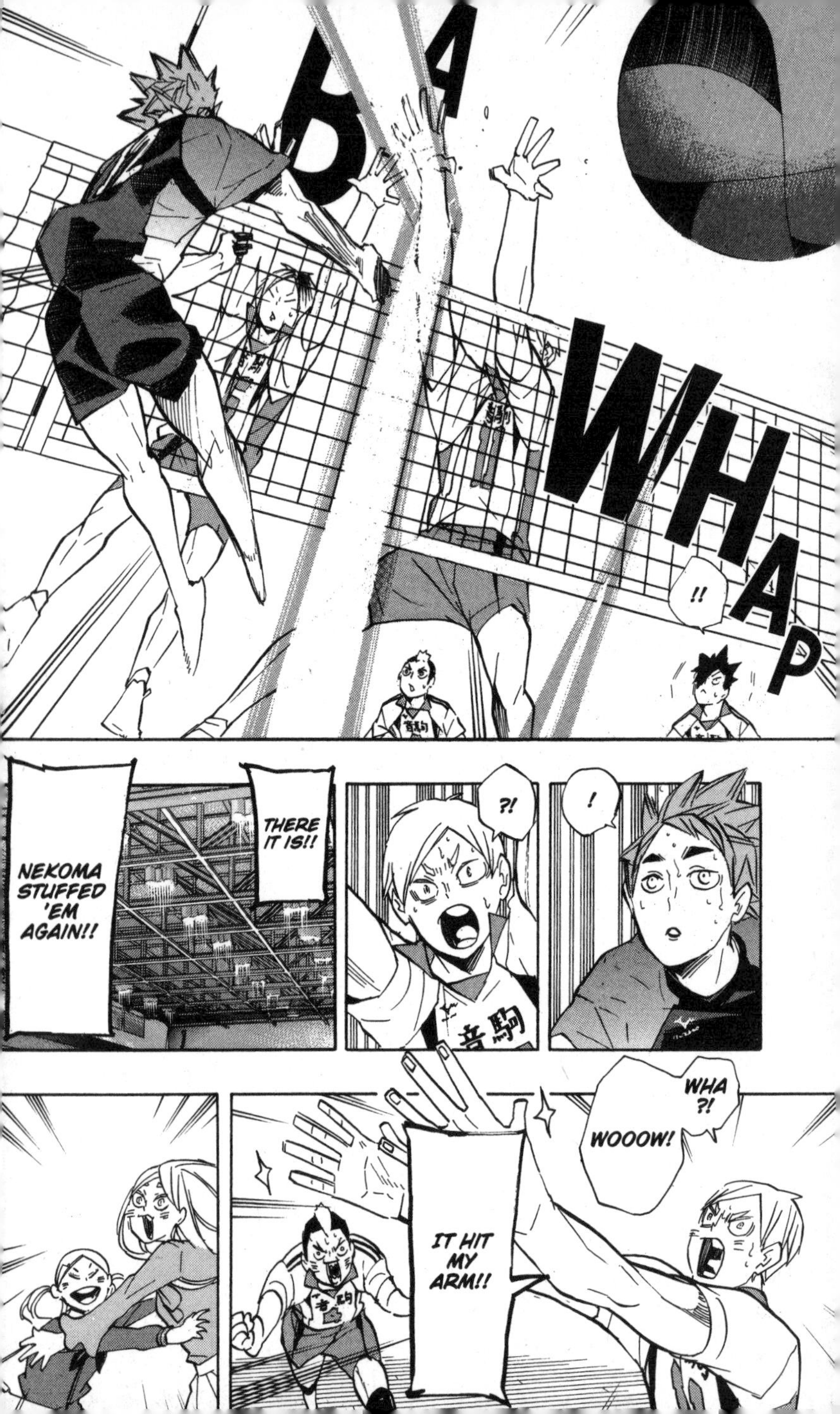
WHAP
!!
!
?!
THERE IT IS!!
NEKOMA STUFFED 'EM AGAIN!!
WHA ?!
WOOOW!
IT HIT MY ARM!!

NEKOMA
SET 1
SET POINT

....

IT WON'T BE A FLUKE WHEN I DO IT AGAIN!

!!

FLUKE! THAT WAS JUST A FLUKE!

TAKACHIHO SERVE

....

BAF

GOT IT!

SORRY!

!

OUT!

NOHEBI	NEKOMA
26	26

DAMMIT!

MAN, NEKOMA'S SETTER IS STAYING COOL AS ICE.

NOHEBI	NEKOMA
26	27

TUMP

BACK AT YOU!

TMP TMP

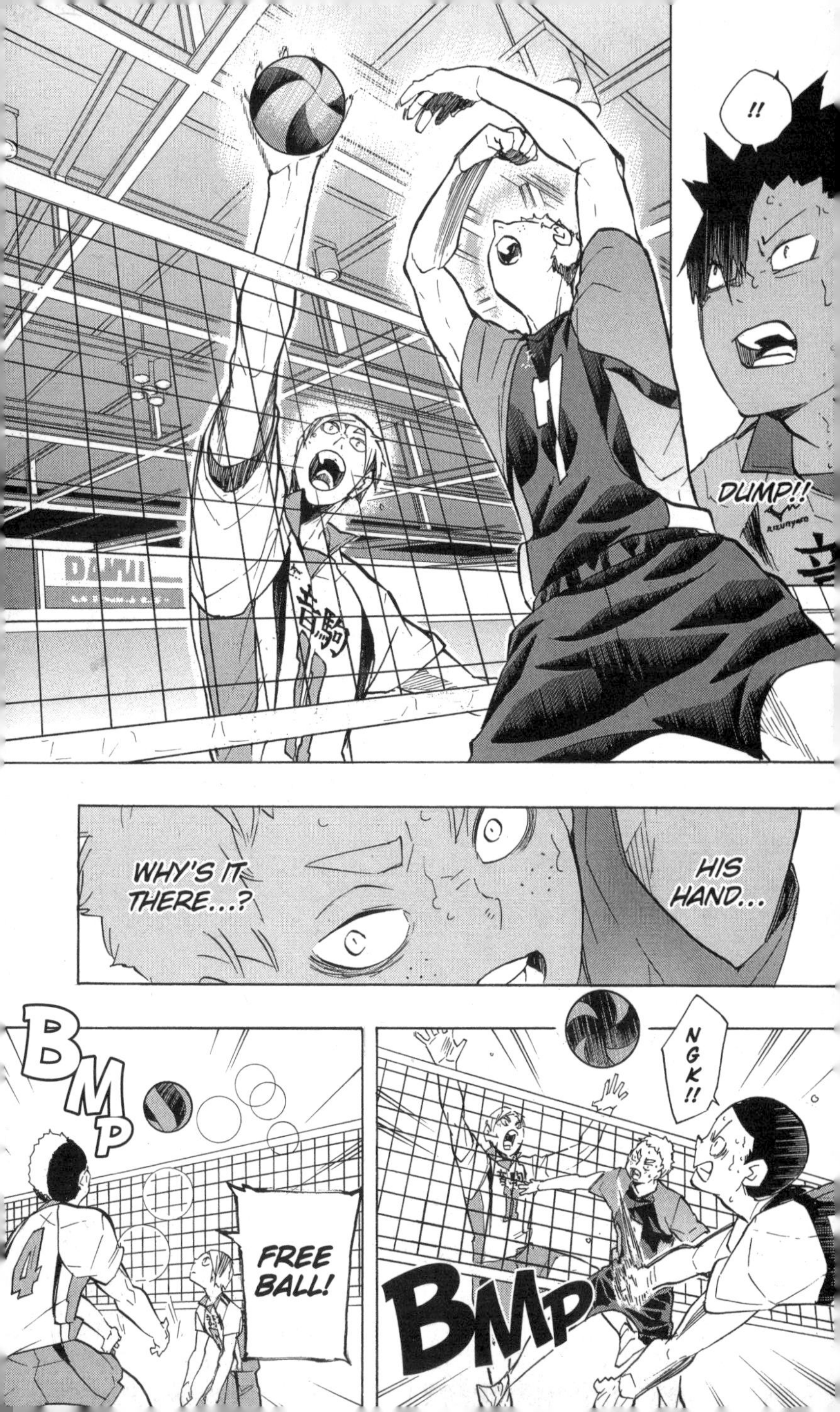
!!
DUMP!!
HIS HAND...
WHY'S IT THERE...?
NGK!!
BMP
BMP
FREE BALL!

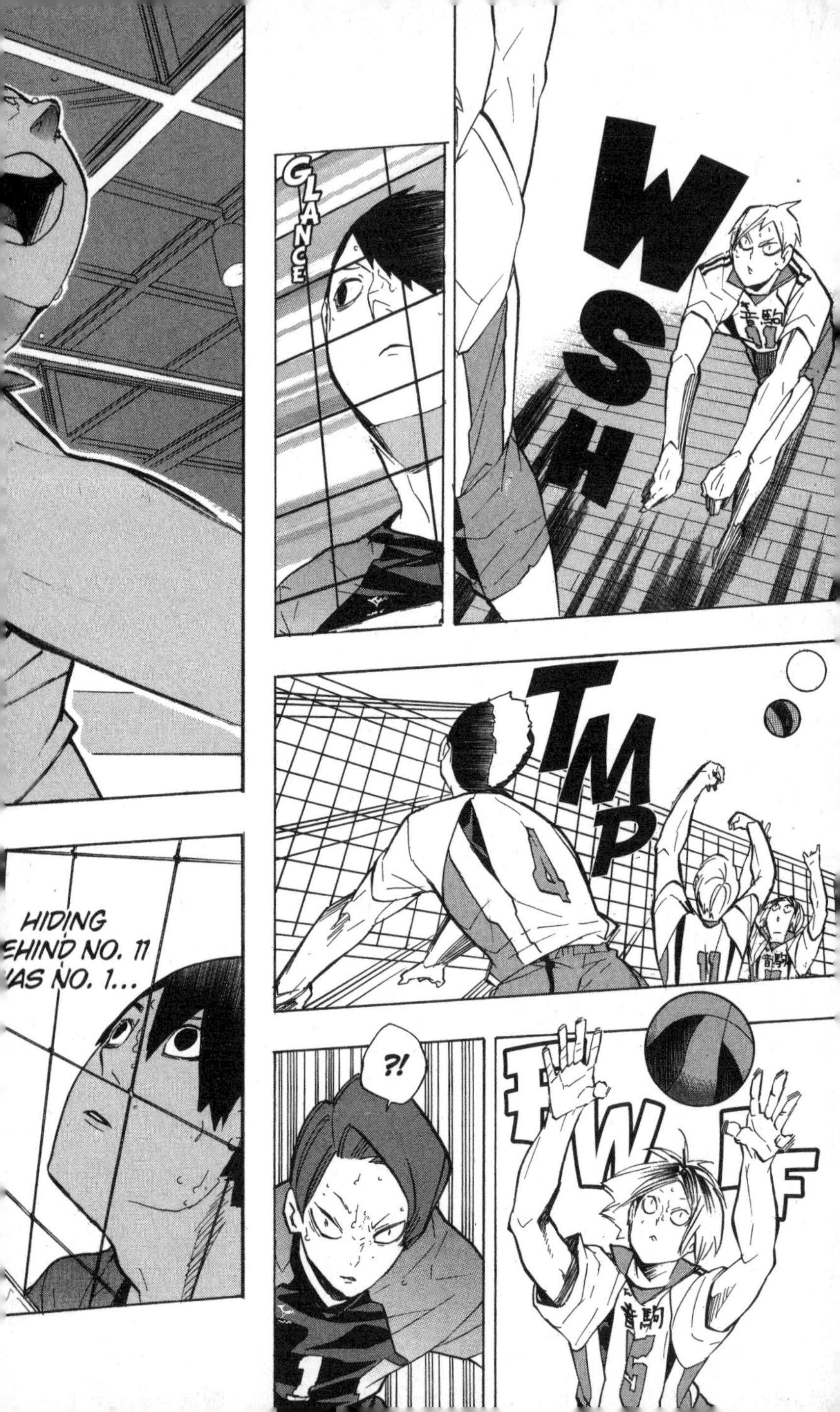
WSH
GLANCE
TMP
FWF
?!
HIDING EHIND NO. 11 VAS NO. 1…

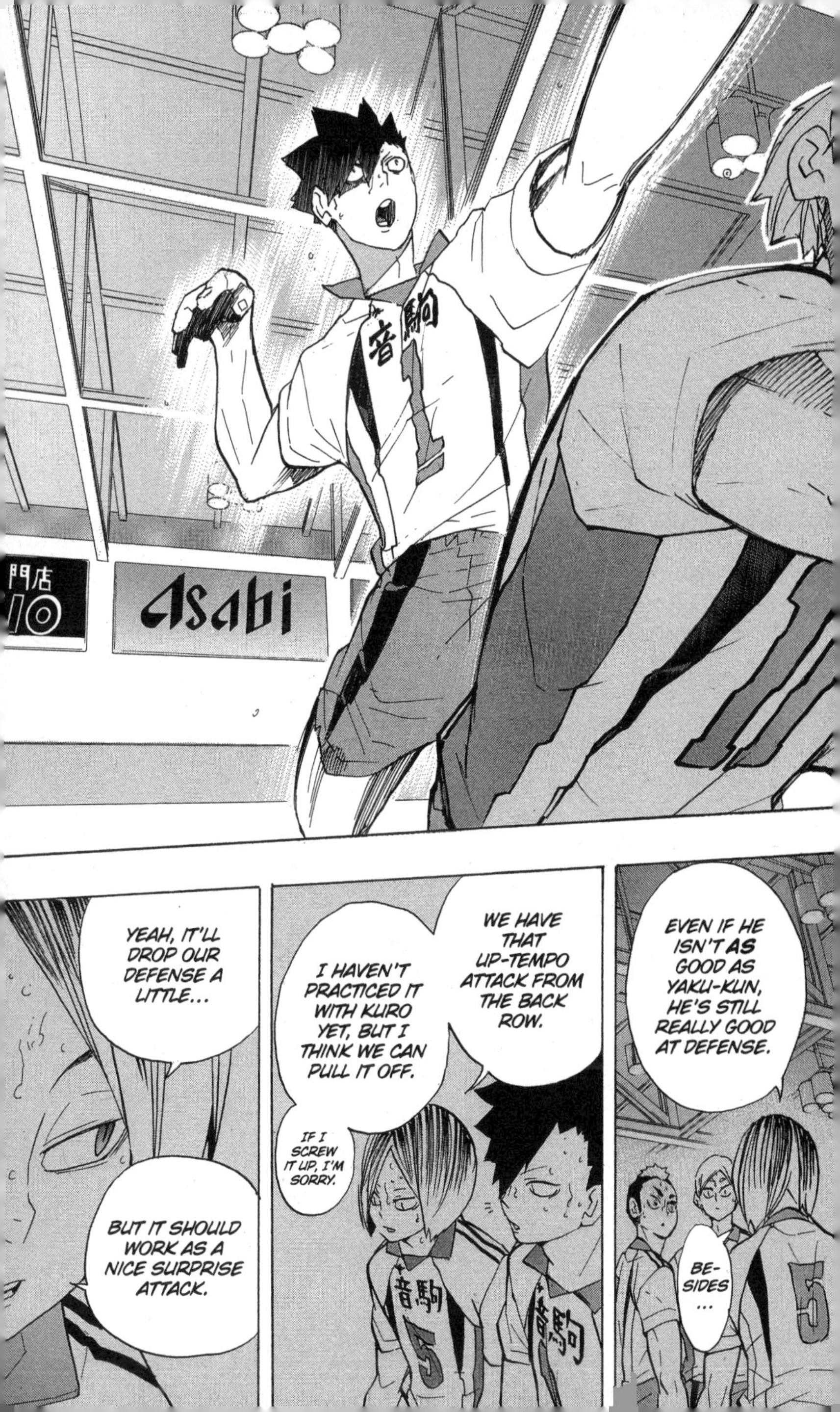

Asabi
EVEN IF HE ISN'T AS GOOD AS YAKU-KUN, HE'S STILL REALLY GOOD AT DEFENSE.
BE-SIDES...
WE HAVE THAT UP-TEMPO ATTACK FROM THE BACK ROW.
I HAVEN'T PRACTICED IT WITH KURO YET, BUT I THINK WE CAN PULL IT OFF.
IF I SCREW IT UP, I'M SORRY.
YEAH, IT'LL DROP OUR DEFENSE A LITTLE...
BUT IT SHOULD WORK AS A NICE SURPRISE ATTACK.

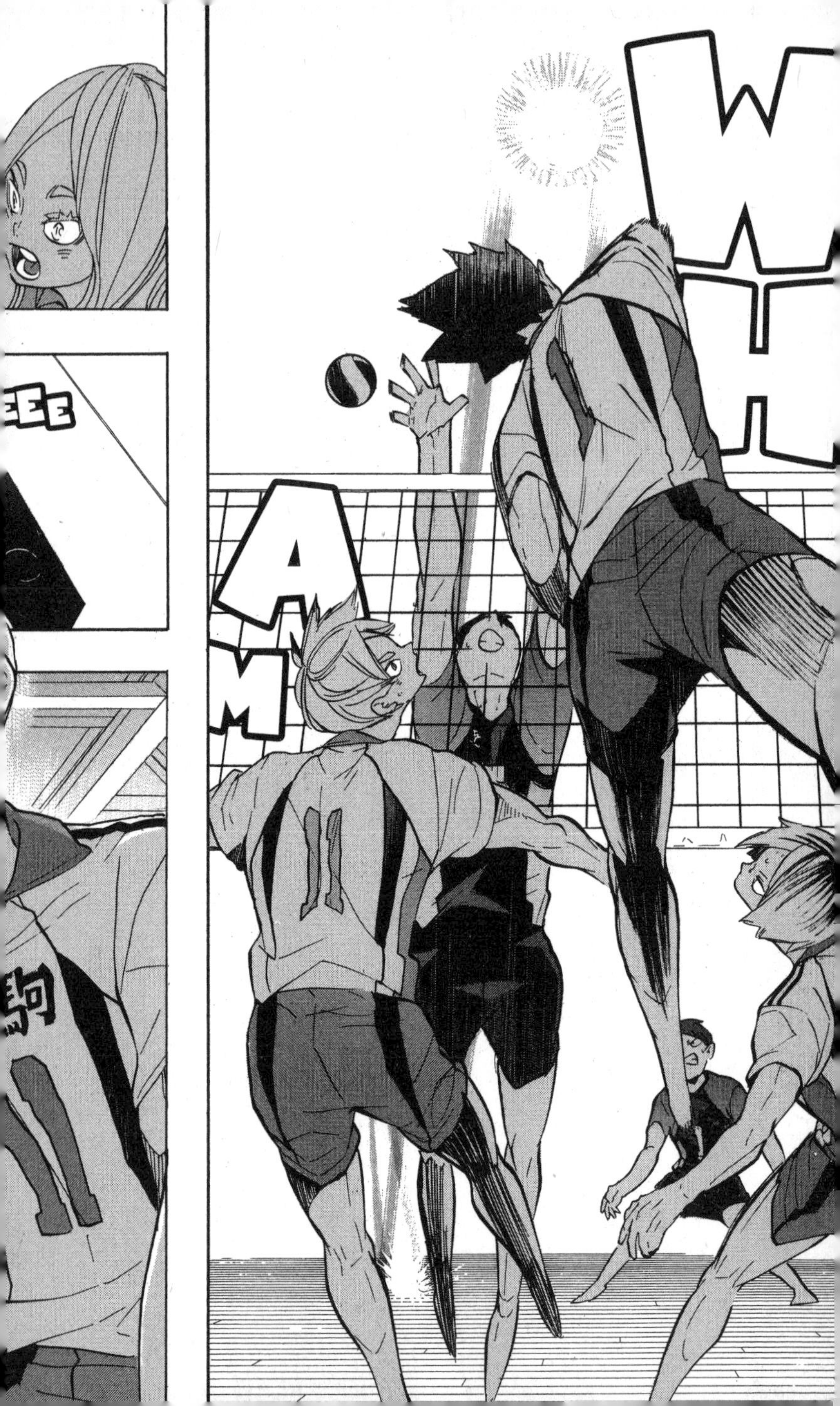
WHAM
EEE

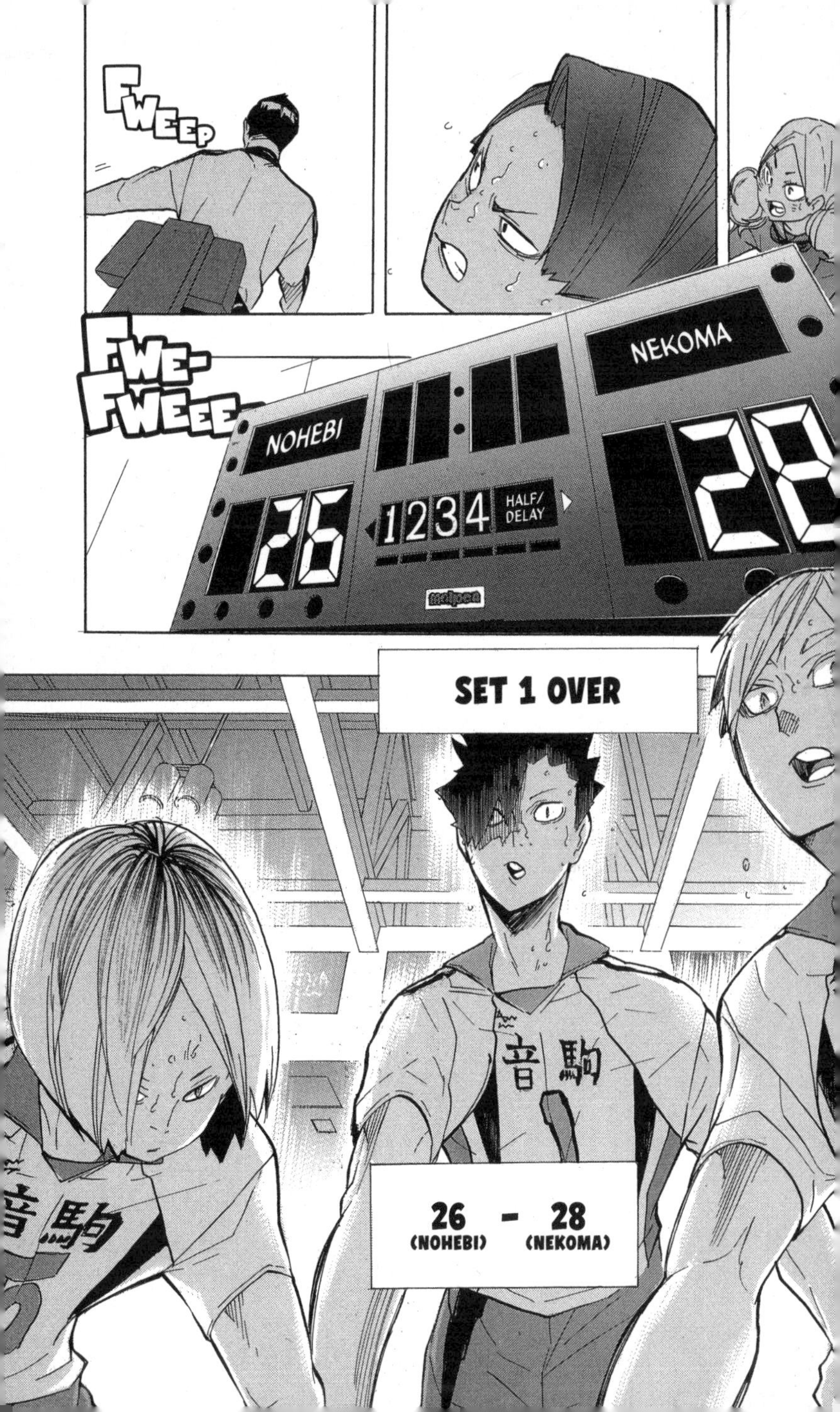
FWEEP
FWE-FWEEE
NOHEBI
NEKOMA
26
1234 HALF/DELAY
28
SET 1 OVER
音駒
音駒
26 - 28
(NOHEBI) (NEKOMA)

ISUMI SAKISHIMA

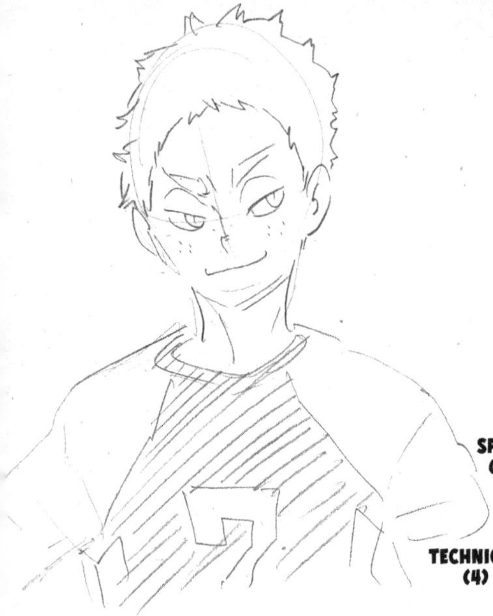

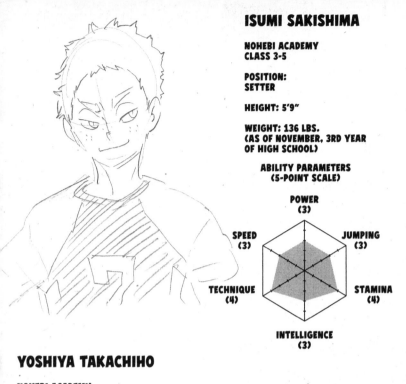

NOHEBI ACADEMY
CLASS 3-5

POSITION:
SETTER

HEIGHT: 5'9"

WEIGHT: 136 LBS.
(AS OF NOVEMBER, 3RD YEAR
OF HIGH SCHOOL)

ABILITY PARAMETERS
(5-POINT SCALE)

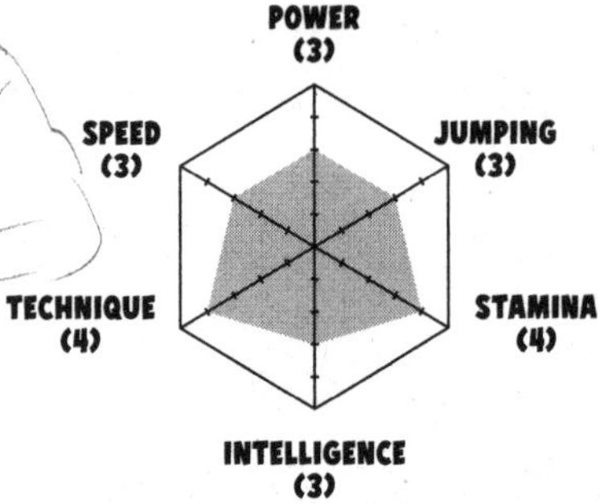
POWER
(3)
JUMPING
(3)
STAMINA
(4)
INTELLIGENCE
(3)
TECHNIQUE
(4)
SPEED
(3)

YOSHIYA TAKACHIHO

NOHEBI ACADEMY
CLASS 3-7

POSITION:
WING SPIKER

HEIGHT: 5'9"

WEIGHT: 139 LBS.
(AS OF NOVEMBER, 3RD YEAR
OF HIGH SCHOOL)

ABILITY PARAMETERS
(5-POINT SCALE)

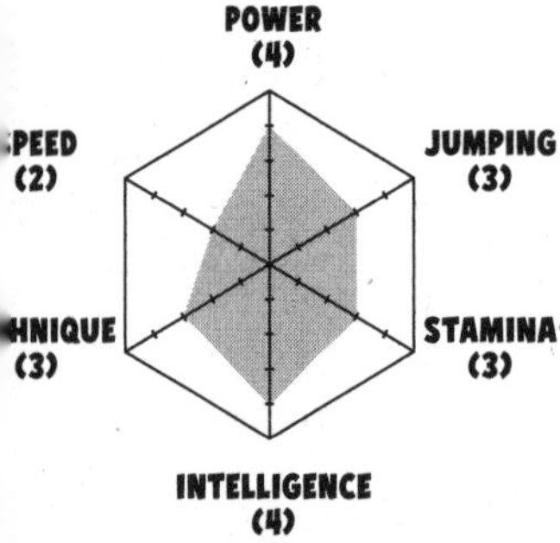
POWER
(4)
JUMPING
(3)
STAMINA
(3)
INTELLIGENCE
(4)
HNIQUE
(3)
PEED
(2)

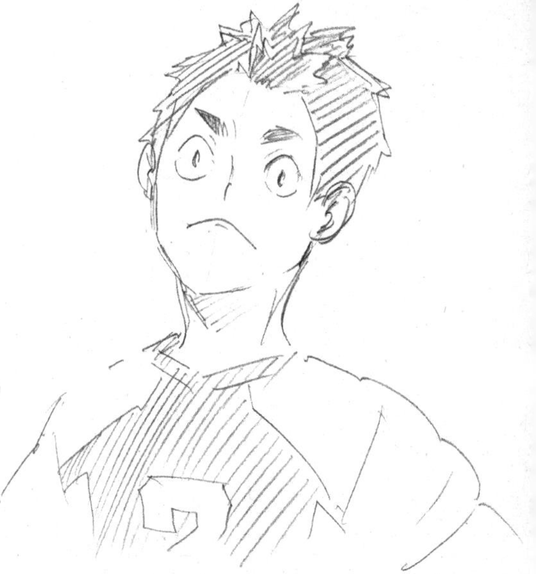

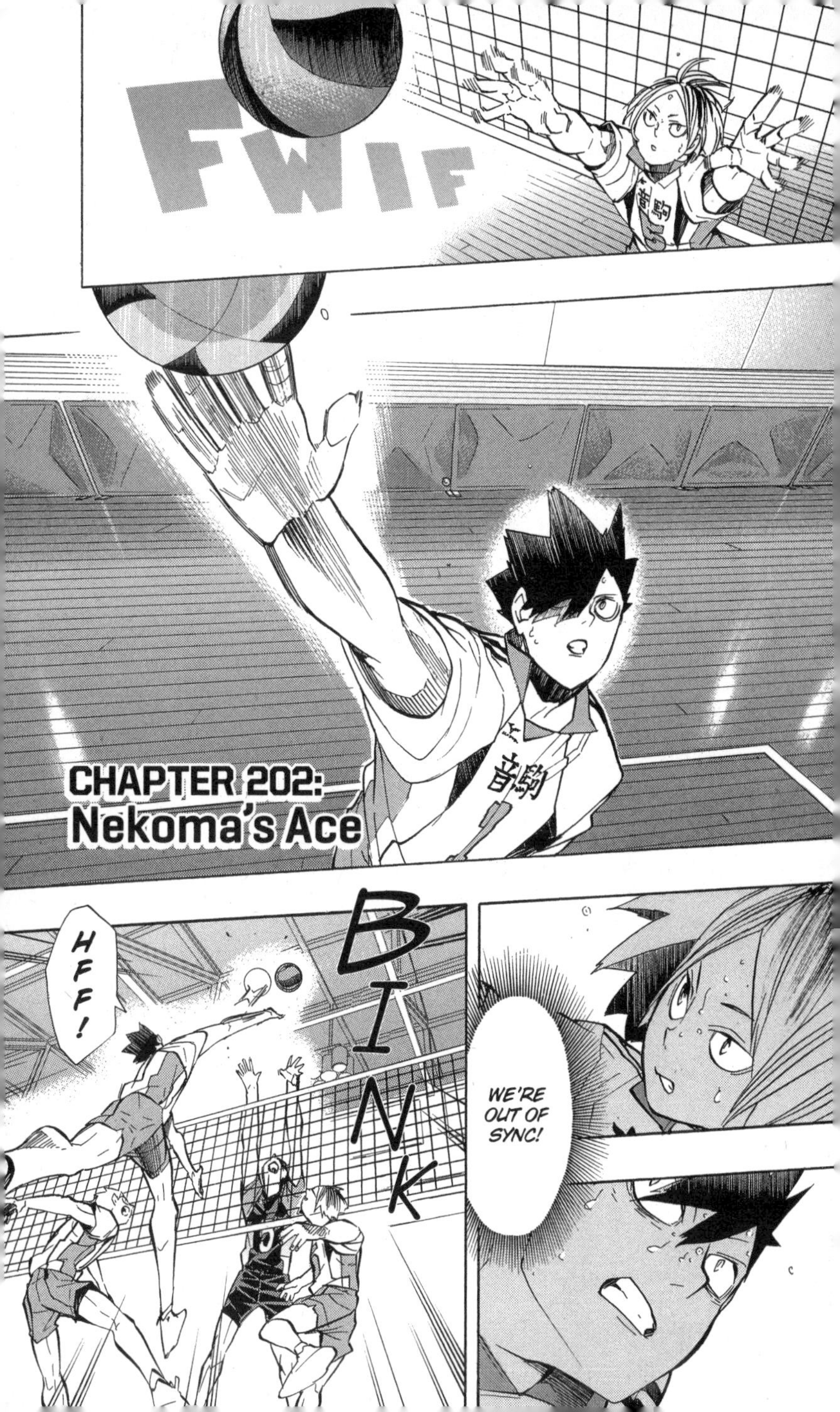
FWIF
CHAPTER 202:
Nekoma's Ace
WE'RE OUT OF SYNC!
BINK
HFF!

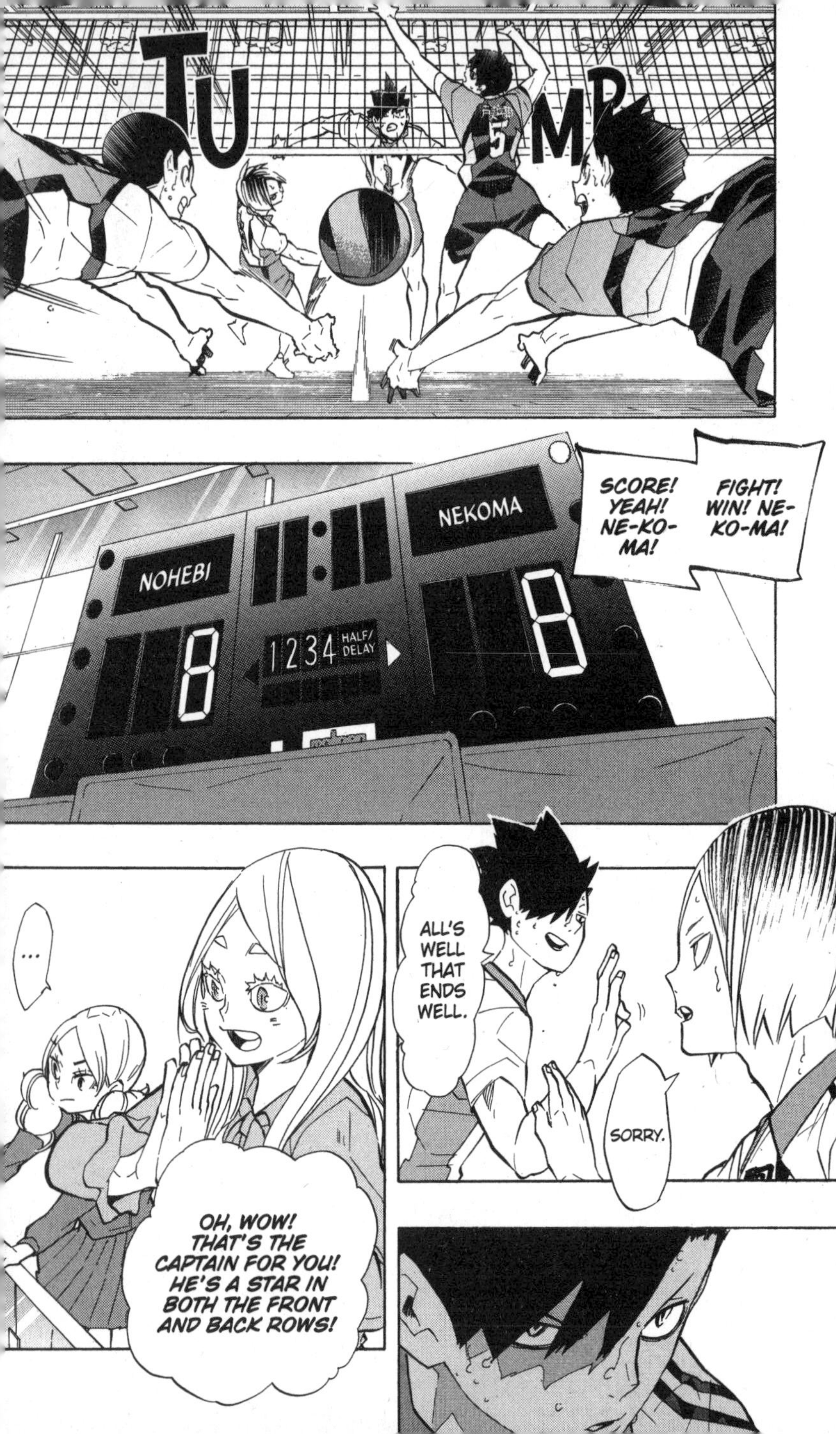
TUMP
FIGHT! WIN! NE-KO-MA!
SCORE! YEAH! NE-KO-MA!
NEKOMA
NOHEBI
8
8
1234 HALF/DELAY
ALL'S WELL THAT ENDS WELL.
SORRY.
...
OH, WOW! THAT'S THE CAPTAIN FOR YOU! HE'S A STAR IN BOTH THE FRONT AND BACK ROWS!

I'M SURE THIS HAS TO BE WAY MORE PRESSURE AND MORE TIRING FOR HIM THAN ANYBODY THINKS.

AND IN OUR CASE, WE'RE MISSING OUR LIBERO. THAT MEANS HE CAN'T GET A BREAK WHEN HE ROTATES INTO THE BACK ROW.

WHETHER IT'S BLOCKING OR HITTING A QUICK SET, MIDDLE BLOCKER IS A POSITION THAT INVOLVES A WHOLE LOT OF MOVING AND JUMPING.

FWEEEEEE

LET'S DO THAT AGAIN!

HANG IN THERE...!

!!

PL DUN AT

KOZUME SERVE

*CURRENT ROTATION

TAKACHIHO	SEGURO (AKAMA)	DAISHO
KUGURI	DAISHO	SAKISHIMA
KAI	YAMAMOTO	HAIBA
KUROO	FUKUNAGA	KOZUME
		SERVE

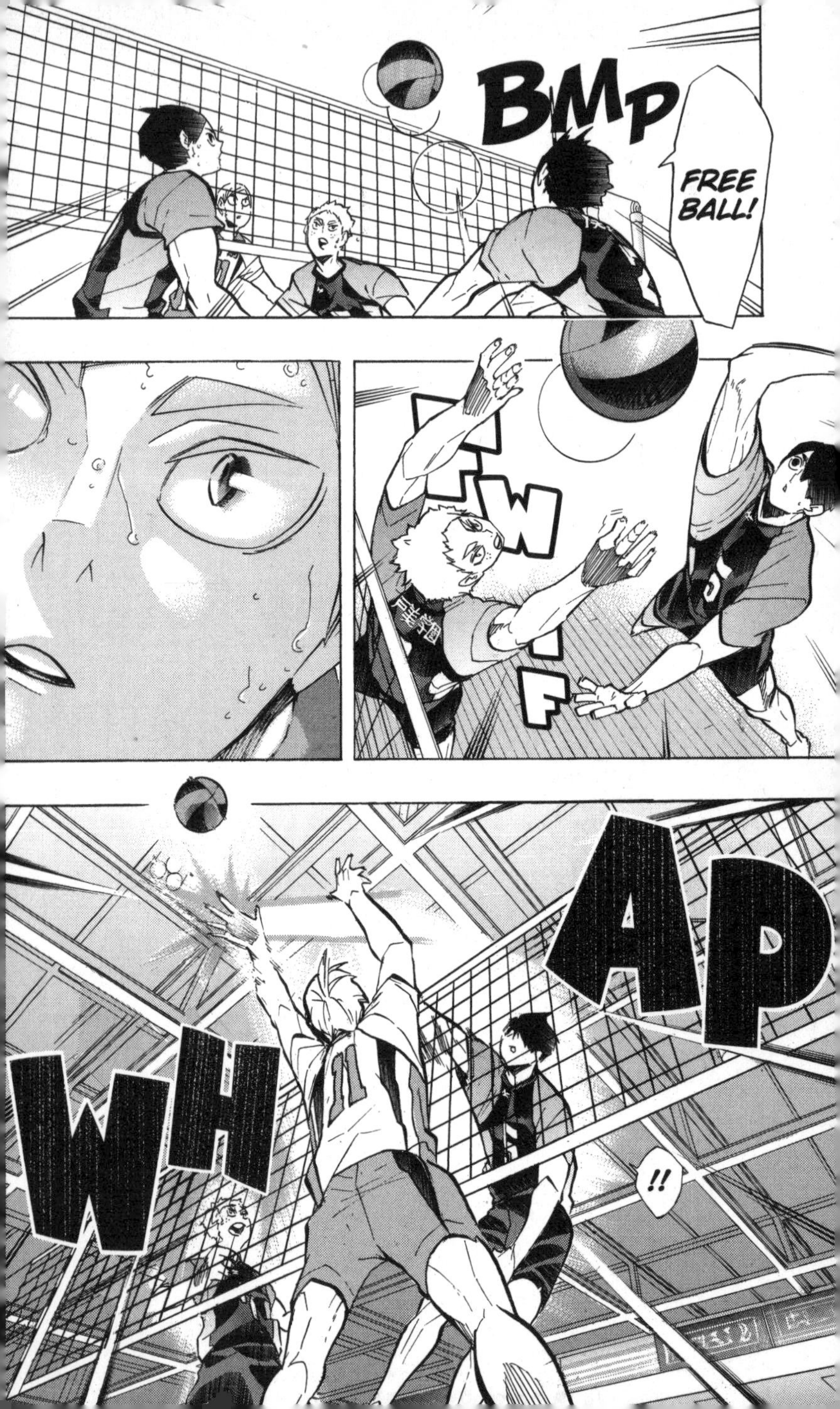
BMP
FREE BALL!
FW
F
WH
AP
!!

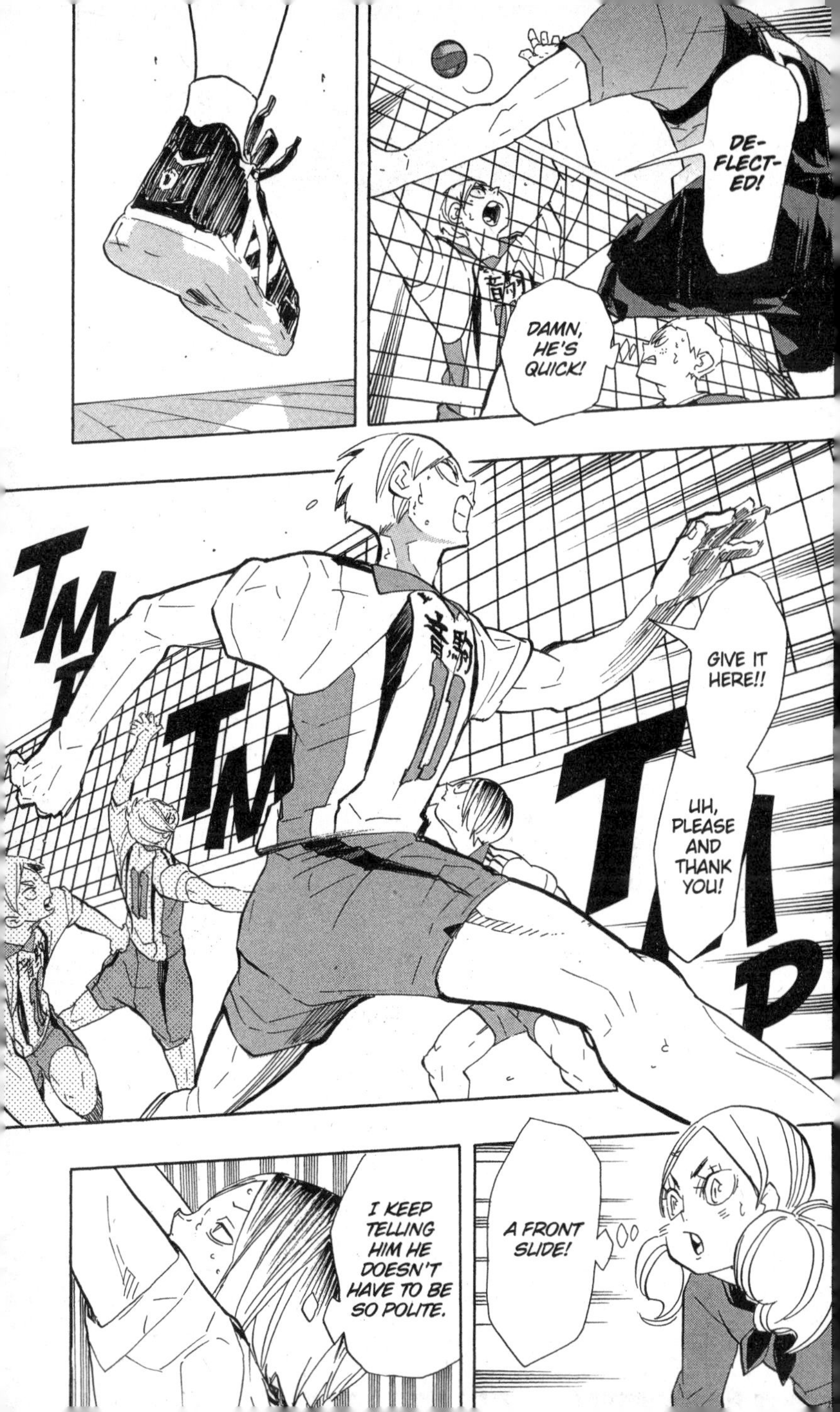
DE-FLECT-ED!
DAMN, HE'S QUICK!
GIVE IT HERE!!
UH, PLEASE AND THANK YOU!
TMP
TM
TM
A FRONT SLIDE!
I KEEP TELLING HIM HE DOESN'T HAVE TO BE SO POLITE.

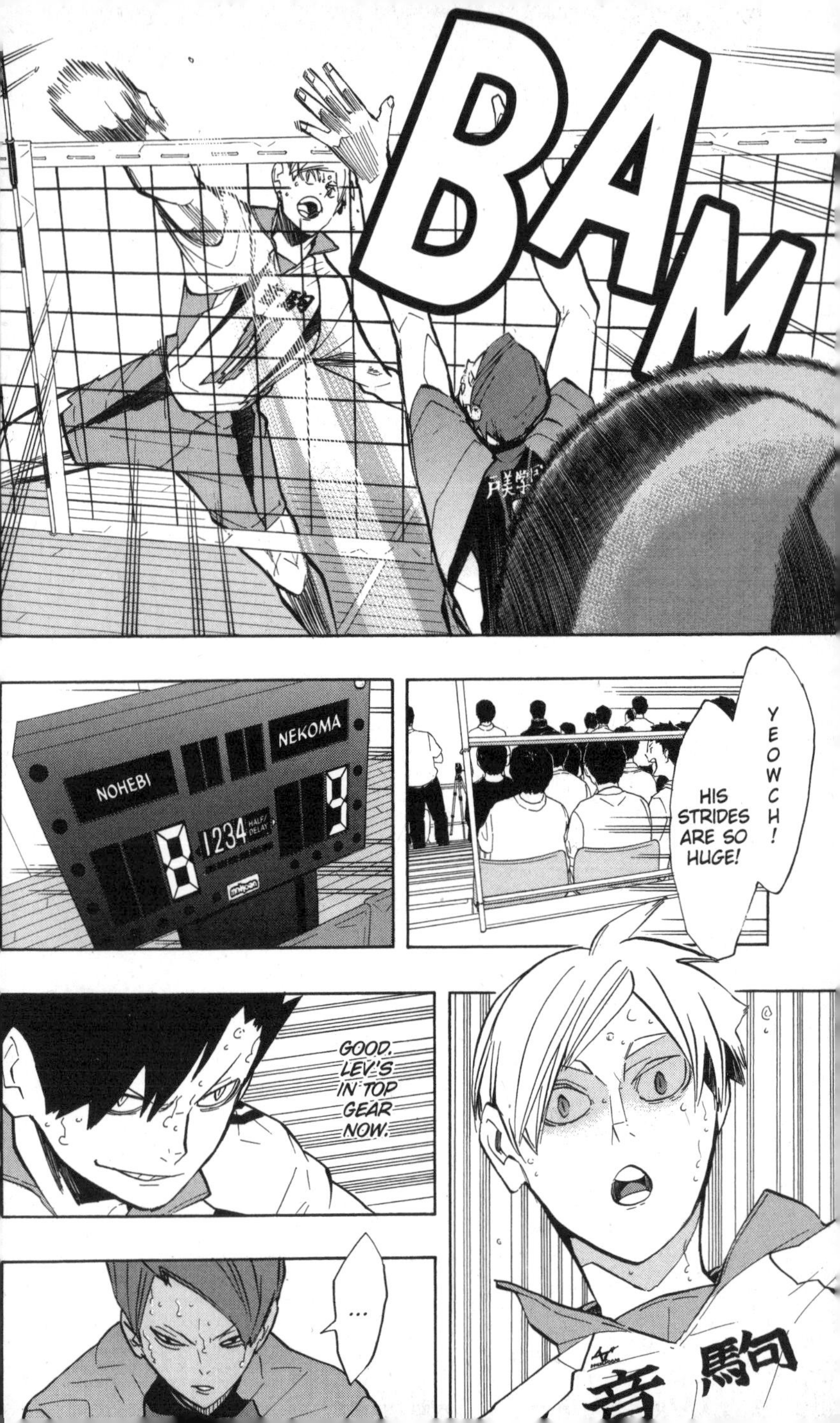
BAM
YEOWCH!
HIS STRIDES ARE SO HUGE!
NEKOMA
NOHEBI
8
1234
HALF/DELAY
9
音駒
GOOD. LEV'S IN TOP GEAR NOW.
...

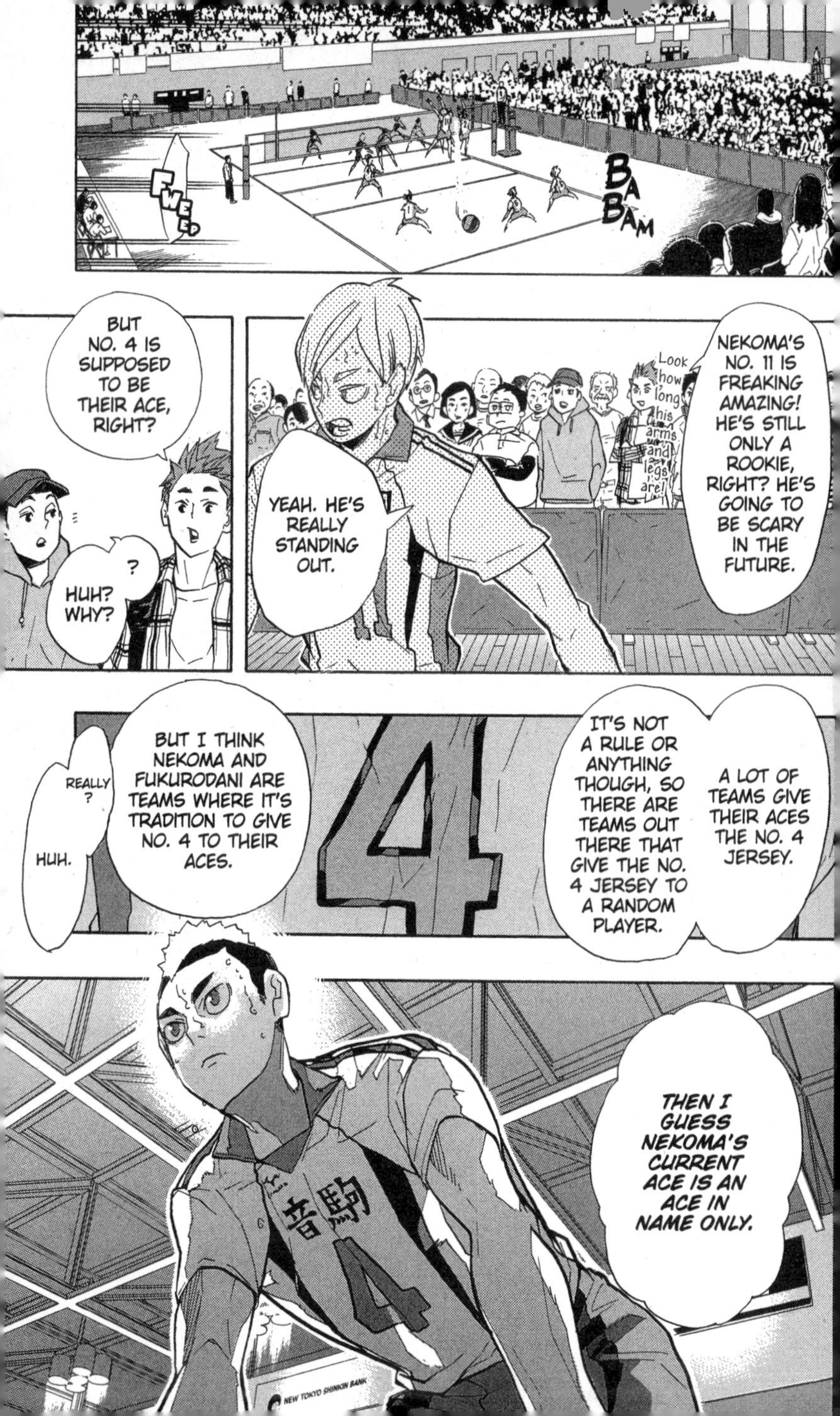
BA BAM
FWEEP
NEKOMA'S NO. 11 IS FREAKING AMAZING! HE'S STILL ONLY A ROOKIE, RIGHT? HE'S GOING TO BE SCARY IN THE FUTURE.
Look how long his arms and legs are!
YEAH. HE'S REALLY STANDING OUT.
BUT NO. 4 IS SUPPOSED TO BE THEIR ACE, RIGHT?
?
HUH? WHY?
A LOT OF TEAMS GIVE THEIR ACES THE NO. 4 JERSEY.
IT'S NOT A RULE OR ANYTHING THOUGH, SO THERE ARE TEAMS OUT THERE THAT GIVE THE NO. 4 JERSEY TO A RANDOM PLAYER.
BUT I THINK NEKOMA AND FUKURODANI ARE TEAMS WHERE IT'S TRADITION TO GIVE NO. 4 TO THEIR ACES.
REALLY?
HUH.
THEN I GUESS NEKOMA'S CURRENT ACE IS AN ACE IN NAME ONLY.
音駒
NEW TOKYO SHINKIN BANK

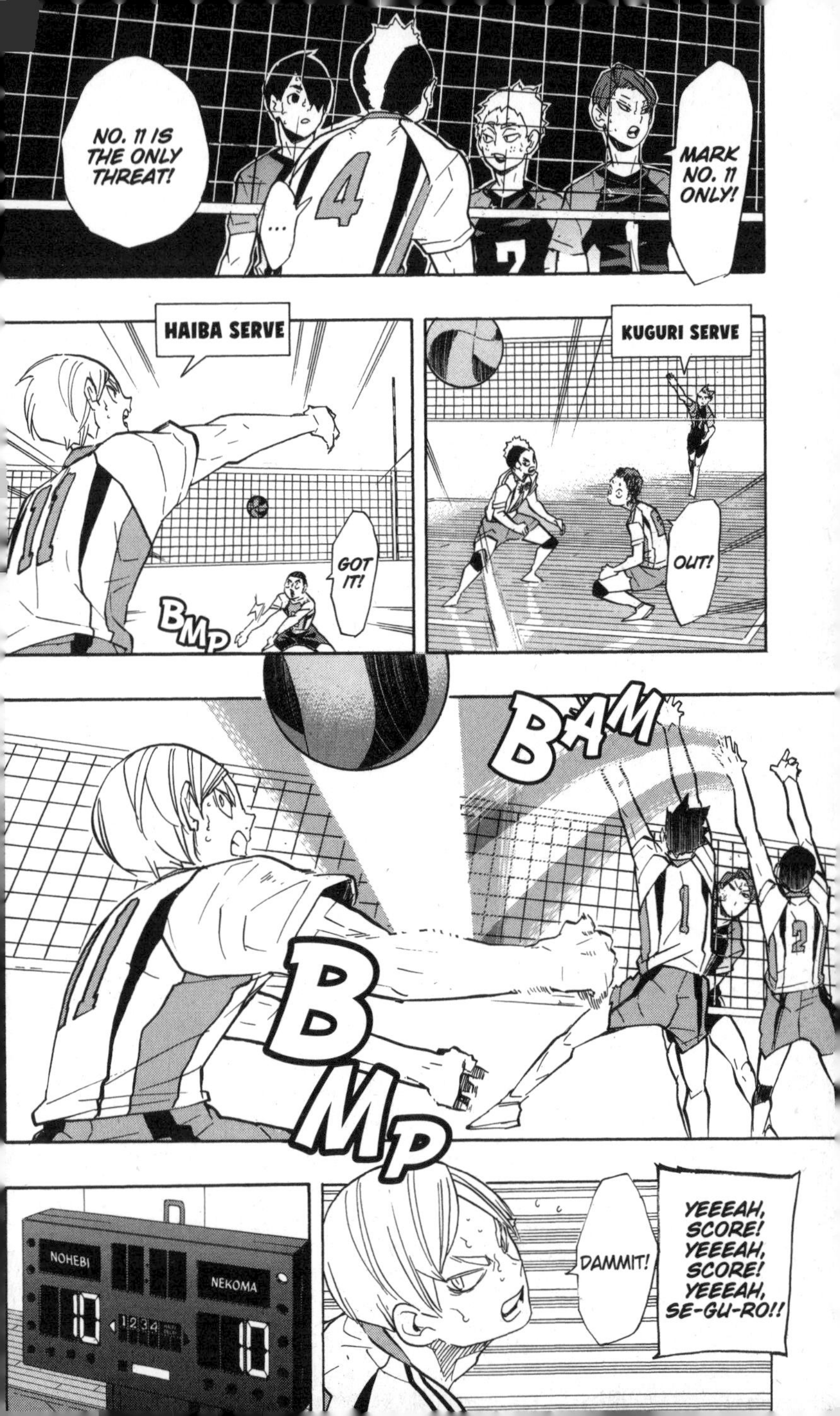
MARK NO. 11 ONLY!
NO. 11 IS THE ONLY THREAT!
...
KUGURI SERVE
OUT!
HAIBA SERVE
GOT IT!
BMP
BAM
BMP
YEEEAH, SCORE! YEEEAH, SCORE! YEEEAH, SE-GU-RO!!
DAMMIT!
NOHEBI
NEKOMA
10
10

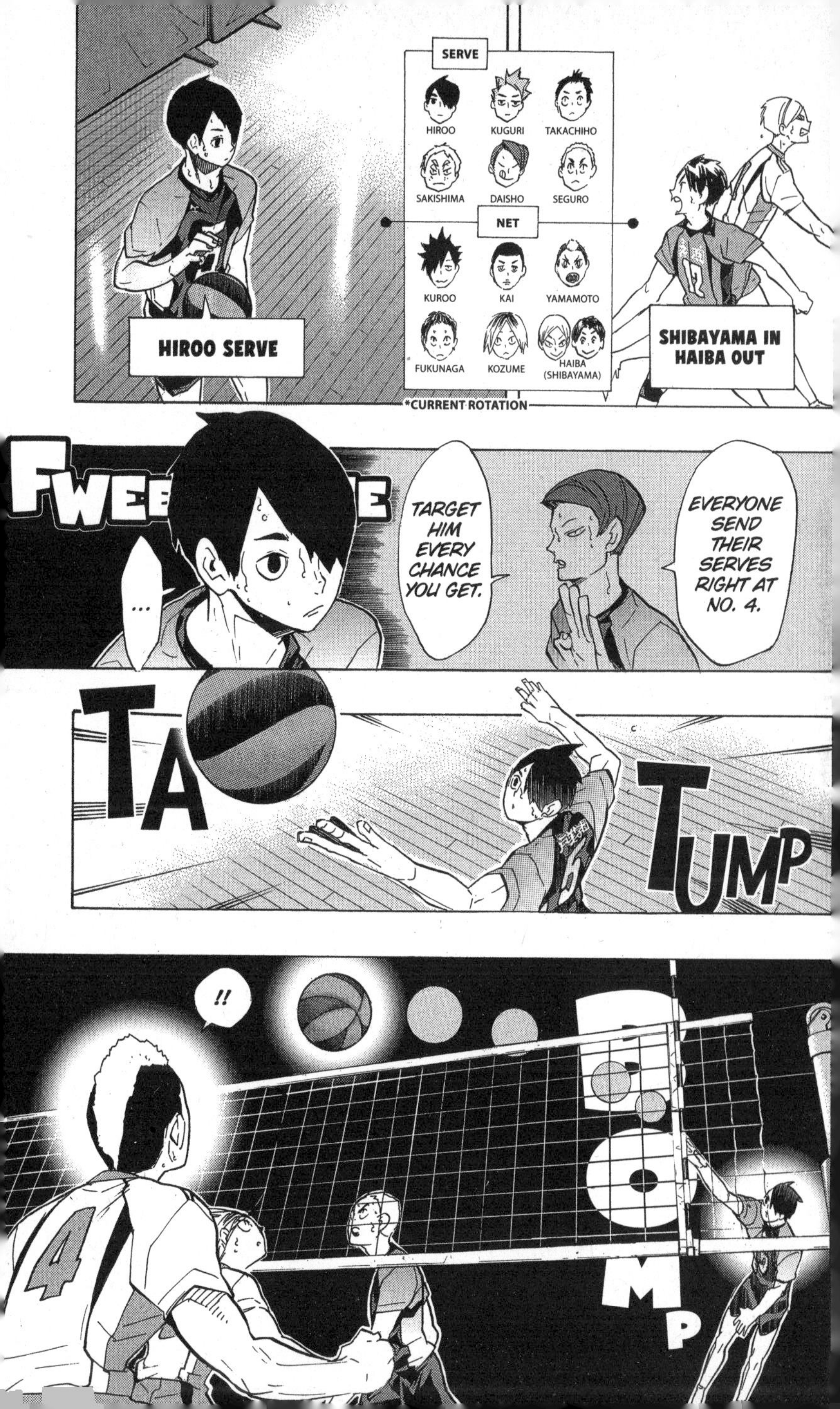

SHIBAYAMA IN HAIBA OUT
SERVE
HIROO
KUGURI
TAKACHIHO
SAKISHIMA
DAISHO
SEGURO
NET
KUROO
KAI
YAMAMOTO
FUKUNAGA
KOZUME
HAIBA (SHIBAYAMA)
*CURRENT ROTATION
HIROO SERVE
EVERYONE SEND THEIR SERVES RIGHT AT NO. 4.
TARGET HIM EVERY CHANCE YOU GET.
...
TUMP
TA
!!

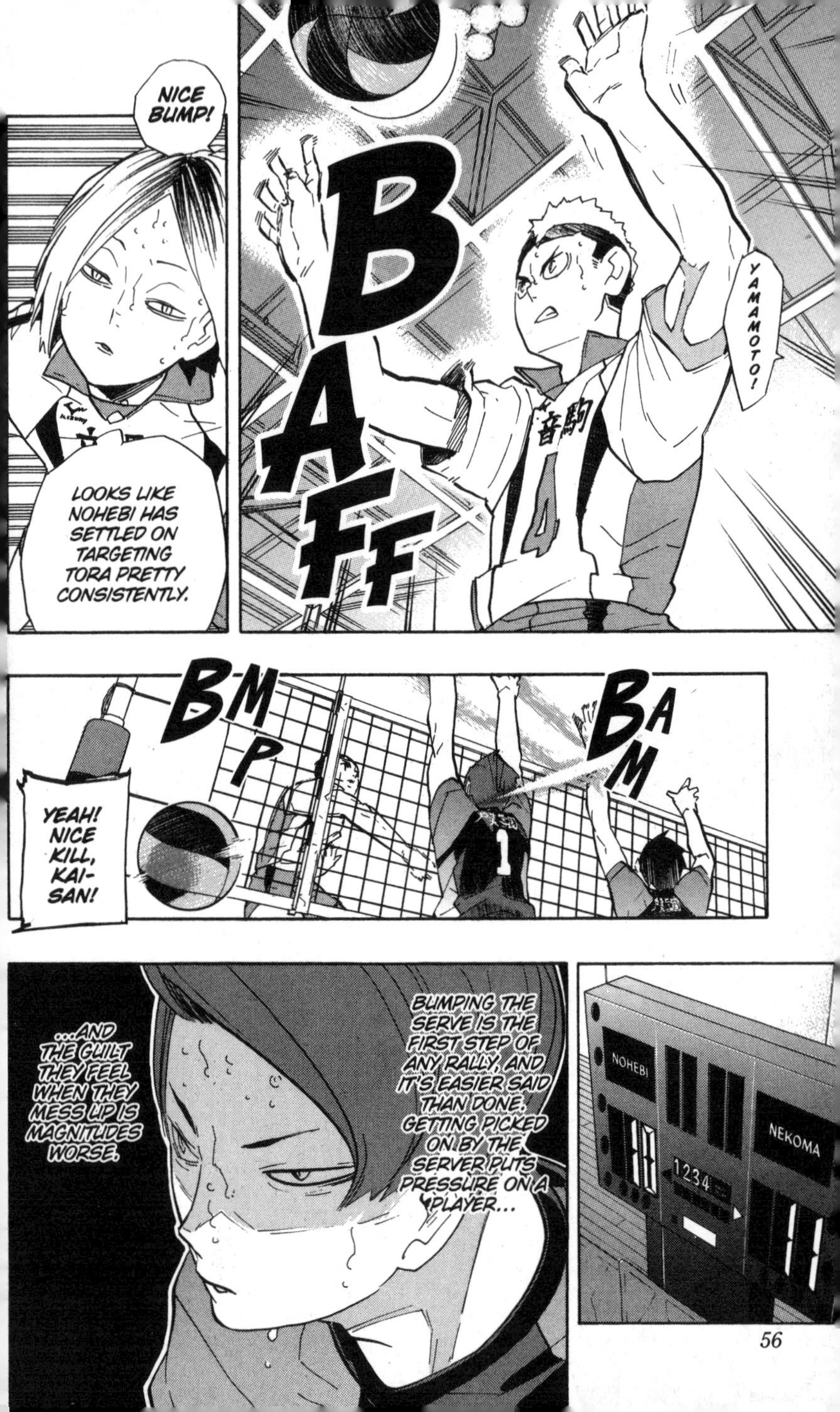
YAMAMOTO!
BAFF
NICE BUMP!
LOOKS LIKE NOHEBI HAS SETTLED ON TARGETING TORA PRETTY CONSISTENTLY.
BAM
BMP
YEAH! NICE KILL, KAI-SAN!
NOHEBI
1234
NEKOMA
BUMPING THE SERVE IS THE FIRST STEP OF ANY RALLY, AND IT'S EASIER SAID THAN DONE. GETTING PICKED ON BY THE SERVER PUTS PRESSURE ON A PLAYER...
...AND THE GUILT THEY FEEL WHEN THEY MESS UP IS MAGNITUDES WORSE.

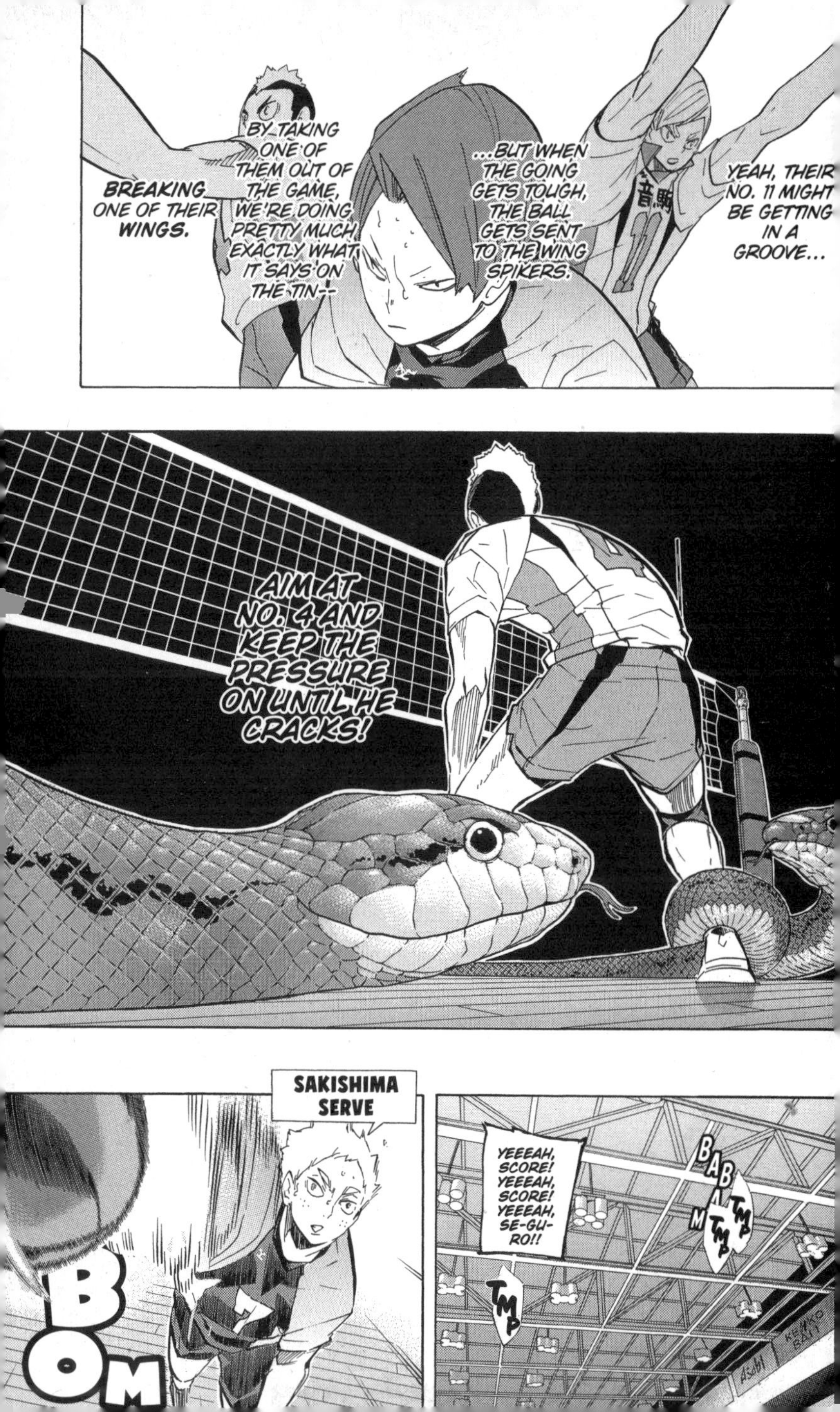
YEAH, THEIR NO. 11 MIGHT BE GETTING IN A GROOVE...
...BUT WHEN THE GOING GETS TOUGH, THE BALL GETS SENT TO THE WING SPIKERS.
BY TAKING ONE OF THEM OUT OF THE GAME, WE'RE DOING PRETTY MUCH EXACTLY WHAT IT SAYS ON THE TIN--
BREAKING ONE OF THEIR WINGS.
AIM AT NO. 4 AND KEEP THE PRESSURE ON UNTIL HE CRACKS!
YEEEAH, SCORE! YEEEAH, SCORE! YEEEAH, SE-GU-RO!!
BABAM
TMP TMP
TMP
SAKISHIMA SERVE
BOM

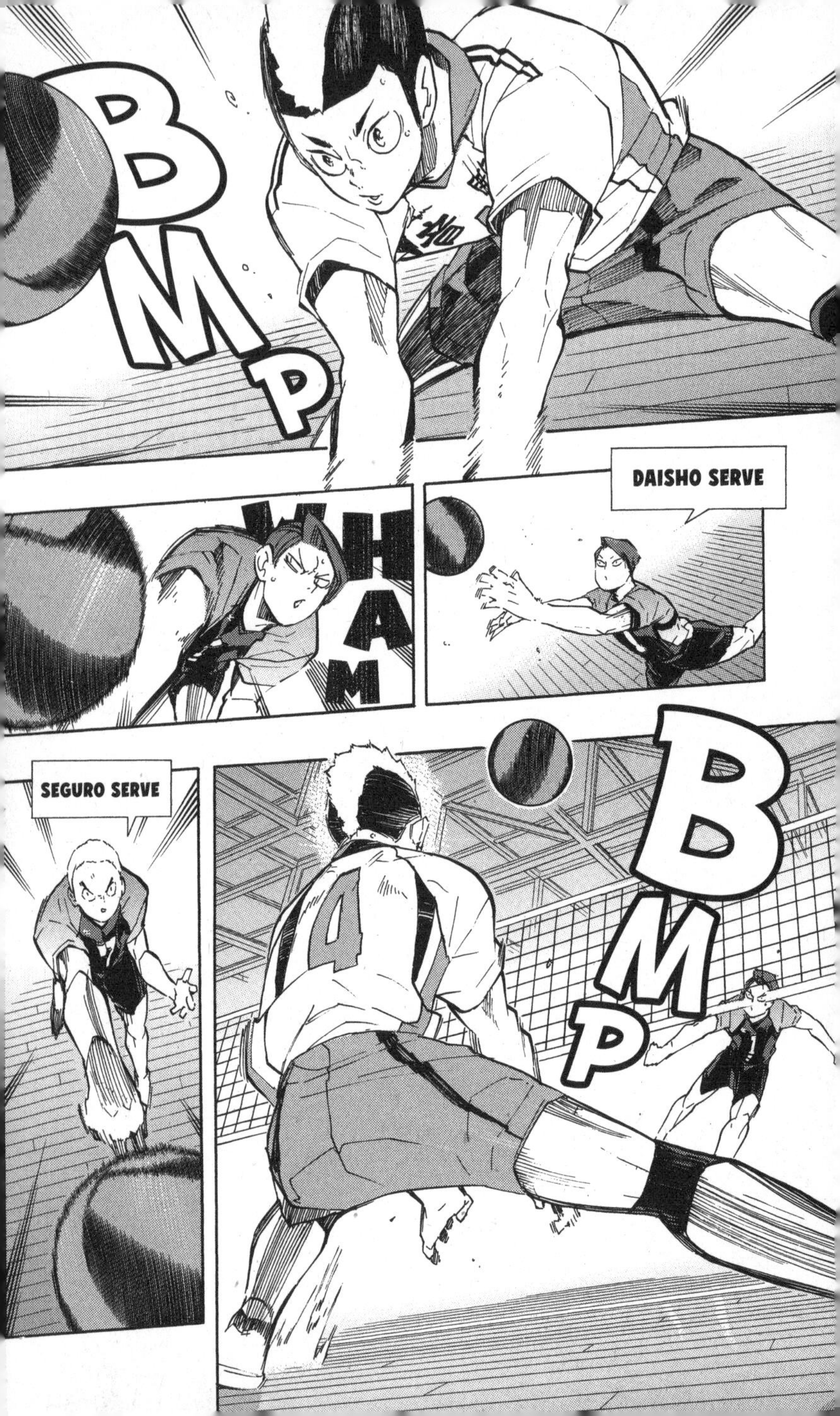
BMP
DAISHO SERVE
WHAM
BMP
SEGURO SERVE

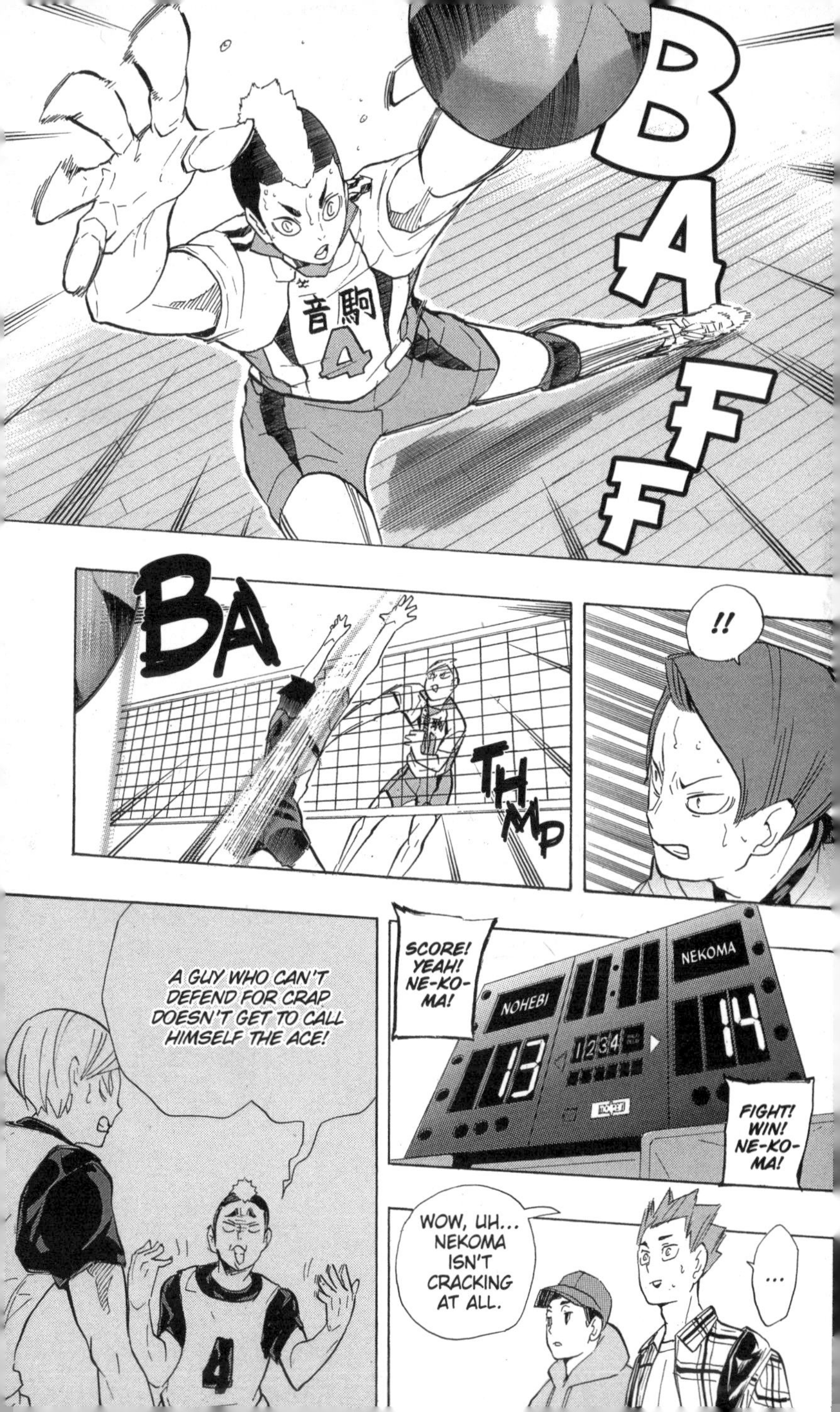
BAFFF
!!
BA
THMP
SCORE! YEAH! NE-KO-MA!
NEKOMA
NOHEBI
13
14
FIGHT! WIN! NE-KO-MA!
WOW, UH... NEKOMA ISN'T CRACKING AT ALL.
...
A GUY WHO CAN'T DEFEND FOR CRAP DOESN'T GET TO CALL HIMSELF THE ACE!

FORGET THE LINE! THERE'S NO THREAT OF A LINE SHOT!

NO. 4 ONLY HITS A CROSS!

FUKUNAGA SERVE

CURRENT ROTATION

SEGURO (AKAMA)	DAISHO	SAKISHIMA
TAKACHIHO	KUGURI	HIROO
	NET	
YAMAMOTO	HAIBA	KOZUME
KAI	KUROO	FUKUNAGA
		SERVE

SO, SORRY, GUYS...

TO BE HONEST, KNOWING YAKU-SAN ISN'T BACK THERE IS REALLY SCARING THE CRAP OUT OF ME.

....?

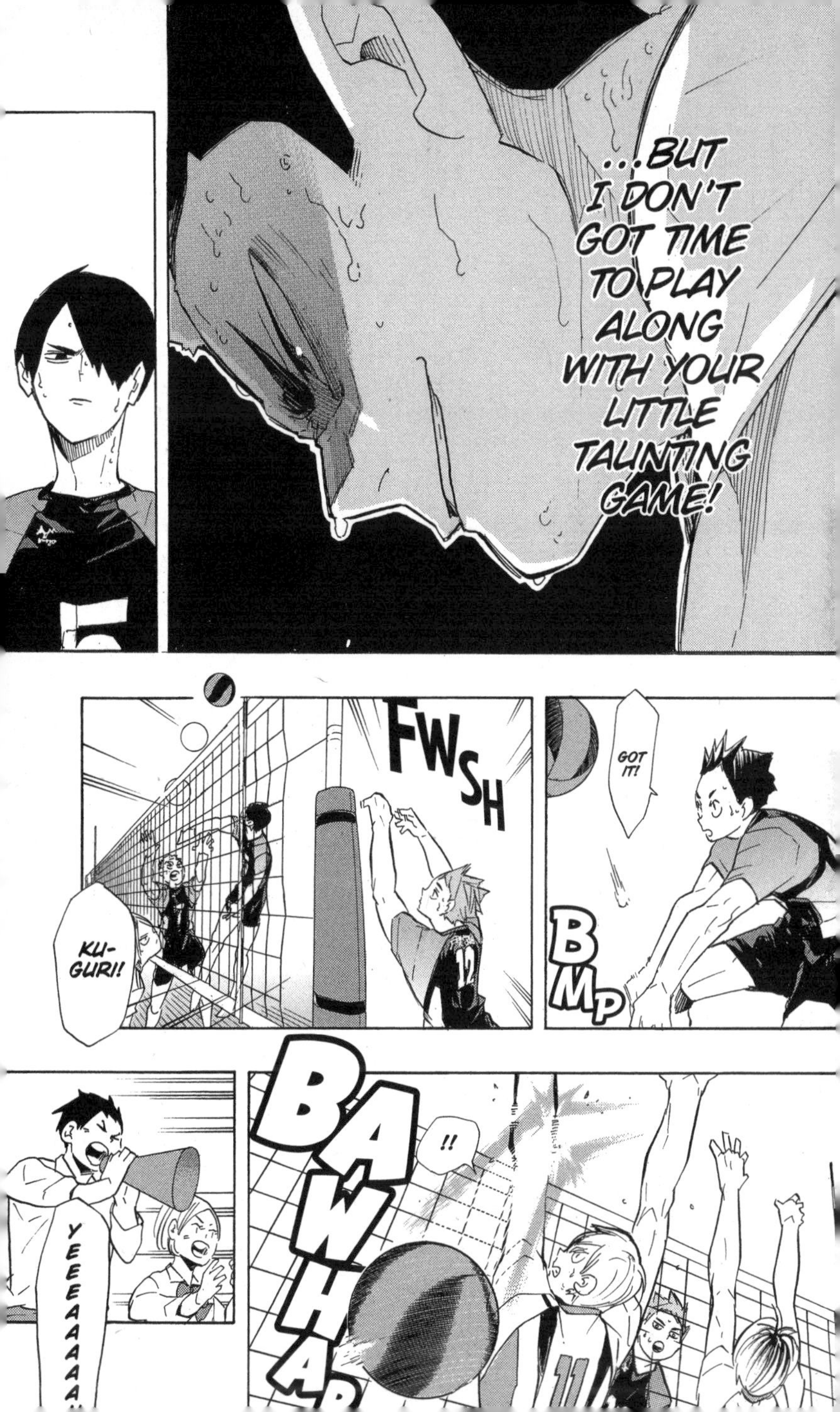
...BUT I DON'T GOT TIME TO PLAY ALONG WITH YOUR LITTLE TAUNTING GAME!
GOT IT!
BMP
FWSH
KU-GURI!
BAWHA
!!
YEEEAAAAAA

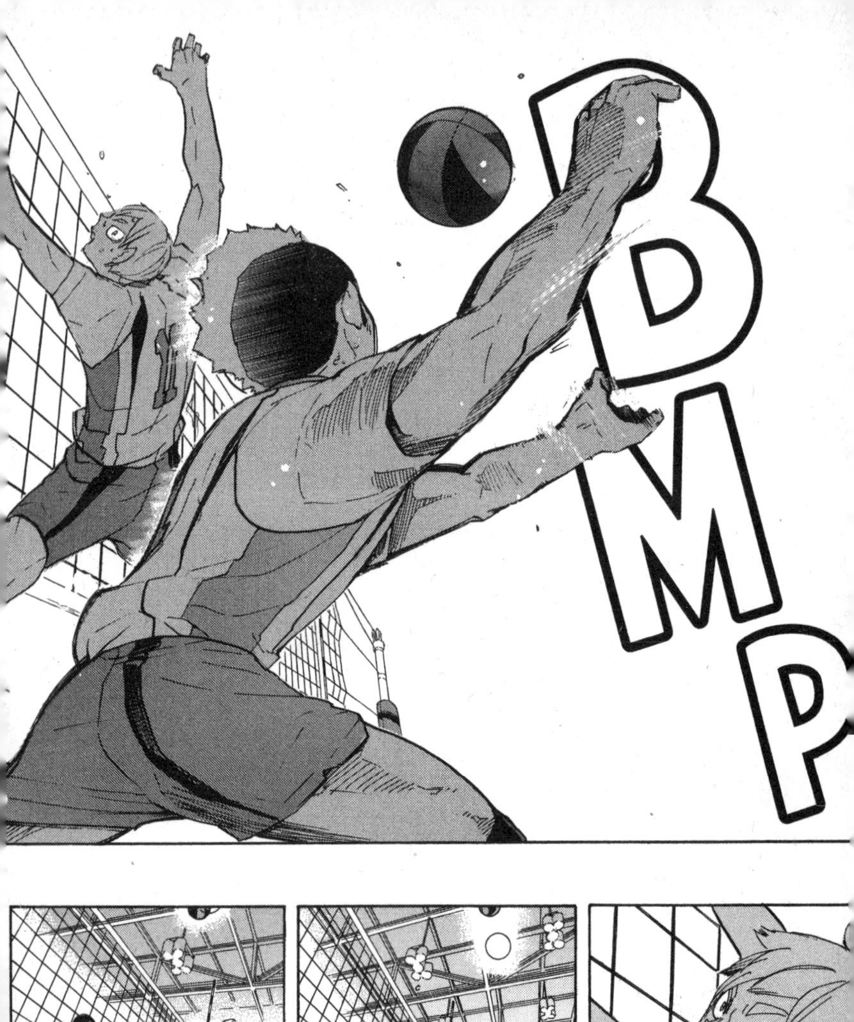
BDMP

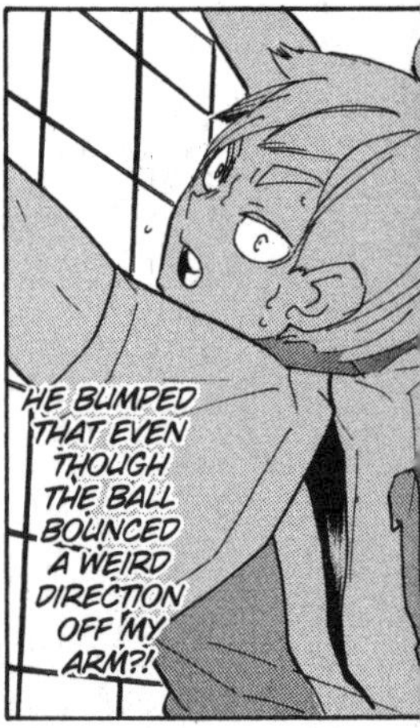
HE BUMPED THAT EVEN THOUGH THE BALL BOUNCED A WEIRD DIRECTION OFF MY ARM?!

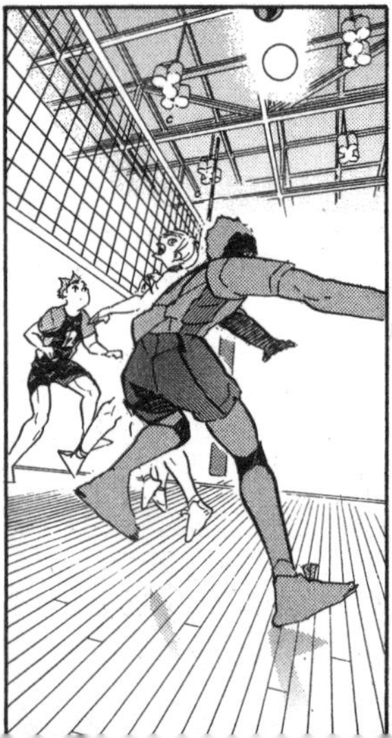

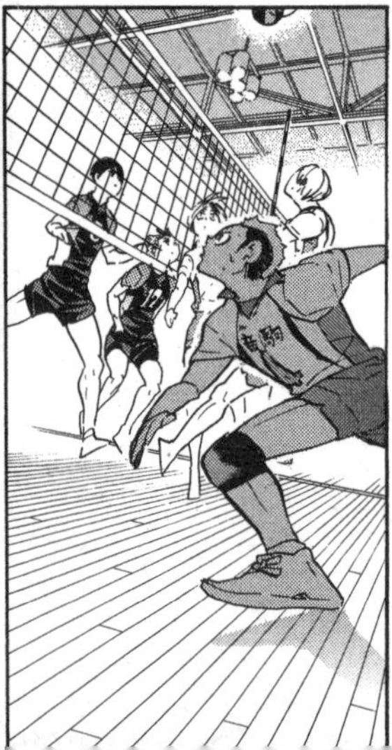

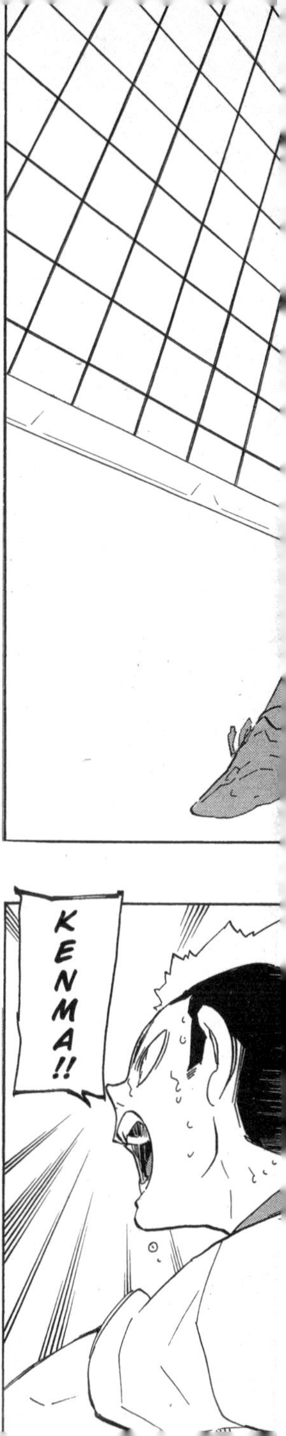
KENMA!!

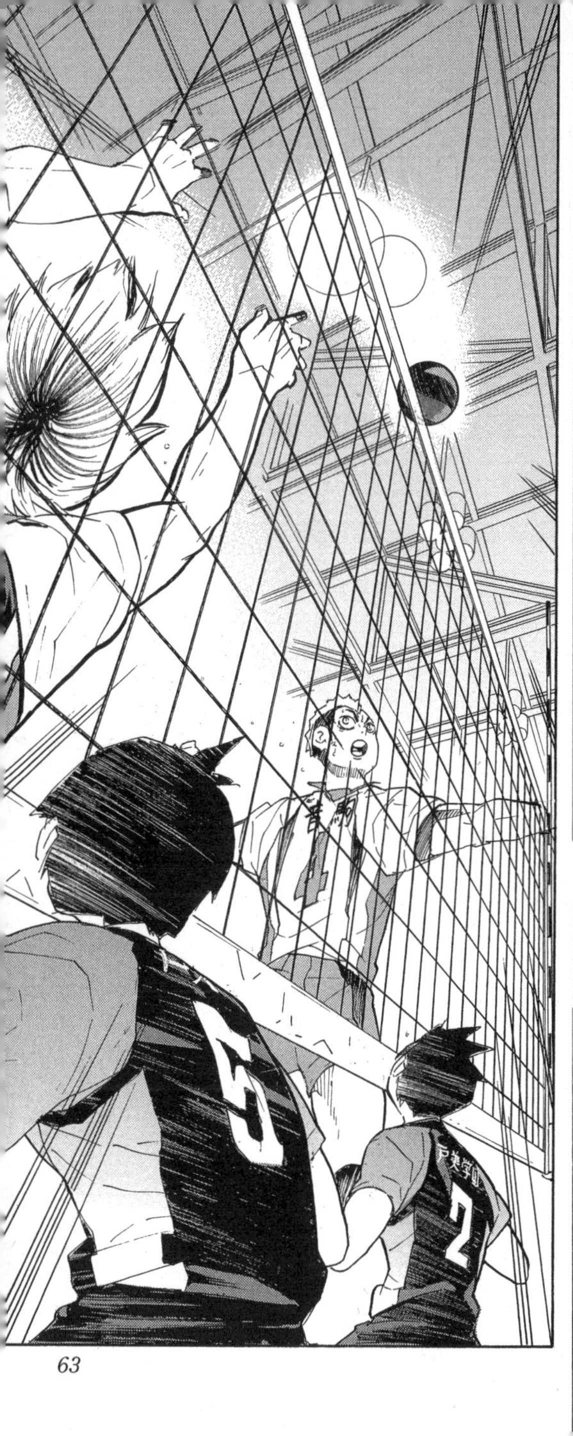

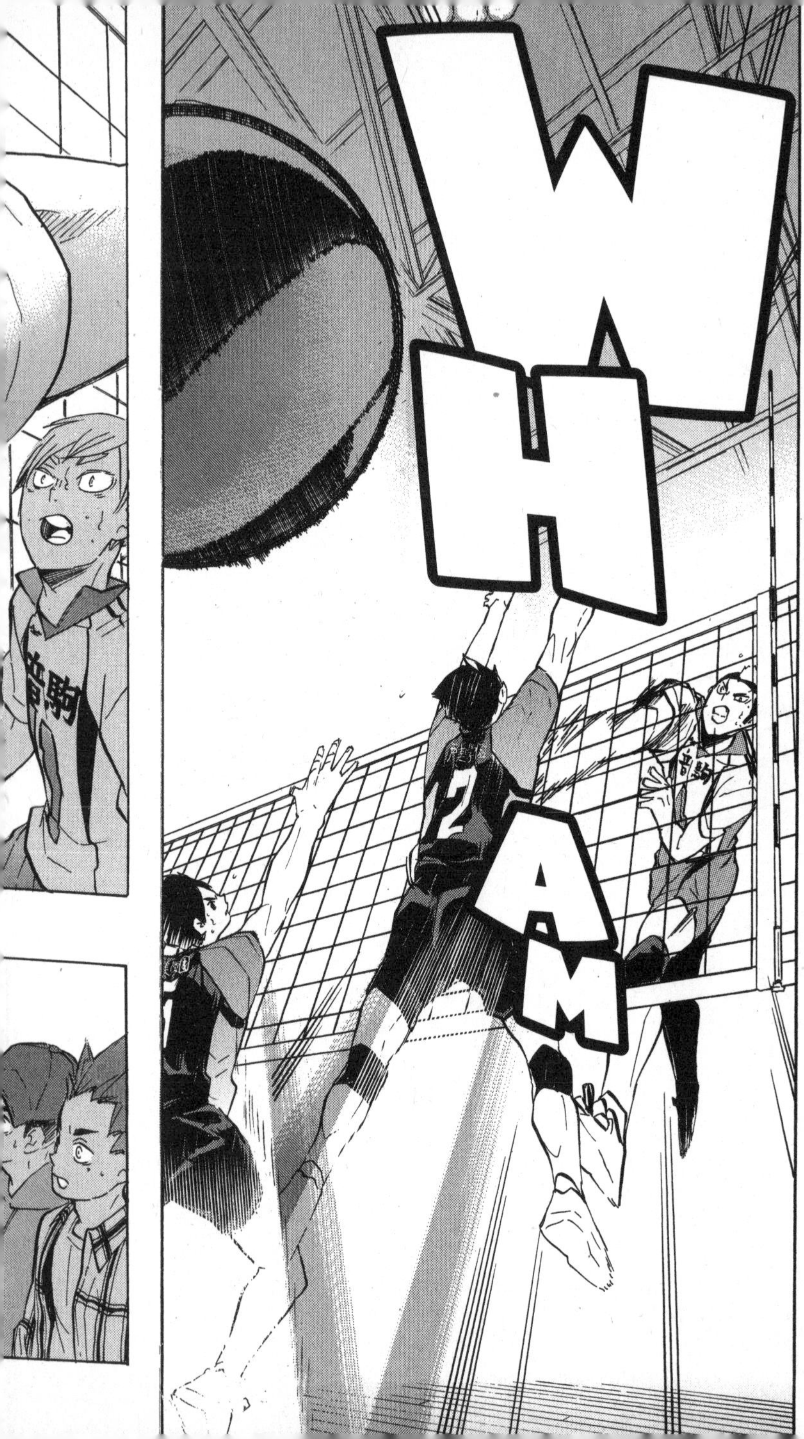
WHAM

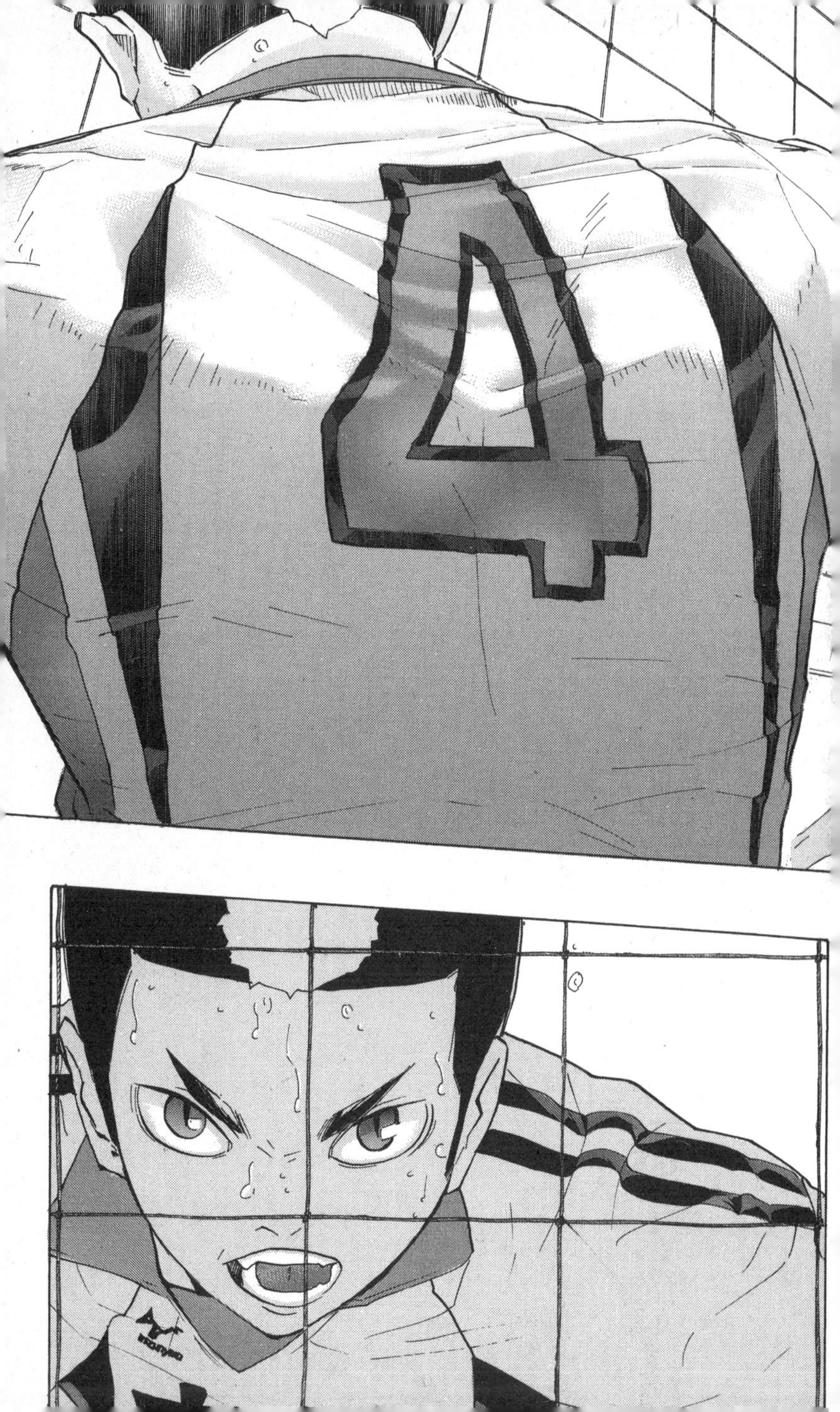

SOU AKAMA

NOHEBI ACADEMY
CLASS 2-10

POSITION:
LIBERO

HEIGHT: 5'8"

WEIGHT: 140 LBS.
(AS OF NOVEMBER, 2ND YEAR
OF HIGH SCHOOL)

ABILITY PARAMETERS
(5-POINT SCALE)

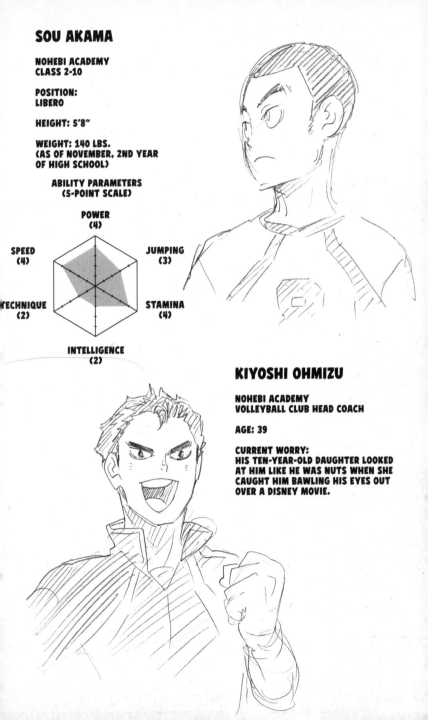

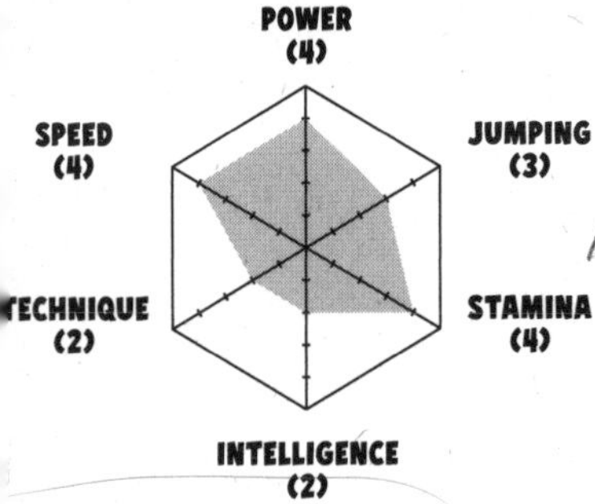
POWER (4)
JUMPING (3)
STAMINA (4)
INTELLIGENCE (2)
TECHNIQUE (2)
SPEED (4)

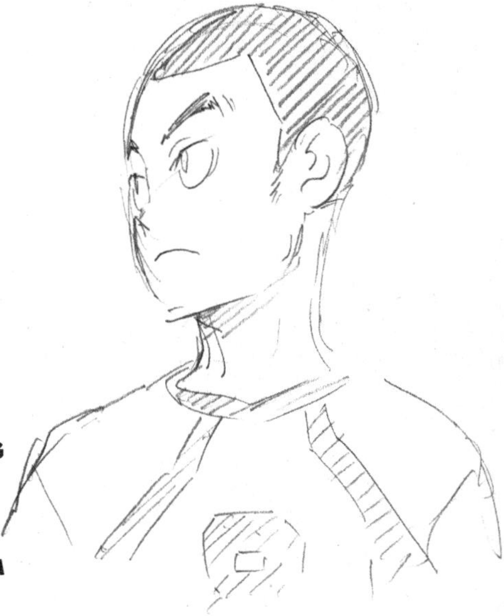

KIYOSHI OHMIZU

NOHEBI ACADEMY
VOLLEYBALL CLUB HEAD COACH

AGE: 39

CURRENT WORRY:
HIS TEN-YEAR-OLD DAUGHTER LOOKED AT HIM LIKE HE WAS NUTS WHEN SHE CAUGHT HIM BAWLING HIS EYES OUT OVER A DISNEY MOVIE.

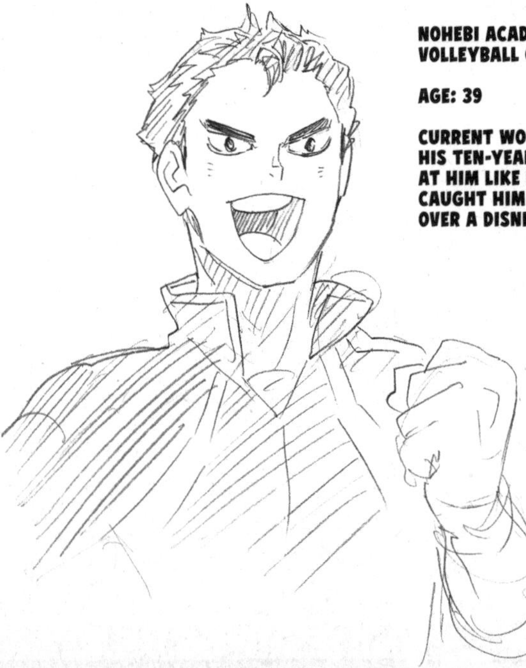

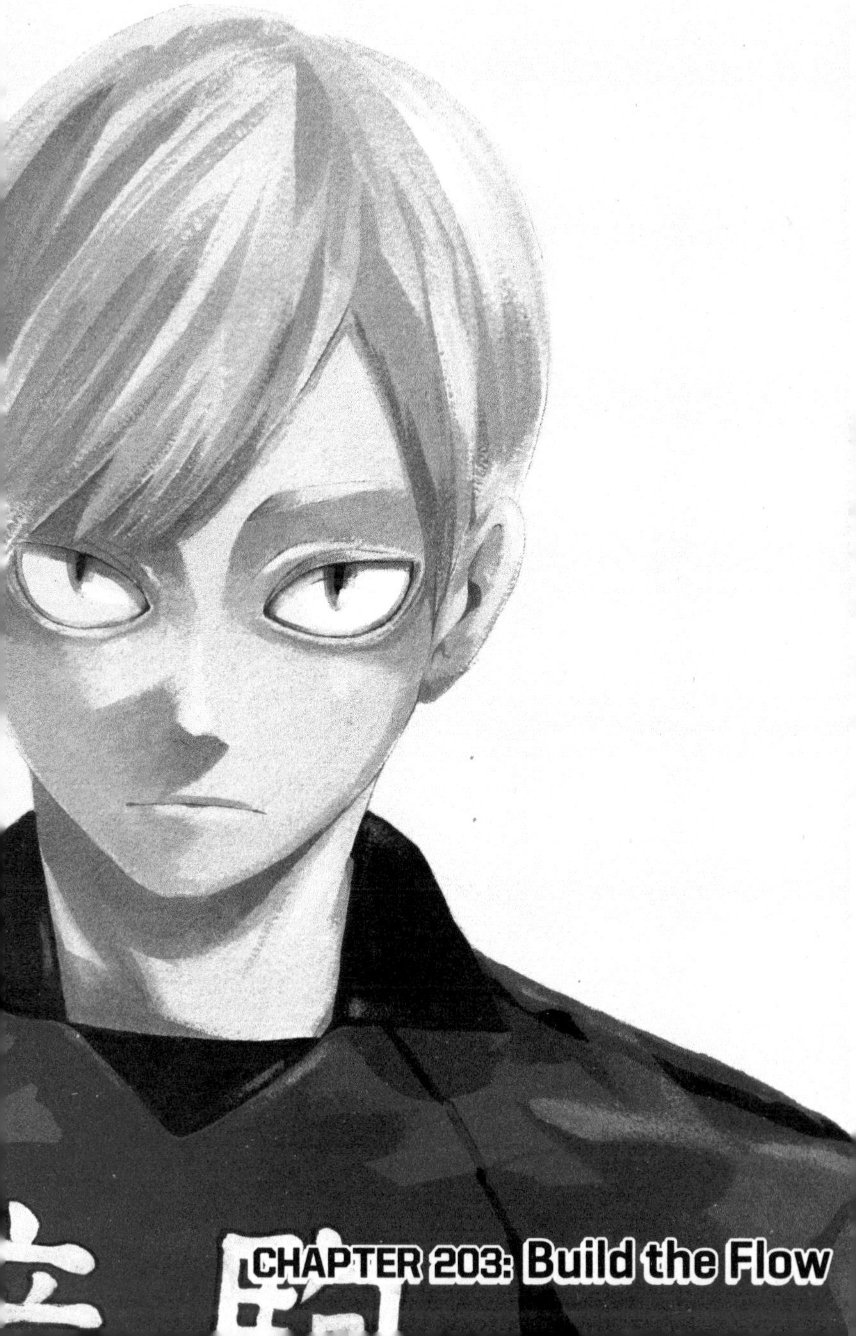

CHAPTER 203: Build the Flow

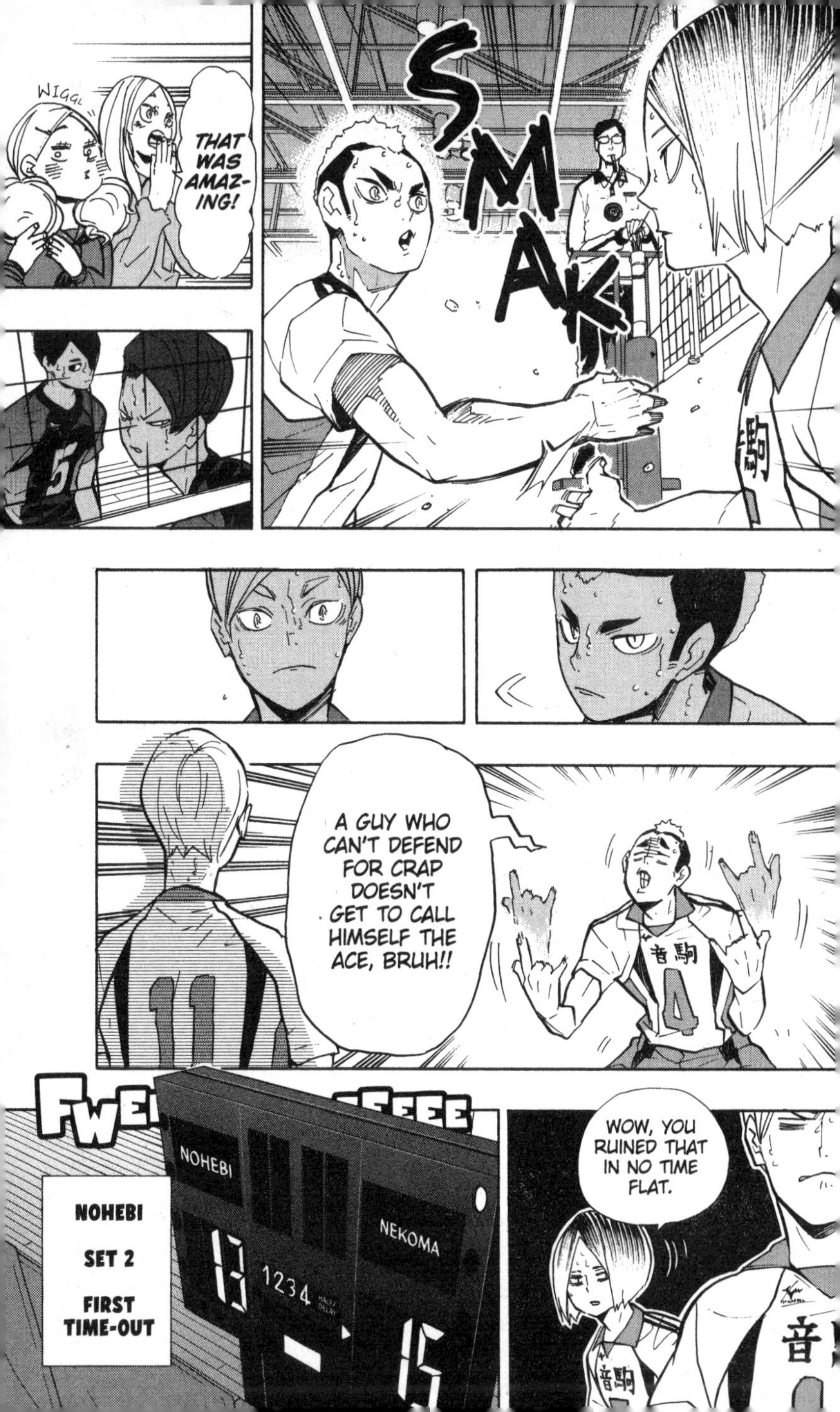
SMAK
THAT WAS AMAZ-ING!
WIGGL
A GUY WHO CAN'T DEFEND FOR CRAP DOESN'T GET TO CALL HIMSELF THE ACE, BRUH!!
WOW, YOU RUINED THAT IN NO TIME FLAT.
FWE
EEEE
NOHEBI
NEKOMA
13
1234
15
NOHEBI SET 2 FIRST TIME-OUT

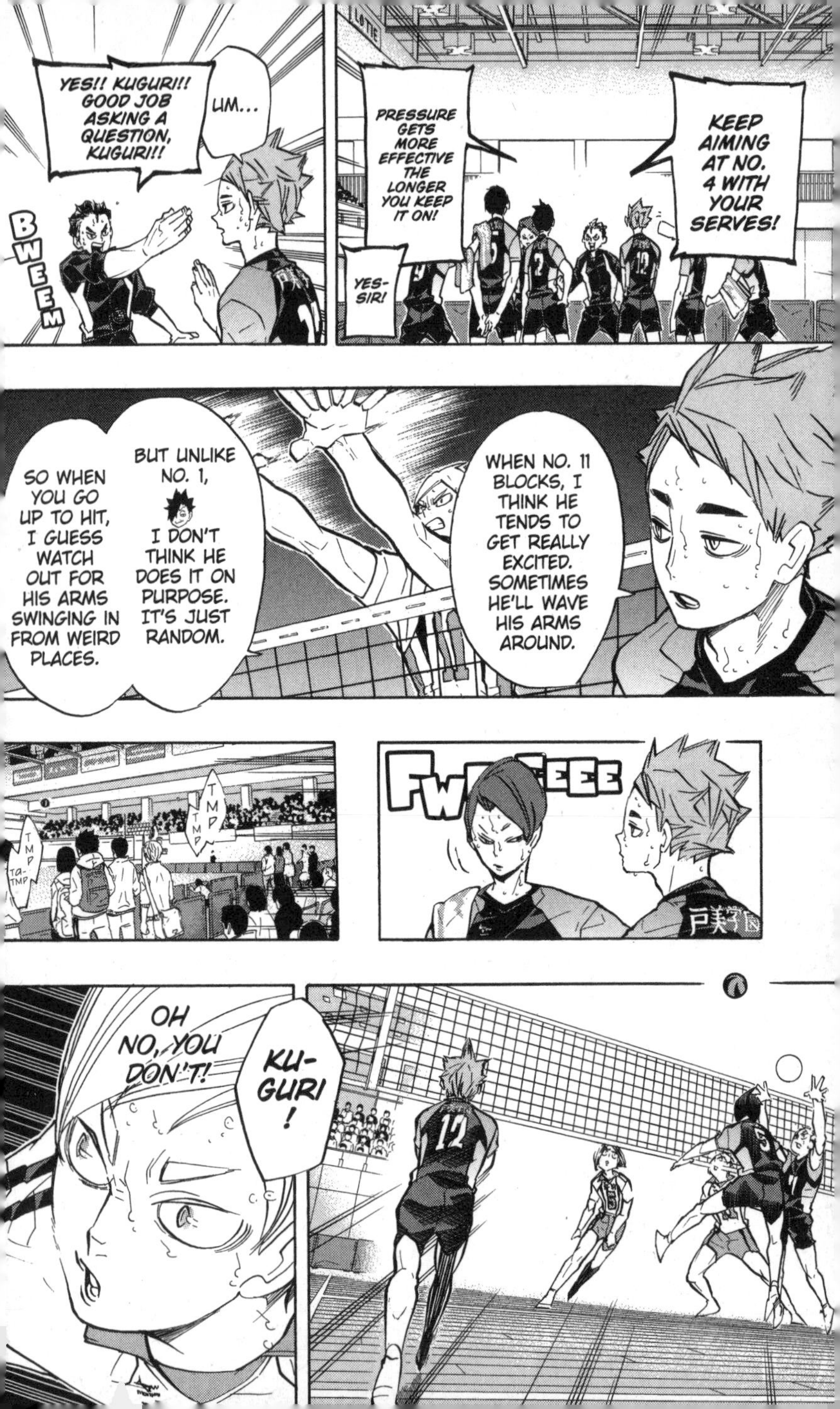
KEEP AIMING AT NO. 4 WITH YOUR SERVES!
PRESSURE GETS MORE EFFECTIVE THE LONGER YOU KEEP IT ON!
YES-SIR!
UM...
YES!! KUGURI!!! GOOD JOB ASKING A QUESTION, KUGURI!!
BWEEM
WHEN NO. 11 BLOCKS, I THINK HE TENDS TO GET REALLY EXCITED. SOMETIMES HE'LL WAVE HIS ARMS AROUND.
BUT UNLIKE NO. 1, I DON'T THINK HE DOES IT ON PURPOSE. IT'S JUST RANDOM.
SO WHEN YOU GO UP TO HIT, I GUESS WATCH OUT FOR HIS ARMS SWINGING IN FROM WEIRD PLACES.
FWEEEE
TMP TMP
TMP TA-TMP
KU-GURI!
OH NO, YOU DON'T!

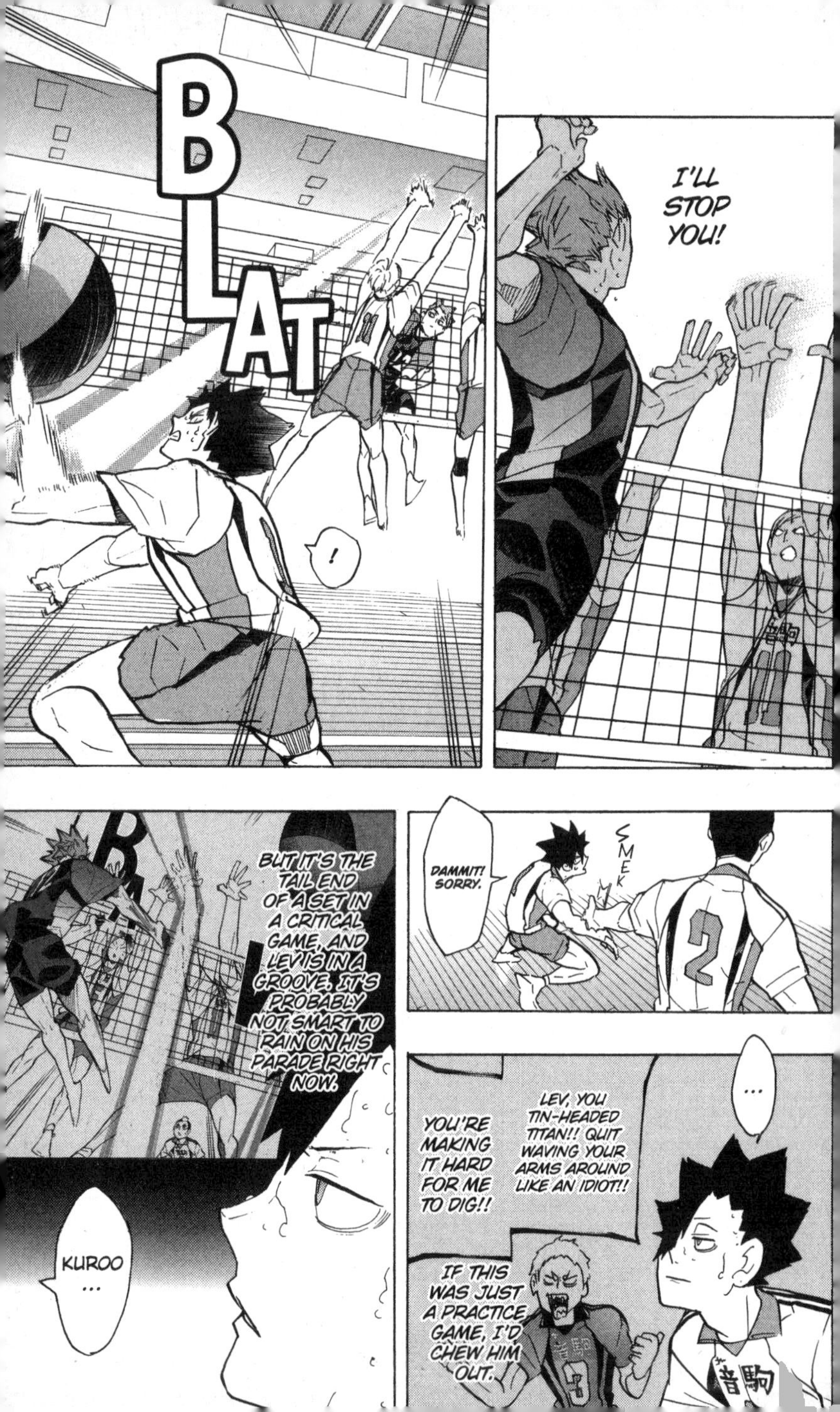

I'LL STOP YOU!
BLAT
!
DAMMIT! SORRY.
SMEK
...
LEV, YOU TIN-HEADED TITAN!! QUIT WAVING YOUR ARMS AROUND LIKE AN IDIOT!!
YOU'RE MAKING IT HARD FOR ME TO DIG!!
IF THIS WAS JUST A PRACTICE GAME, I'D CHEW HIM OUT.
BUT IT'S THE TAIL END OF A SET IN A CRITICAL GAME, AND LEV IS IN A GROOVE. IT'S PROBABLY NOT SMART TO RAIN ON HIS PARADE RIGHT NOW.
KUROO ...

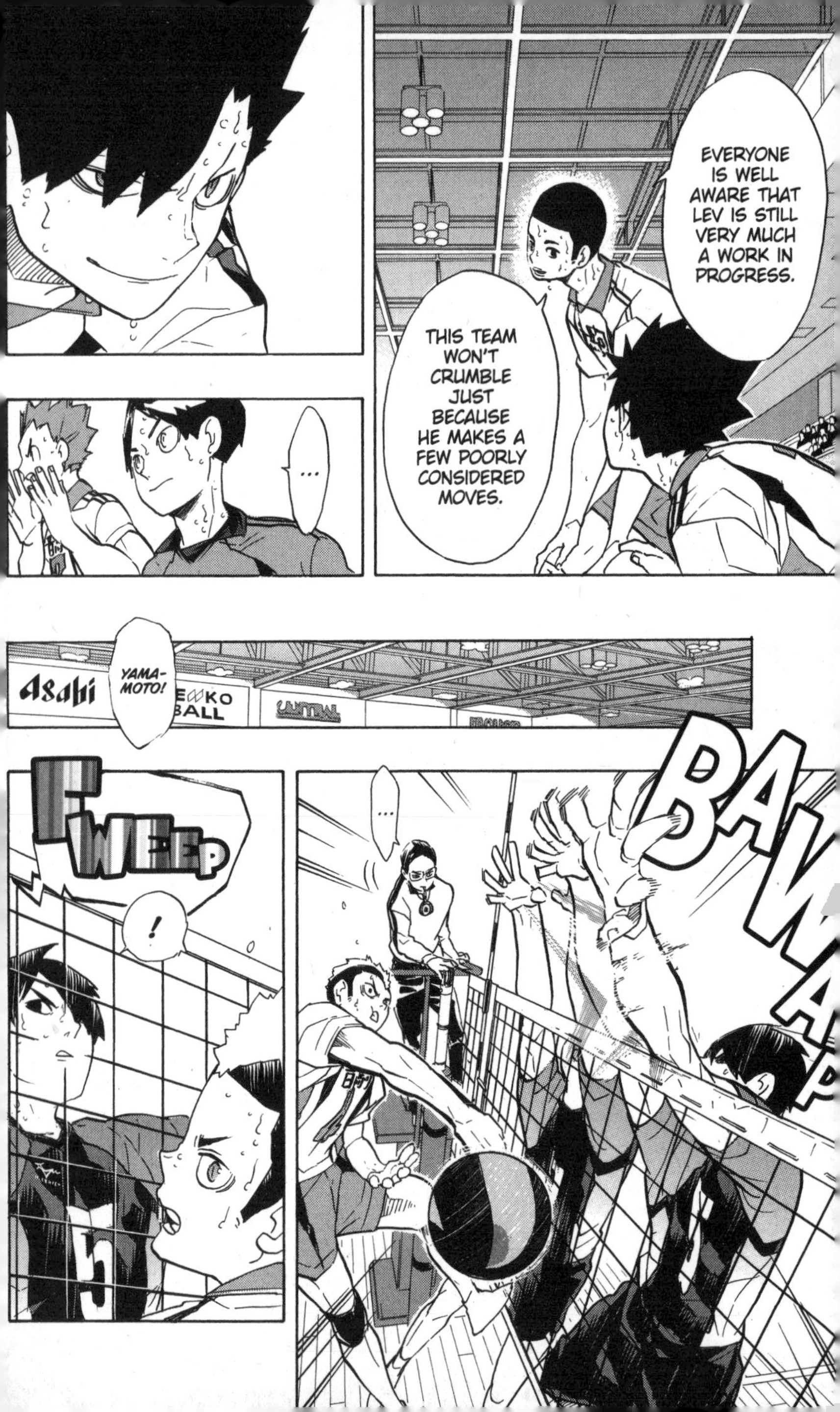
EVERYONE IS WELL AWARE THAT LEV IS STILL VERY MUCH A WORK IN PROGRESS.
THIS TEAM WON'T CRUMBLE JUST BECAUSE HE MAKES A FEW POORLY CONSIDERED MOVES.
...
YAMA-MOTO!
asahi
BAWAP
...
FWEEP
!

LOOK AT THAT. THEY'RE AT IT AGAIN.

UGH.

TMP TMP

BOW!

THEIR FAKE GOODY-TWO-SHOES ACT.

NET FOUL: NOHEBI NO. 5

YES, SIR! I TOUCHED IT!

NOHEBI	NEKOMA
15	17

...

YEAH. THEIR OPPONENTS ARE THE ONLY ONES WHO SEE THEM FOR THE SLEAZY CHEATERS THEY ARE.

THE AUDIENCE ALWAYS SEEMS TO LOVE THEM. THEY JUST DON'T KNOW.

Asahi

LEFT! LEFT!

TMP TMP TMP

CROSS SHOT!

KU-GURI!

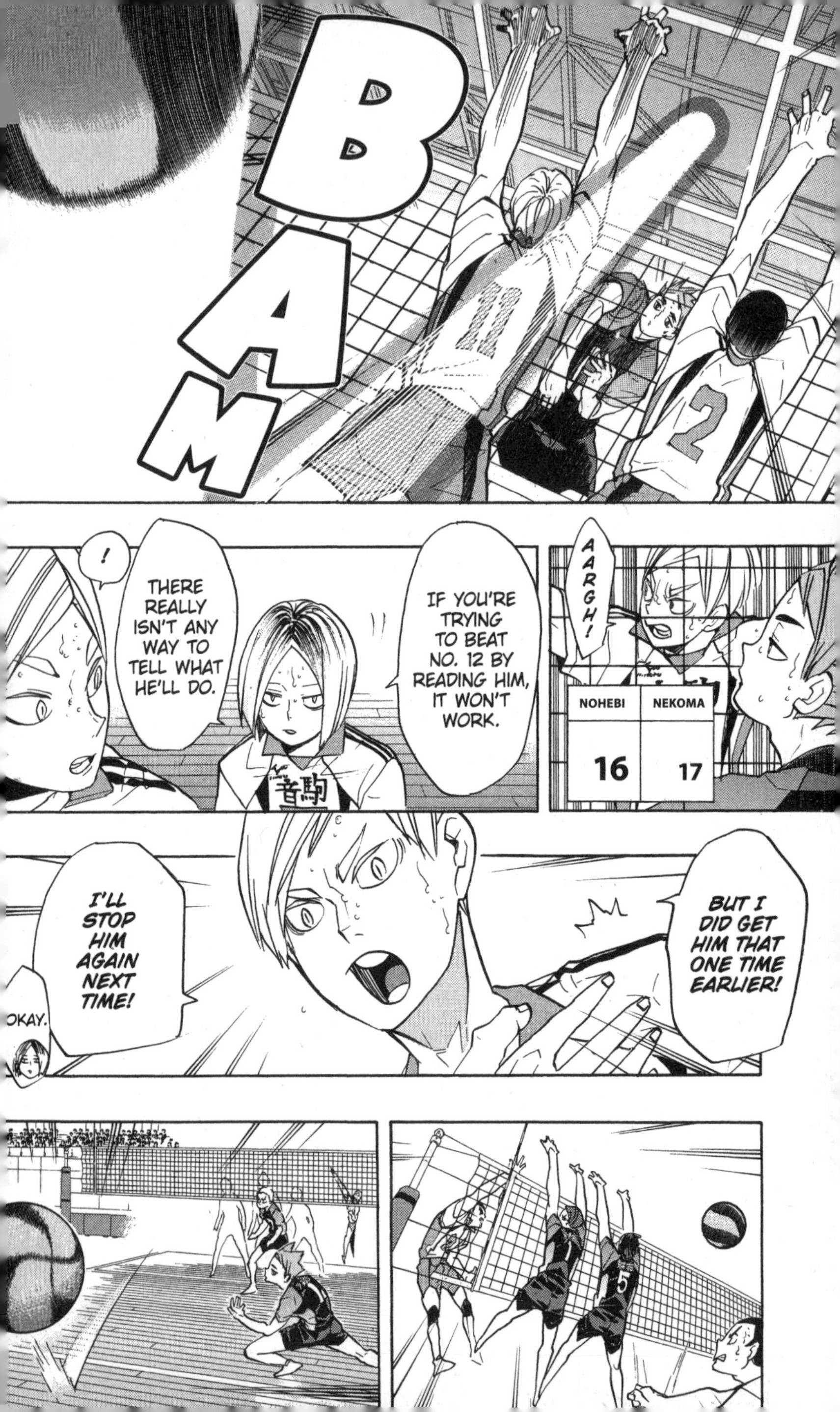
BAM
AARGH!
NOHEBI 16
NEKOMA 17
IF YOU'RE TRYING TO BEAT NO. 12 BY READING HIM, IT WON'T WORK.
THERE REALLY ISN'T ANY WAY TO TELL WHAT HE'LL DO.
!
BUT I DID GET HIM THAT ONE TIME EARLIER!
I'LL STOP HIM AGAIN NEXT TIME!
OKAY.

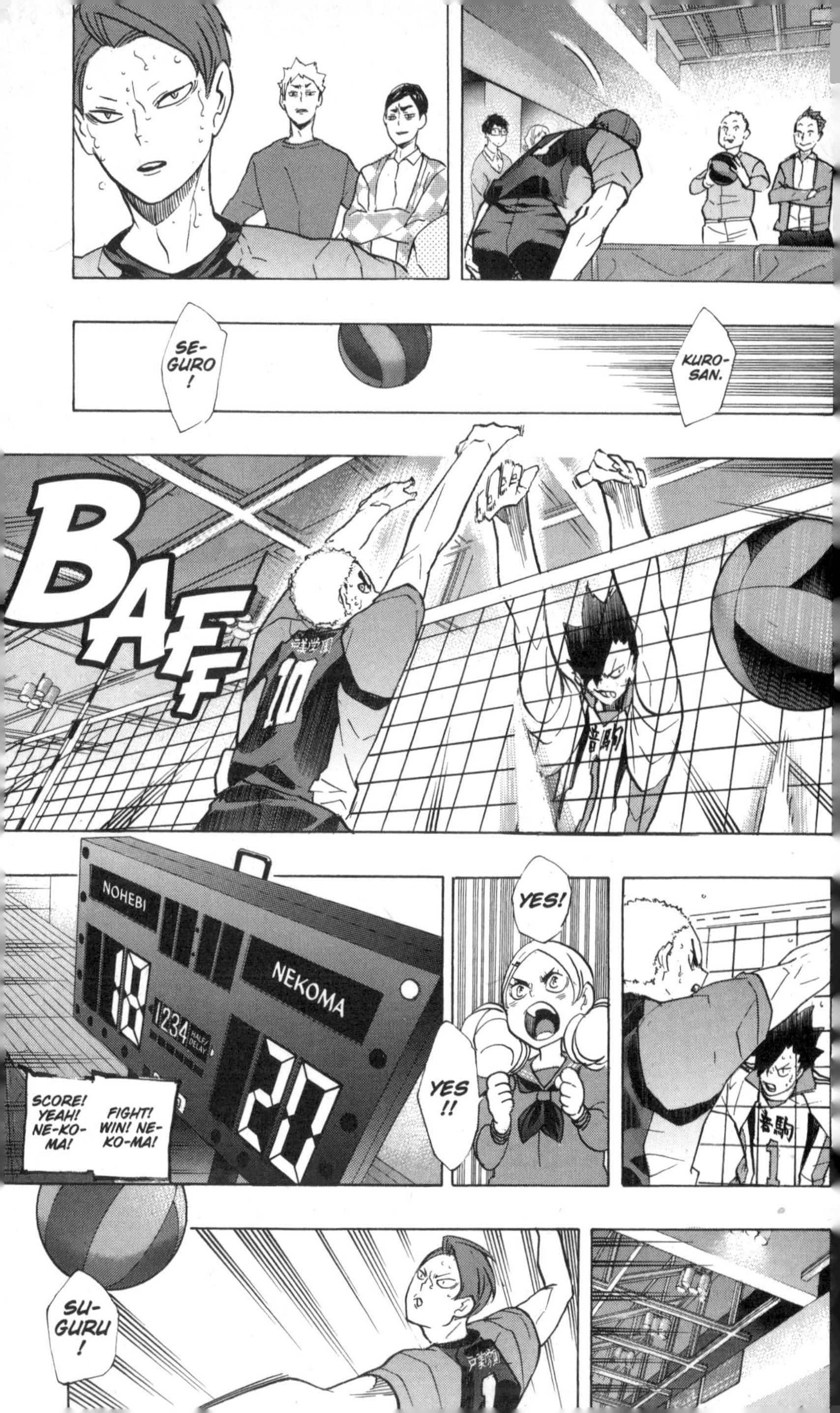
KURO-SAN.
SE-GURO!
BAFF
YES!
YES!!
NOHEBI
18
1234 HALF/DELAY
NEKOMA
20
SCORE! YEAH! NE-KO-MA!
FIGHT! WIN! NE-KO-MA!
SU-GURU!

SK

TCH.

THMP

!!

THAT'S AMAZING, BUT IT'S SO UNFAIR!

HE'S WAY TOO GOOD AT ABUSING BLOCKERS!

ARGH!

NOHEBI	NEKOMA
19	20

YEAAAH!!

FWEEEEEE

*CURRENT ROTATION

SERVE		
SAKISHIMA	HIROO (AKAMA)	KUGURI
DAISHO	SEGURO	TAKACHIHO
NET		
FUKUNAGA	KUROO	KAI
KOZUME	HAIBA (SHIBAYAMA)	YAMAMOTO

NOHEBI PLAYER SUBSTITUTION

IN   NO. 4   NUMAI (WS)
OUT NO. 7   SAKISHIMA (S)

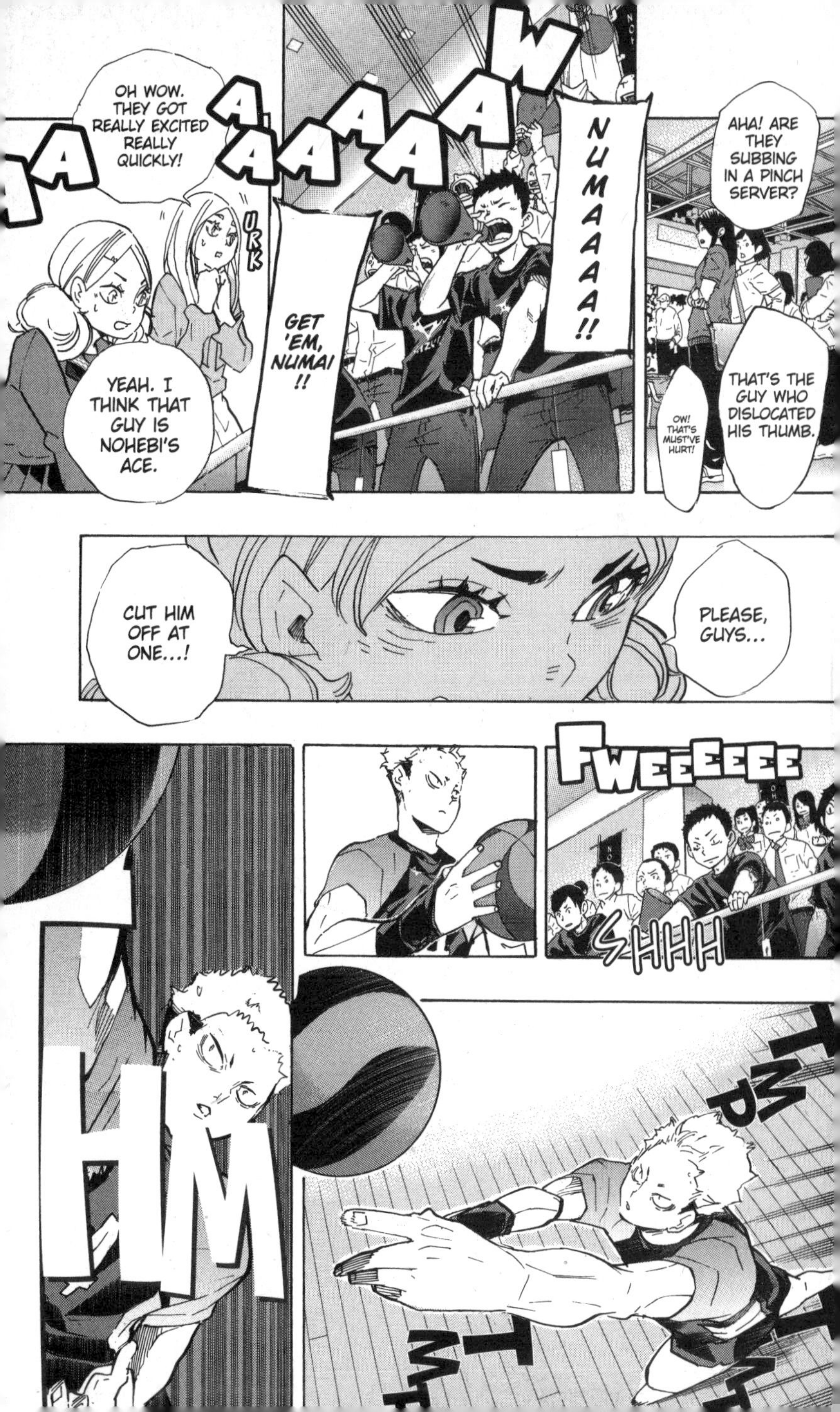
AHA! ARE THEY SUBBING IN A PINCH SERVER?
THAT'S THE GUY WHO DISLOCATED HIS THUMB.
OW! THAT'S MUST'VE HURT!
AAAAAAAW
NUMAAAAAAA!!
GET 'EM, NUMAI!!
OH WOW. THEY GOT REALLY EXCITED REALLY QUICKLY!
URK
YEAH. I THINK THAT GUY IS NOHEBI'S ACE.
PLEASE, GUYS...
CUT HIM OFF AT ONE...!
FWEEEEEE
SHHH
HM
TMP
TMP

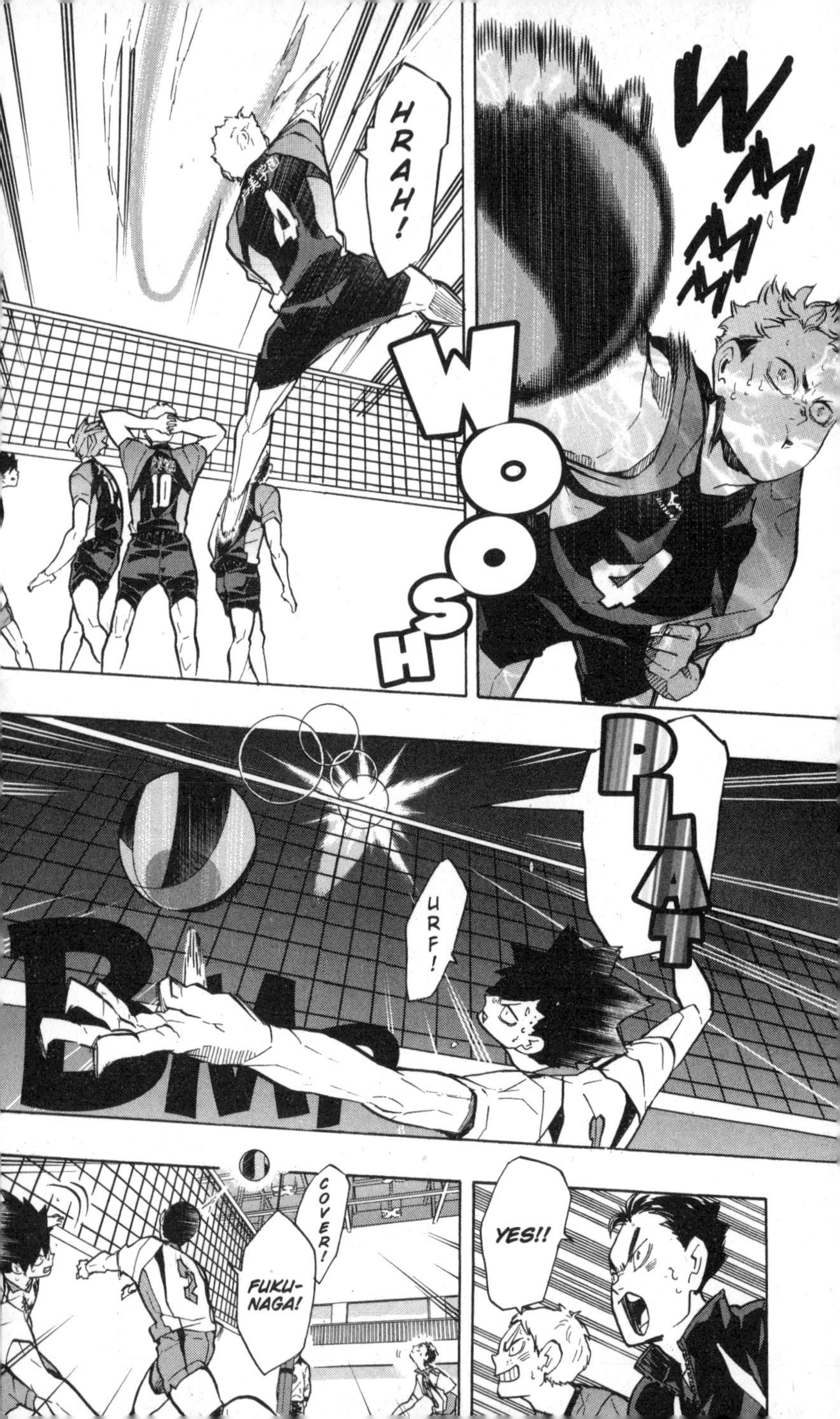
WOOOSH
HRAH!
PLAP
URF!
BMP
YES!!
COVER!
FUKU-NAGA!

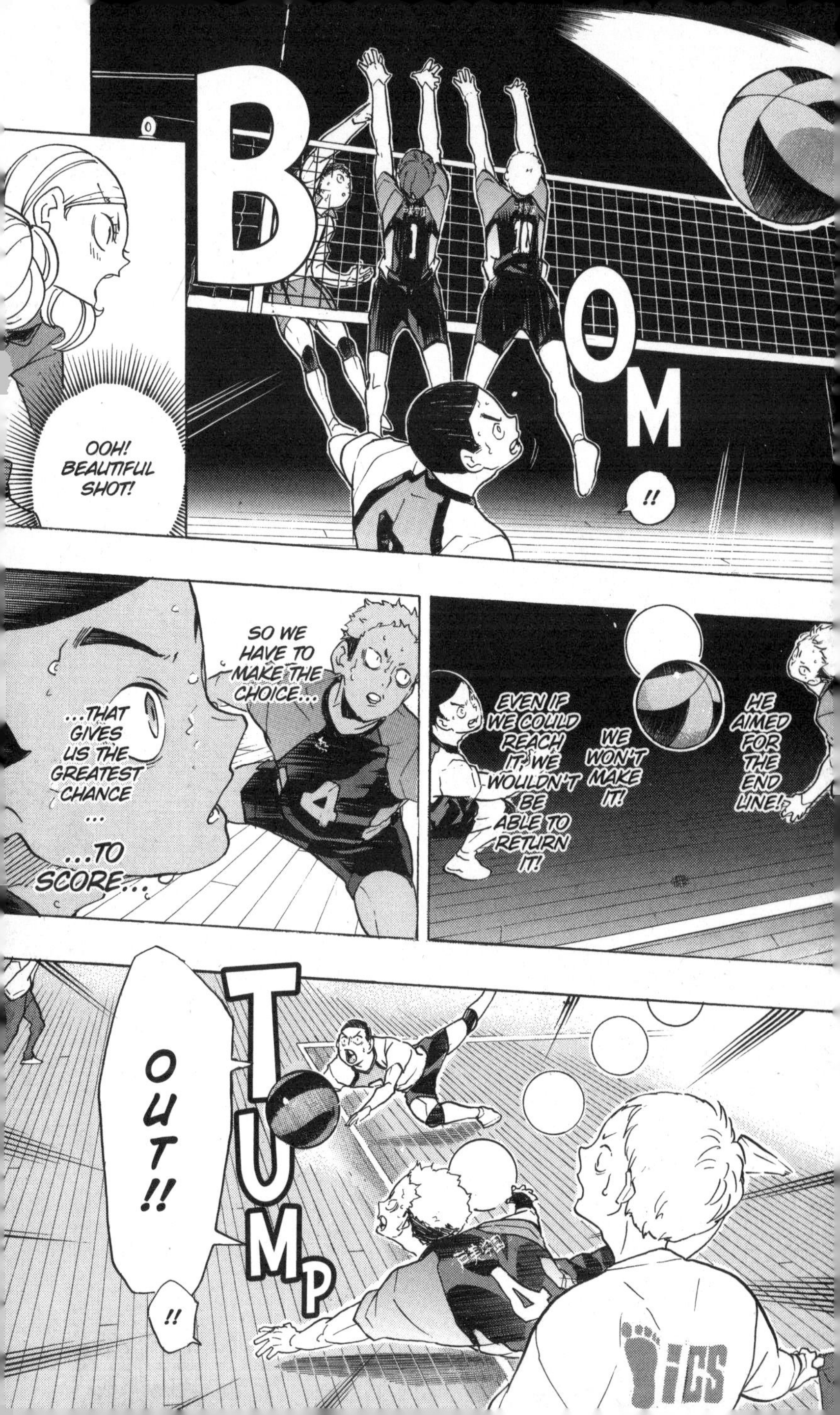
BOOM
!!
OOH! BEAUTIFUL SHOT!
HE AIMED FOR THE END LINE!
WE WON'T MAKE IT!
EVEN IF WE COULD REACH IT, WE WOULDN'T BE ABLE TO RETURN IT!
SO WE HAVE TO MAKE THE CHOICE...
...THAT GIVES US THE GREATEST CHANCE...
...TO SCORE...
TUMP
OUT!!
!!

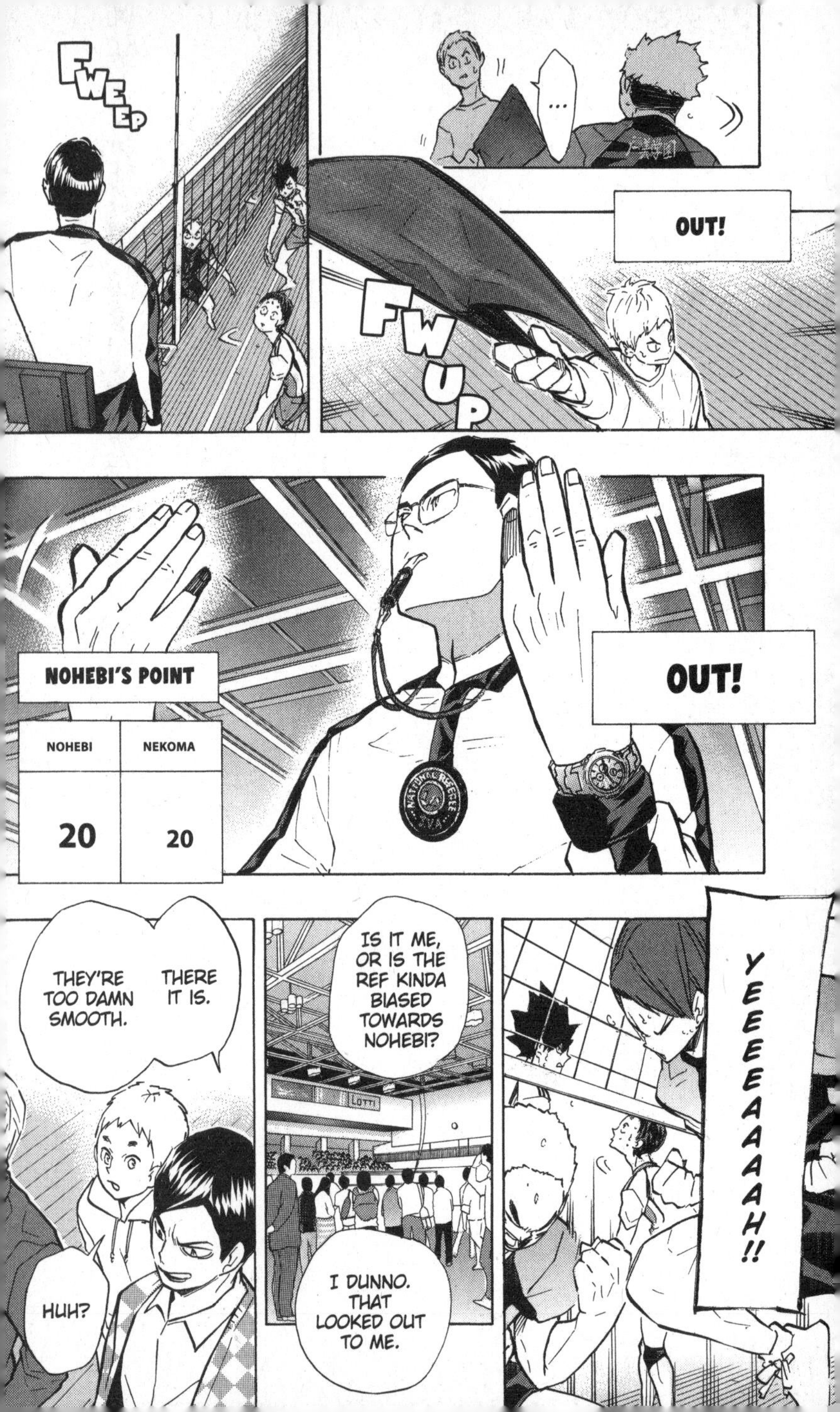
...
OUT!
FWUP
FWEEP
OUT!
NOHEBI'S POINT
NOHEBI 20
NEKOMA 20
YEEEEAAAAAH!!
IS IT ME, OR IS THE REF KINDA BIASED TOWARDS NOHEBI?
I DUNNO. THAT LOOKED OUT TO ME.
THERE IT IS.
THEY'RE TOO DAMN SMOOTH.
HUH?

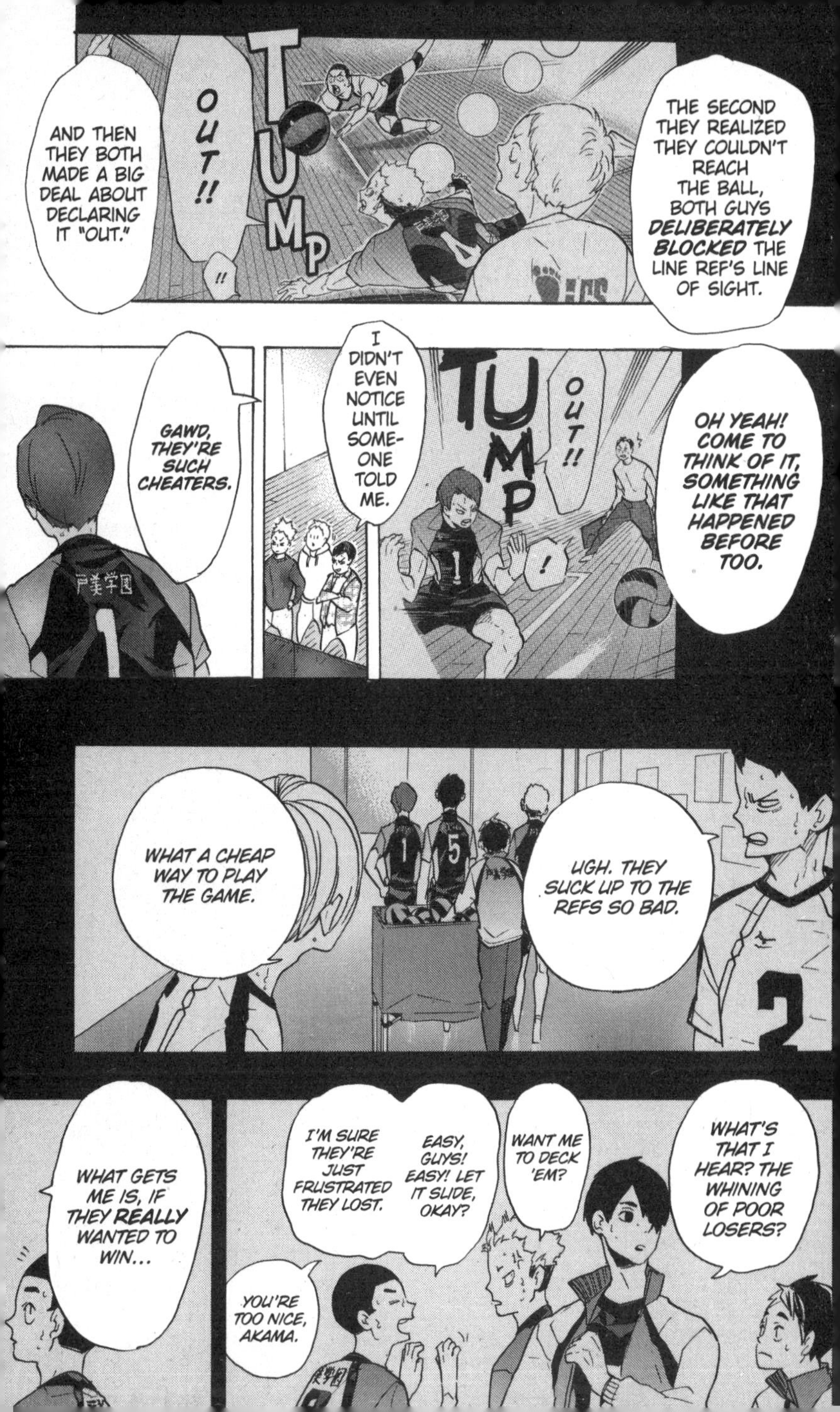
THE SECOND THEY REALIZED THEY COULDN'T REACH THE BALL, BOTH GUYS **DELIBERATELY BLOCKED** THE LINE REF'S LINE OF SIGHT.
OUT!!
TUMP
!!
AND THEN THEY BOTH MADE A BIG DEAL ABOUT DECLARING IT "OUT."
OH YEAH! COME TO THINK OF IT, SOMETHING LIKE THAT HAPPENED BEFORE TOO.
OUT!!
TUMP
!
I DIDN'T EVEN NOTICE UNTIL SOME-ONE TOLD ME.
GAWD, THEY'RE SUCH CHEATERS.
UGH. THEY SUCK UP TO THE REFS SO BAD.
WHAT A CHEAP WAY TO PLAY THE GAME.
WHAT'S THAT I HEAR? THE WHINING OF POOR LOSERS?
WANT ME TO DECK 'EM?
EASY, GUYS! EASY! LET IT SLIDE, OKAY?
I'M SURE THEY'RE JUST FRUSTRATED THEY LOST.
YOU'RE TOO NICE, AKAMA.
WHAT GETS ME IS, IF THEY **REALLY** WANTED TO WIN...

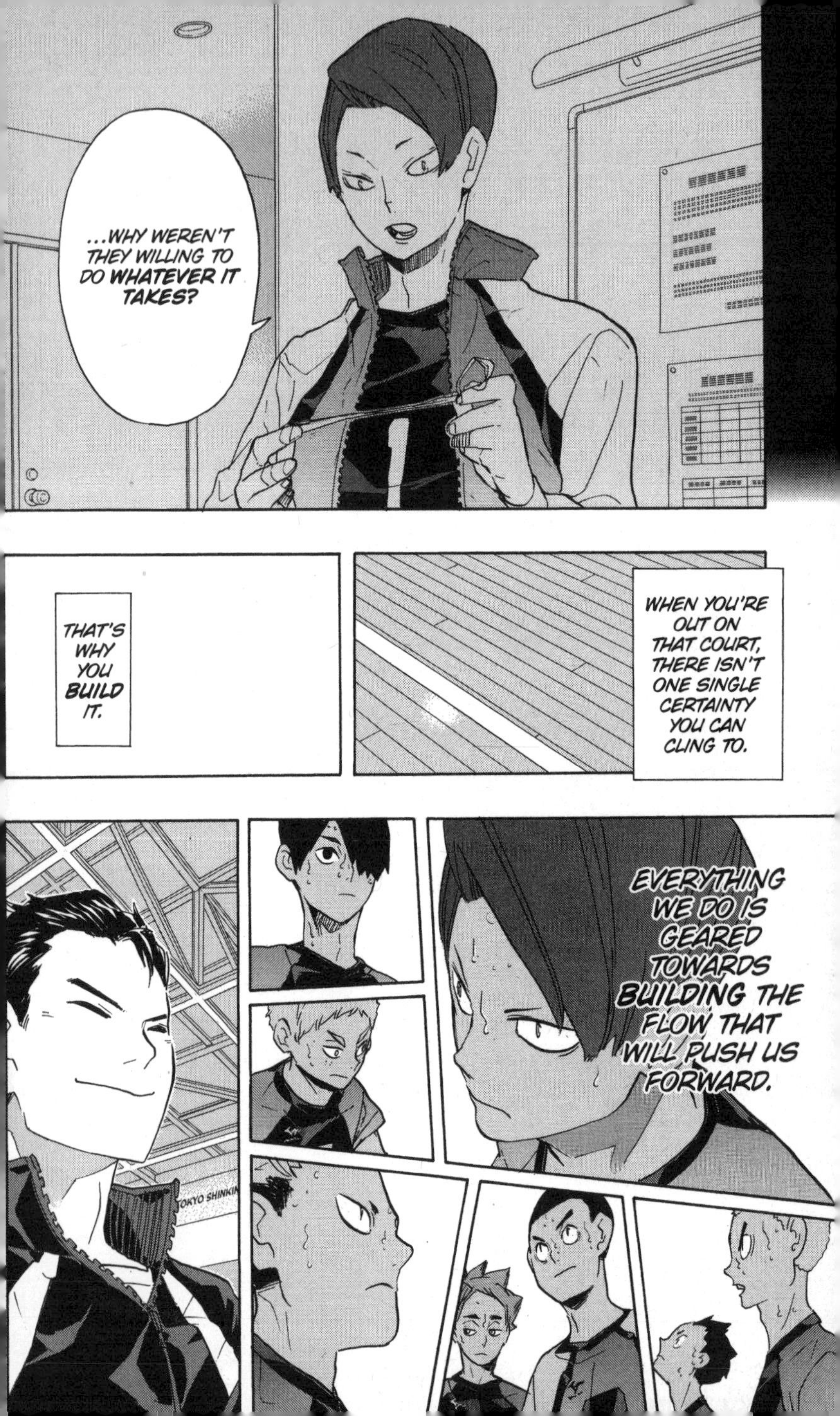
...WHY WEREN'T THEY WILLING TO DO WHATEVER IT TAKES?
WHEN YOU'RE OUT ON THAT COURT, THERE ISN'T ONE SINGLE CERTAINTY YOU CAN CLING TO.
THAT'S WHY YOU BUILD IT.
EVERYTHING WE DO IS GEARED TOWARDS BUILDING THE FLOW THAT WILL PUSH US FORWARD.

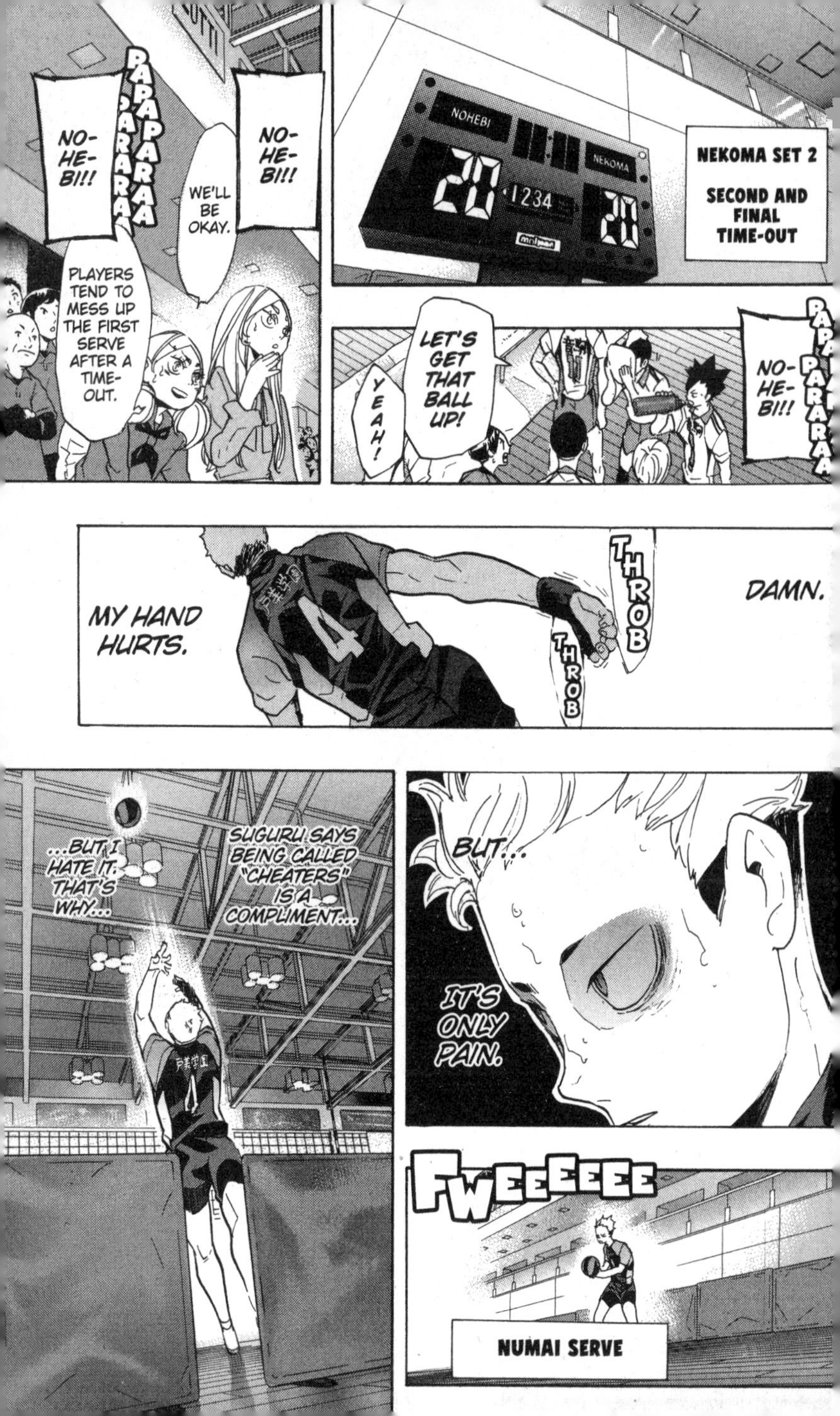
NOHEBI
NEKOMA
20
20
NEKOMA SET 2
SECOND AND FINAL TIME-OUT
PAPAPARARARAA
NO-HE-BI!!
LET'S GET THAT BALL UP!
YEAH!
NO-HE-BI!!
PAPAPARARARAA
WE'LL BE OKAY.
NO-HE-BI!!
PLAYERS TEND TO MESS UP THE FIRST SERVE AFTER A TIME-OUT.
DAMN.
THROB
THROB
MY HAND HURTS.
BUT...
IT'S ONLY PAIN.
FWEEEEEE
NUMAI SERVE
SUGURU SAYS BEING CALLED "CHEATERS" IS A COMPLIMENT...
...BUT I HATE IT. THAT'S WHY...

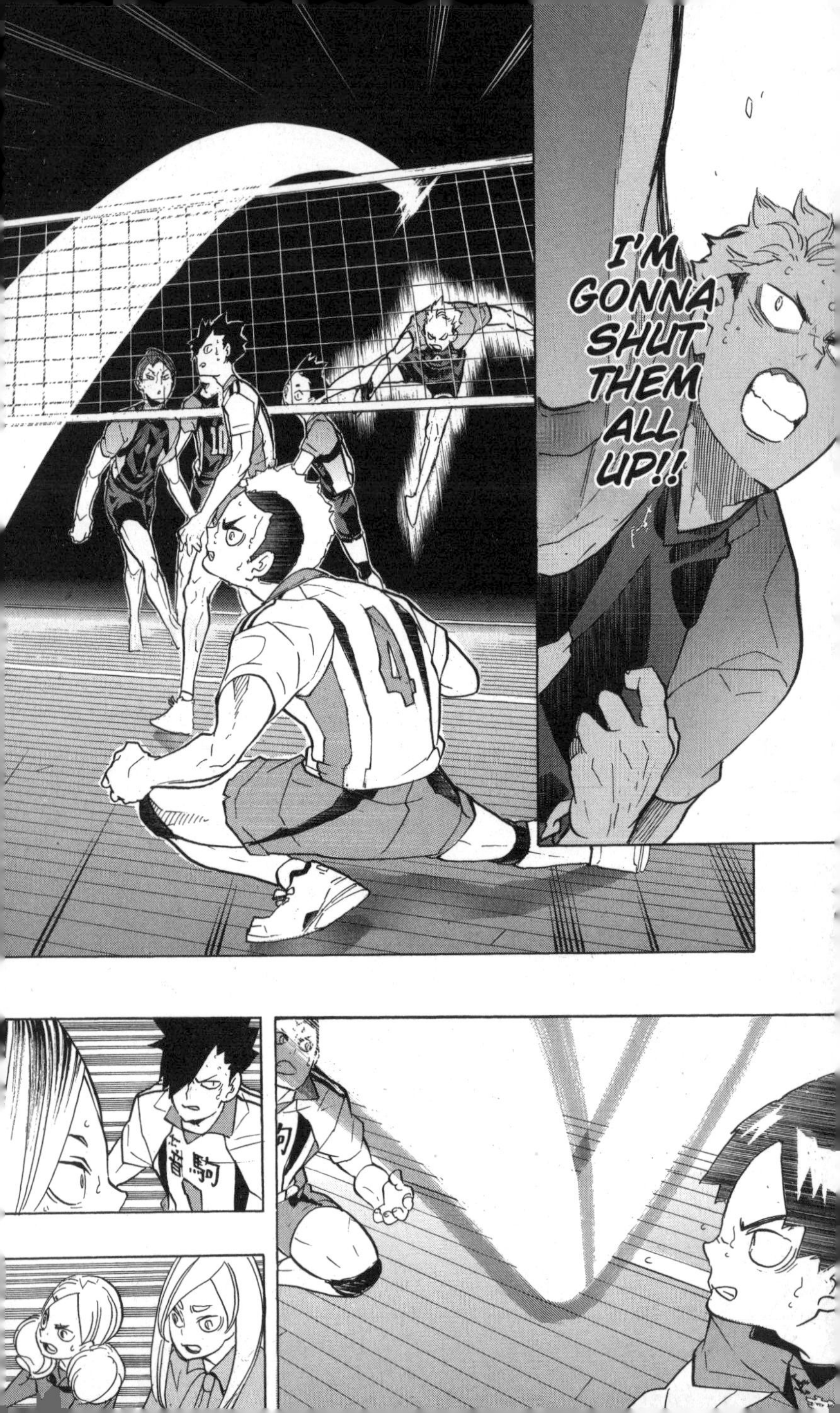
I'M GONNA SHUT THEM ALL UP!!

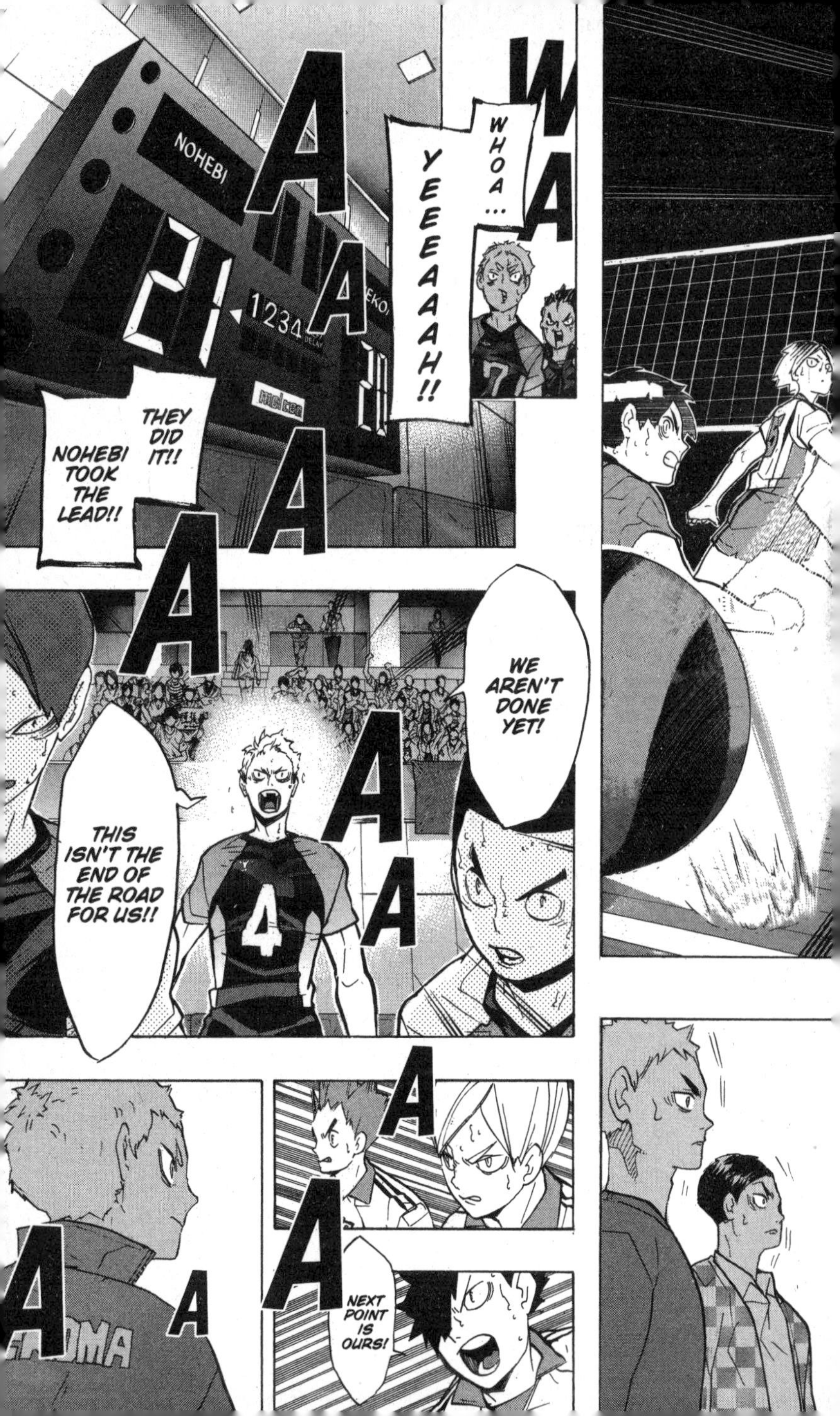
WAAAAAAAAAAAA
WHOA...
YEEEAAAAH!!
NOHEBI
21
THEY DID IT!!
NOHEBI TOOK THE LEAD!!
WE AREN'T DONE YET!
THIS ISN'T THE END OF THE ROAD FOR US!!
NEXT POINT IS OURS!

KAZUMA NUMAI

NOHEBI ACADEMY
CLASS 3-1

POSITION:
WING SPIKER

HEIGHT: 5'10"

WEIGHT: 158 LBS.
(AS OF NOVEMBER, 3RD YEAR OF HIGH SCHOOL)

BIRTHDAY: AUGUST 4

FAVORITE FOOD:
TAKANA **FRIED RICE**

CURRENT WORRY:
THE ROOKIES AND SECOND YEARS ON THE TEAM DON'T HAVE ENOUGH GUTS!

ABILITY PARAMETERS
(5-POINT SCALE)

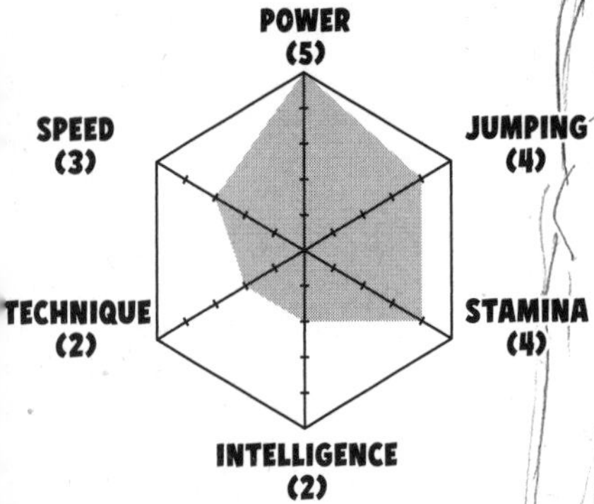
POWER
(5)
JUMPING
(4)
STAMINA
(4)
INTELLIGENCE
(2)
TECHNIQUE
(2)
SPEED
(3)

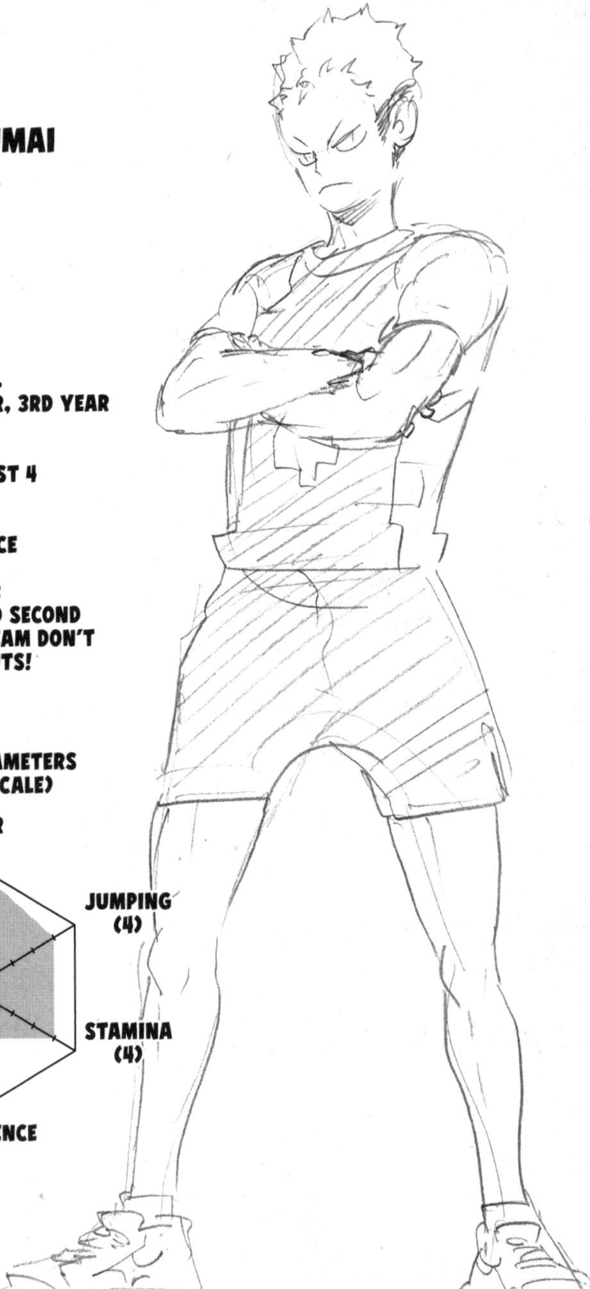

CHAPTER 204: Volleyball Even Idiots Understand

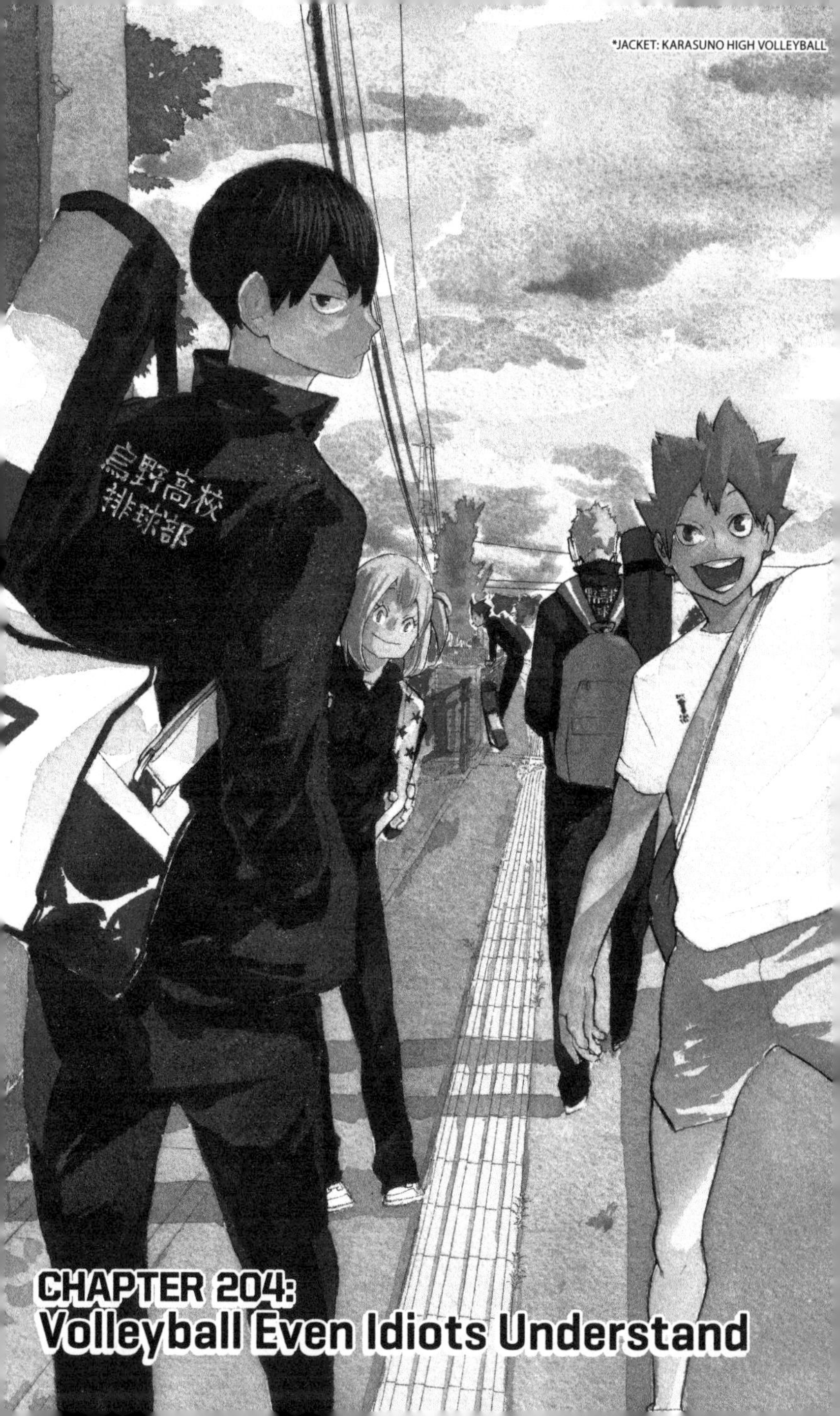
*JACKET: KARASUNO HIGH VOLLEYBALL
烏野高校
排球部

HAIKYU!!

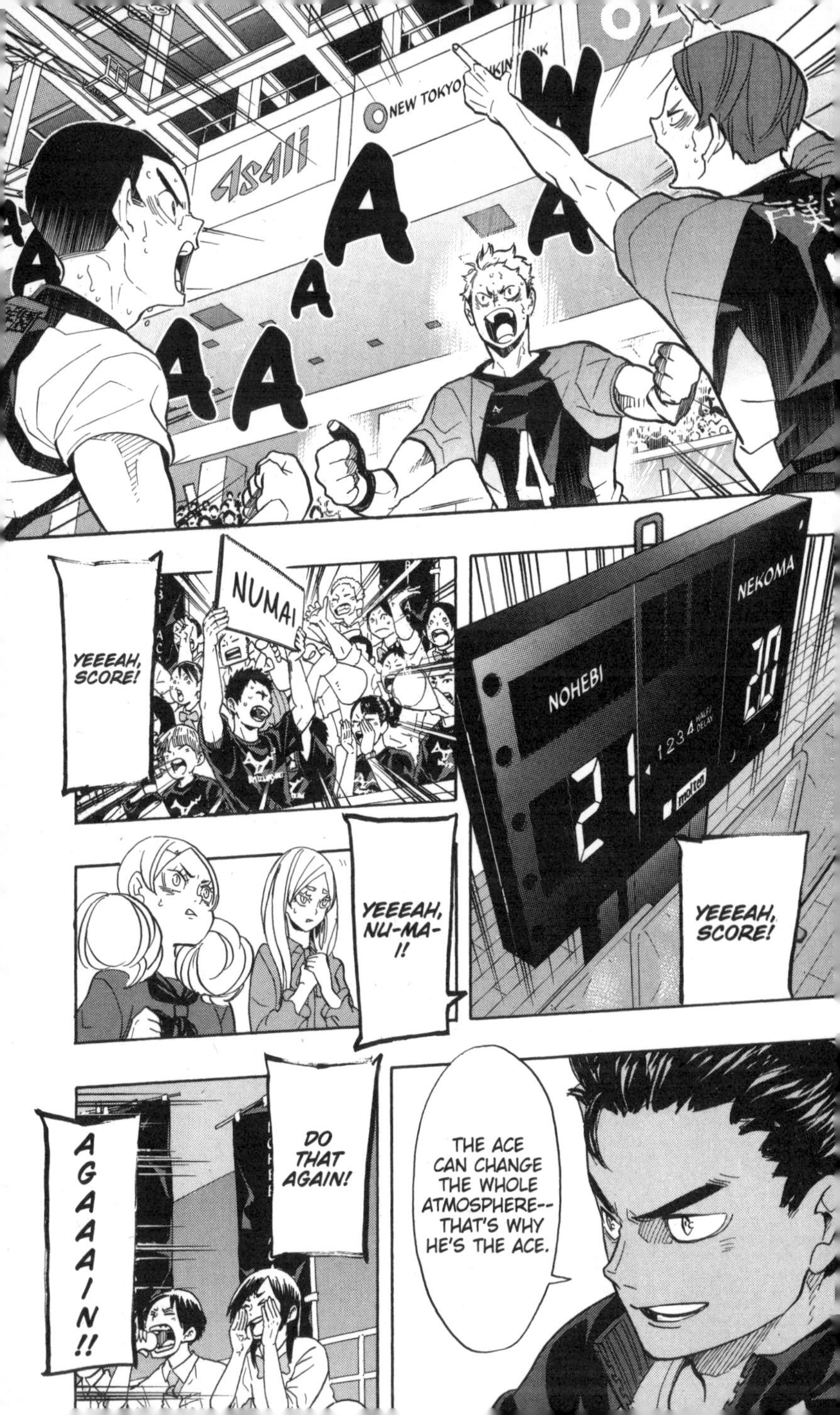

AAAAAAAAW
NEW TOKYO
NEKOMA
NOHEBI
20
21
1 2 3 4 HALF/DELAY
molten
YEEEAH, SCORE!
NUMAI
YEEEAH, SCORE!
YEEEAH, NU-MA-I!
THE ACE CAN CHANGE THE WHOLE ATMOSPHERE-- THAT'S WHY HE'S THE ACE.
DO THAT AGAIN!
AGAAAAIN!!

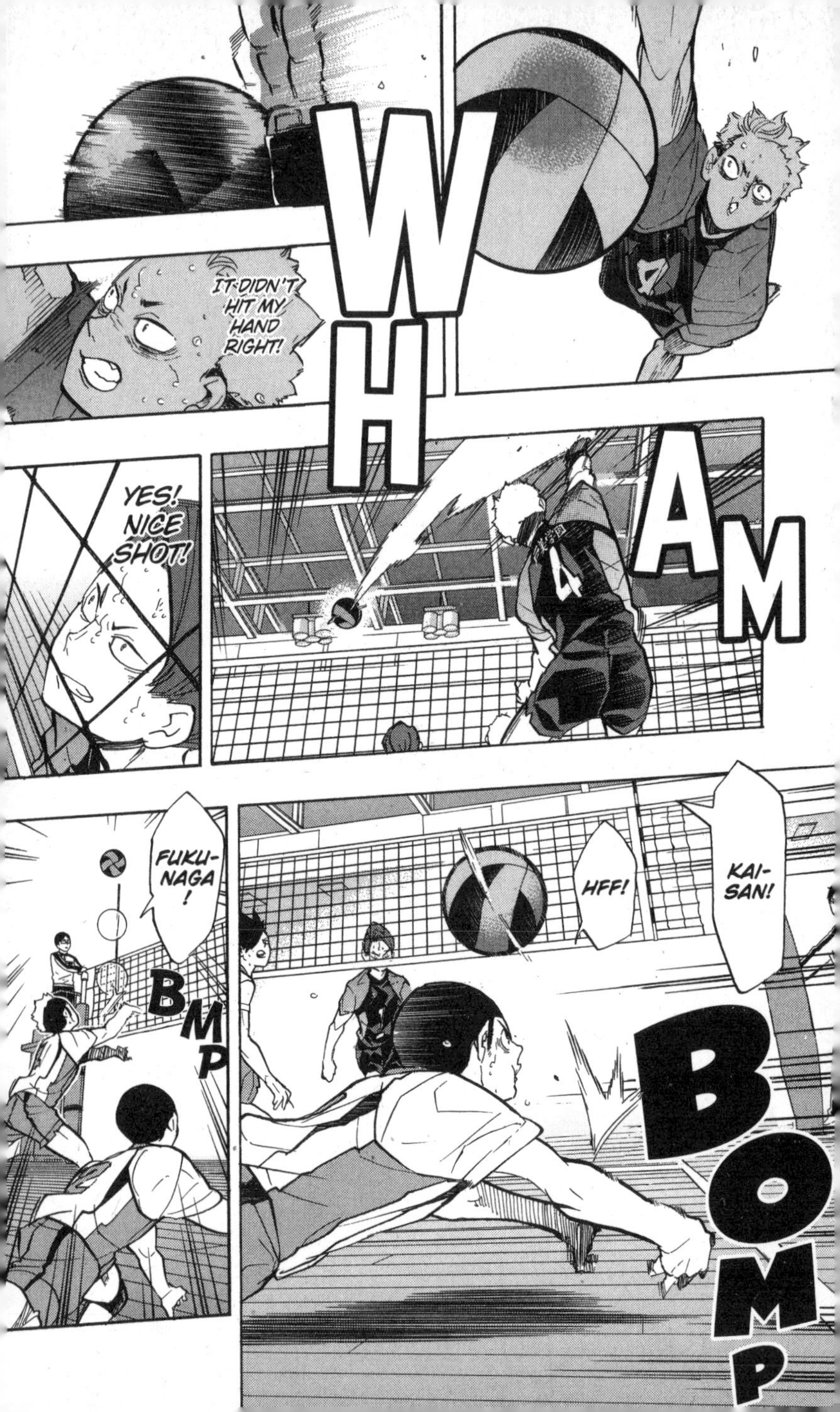
WHAM
IT DIDN'T HIT MY HAND RIGHT!
YES! NICE SHOT!
KAI-SAN!
HFF!
BOMP
FUKU-NAGA!
BMP

TUMP

OUT!!

IN

WHEW

WELL AIMED, WELL AIMED.

CLAP CLAP

FWUP

IT'S IN YOUR HANDS NOW, GUYS.

NOHEBI PLAYER SUBSTITUTION

IN	NO. 7	SAKISHIMA (S)
OUT	NO. 4	NUMAI (WS)

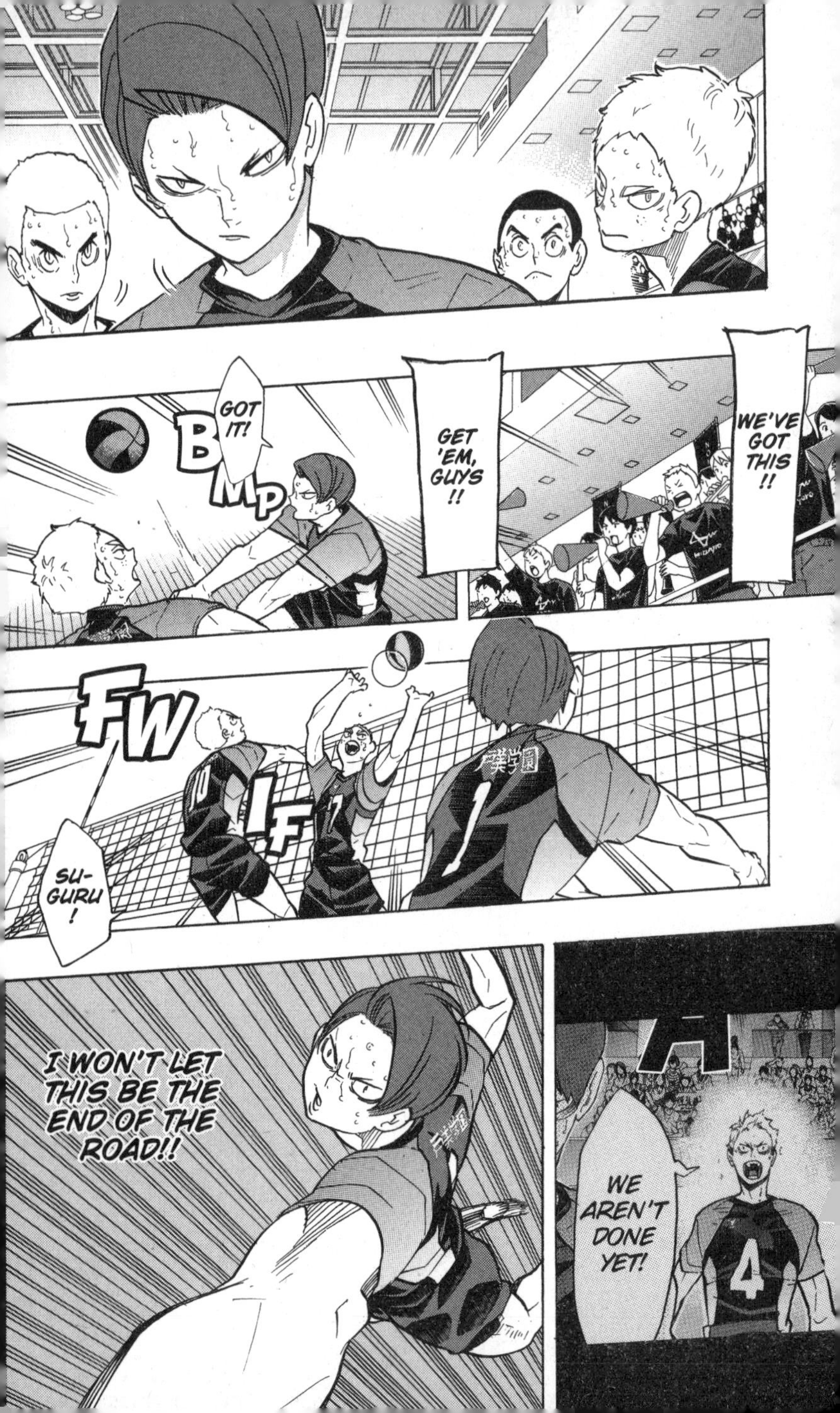
WE'VE GOT THIS!!
GET 'EM, GUYS!!
GOT IT!
BMP
FWIF
SU-GURU!
WE AREN'T DONE YET!
I WON'T LET THIS BE THE END OF THE ROAD!!

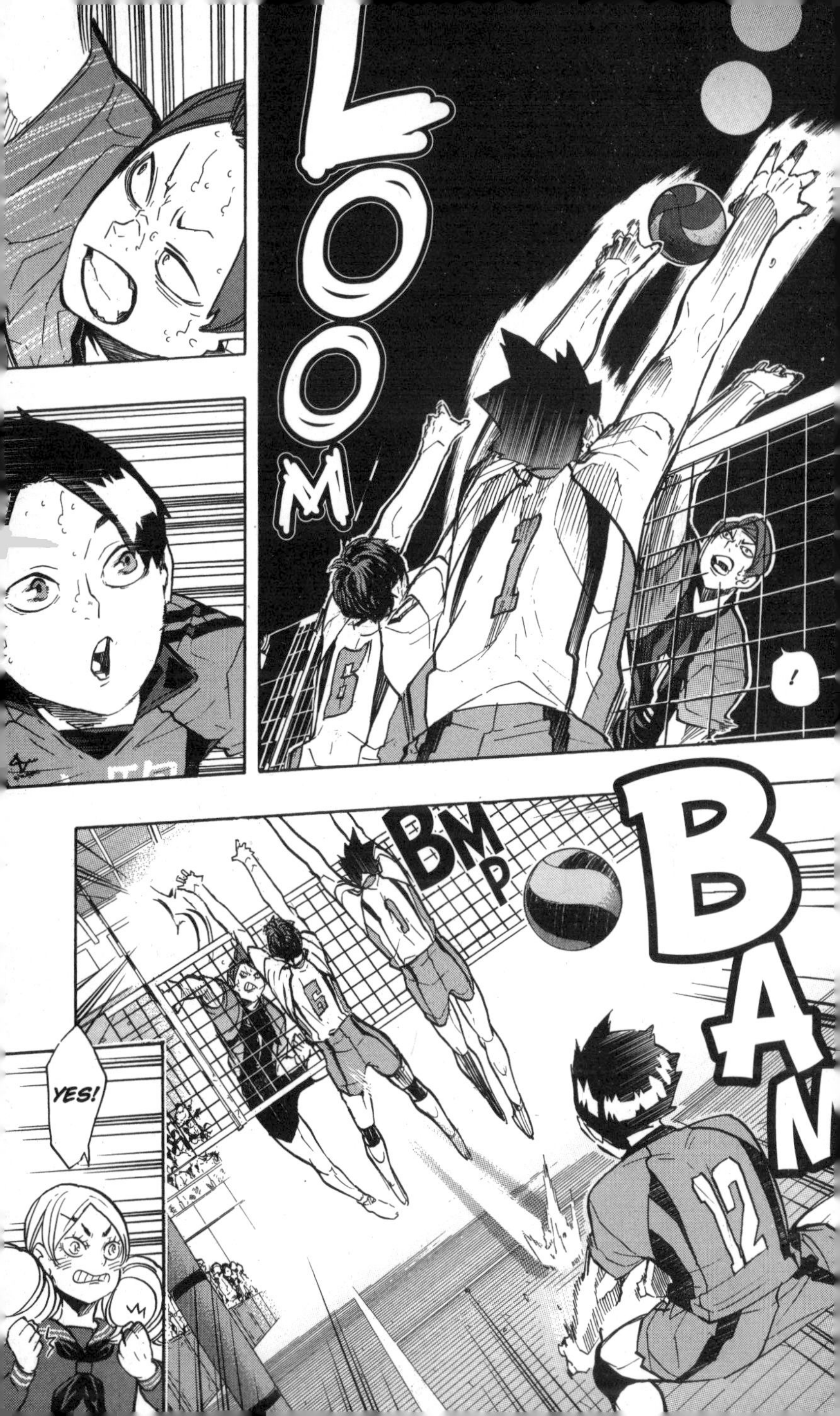
LOOOM
!
BAM
BMP
YES!

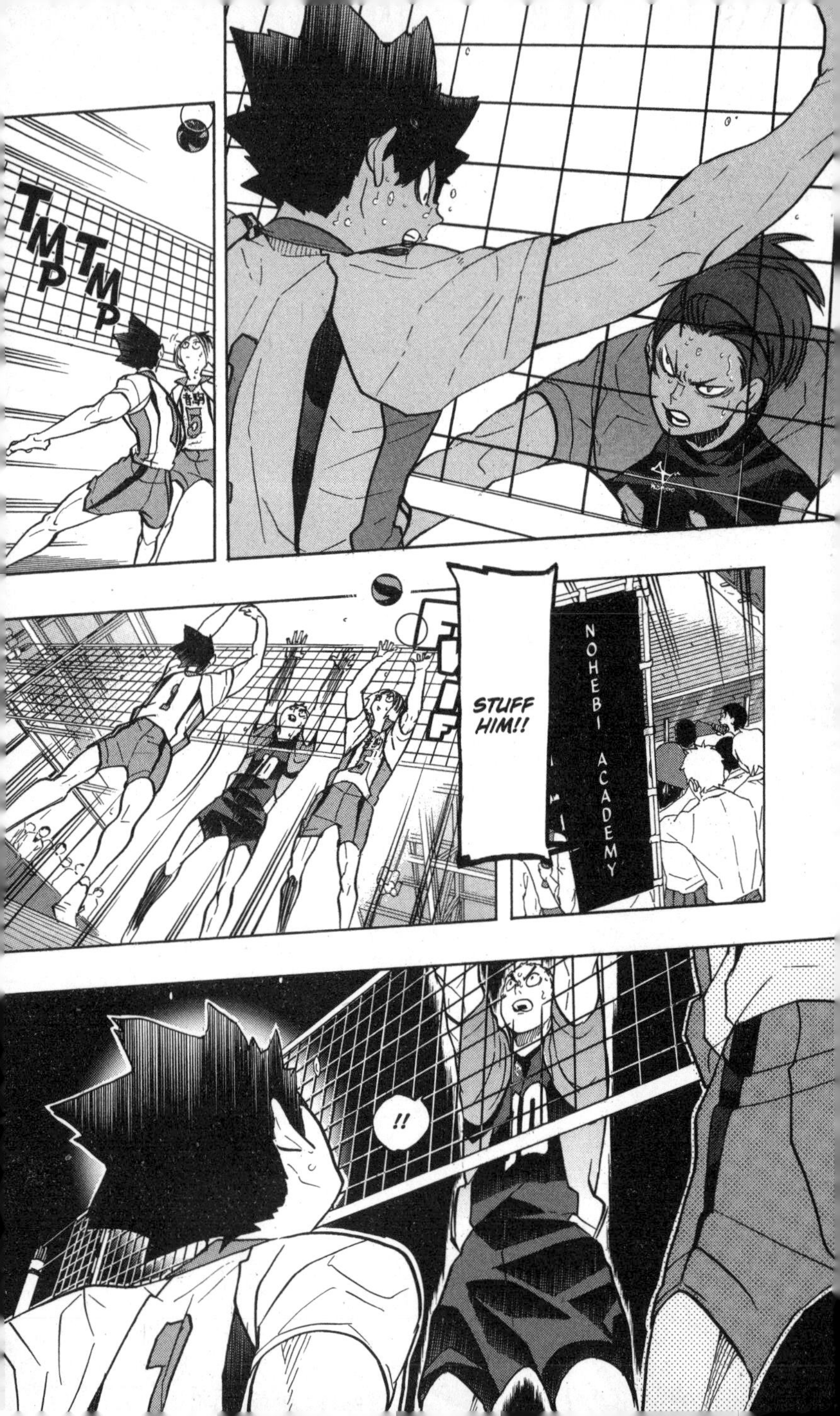
TMP TMP
STUFF HIM!!
NOHEBI ACADEMY
!!

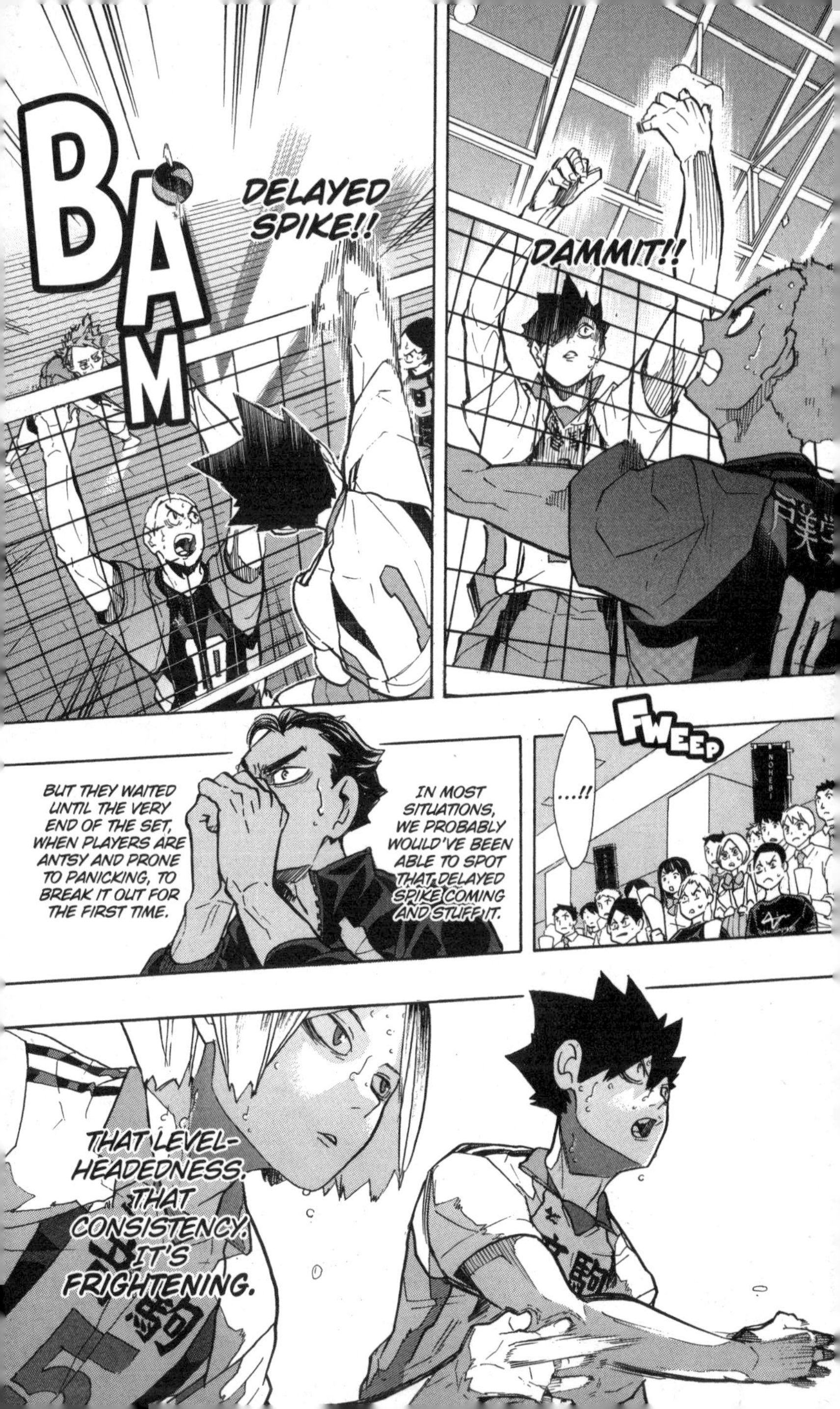
DAMMIT!!
BAM
DELAYED SPIKE!!
FWEEP
...!!
IN MOST SITUATIONS, WE PROBABLY WOULD'VE BEEN ABLE TO SPOT THAT DELAYED SPIKE COMING AND STUFF IT.
BUT THEY WAITED UNTIL THE VERY END OF THE SET, WHEN PLAYERS ARE ANTSY AND PRONE TO PANICKING, TO BREAK IT OUT FOR THE FIRST TIME.
THAT LEVEL-HEADEDNESS. THAT CONSISTENCY. IT'S FRIGHTENING.

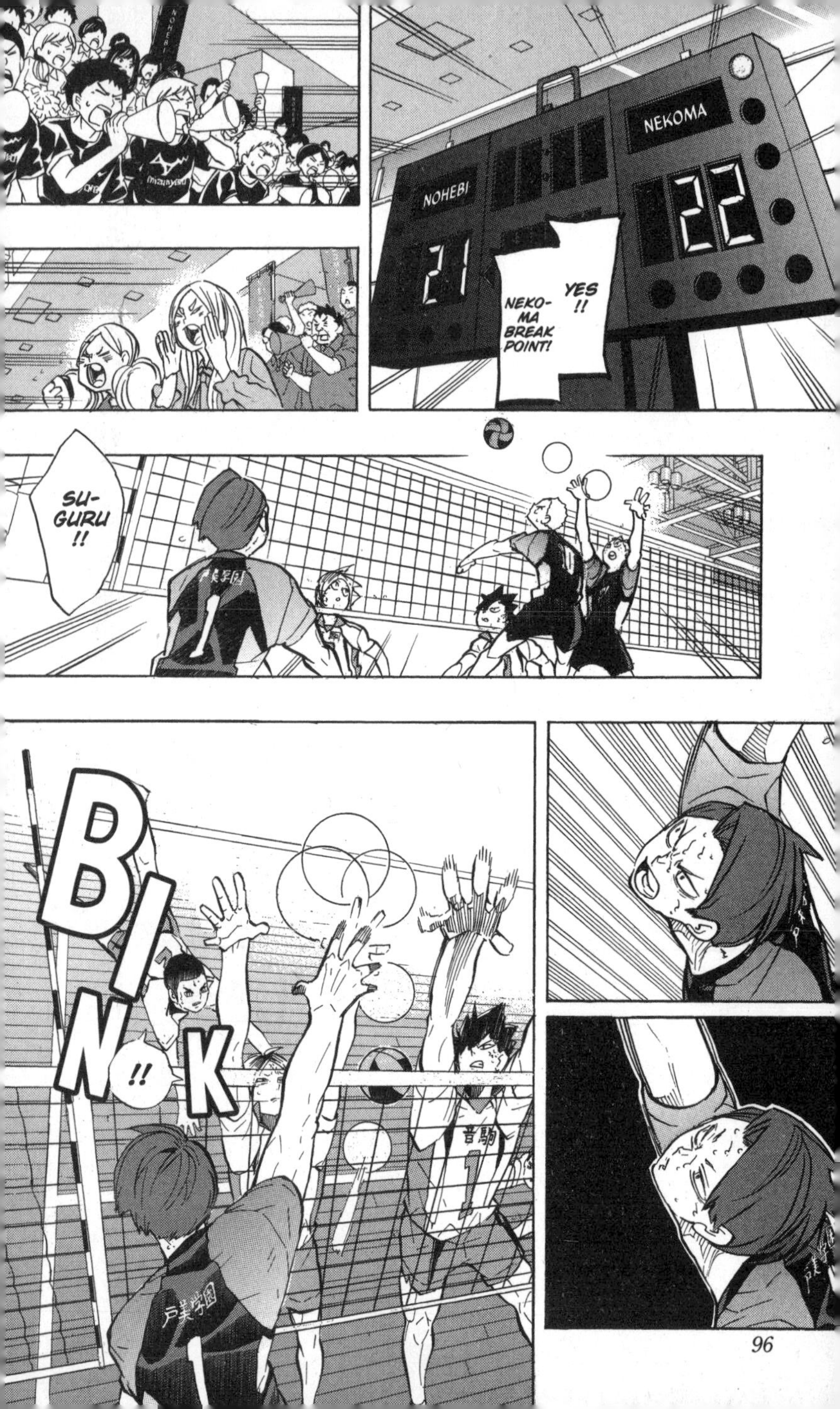
NEKOMA
NOHEBI
21
22
YES!!
NEKOMA BREAK POINT!
SUGURU!!
BINK
!!

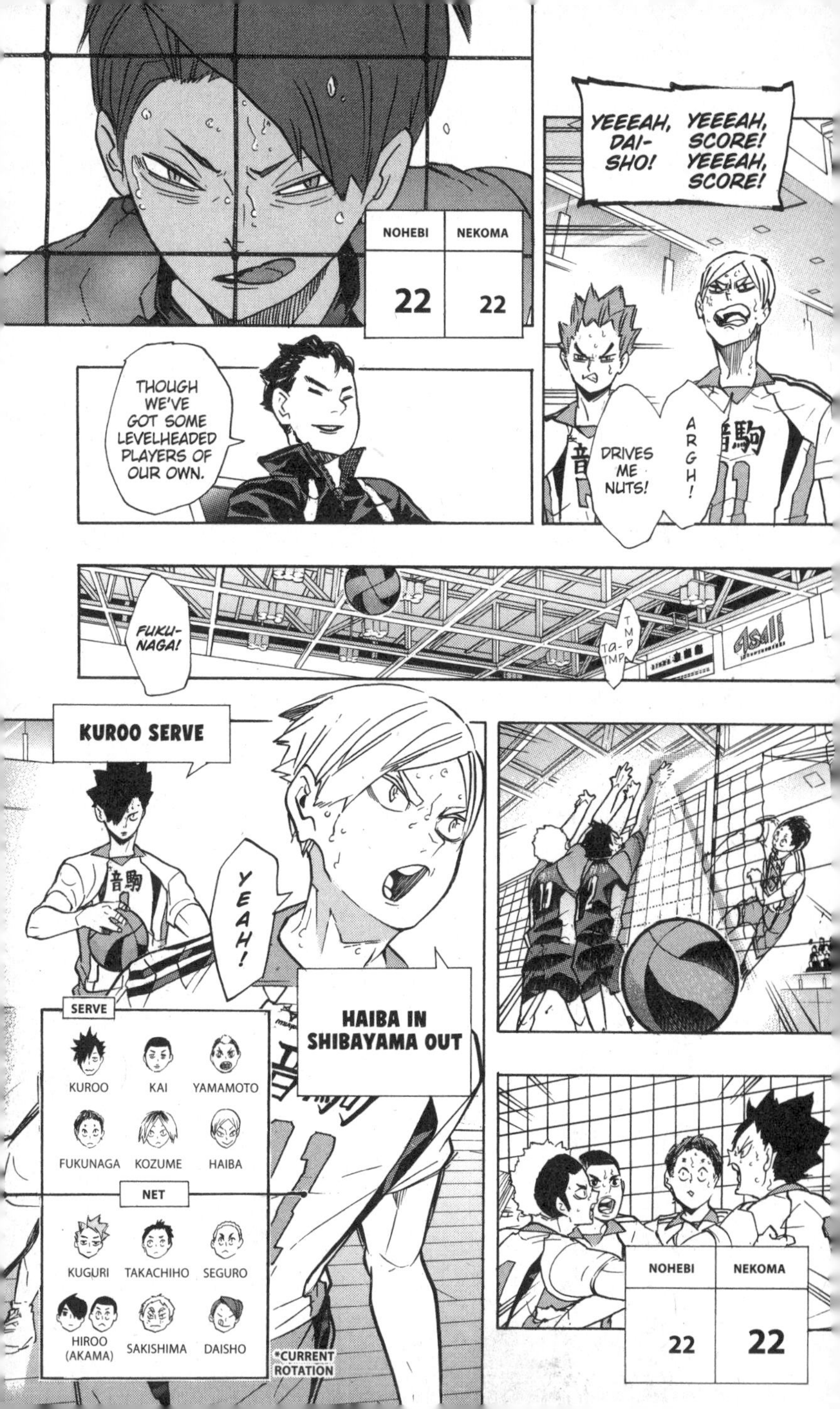
YEEEAH, YEEEAH, SCORE! YEEEAH, SCORE!
YEEEAH, DAI-SHO!
ARGH!
DRIVES ME NUTS!
NOHEBI 22
NEKOMA 22
THOUGH WE'VE GOT SOME LEVELHEADED PLAYERS OF OUR OWN.
TMP
Ta-P TMP
FUKU-NAGA!
NOHEBI 22
NEKOMA 22
KUROO SERVE
YEAH!
HAIBA IN SHIBAYAMA OUT
SERVE
KUROO
KAI
YAMAMOTO
FUKUNAGA
KOZUME
HAIBA
NET
KUGURI
TAKACHIHO
SEGURO
HIROO (AKAMA)
SAKISHIMA
DAISHO
*CURRENT ROTATION

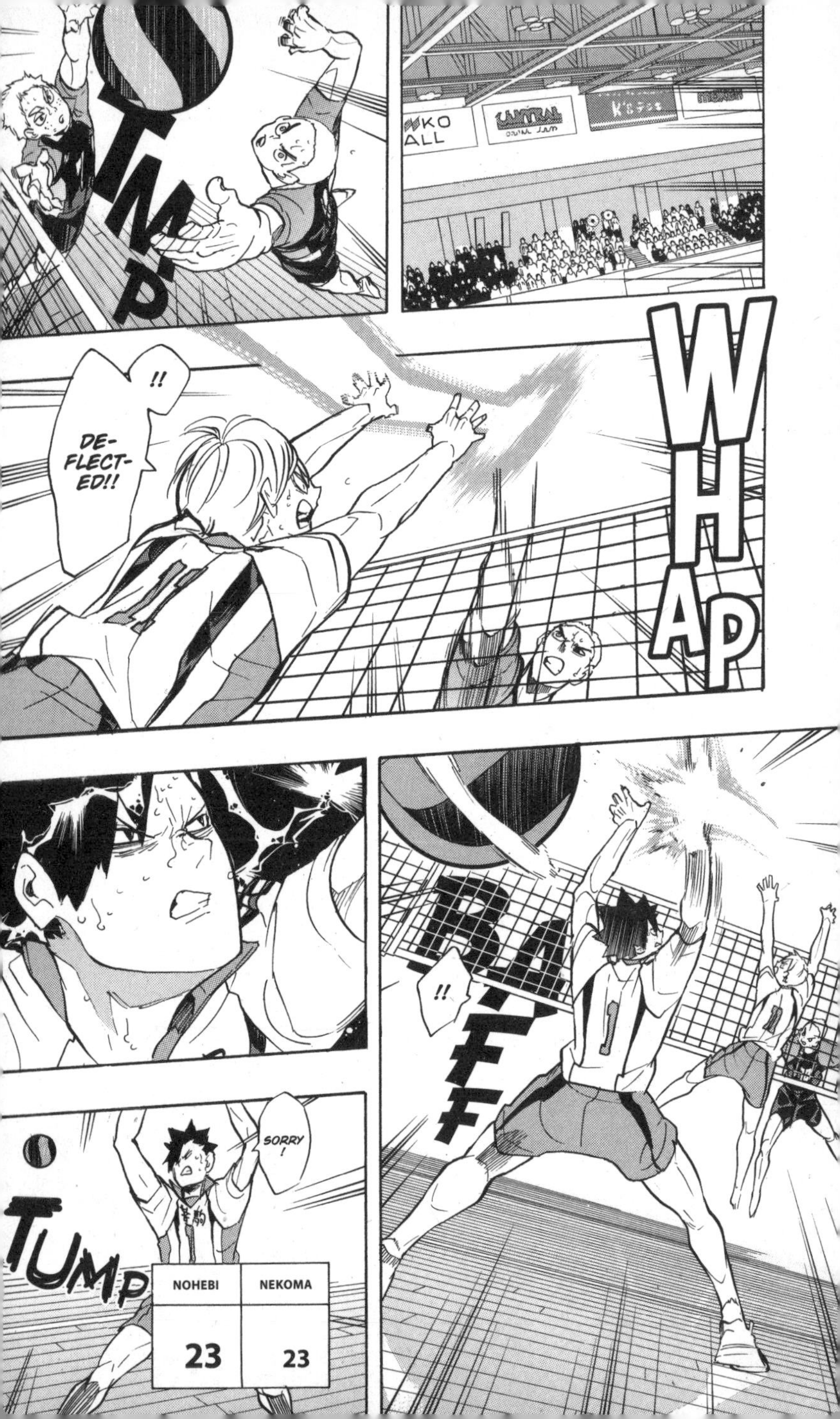
TMP
WHAP
!!
DE-FLECTED!!
BAFF
!!
SORRY!
TUMP
NOHEBI 23
NEKOMA 23

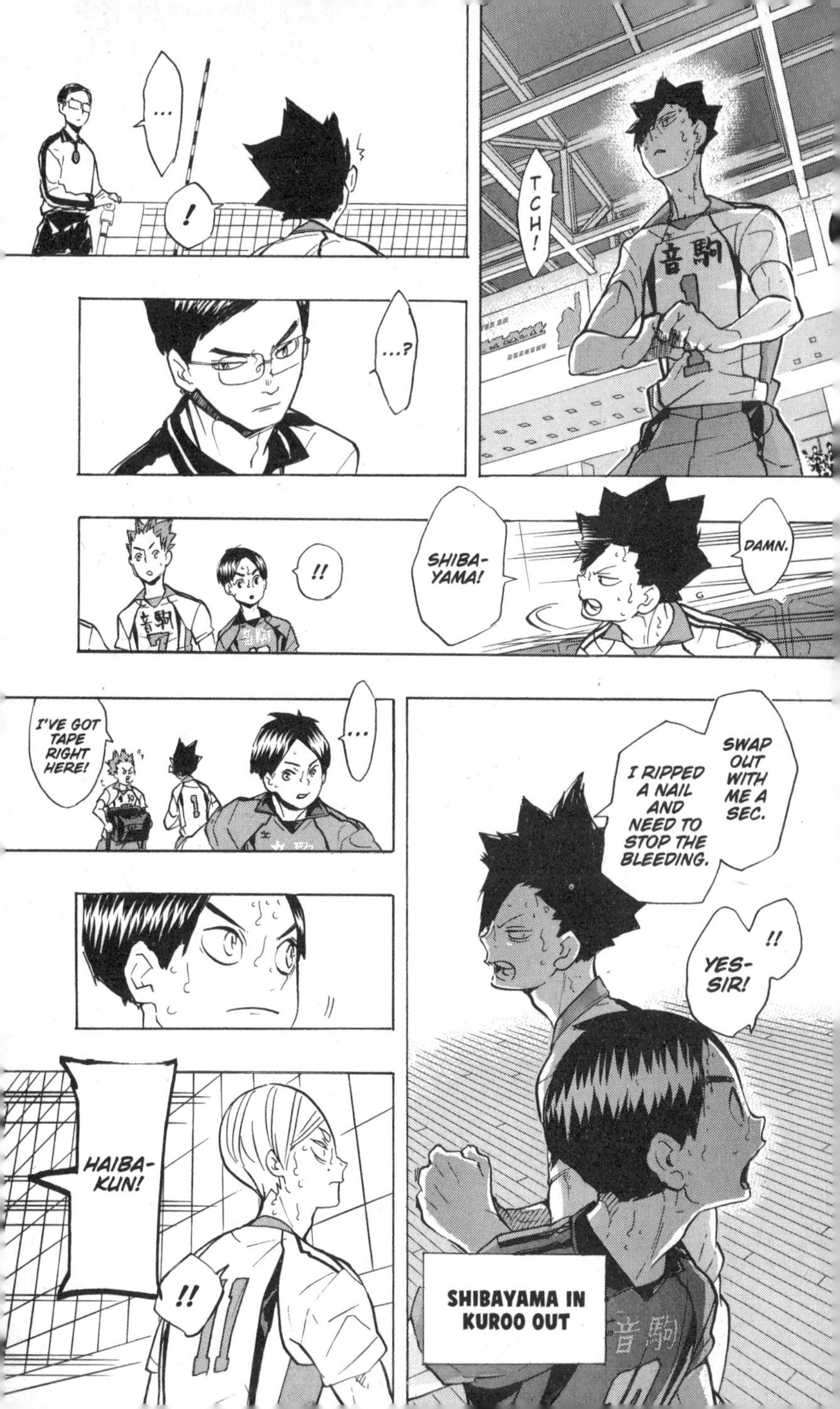
TCH!
...
!
...?
DAMN.
SHIBA-YAMA!
!!
SWAP OUT WITH ME A SEC.
I RIPPED A NAIL AND NEED TO STOP THE BLEEDING.
!!
YES-SIR!
SHIBAYAMA IN KUROO OUT
...
I'VE GOT TAPE RIGHT HERE!
HAIBA-KUN!
!!

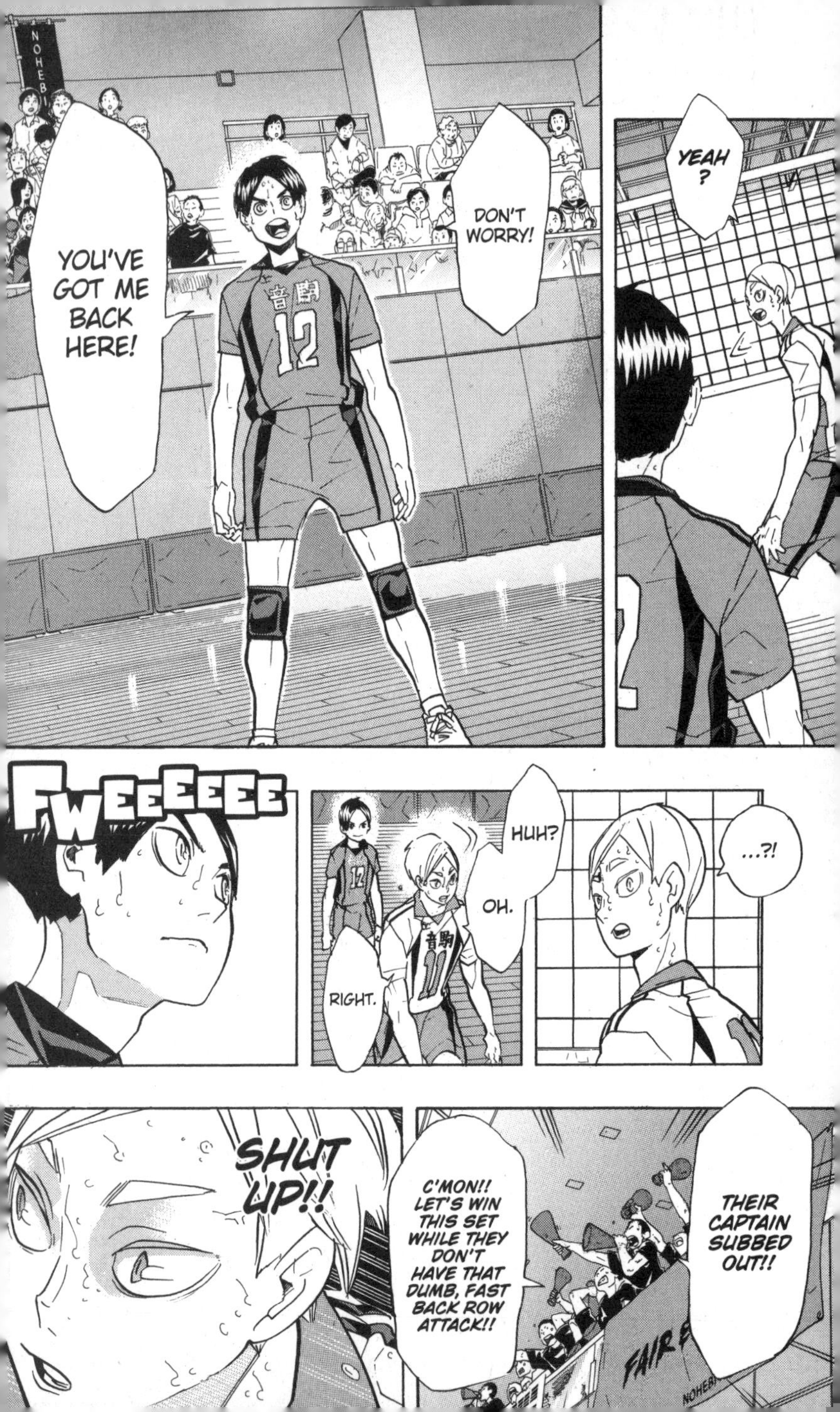
YEAH?
NOHEBI
DON'T WORRY!
YOU'VE GOT ME BACK HERE!
...?!
HUH?
OH.
RIGHT.
FWEEEEEE
THEIR CAPTAIN SUBBED OUT!!
C'MON!! LET'S WIN THIS SET WHILE THEY DON'T HAVE THAT DUMB, FAST BACK ROW ATTACK!!
SHUT UP!!

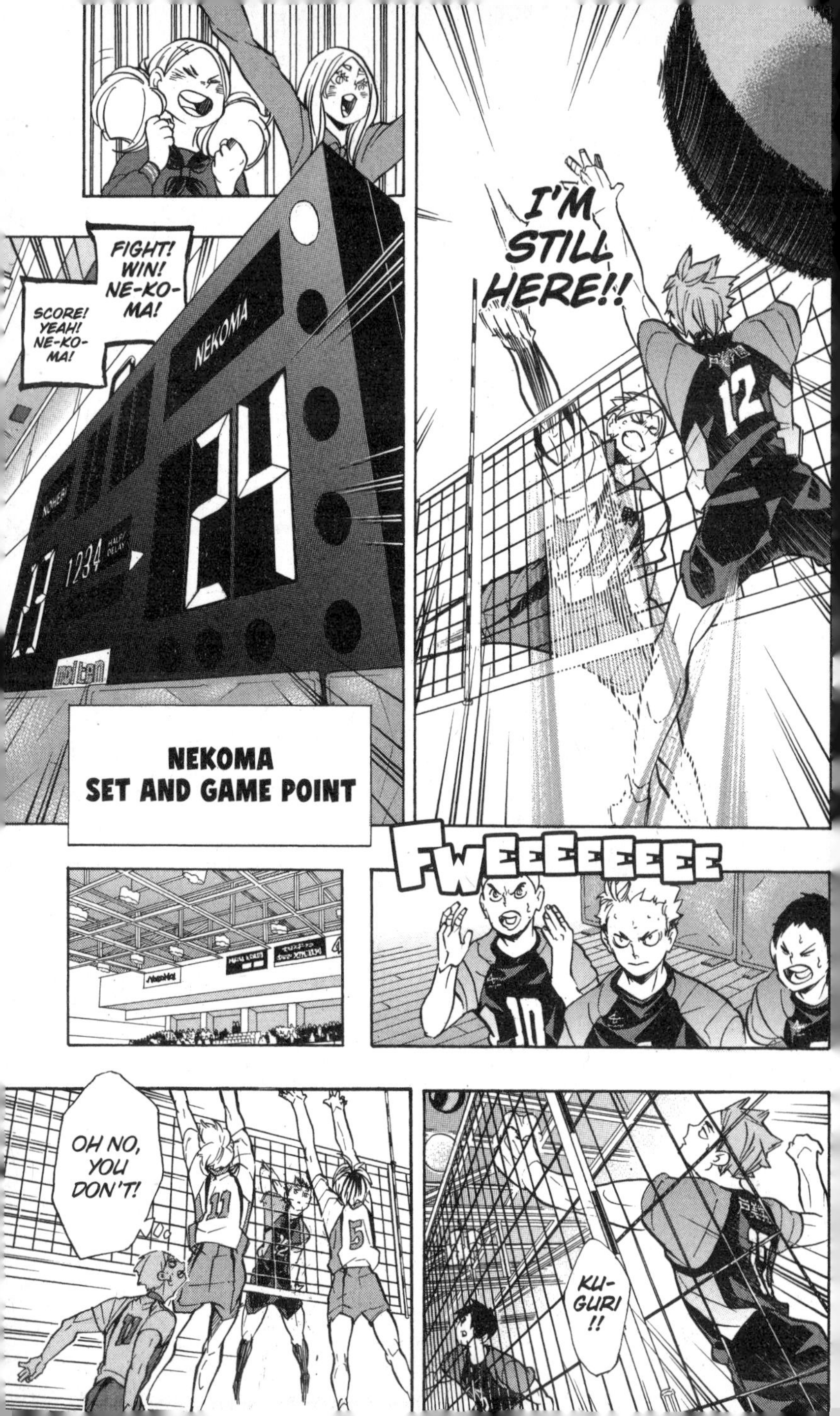

I'M STILL HERE!!
FIGHT! WIN! NE-KO-MA!
SCORE! YEAH! NE-KO-MA!
NEKOMA
24
NEKOMA SET AND GAME POINT
FWEEEEEEEE
KU-GURI!!
OH NO, YOU DON'T!

I'LL STOP YOU!!

HE'S TOO GOOD...!

DAM- MIT.

YEEEAH, SCORE! YEEEAH, SCORE! YEEEAH, KU-GU-RI-!

NOHEBI	NEKOMA
14	13

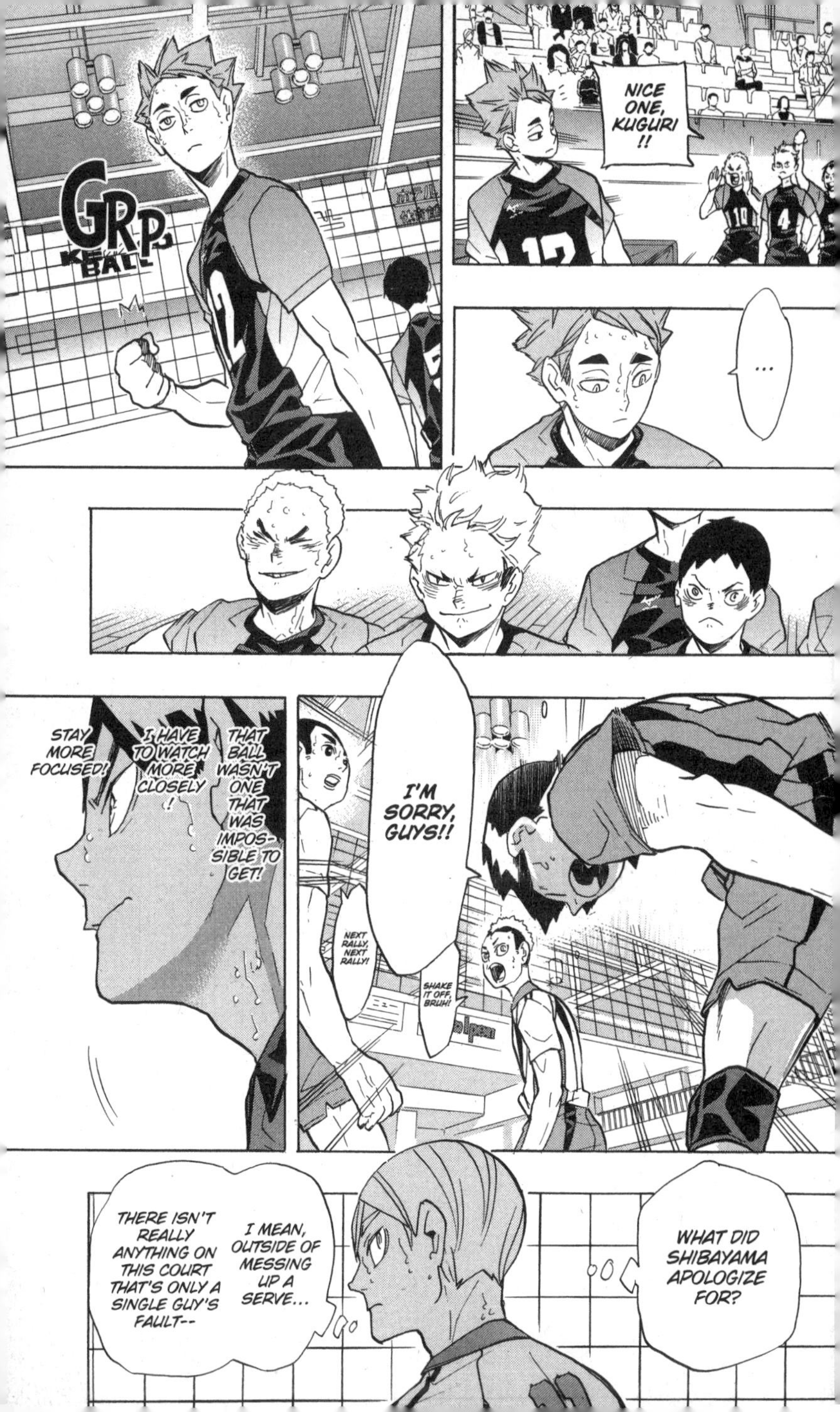
NICE ONE, KUGURI!!
...
GRP
I'M SORRY, GUYS!!
SHAKE IT OFF, BRUH!
NEXT RALLY, NEXT RALLY!
THAT BALL WASN'T ONE THAT WAS IMPOSSIBLE TO GET!
I HAVE TO WATCH MORE CLOSELY!
STAY MORE FOCUSED!
WHAT DID SHIBAYAMA APOLOGIZE FOR?
I MEAN, OUTSIDE OF MESSING UP A SERVE...
THERE ISN'T REALLY ANYTHING ON THIS COURT THAT'S ONLY A SINGLE GUY'S FAULT--

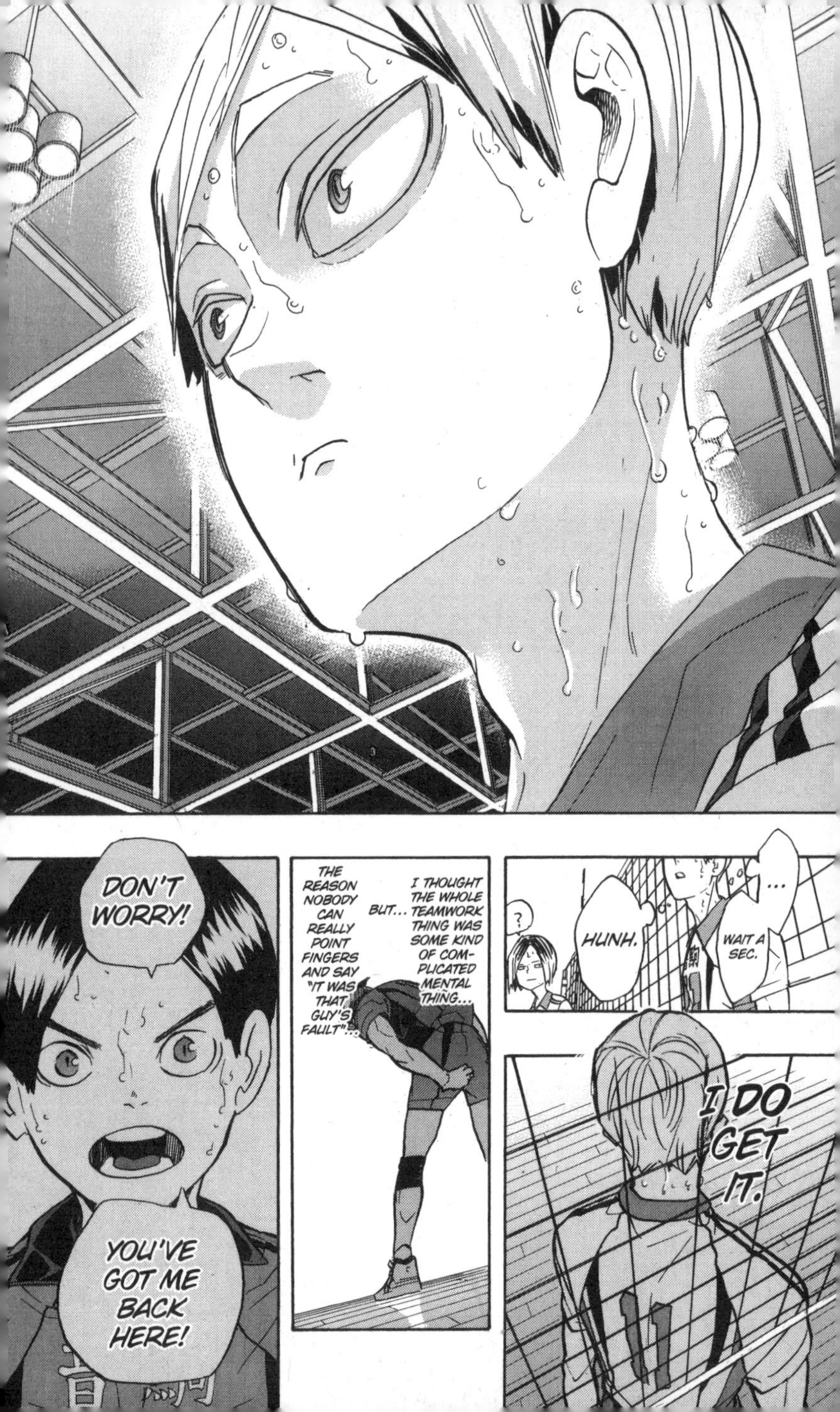
...
WAIT A SEC.
HUNH.
?
I DO GET IT.
I THOUGHT THE WHOLE TEAMWORK THING WAS SOME KIND OF COMPLICATED MENTAL THING...
BUT...
THE REASON NOBODY CAN REALLY POINT FINGERS AND SAY "IT WAS THAT GUY'S FAULT"...
DON'T WORRY!
YOU'VE GOT ME BACK HERE!

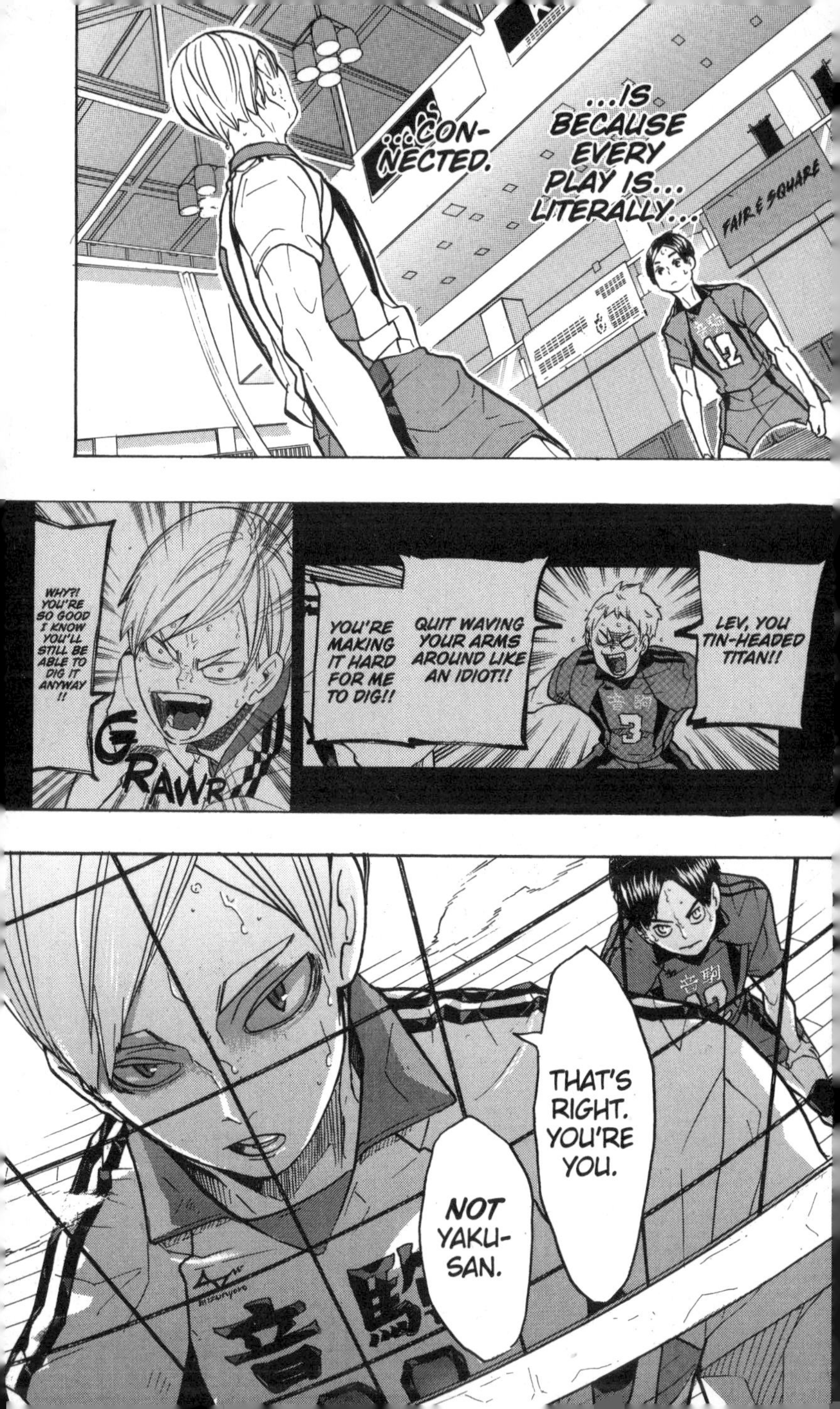

...IS BECAUSE EVERY PLAY IS... LITERALLY...
FAIR & SQUARE
...CON-NECTED.
LEV, YOU TIN-HEADED TITAN!!
QUIT WAVING YOUR ARMS AROUND LIKE AN IDIOT!!
YOU'RE MAKING IT HARD FOR ME TO DIG!!
WHY?! YOU'RE SO GOOD I KNOW YOU'LL STILL BE ABLE TO DIG IT ANYWAY!!
GRAWR
THAT'S RIGHT. YOU'RE YOU.
NOT YAKU-SAN.

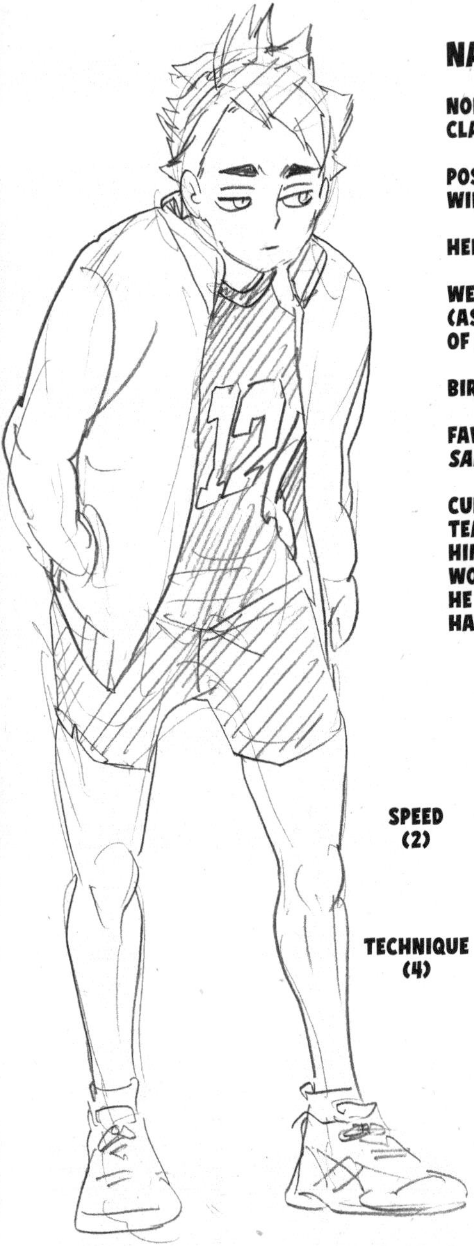

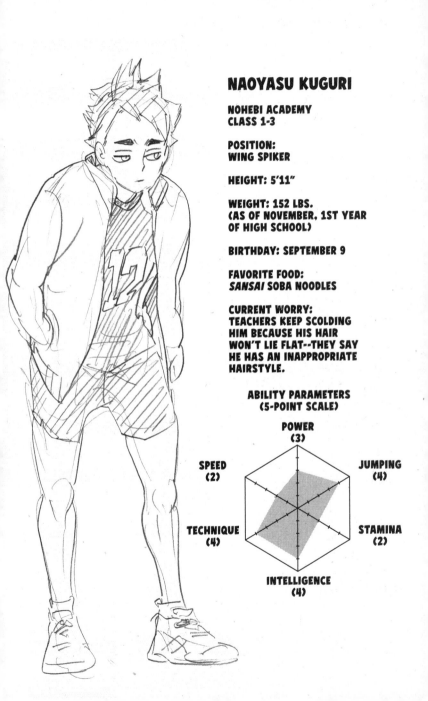

NAOYASU KUGURI

NOHEBI ACADEMY
CLASS 1-3

POSITION:
WING SPIKER

HEIGHT: 5'11"

WEIGHT: 152 LBS.
(AS OF NOVEMBER, 1ST YEAR OF HIGH SCHOOL)

BIRTHDAY: SEPTEMBER 9

FAVORITE FOOD:
***SANSAI* SOBA NOODLES**

CURRENT WORRY:
TEACHERS KEEP SCOLDING HIM BECAUSE HIS HAIR WON'T LIE FLAT--THEY SAY HE HAS AN INAPPROPRIATE HAIRSTYLE.

ABILITY PARAMETERS
(5-POINT SCALE)

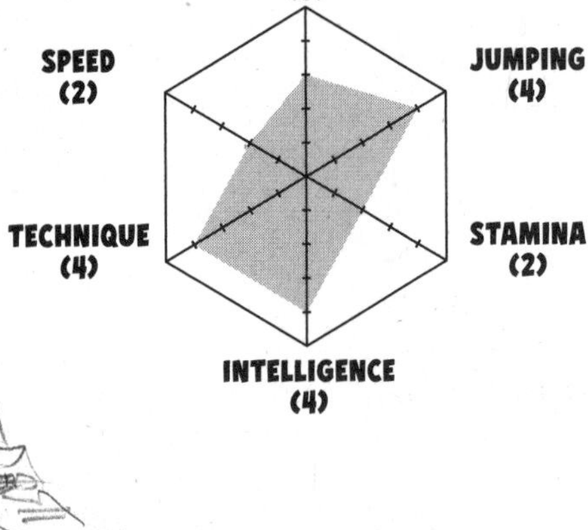
POWER (3)
JUMPING (4)
STAMINA (2)
INTELLIGENCE (4)
TECHNIQUE (4)
SPEED (2)

CHAPTER 205: The Ball's Path

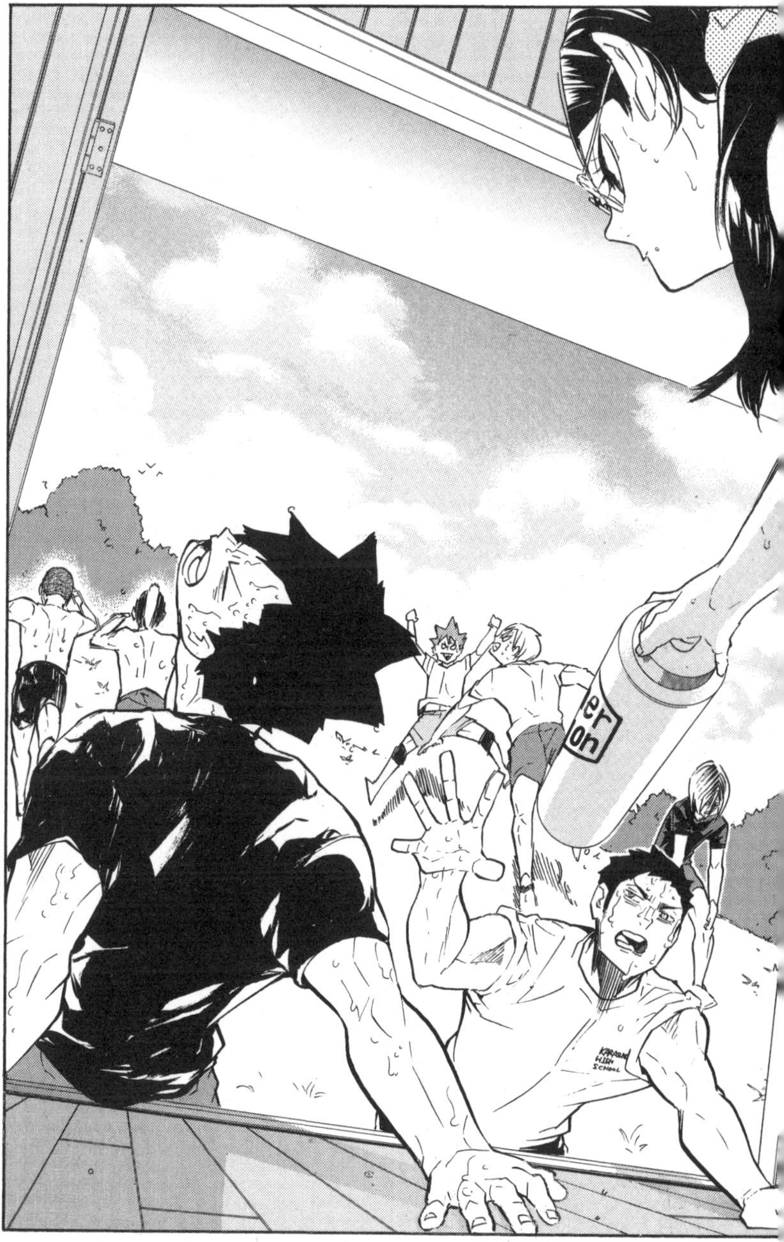

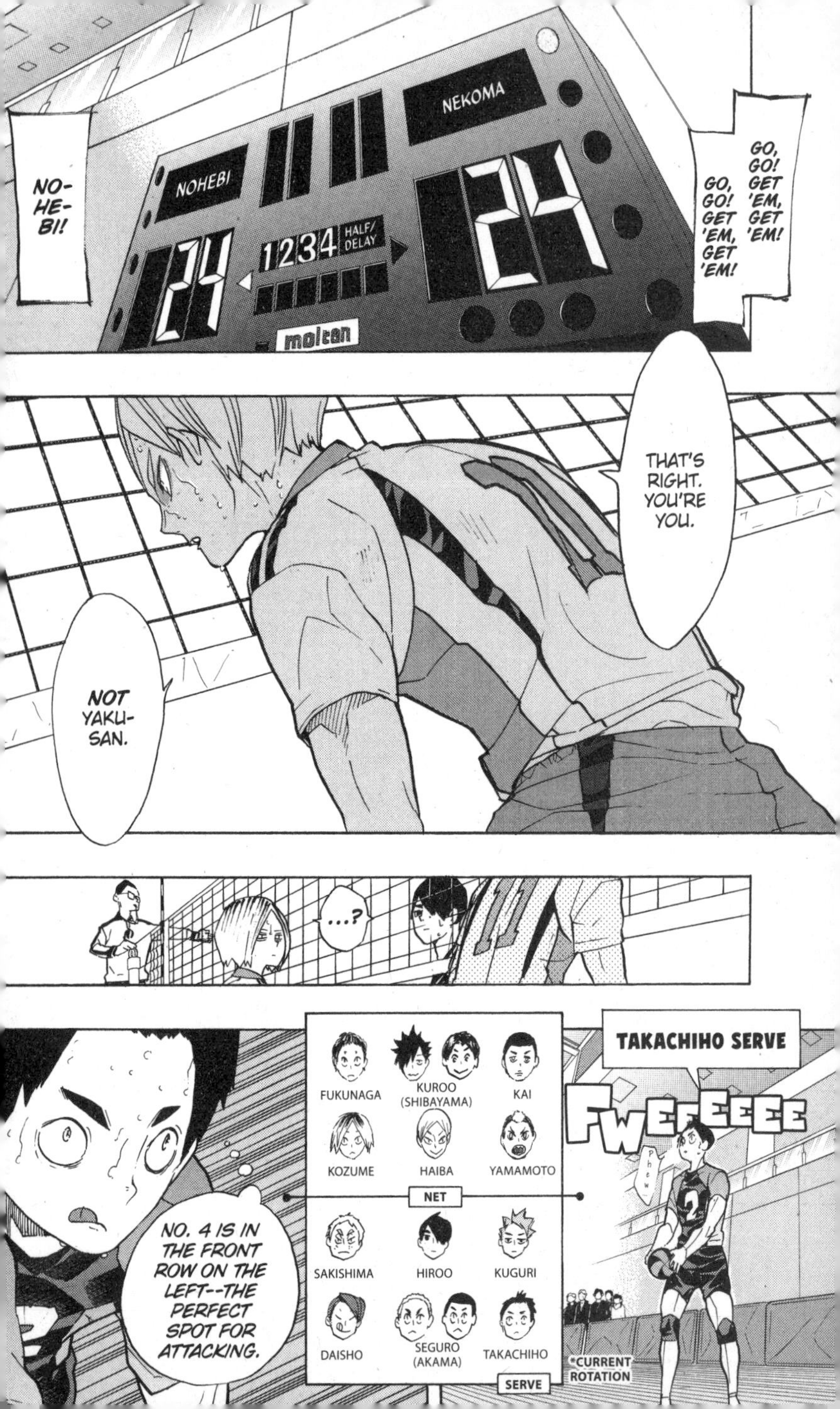

GO, GO! GET 'EM, GET 'EM!
GO, GO! GET 'EM, GET 'EM!
NEKOMA
24
1234 HALF/ DELAY
NOHEBI
24
NO-HE-BI!
THAT'S RIGHT. YOU'RE YOU.
NOT YAKU-SAN.
...?
TAKACHIHO SERVE
FWEEEEE
Phew...
*CURRENT ROTATION
FUKUNAGA
KUROO (SHIBAYAMA)
KAI
KOZUME
HAIBA
YAMAMOTO
NET
SAKISHIMA
HIROO
KUGURI
DAISHO
SEGURO (AKAMA)
TAKACHIHO
SERVE
NO. 4 IS IN THE FRONT ROW ON THE LEFT--THE PERFECT SPOT FOR ATTACKING.

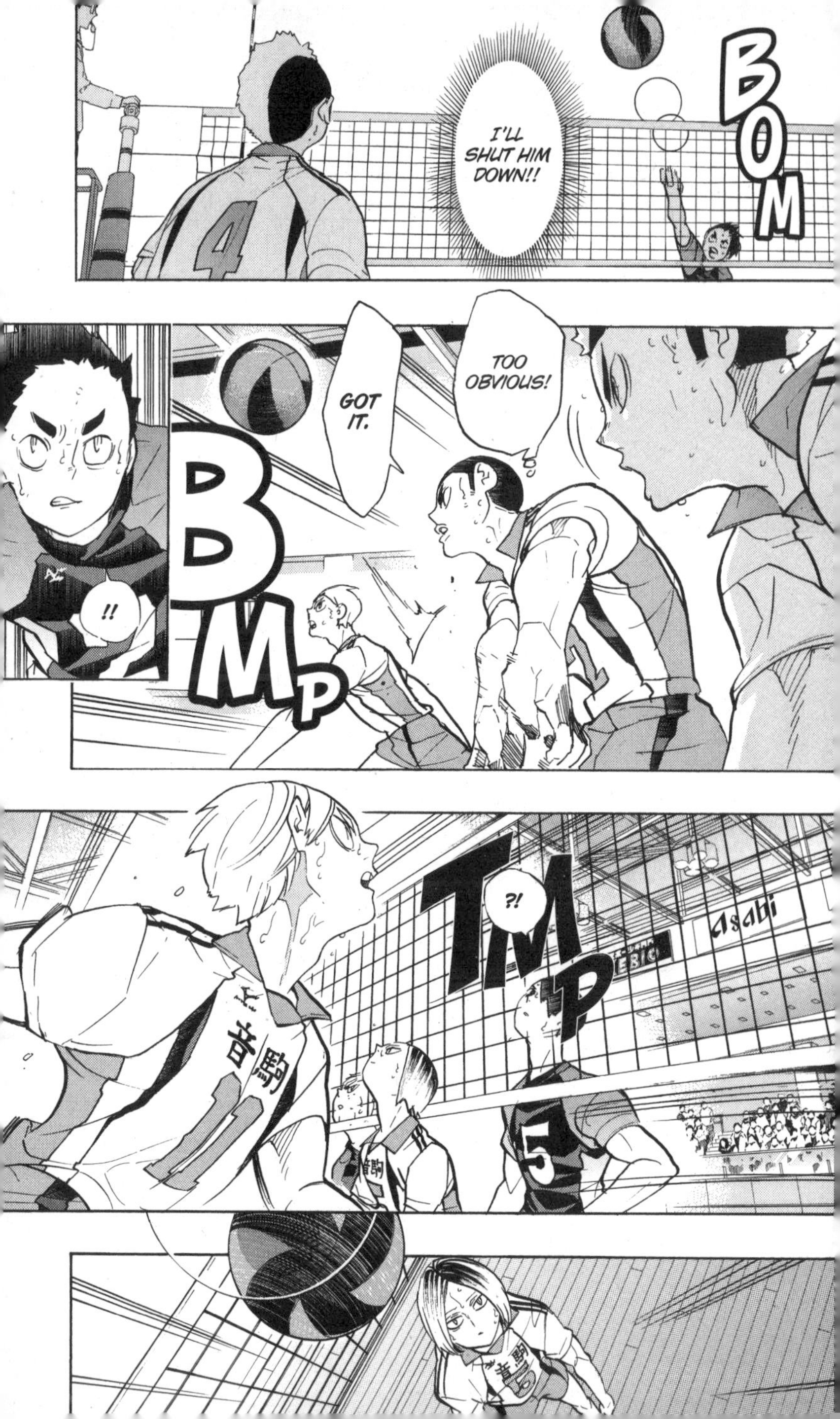
BOM
I'LL SHUT HIM DOWN!!
TOO OBVIOUS!
GOT IT.
BMP
!!
TMP
?!

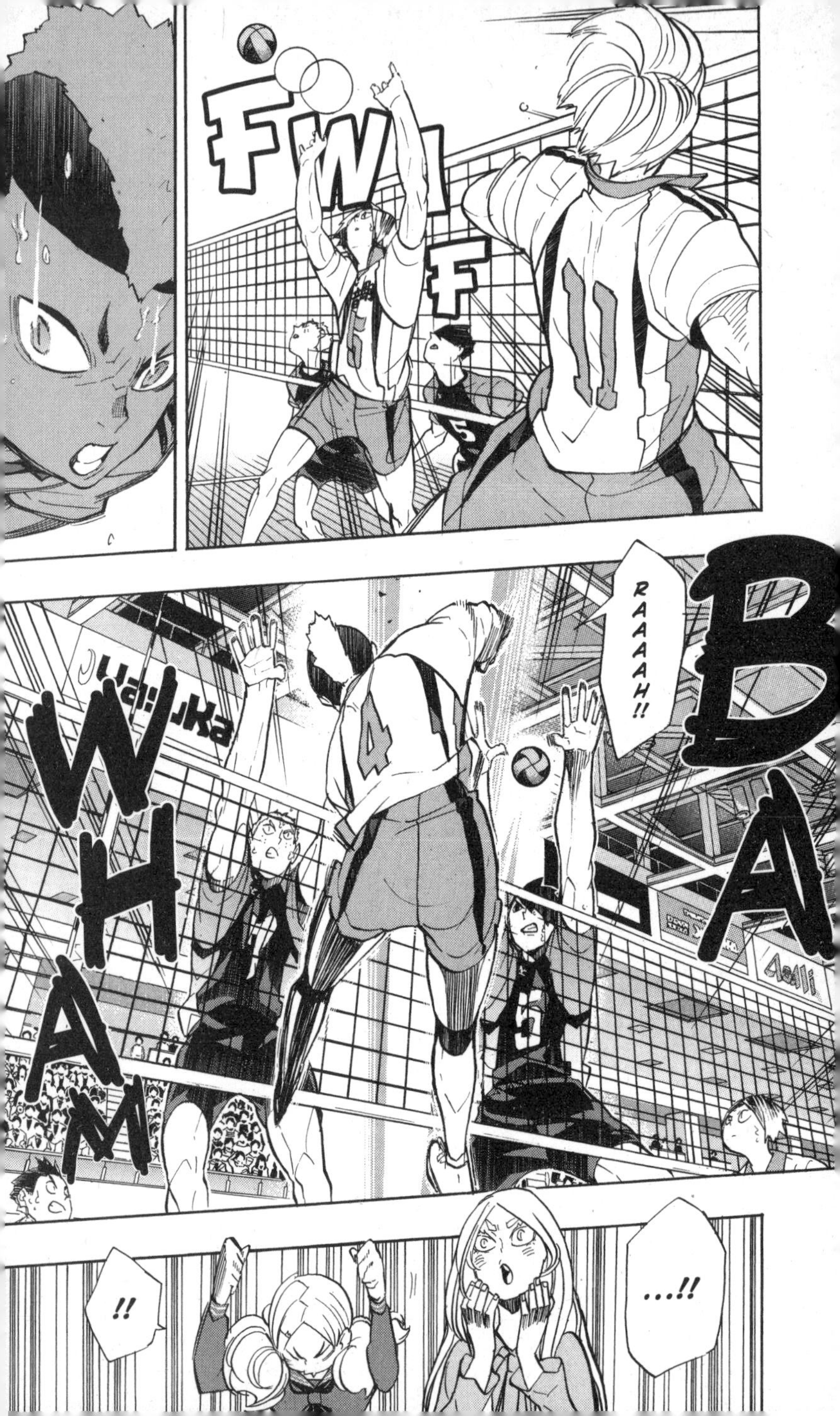
FWIF
RAAAAAH!!
BAM
WHAM
...!!
!!

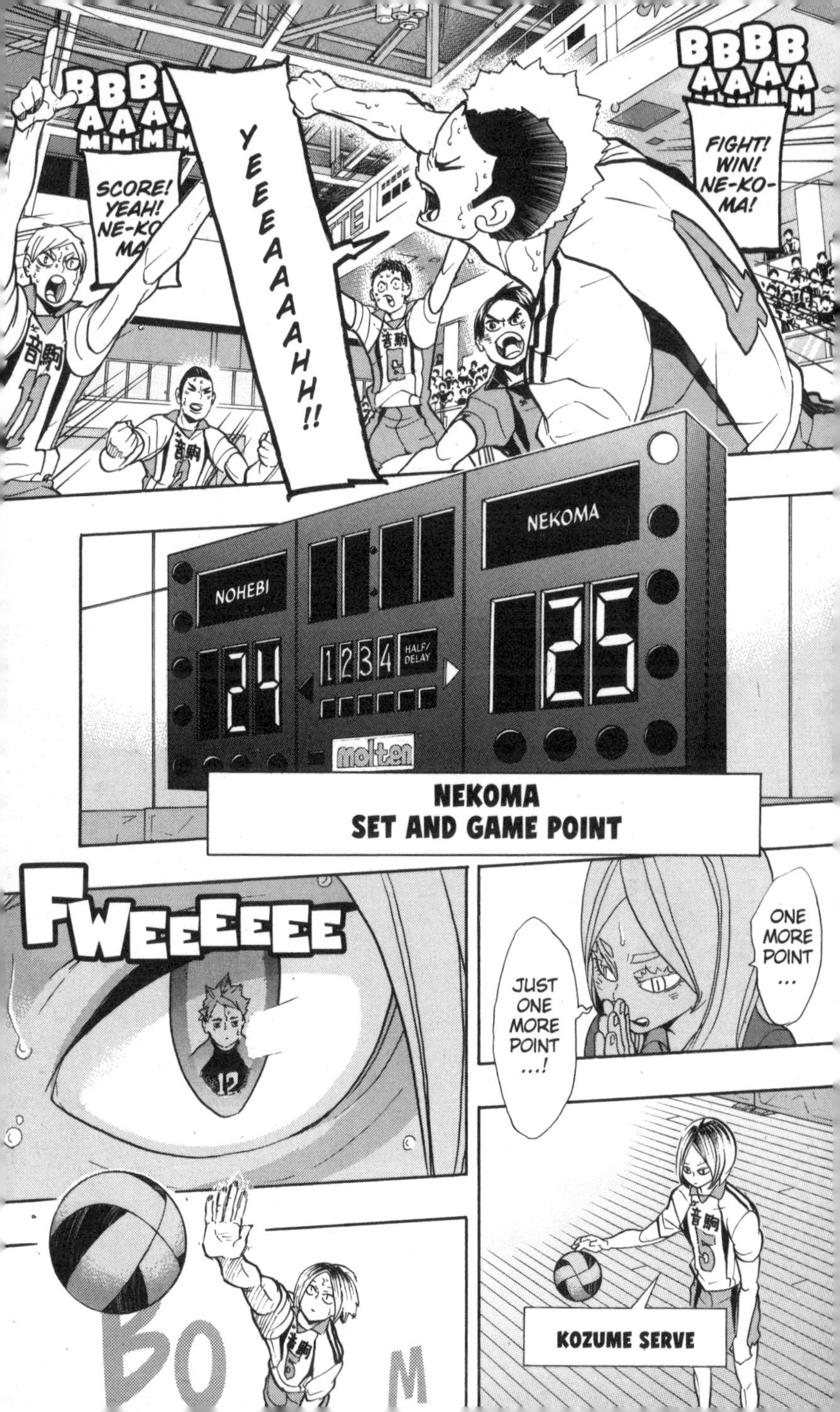
BBBB AAAA MMMM
FIGHT! WIN! NE-KO-MA!
YEEEAAAAAHH!!
BBB AAAA MMMM
SCORE! YEAH! NE-KO MA
NEKOMA
NOHEBI
24
25
1234
HALF/ DELAY
NEKOMA SET AND GAME POINT
ONE MORE POINT ...
JUST ONE MORE POINT ...!
FWEEEEEE
12
KOZUME SERVE
BO M

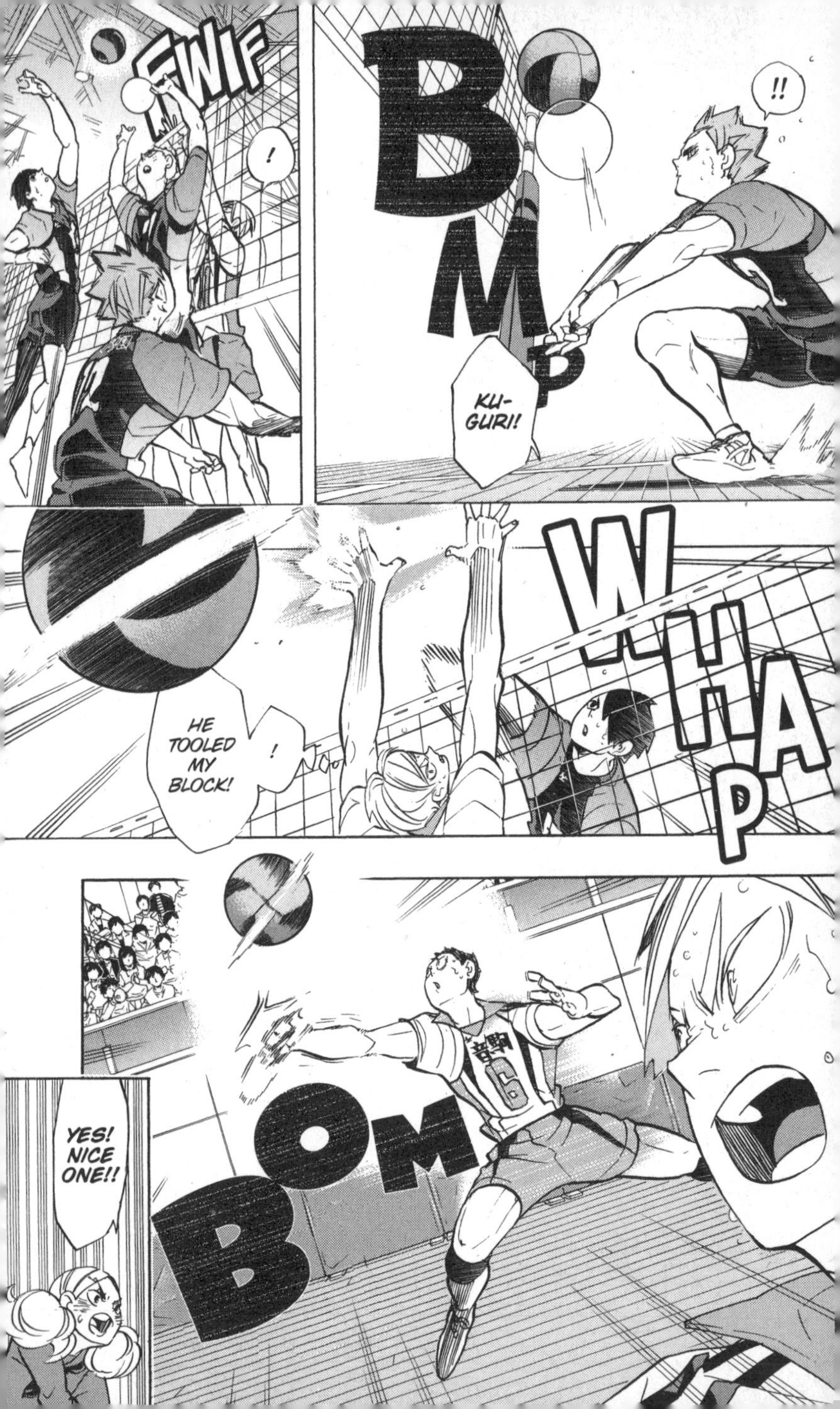
!!
BMP
KU-GURI!
FWIF
!
WHAP
!
HE TOOLED MY BLOCK!
BOOM
YES! NICE ONE!!

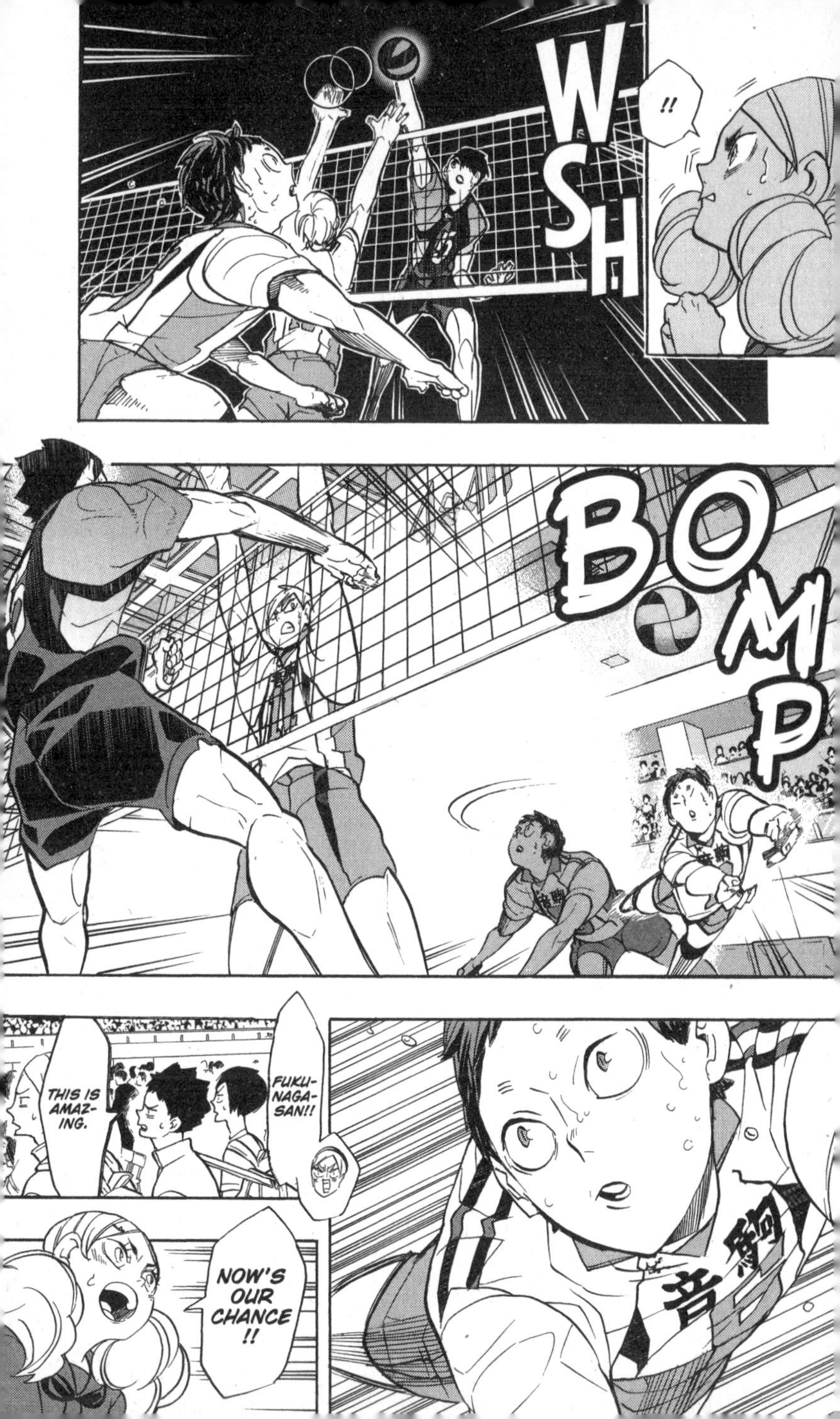
!!
WSH
BOMP
FUKU-NAGA-SAN!!
THIS IS AMAZ-ING.
NOW'S OUR CHANCE!!

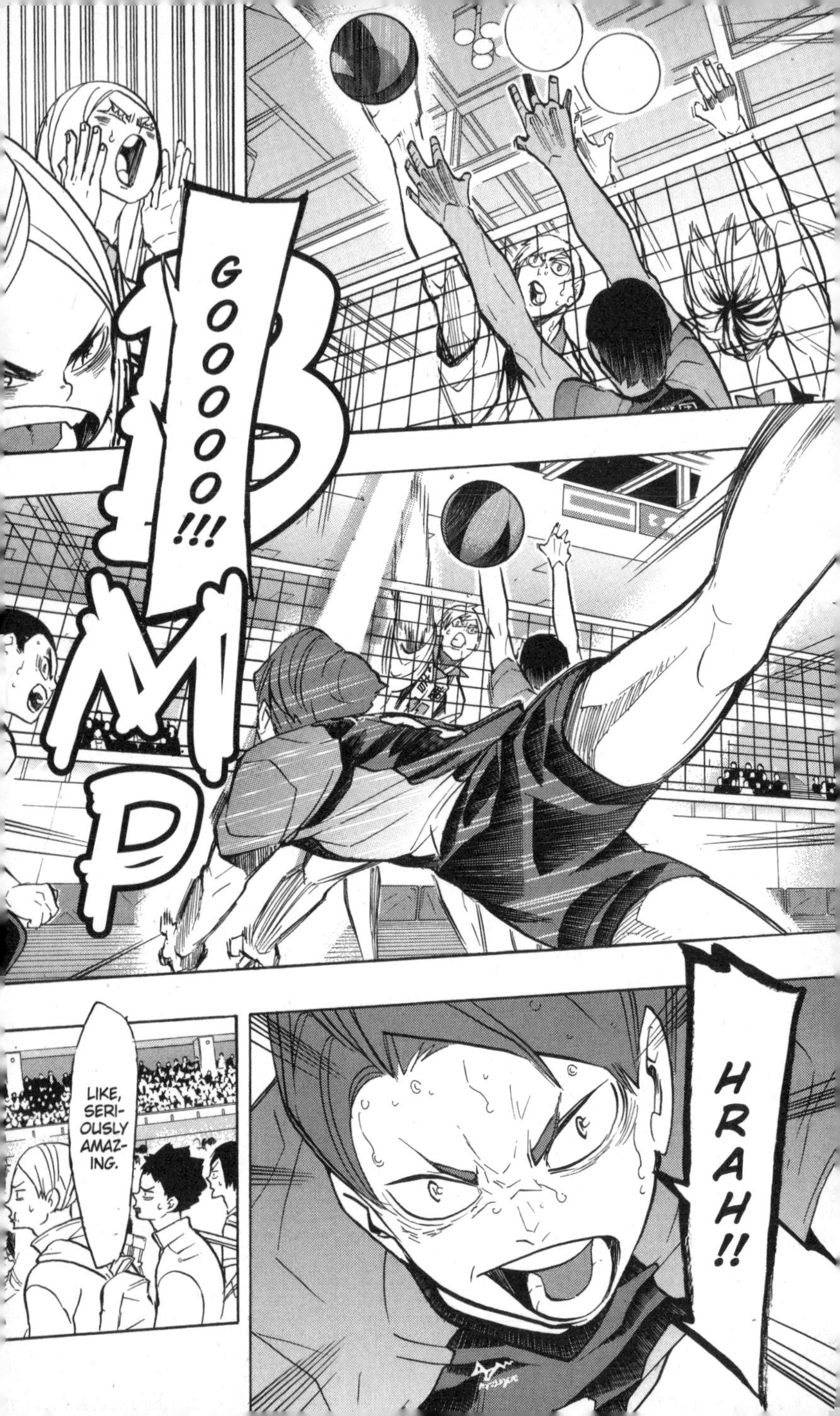
GOOOOOO!!!
BMP
HRAH!!
LIKE, SERIOUSLY AMAZING.

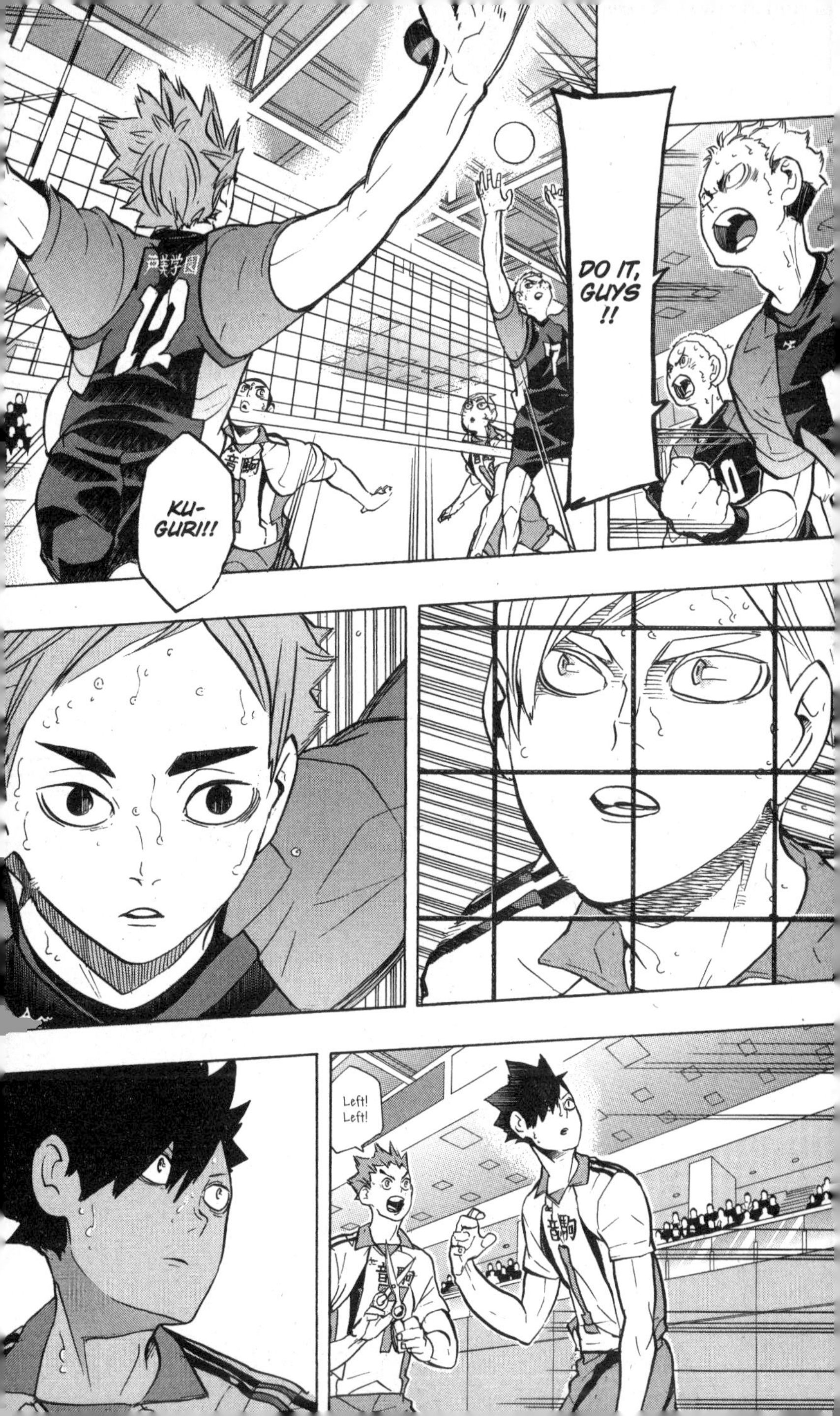
DO IT, GUYS!!
KU-GURI!!
Left! Left!

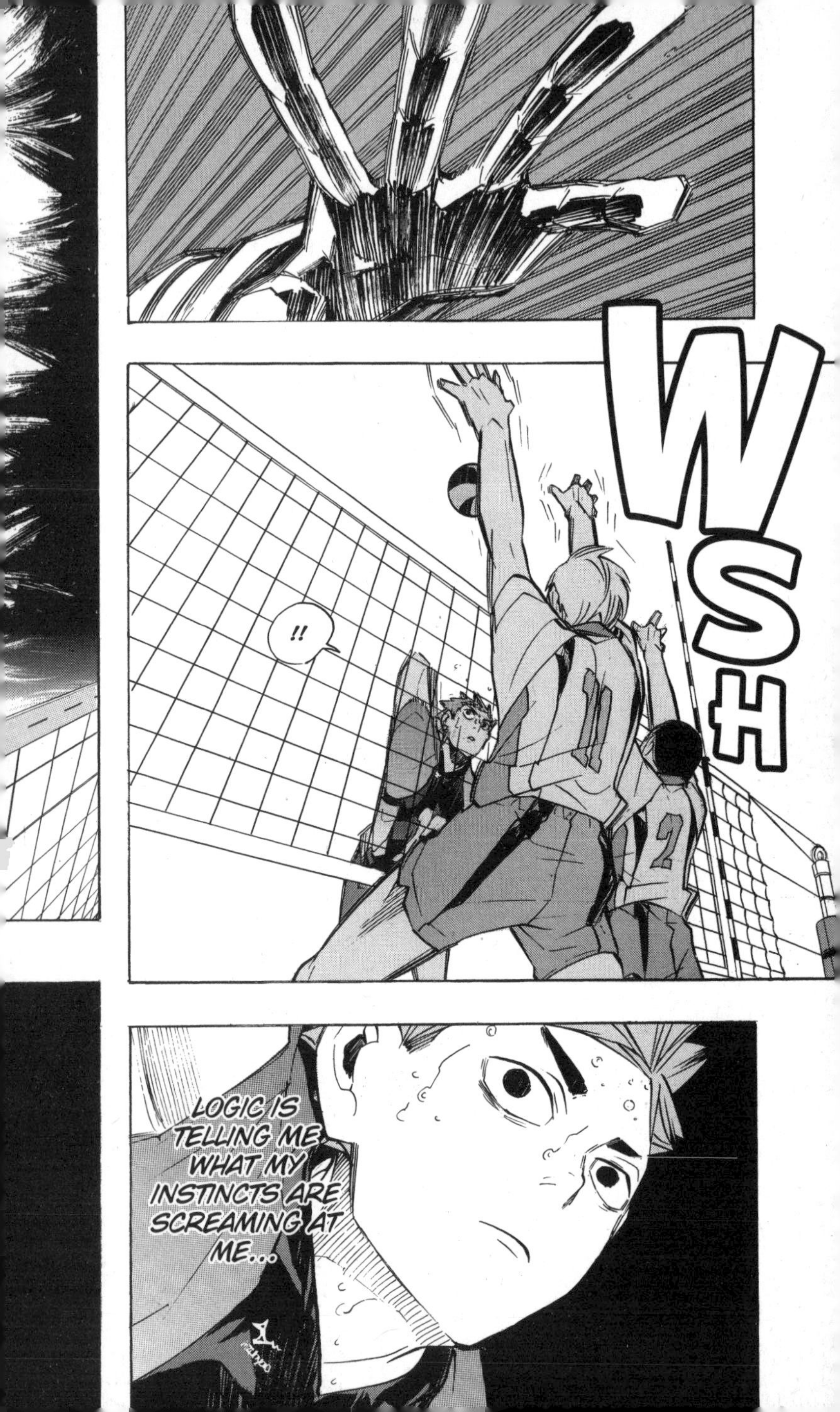
WSH
!!
LOGIC IS TELLING ME WHAT MY INSTINCTS ARE SCREAMING AT ME...

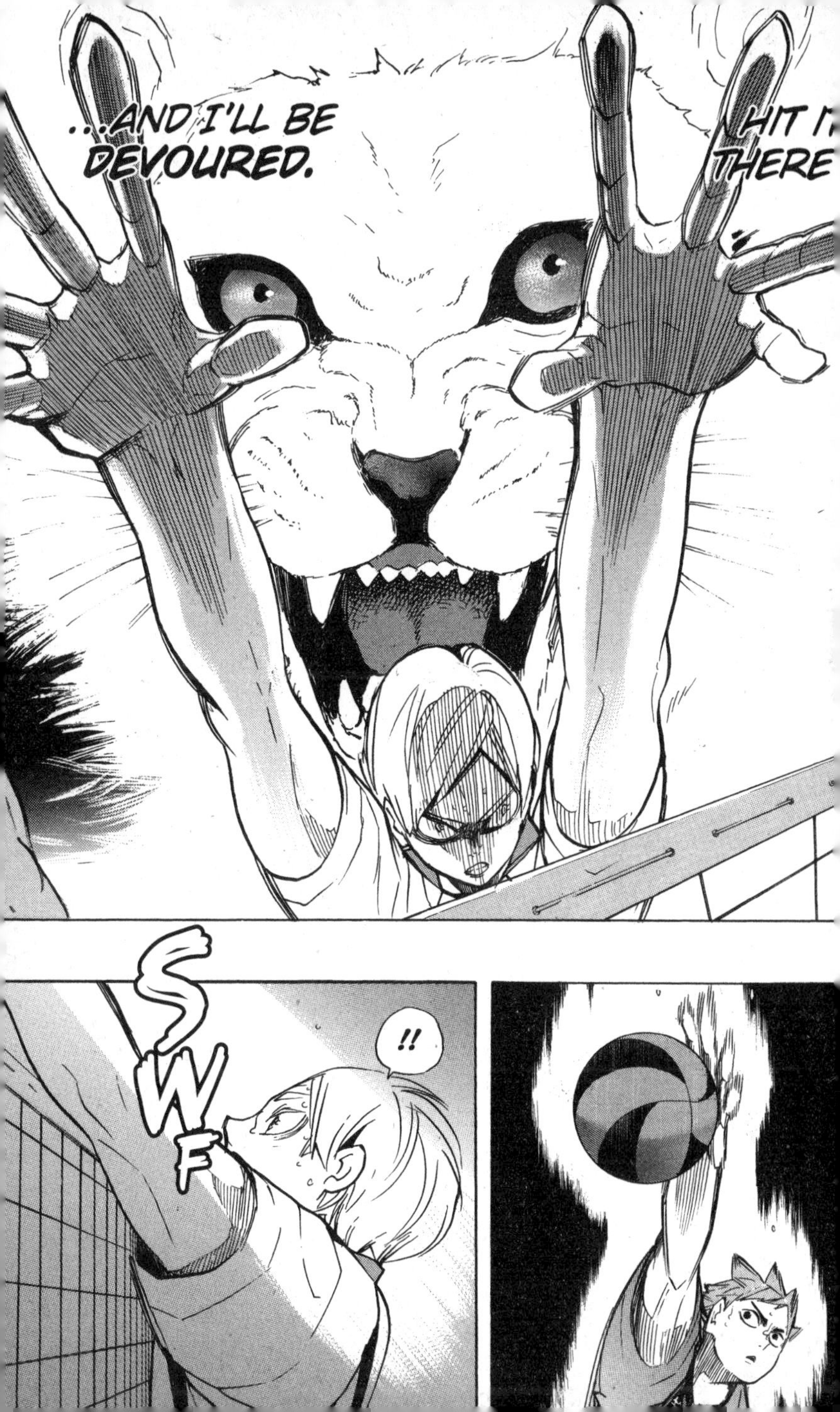
HIT I THERE
...AND I'LL BE DEVOURED.
SWF
!!

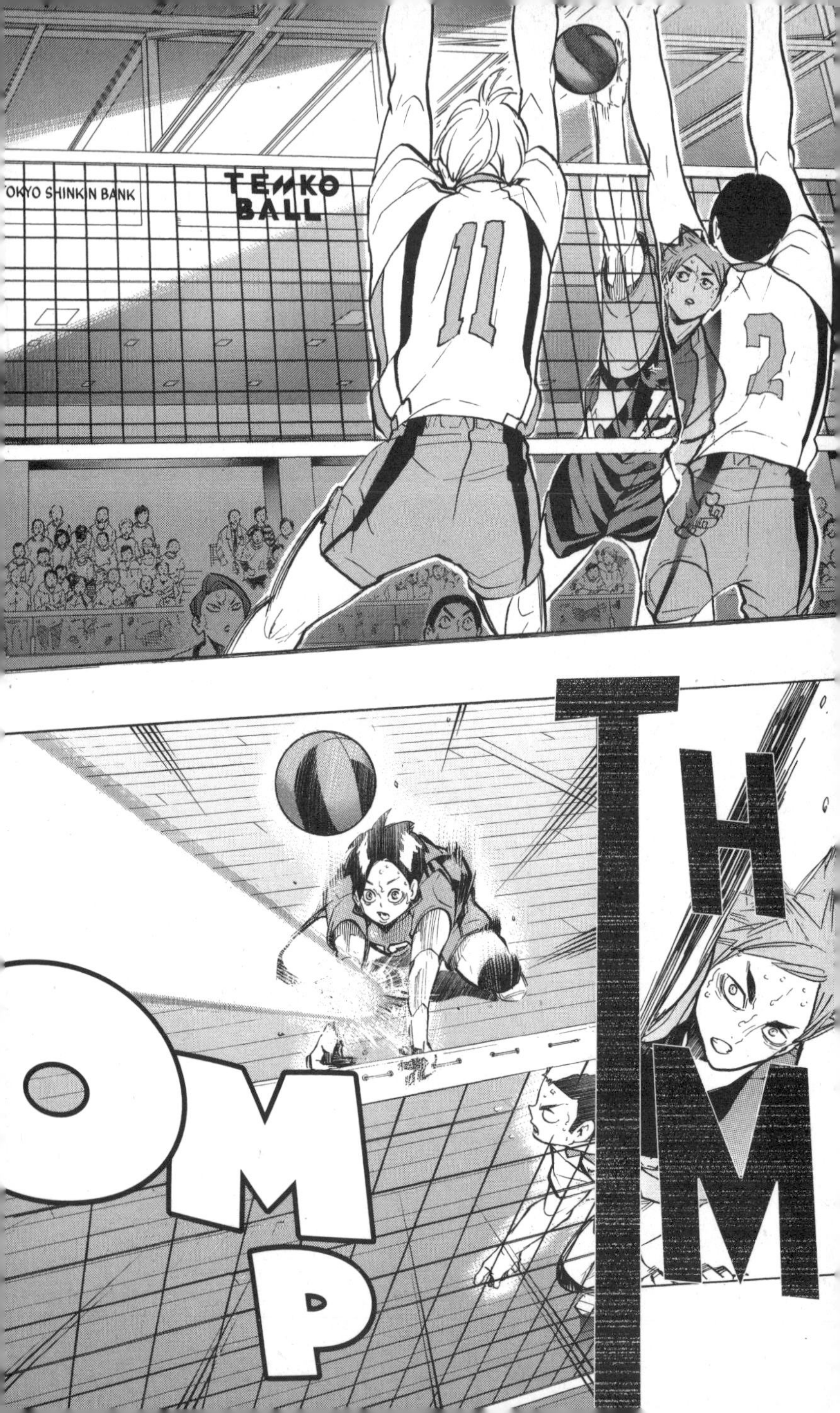
TOKYO SHINKIN BANK
TENKO BALL
THM
OMP

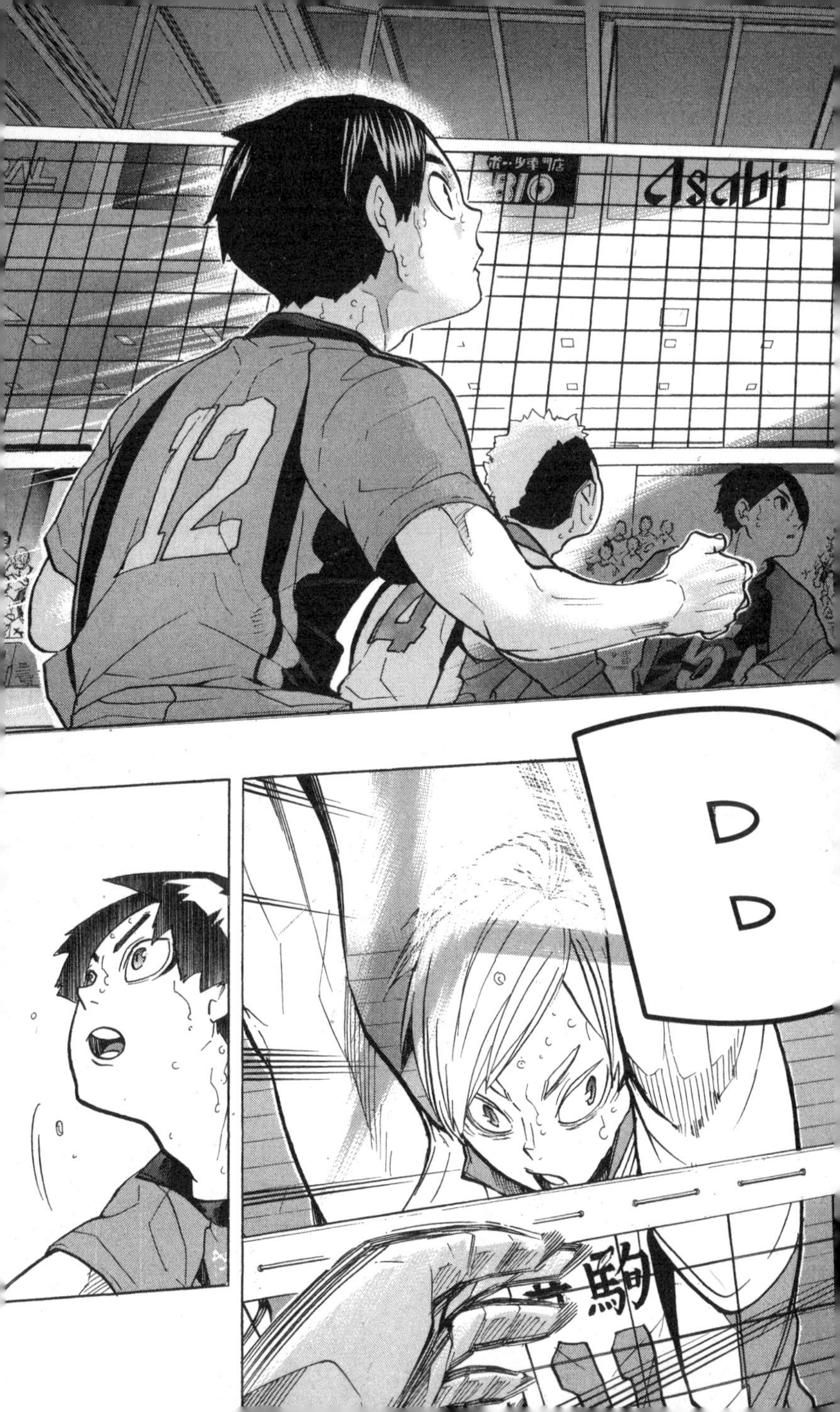
Asabi
D
D

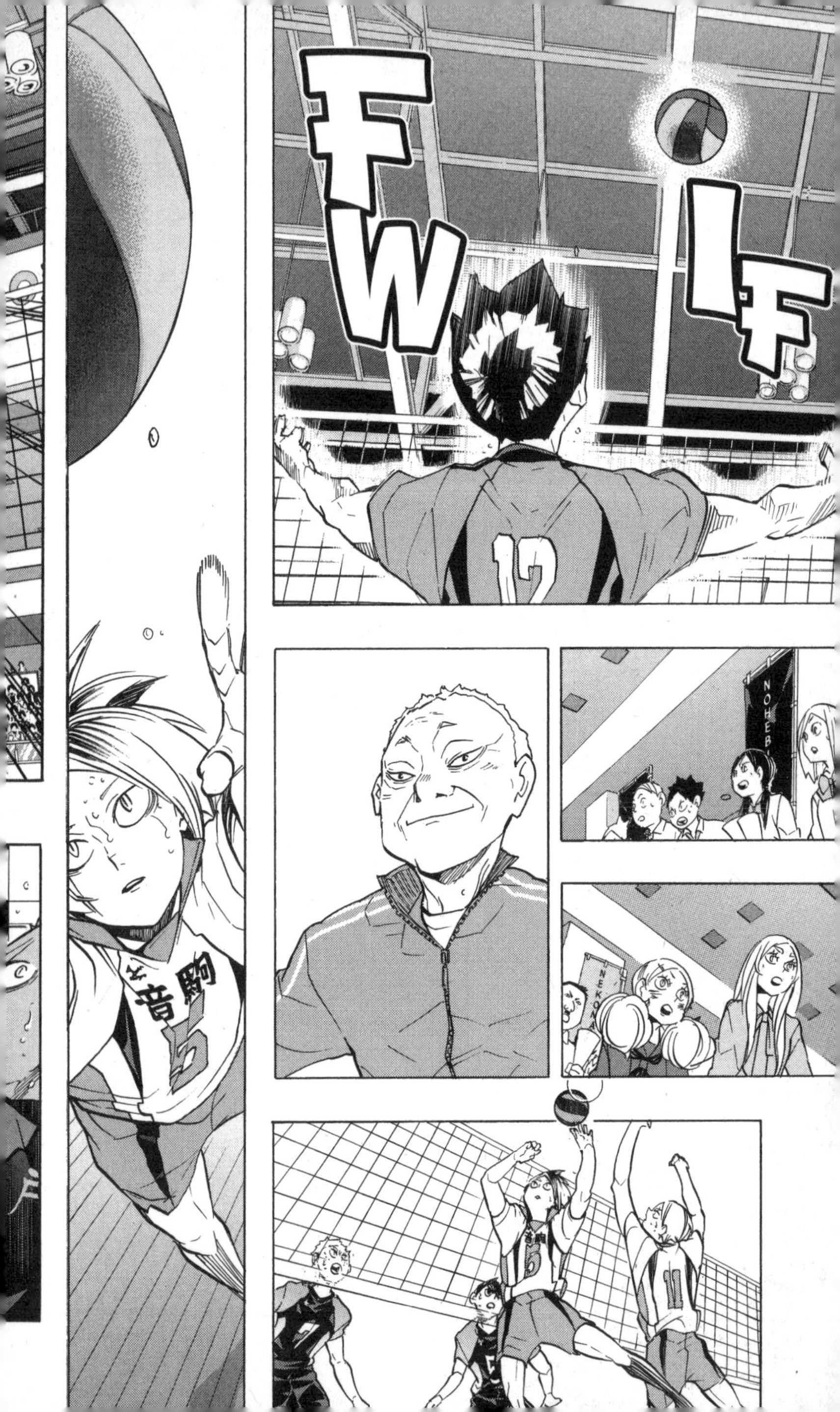

FWIF

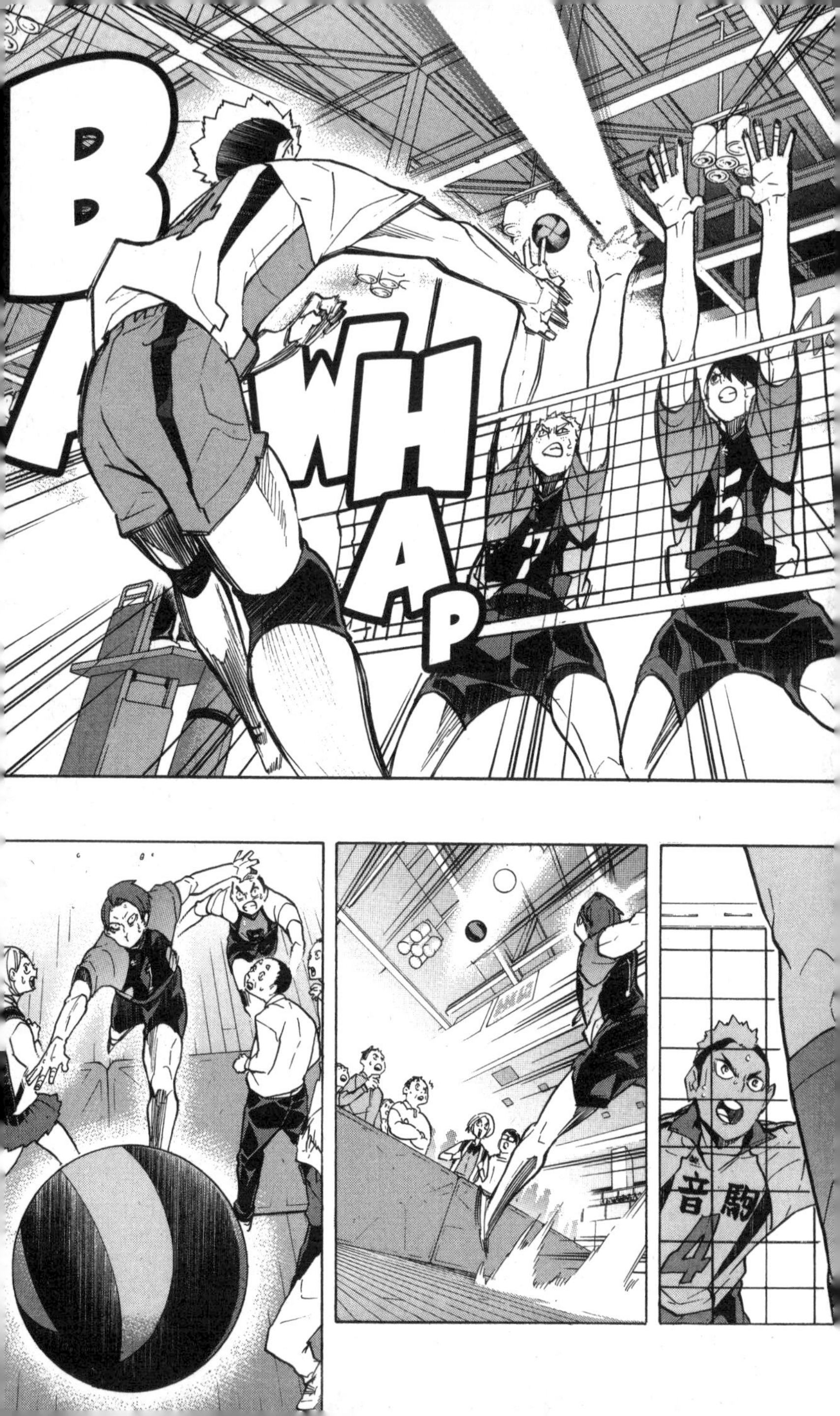
WHAP
音駒

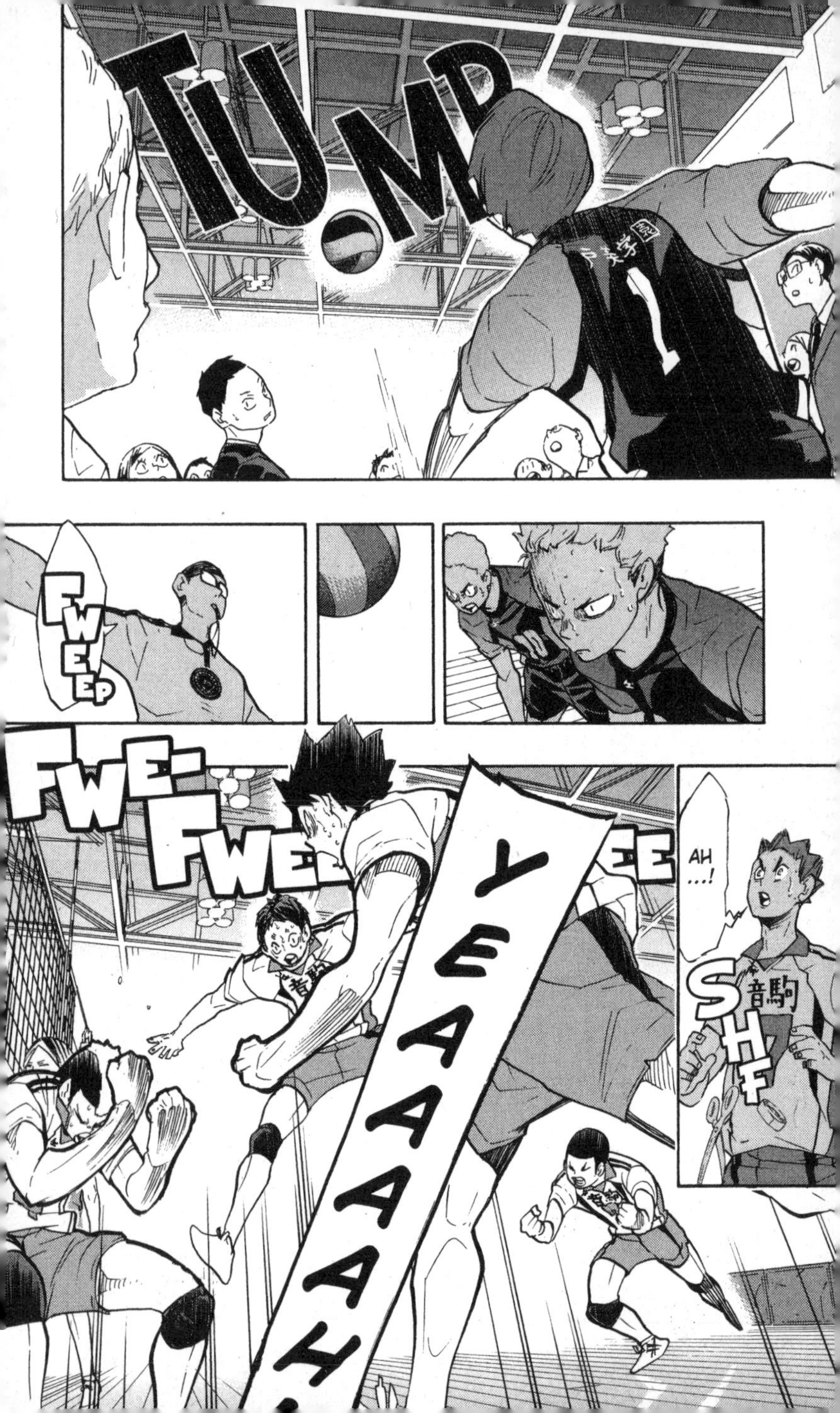
THUMP
FWEEEP
AH ...!
SHF
FWE-FWEE EE
YEAAAAAH!

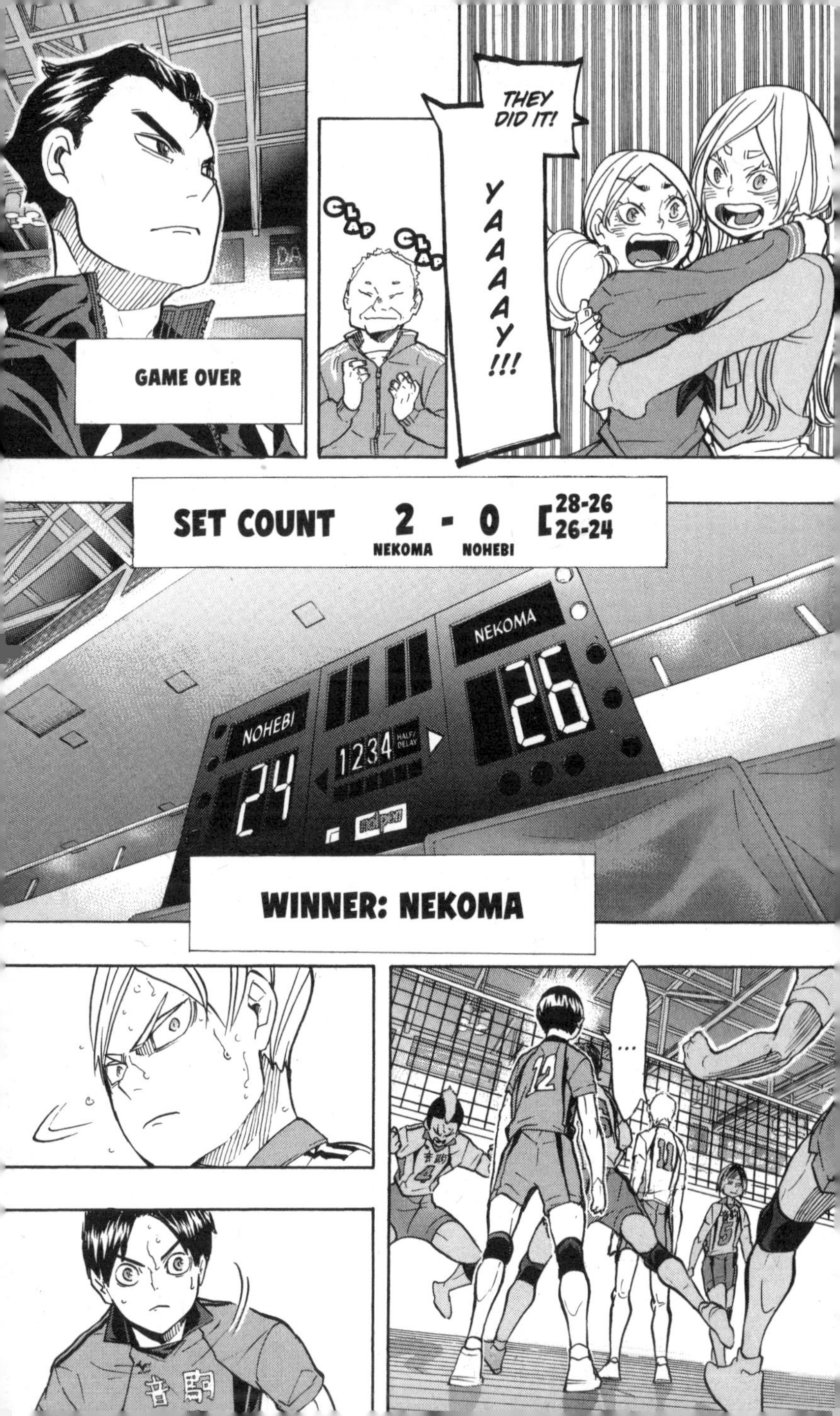
THEY DID IT!
YAAAAAY!!!
CLAP CLAP
GAME OVER
SET COUNT 2 - 0 [28-26 26-24
NEKOMA NOHEBI
NEKOMA
26
NOHEBI
24
WINNER: NEKOMA
...

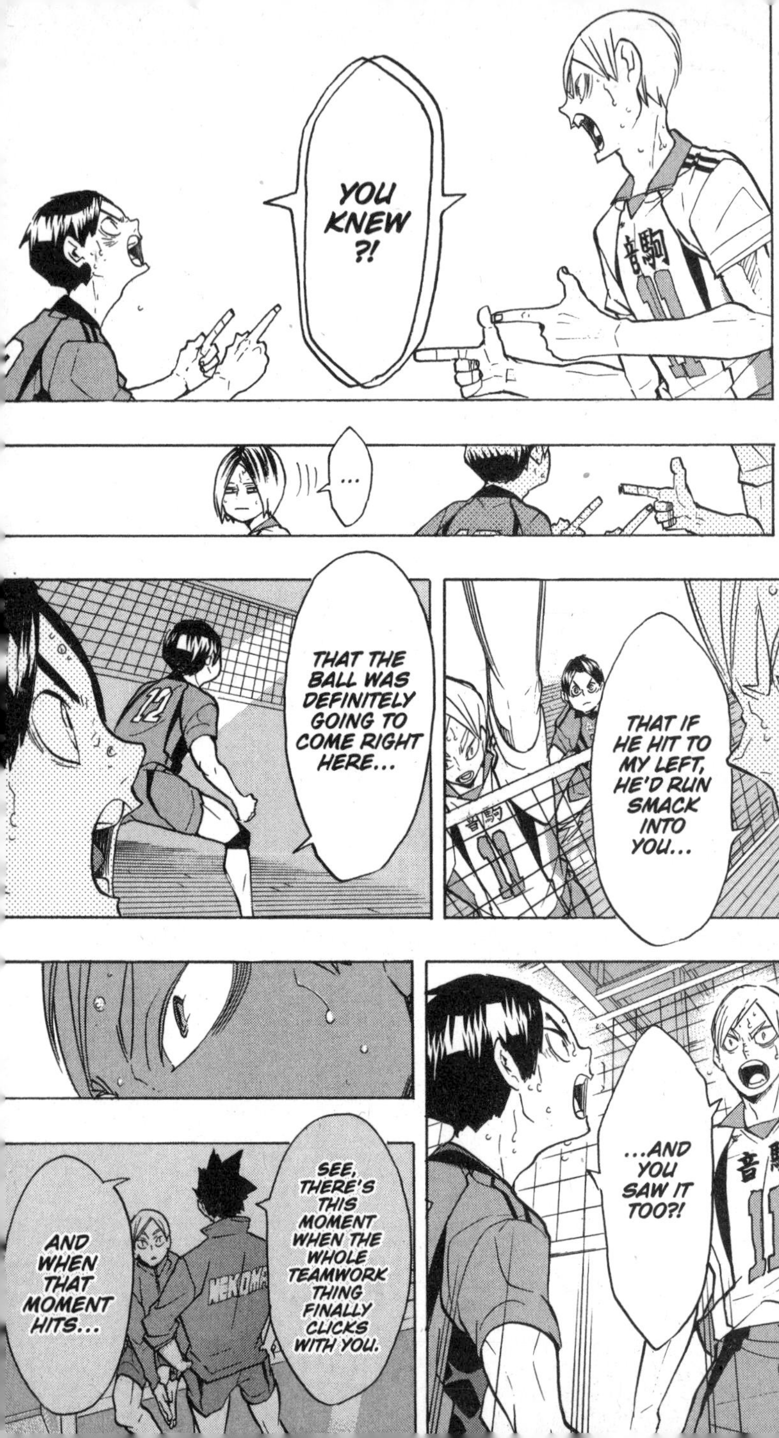
YOU KNEW ?!
...
THAT IF HE HIT TO MY LEFT, HE'D RUN SMACK INTO YOU...
THAT THE BALL WAS DEFINITELY GOING TO COME RIGHT HERE...
...AND YOU SAW IT TOO?!
SEE, THERE'S THIS MOMENT WHEN THE WHOLE TEAMWORK THING FINALLY CLICKS WITH YOU.
AND WHEN THAT MOMENT HITS...

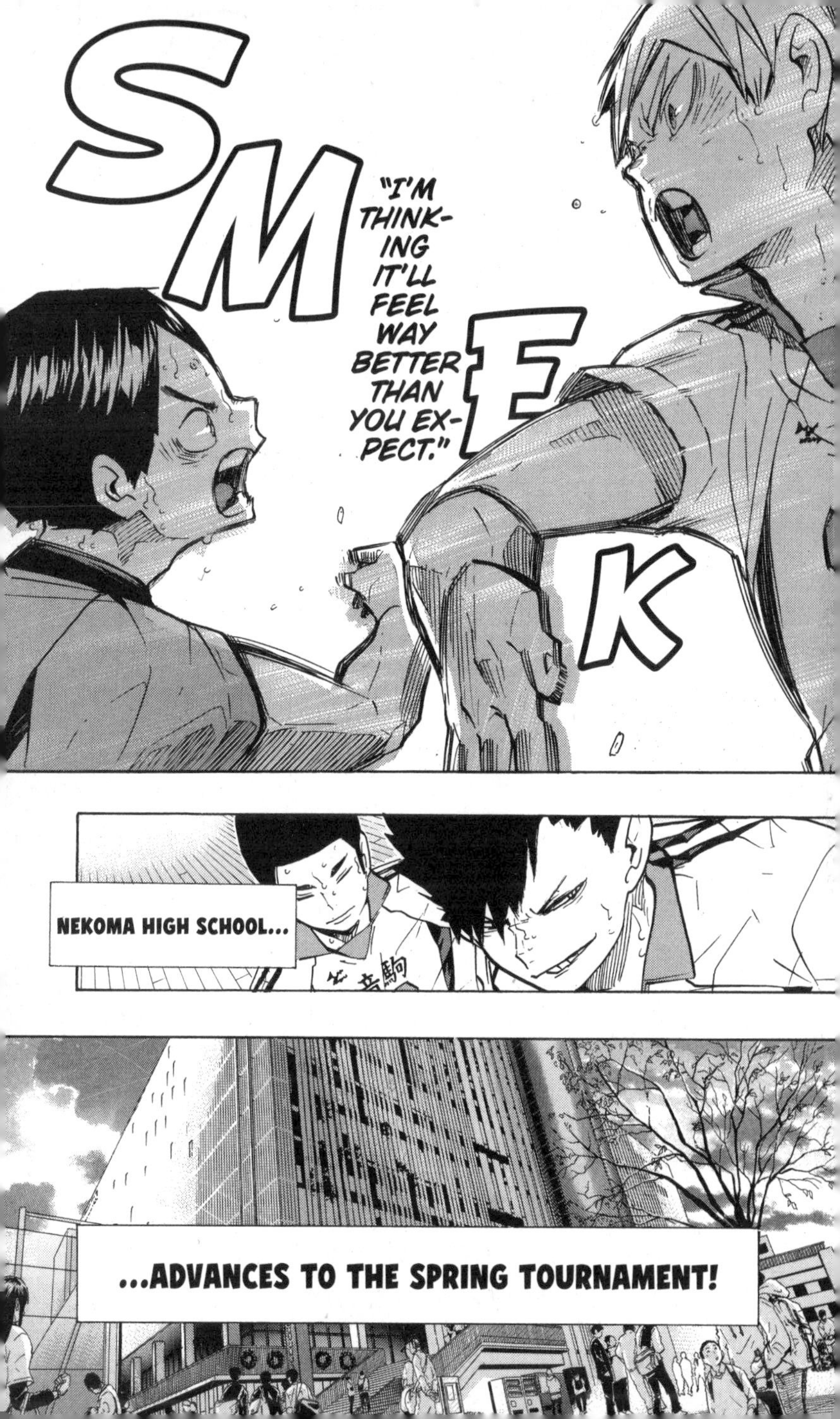
"I'M THINKING IT'LL FEEL WAY BETTER THAN YOU EXPECT."
SMEK
NEKOMA HIGH SCHOOL...
...ADVANCES TO THE SPRING TOURNAMENT!

TWO NEW PAGES HAVE BEEN ADDED TO THIS
CHAPTER FROM THE VERSION THAT ORIGINALLY
RAN IN *WEEKLY SHONEN JUMP*.

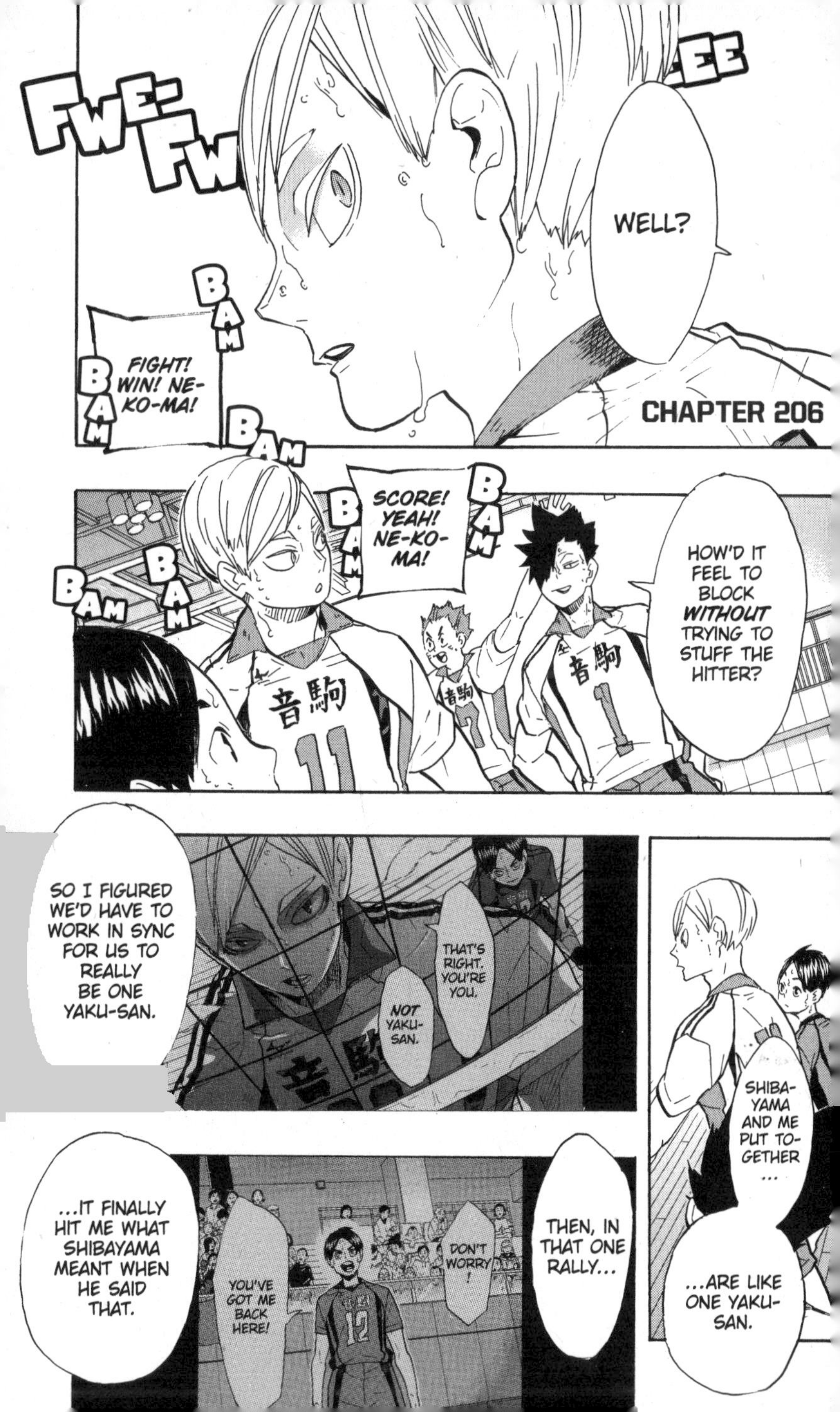
EEE
FWE-FW
WELL?
CHAPTER 206
FIGHT! WIN! NE-KO-MA!
BAM
BAM
BAM
HOW'D IT FEEL TO BLOCK WITHOUT TRYING TO STUFF THE HITTER?
BAM
SCORE! YEAH! NE-KO-MA!
BAM
BAM
BAM
SHIBAYAMA AND ME PUT TOGETHER...
...ARE LIKE ONE YAKU-SAN.
THAT'S RIGHT. YOU'RE YOU.
NOT YAKU-SAN.
SO I FIGURED WE'D HAVE TO WORK IN SYNC FOR US TO REALLY BE ONE YAKU-SAN.
THEN, IN THAT ONE RALLY...
DON'T WORRY!
YOU'VE GOT ME BACK HERE!
...IT FINALLY HIT ME WHAT SHIBAYAMA MEANT WHEN HE SAID THAT.

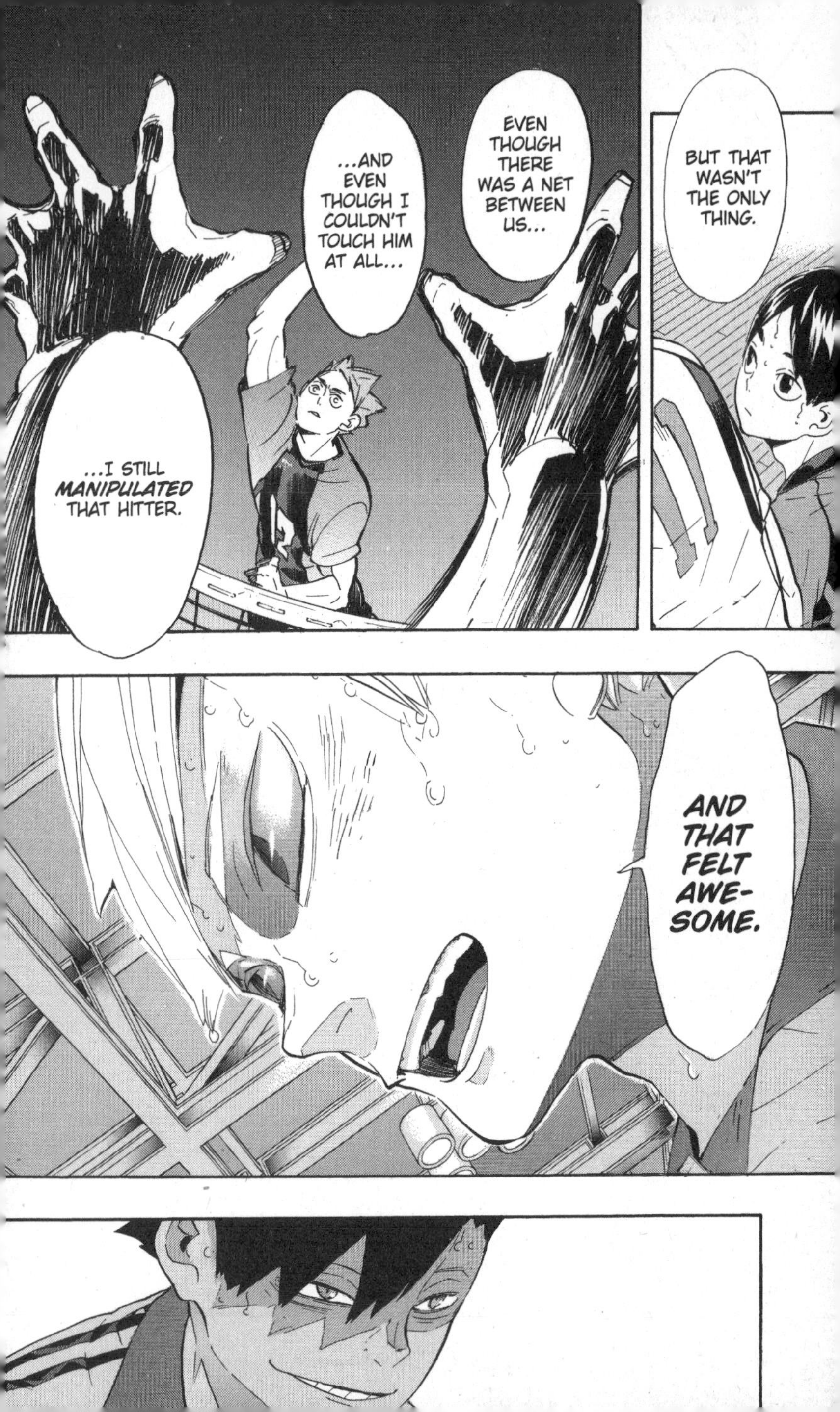
BUT THAT WASN'T THE ONLY THING.
EVEN THOUGH THERE WAS A NET BETWEEN US...
...AND EVEN THOUGH I COULDN'T TOUCH HIM AT ALL...
...I STILL *MANIPULATED* THAT HITTER.
AND THAT FELT AWESOME.

CHAPTER 206: Results

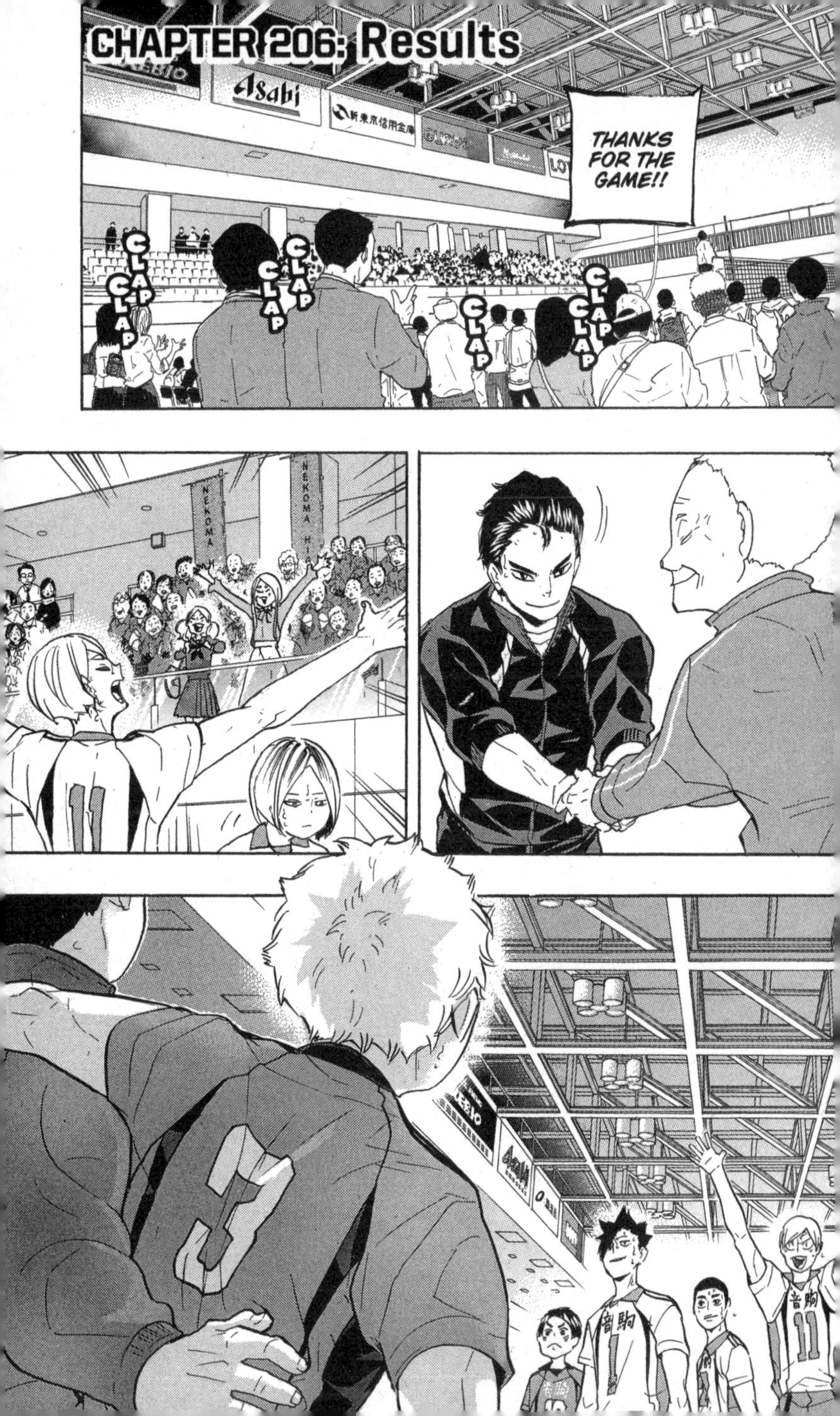
THANKS FOR THE GAME!!
CLAP
CLAP
CLAP
CLAP
CLAP
CLAP
CLAP
Asahi
新東京信用金庫

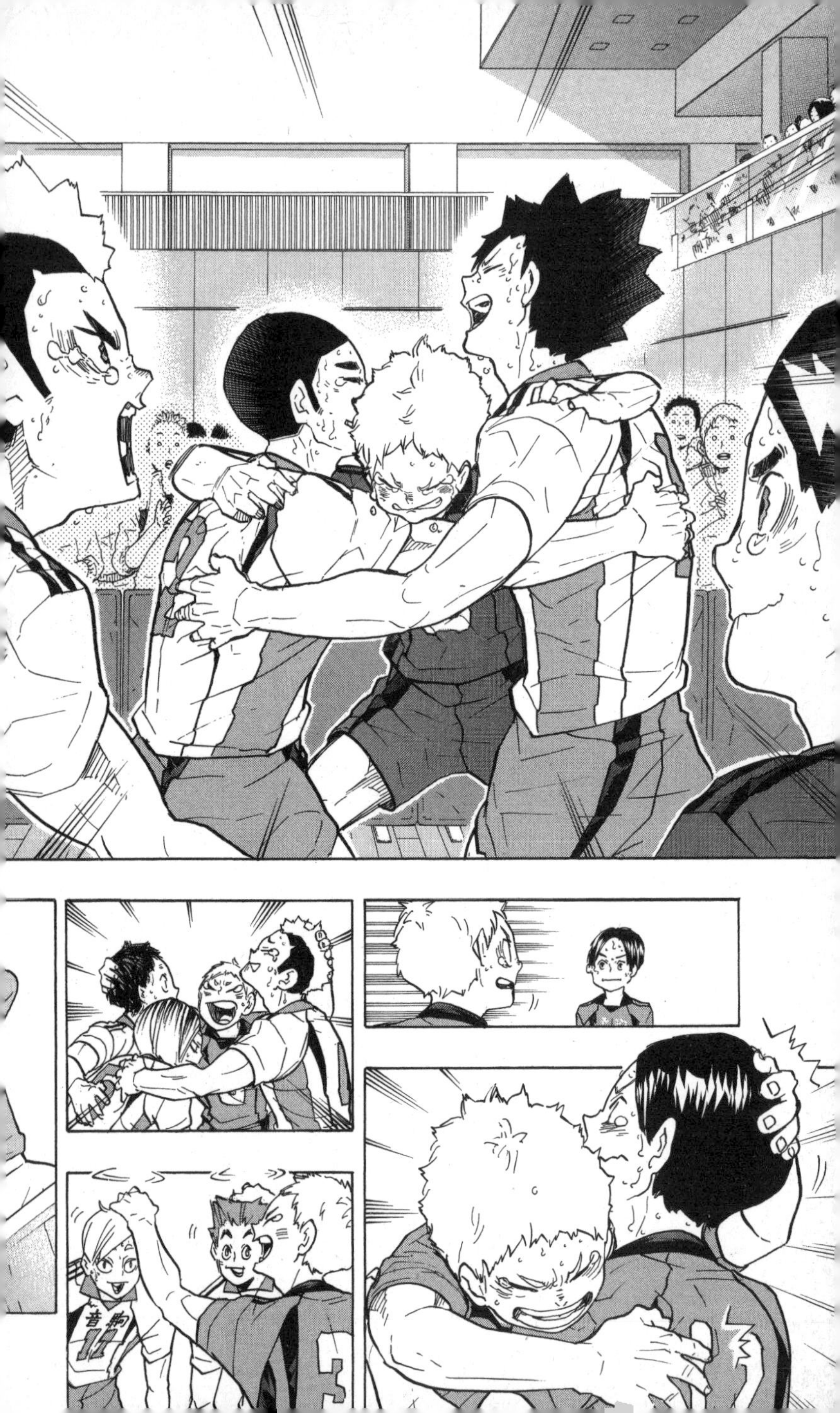
音駒

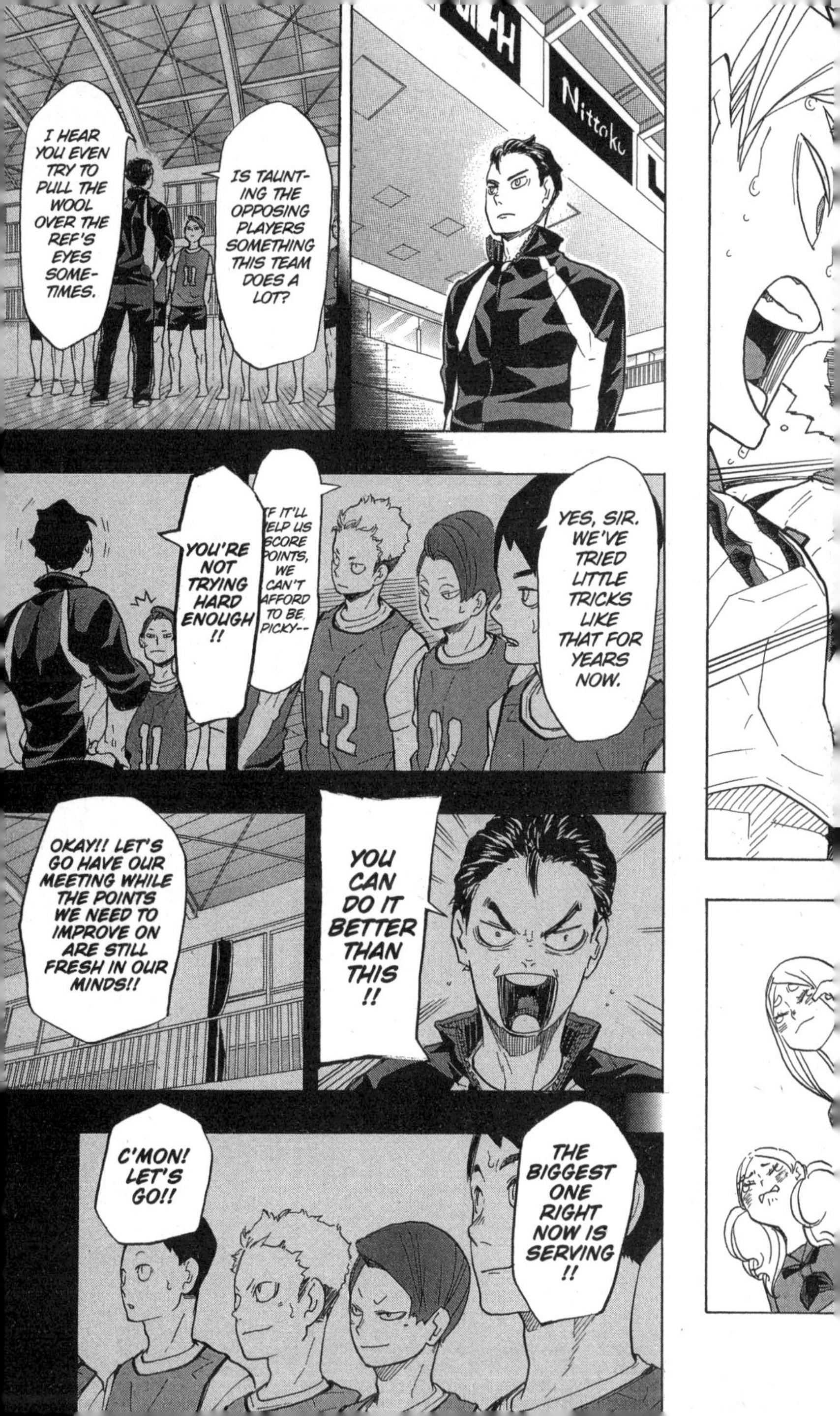
Nittoku
IS TAUNTING THE OPPOSING PLAYERS SOMETHING THIS TEAM DOES A LOT?
I HEAR YOU EVEN TRY TO PULL THE WOOL OVER THE REF'S EYES SOMETIMES.
YES, SIR. WE'VE TRIED LITTLE TRICKS LIKE THAT FOR YEARS NOW.
IF IT'LL HELP US SCORE POINTS, WE CAN'T AFFORD TO BE PICKY--
YOU'RE NOT TRYING HARD ENOUGH!!
YOU CAN DO IT BETTER THAN THIS!!
OKAY!! LET'S GO HAVE OUR MEETING WHILE THE POINTS WE NEED TO IMPROVE ON ARE STILL FRESH IN OUR MINDS!!
THE BIGGEST ONE RIGHT NOW IS SERVING!!
C'MON! LET'S GO!!

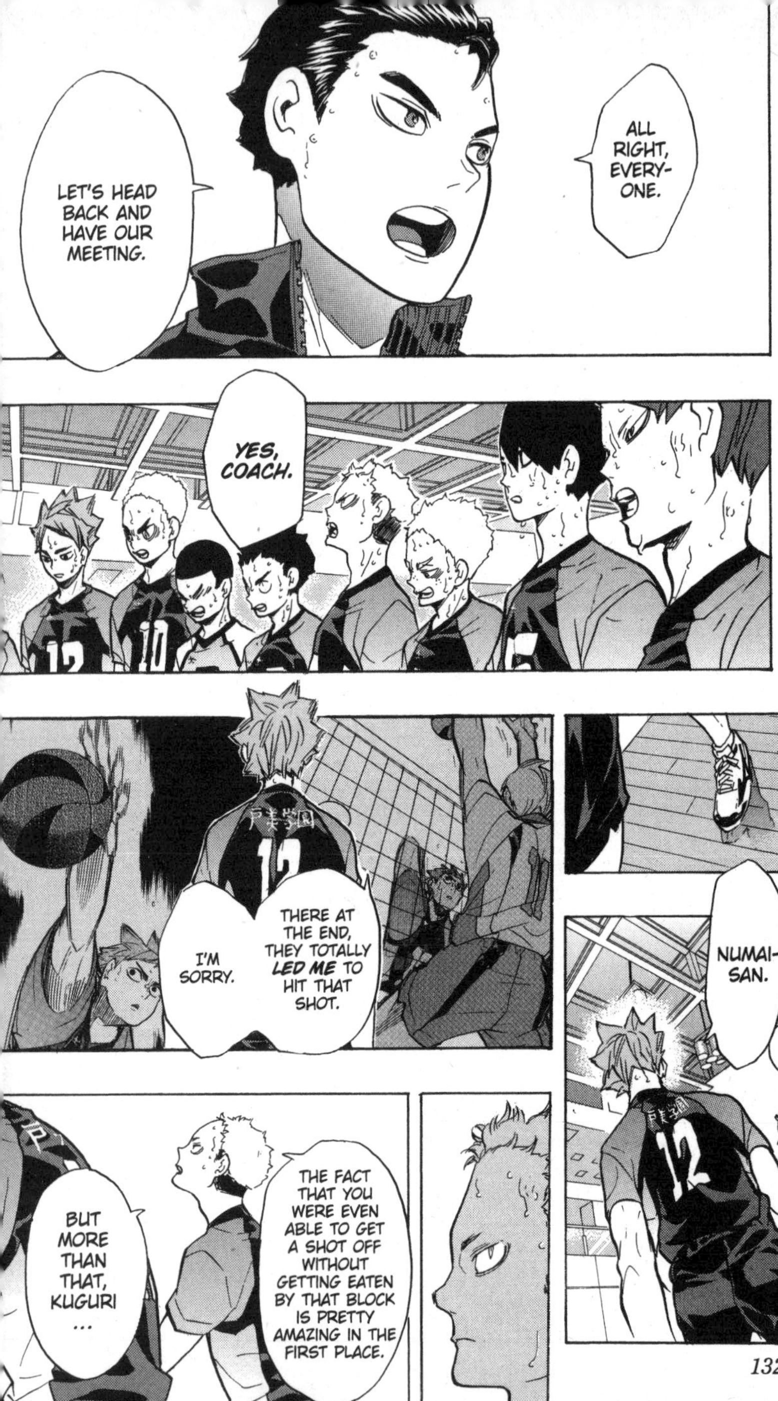
ALL RIGHT, EVERYONE.
LET'S HEAD BACK AND HAVE OUR MEETING.
YES, COACH.
NUMAI-SAN.
?
THERE AT THE END, THEY TOTALLY *LED ME* TO HIT THAT SHOT.
I'M SORRY.
THE FACT THAT YOU WERE EVEN ABLE TO GET A SHOT OFF WITHOUT GETTING EATEN BY THAT BLOCK IS PRETTY AMAZING IN THE FIRST PLACE.
BUT MORE THAN THAT, KUGURI ...

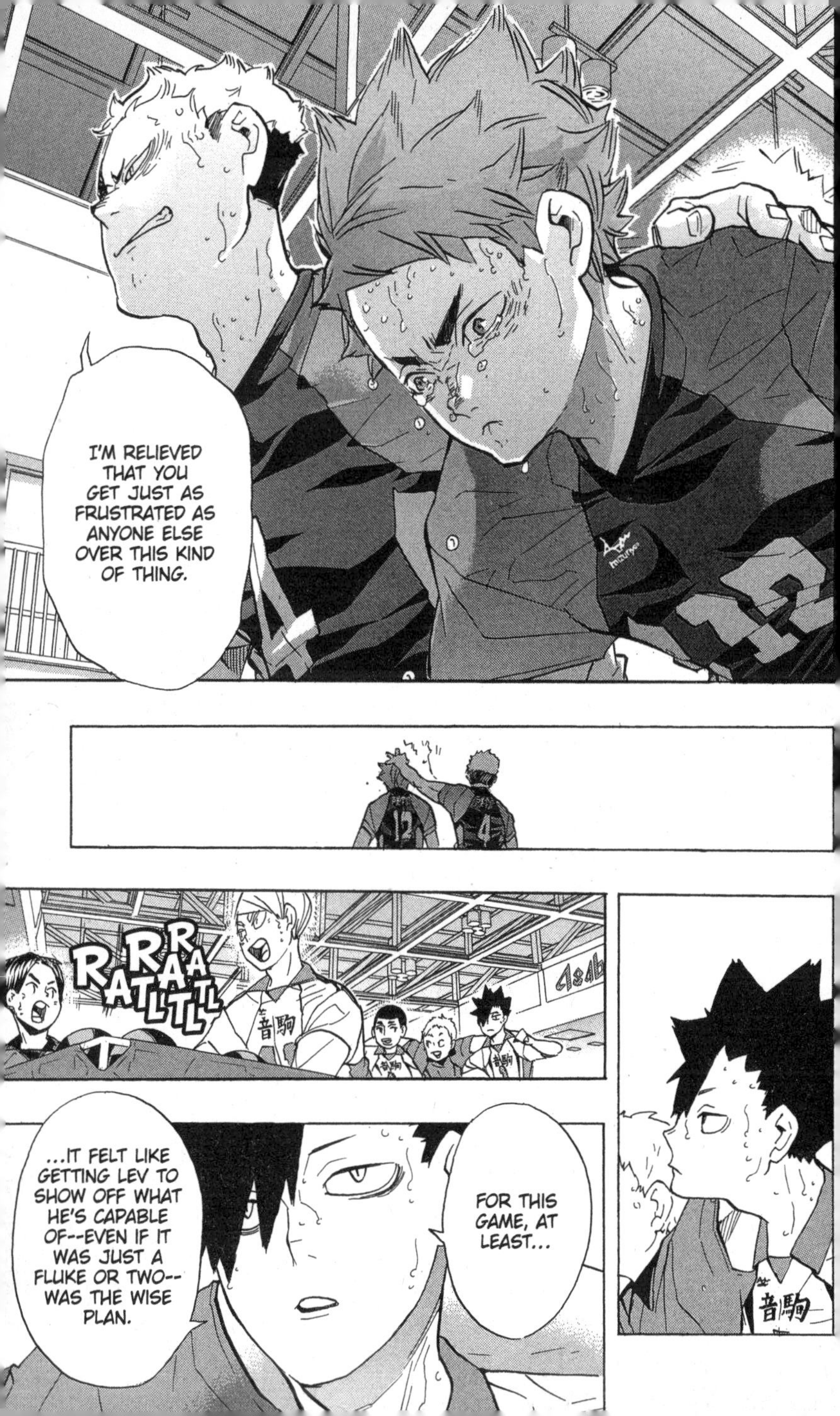
I'M RELIEVED THAT YOU GET JUST AS FRUSTRATED AS ANYONE ELSE OVER THIS KIND OF THING.
RATTL RATTL RATTL
FOR THIS GAME, AT LEAST...
...IT FELT LIKE GETTING LEV TO SHOW OFF WHAT HE'S CAPABLE OF--EVEN IF IT WAS JUST A FLUKE OR TWO--WAS THE WISE PLAN.

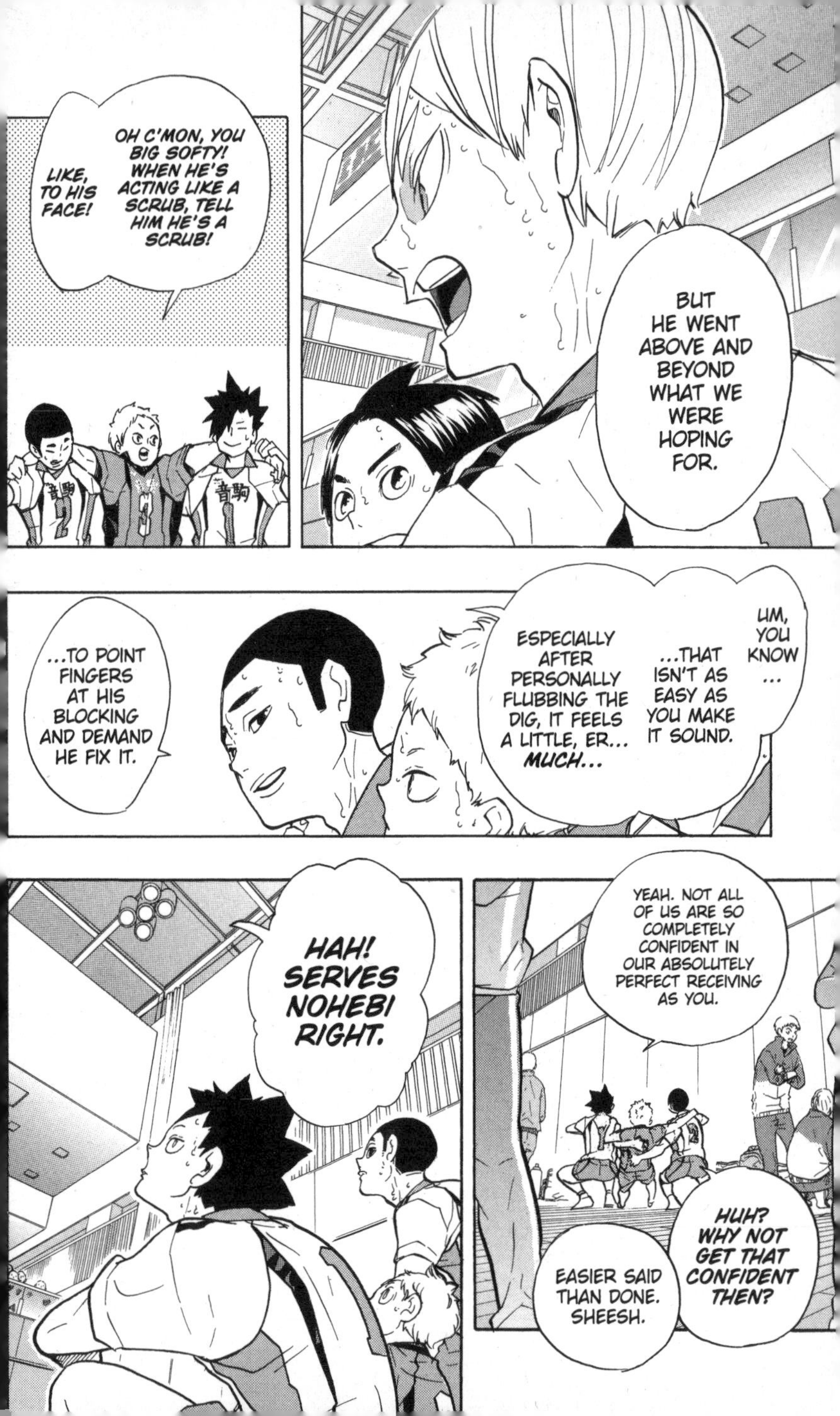
BUT HE WENT ABOVE AND BEYOND WHAT WE WERE HOPING FOR.
OH C'MON, YOU BIG SOFTY! WHEN HE'S ACTING LIKE A SCRUB, TELL HIM HE'S A SCRUB!
LIKE, TO HIS FACE!
UM, YOU KNOW...
...THAT ISN'T AS EASY AS YOU MAKE IT SOUND.
ESPECIALLY AFTER PERSONALLY FLUBBING THE DIG, IT FEELS A LITTLE, ER... MUCH...
...TO POINT FINGERS AT HIS BLOCKING AND DEMAND HE FIX IT.
YEAH. NOT ALL OF US ARE SO COMPLETELY CONFIDENT IN OUR ABSOLUTELY PERFECT RECEIVING AS YOU.
HUH? WHY NOT GET THAT CONFIDENT THEN?
EASIER SAID THAN DONE. SHEESH.
HAH! SERVES NOHEBI RIGHT.

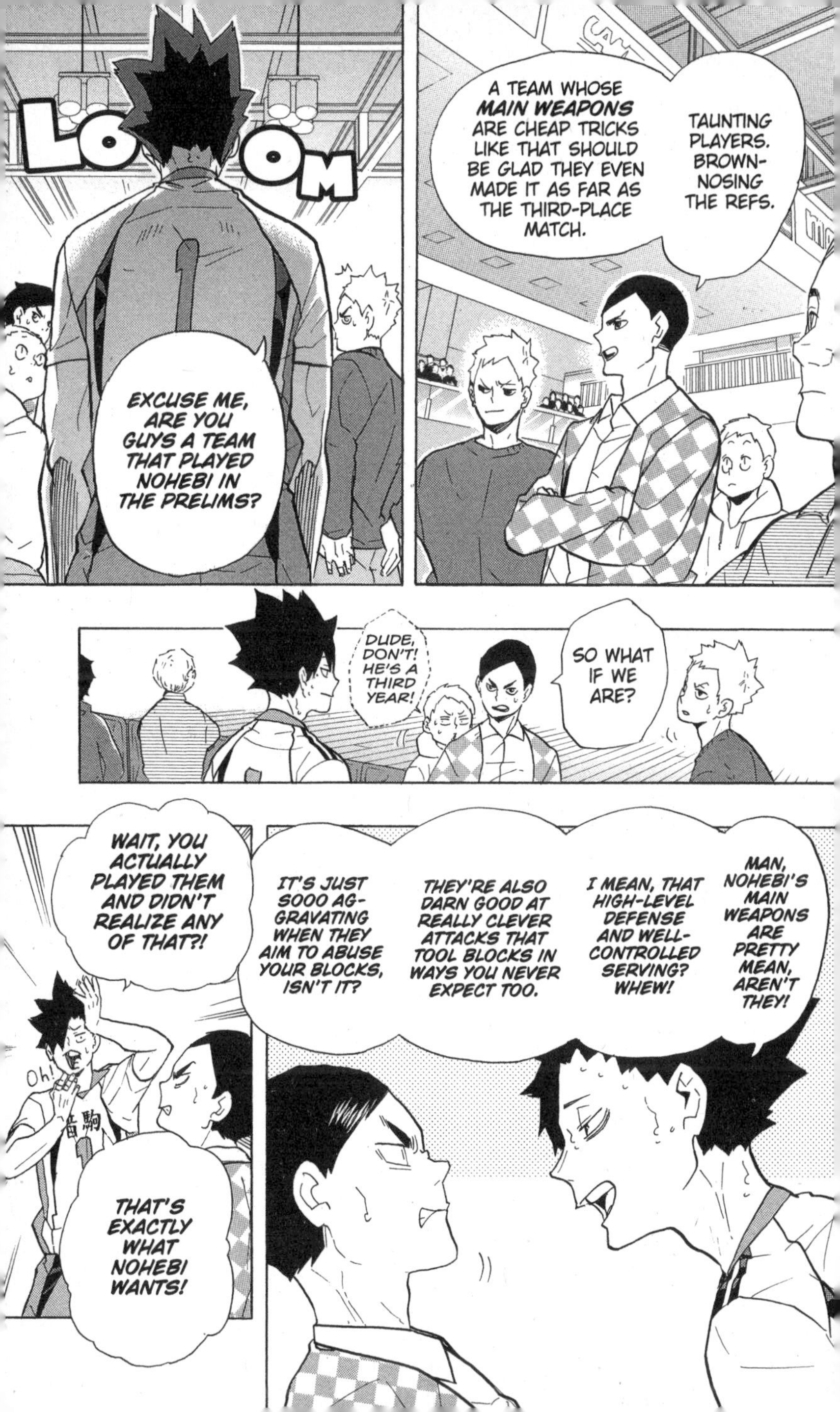
TAUNTING PLAYERS. BROWN-NOSING THE REFS.
A TEAM WHOSE MAIN WEAPONS ARE CHEAP TRICKS LIKE THAT SHOULD BE GLAD THEY EVEN MADE IT AS FAR AS THE THIRD-PLACE MATCH.
LOOM
EXCUSE ME, ARE YOU GUYS A TEAM THAT PLAYED NOHEBI IN THE PRELIMS?
SO WHAT IF WE ARE?
DUDE, DON'T! HE'S A THIRD YEAR!
MAN, NOHEBI'S MAIN WEAPONS ARE PRETTY MEAN, AREN'T THEY!
I MEAN, THAT HIGH-LEVEL DEFENSE AND WELL-CONTROLLED SERVING? WHEW!
THEY'RE ALSO DARN GOOD AT REALLY CLEVER ATTACKS THAT TOOL BLOCKS IN WAYS YOU NEVER EXPECT TOO.
IT'S JUST SOOO AG-GRAVATING WHEN THEY AIM TO ABUSE YOUR BLOCKS, ISN'T IT?
WAIT, YOU ACTUALLY PLAYED THEM AND DIDN'T REALIZE ANY OF THAT?!
Oh!
THAT'S EXACTLY WHAT NOHEBI WANTS!

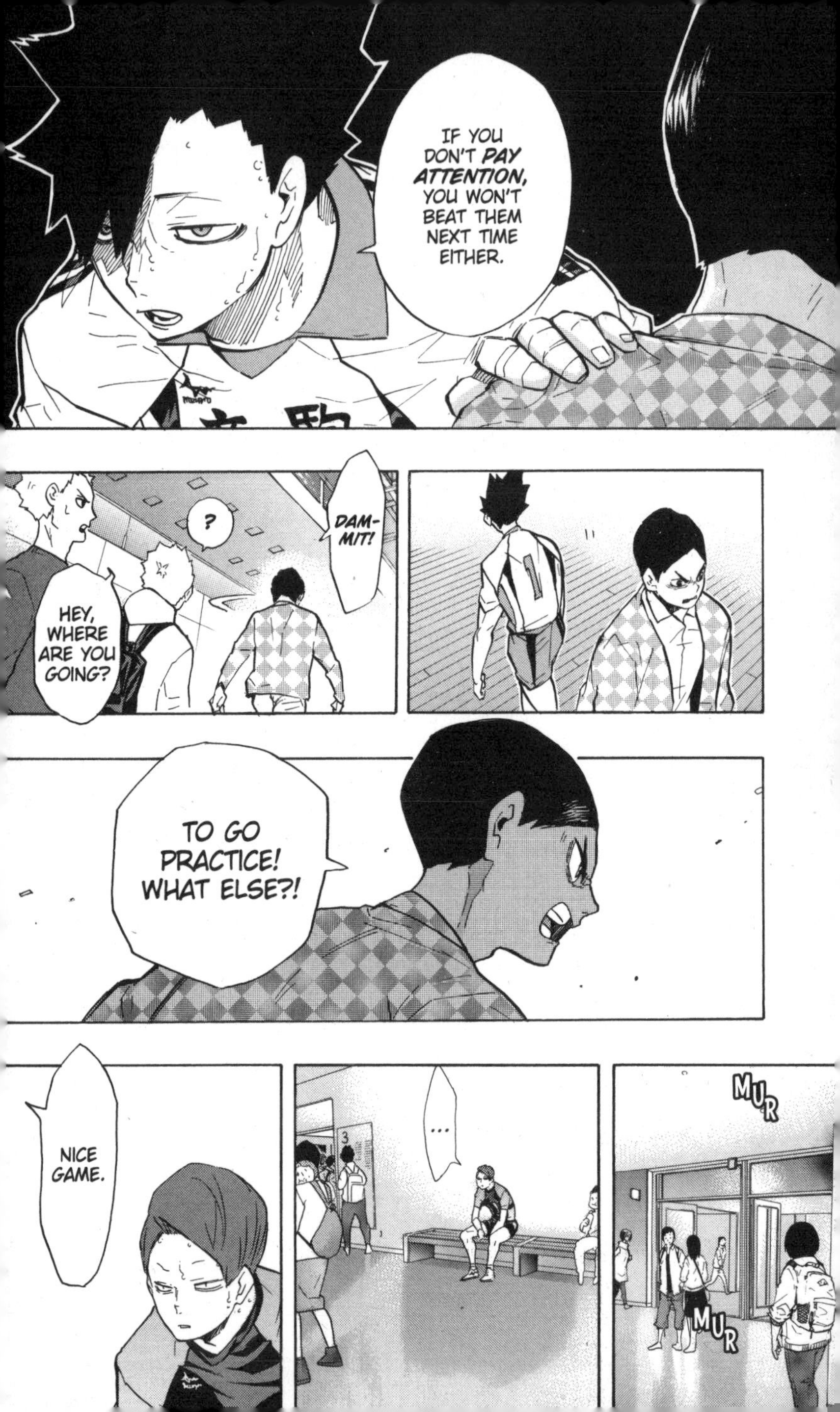
IF YOU DON'T **PAY ATTENTION,** YOU WON'T BEAT THEM NEXT TIME EITHER.
DAM-MIT!
?
HEY, WHERE ARE YOU GOING?
TO GO PRACTICE! WHAT ELSE?!
MUR
MUR
...
NICE GAME.

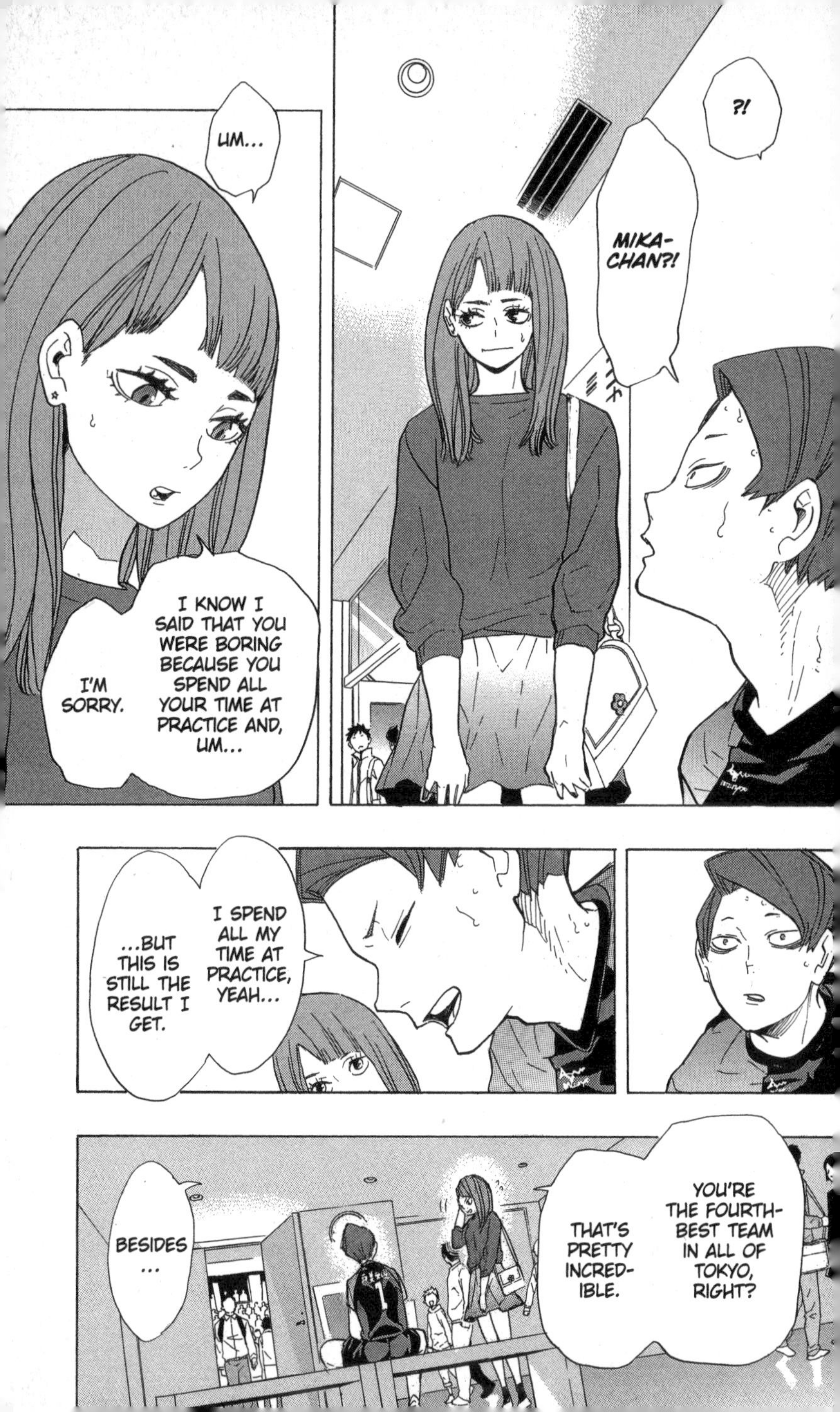
?!
MIKA-CHAN?!
UM...
I KNOW I SAID THAT YOU WERE BORING BECAUSE YOU SPEND ALL YOUR TIME AT PRACTICE AND, UM...
I'M SORRY.
I SPEND ALL MY TIME AT PRACTICE, YEAH...
...BUT THIS IS STILL THE RESULT I GET.
YOU'RE THE FOURTH-BEST TEAM IN ALL OF TOKYO, RIGHT?
THAT'S PRETTY INCREDIBLE.
BESIDES...

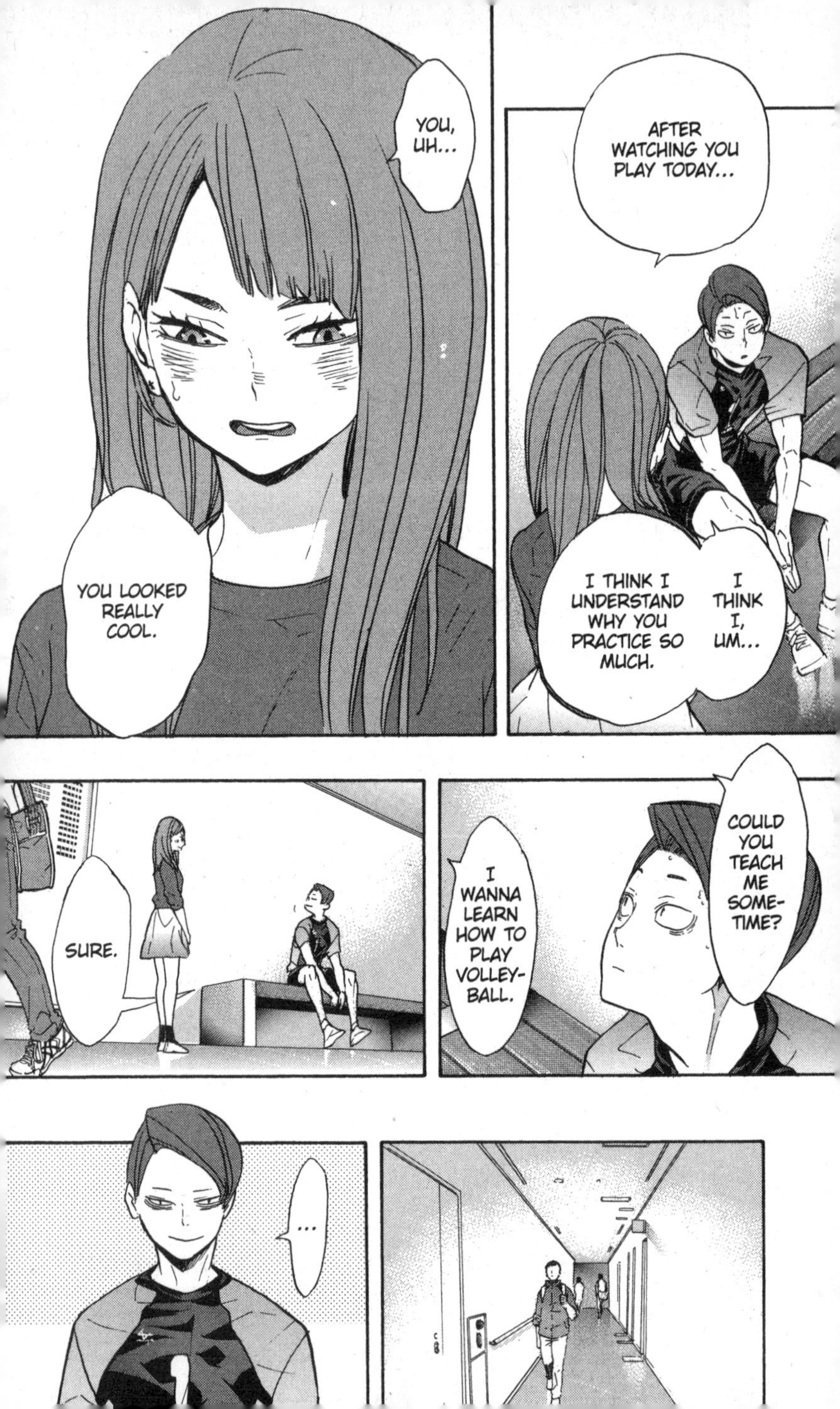
AFTER WATCHING YOU PLAY TODAY...
I THINK I, UM...
I THINK I UNDERSTAND WHY YOU PRACTICE SO MUCH.
YOU, UH...
YOU LOOKED REALLY COOL.
COULD YOU TEACH ME SOME-TIME?
I WANNA LEARN HOW TO PLAY VOLLEY-BALL.
SURE.
...

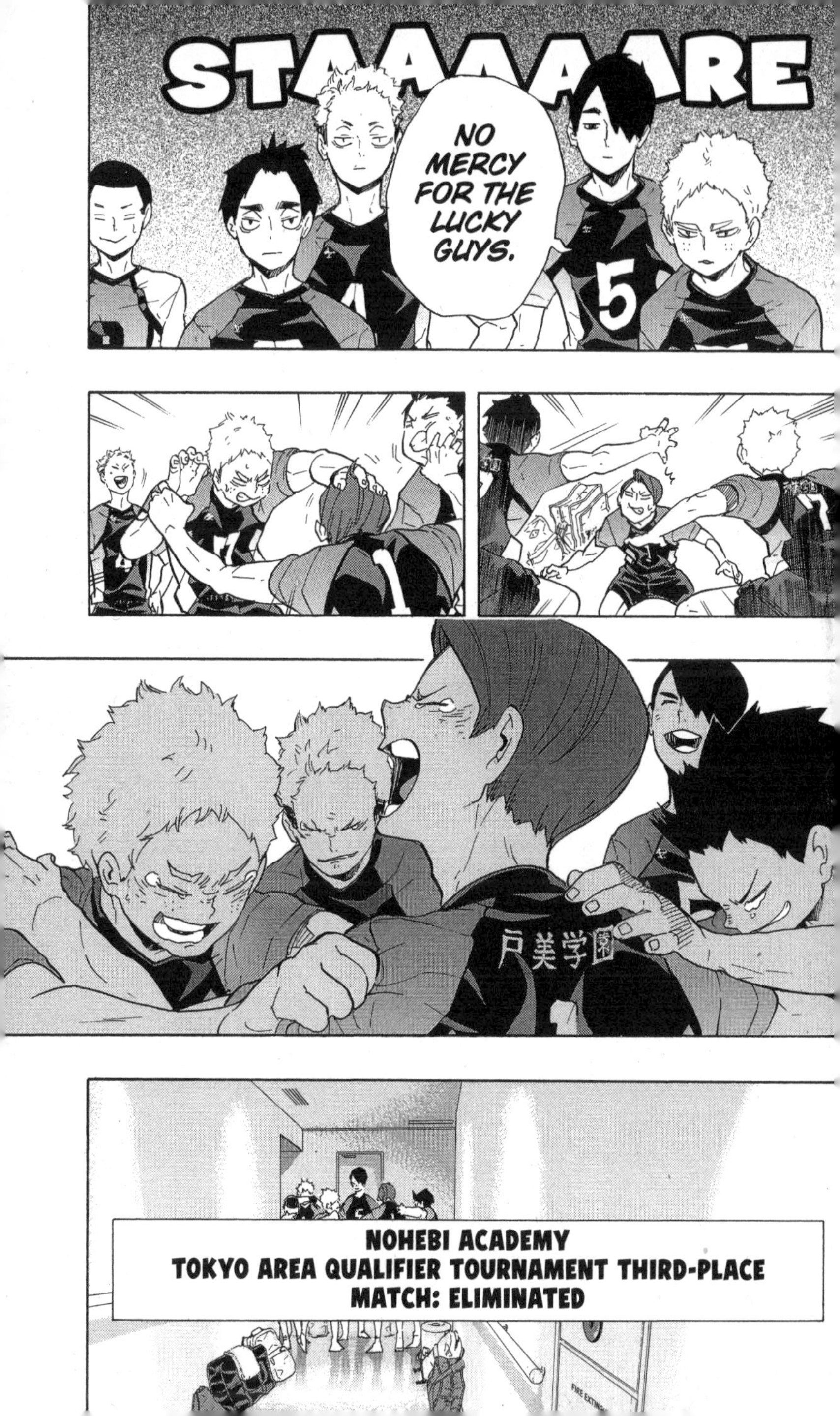
STAAAAARE
NO MERCY FOR THE LUCKY GUYS.
戸美学園
NOHEBI ACADEMY
TOKYO AREA QUALIFIER TOURNAMENT THIRD-PLACE
MATCH: ELIMINATED

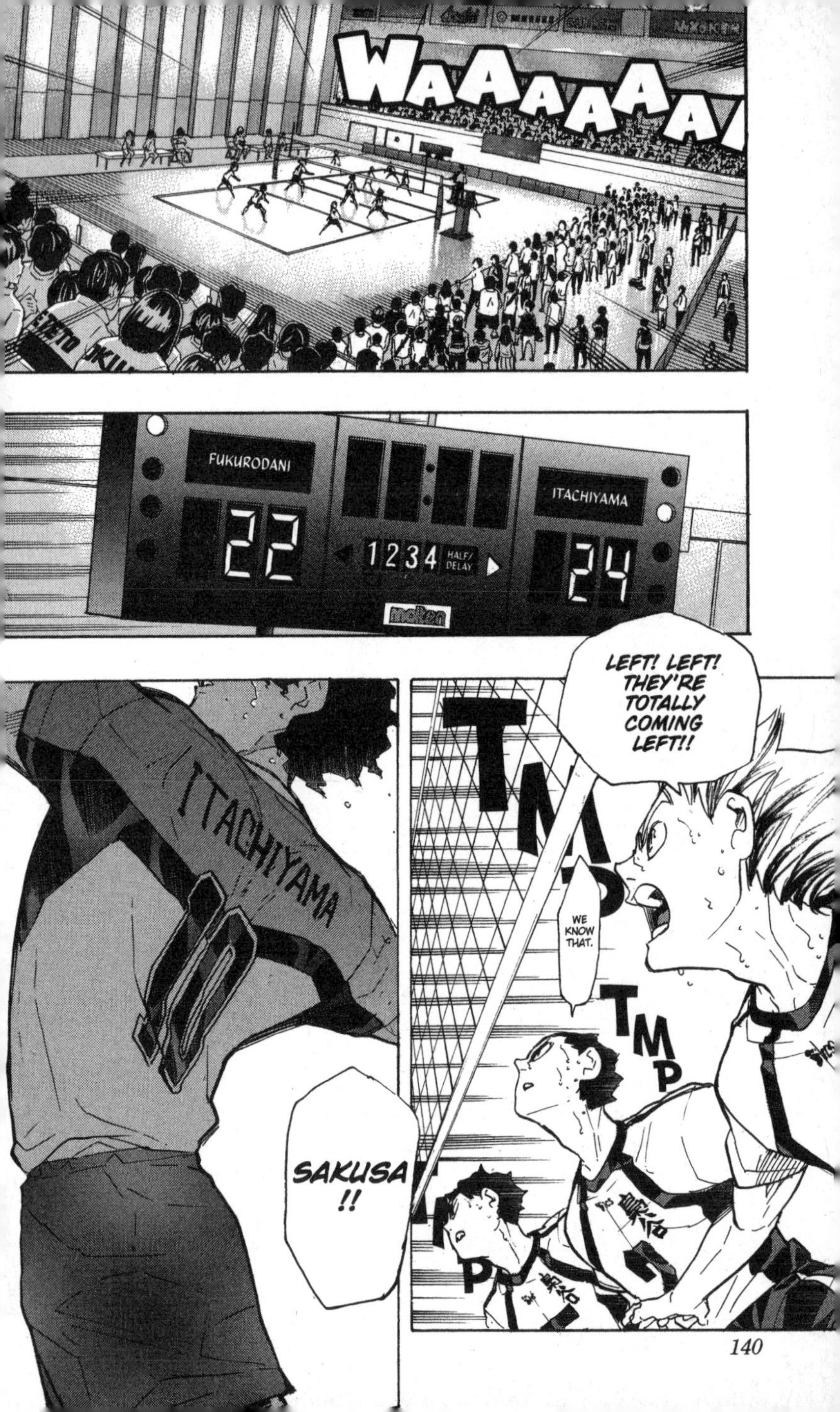
WAAAAAA!
FUKURODANI
22
1234
HALF/ DELAY
ITACHIYAMA
24
LEFT! LEFT! THEY'RE TOTALLY COMING LEFT!!
TMP
WE KNOW THAT.
TMP
TMP
ITACHIYAMA
SAKUSA!!

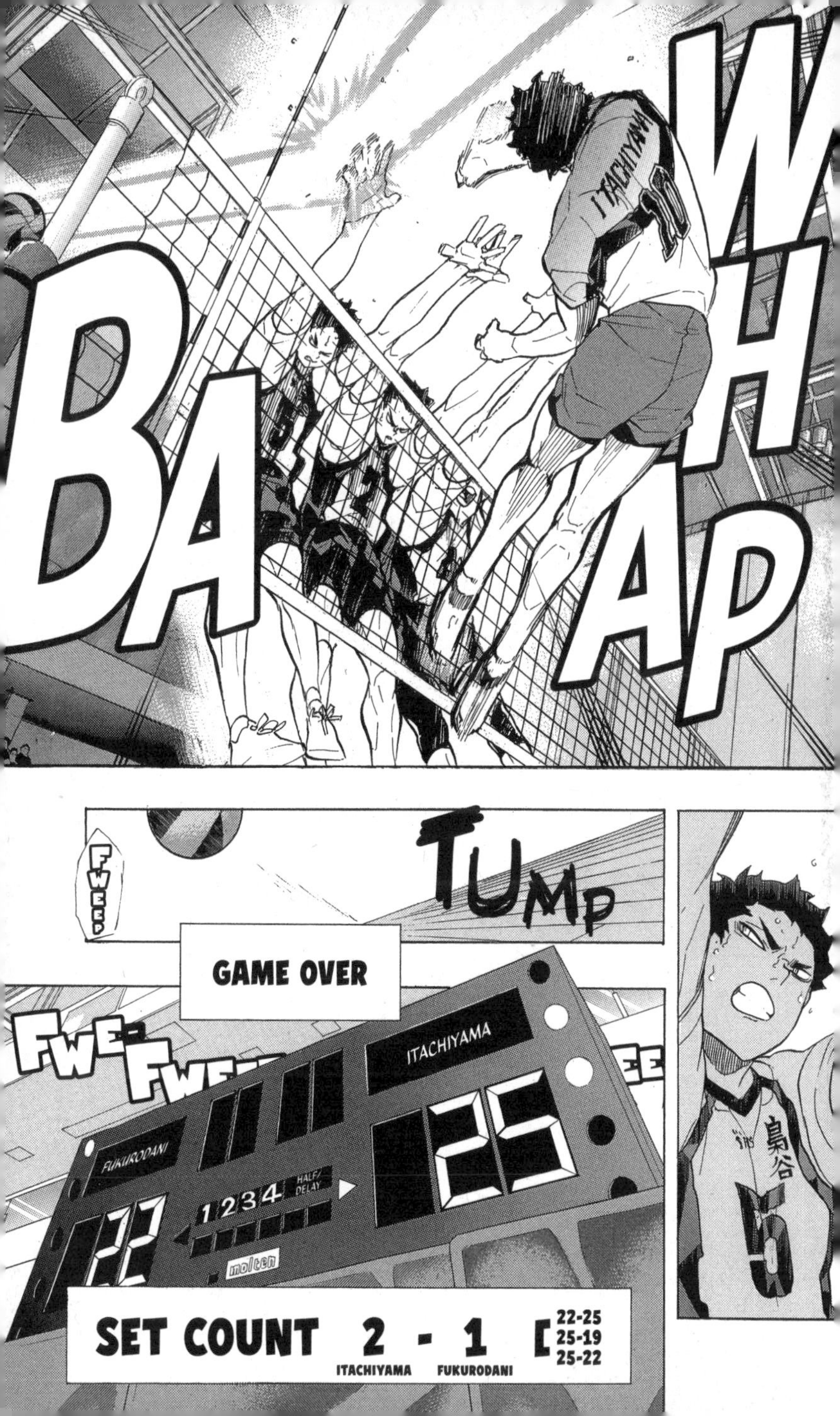
ITACHIYAMA
BA
WHAP
TUMP
FWEEP
GAME OVER
FWE-FWEE
EE
ITACHIYAMA
FUKURODANI
25
22
1234
HALF/DELAY
molten
SET COUNT 2 - 1
ITACHIYAMA FUKURODANI
22-25
25-19
25-22

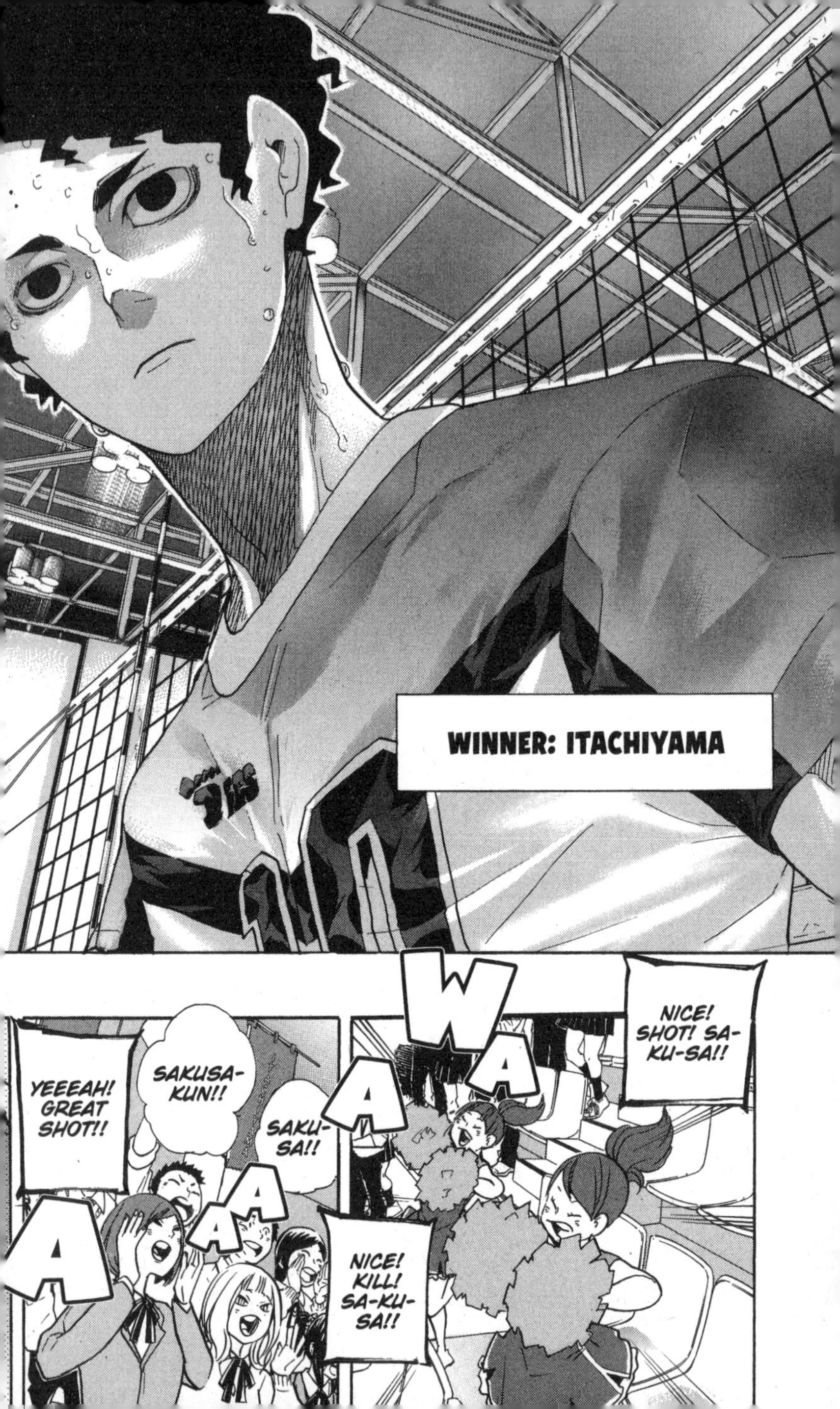
WINNER: ITACHIYAMA
NICE! SHOT! SA-KU-SA!!
NICE! KILL! SA-KU-SA!!
WAAAAAA
SAKU-SA!!
SAKUSA-KUN!!
YEEEAH! GREAT SHOT!!

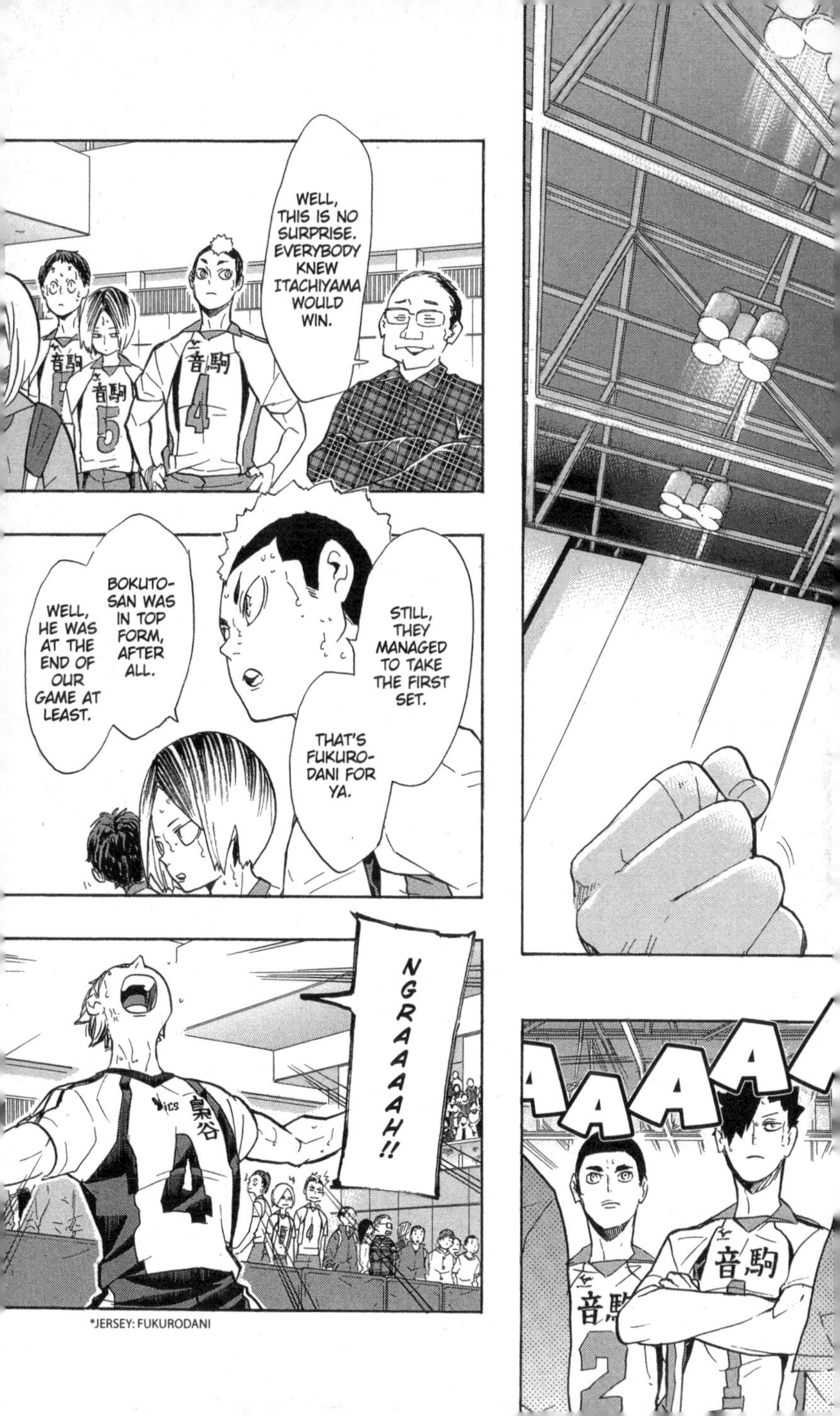
WELL, THIS IS NO SURPRISE. EVERYBODY KNEW ITACHIYAMA WOULD WIN.
STILL, THEY MANAGED TO TAKE THE FIRST SET.
THAT'S FUKURO-DANI FOR YA.
BOKUTO-SAN WAS IN TOP FORM, AFTER ALL.
WELL, HE WAS AT THE END OF OUR GAME AT LEAST.
NGRAAAAAAH!!
AAAAA
*JERSEY: FUKURODANI

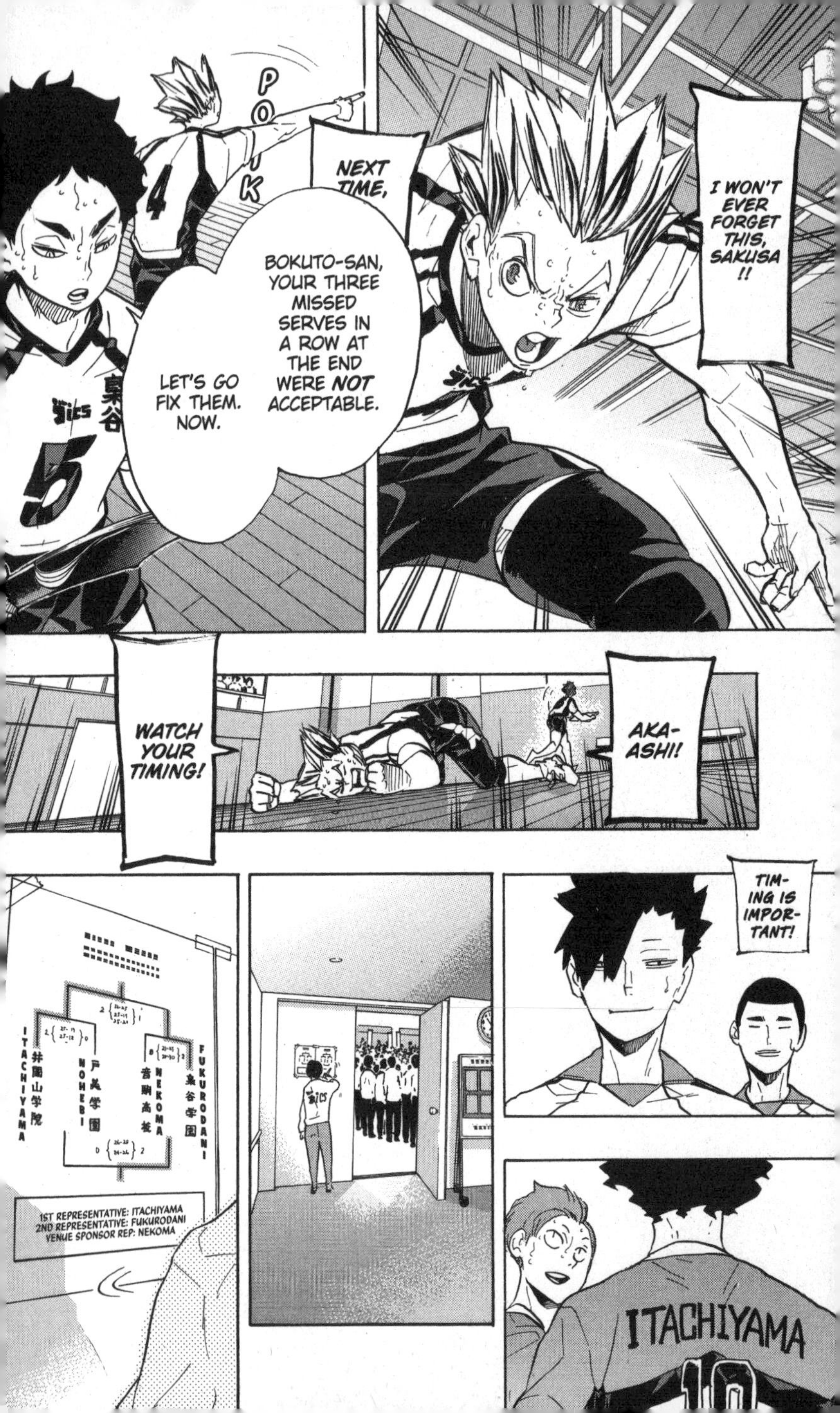

I WON'T EVER FORGET THIS, SAKUSA !!
NEXT TIME,
POKE
BOKUTO-SAN, YOUR THREE MISSED SERVES IN A ROW AT THE END WERE NOT ACCEPTABLE.
LET'S GO FIX THEM. NOW.
AKA-ASHI!
WATCH YOUR TIMING!
TIM-ING IS IMPOR-TANT!
ITACHIYAMA
FUKURODANI
梟谷学園
NEKOMA
音駒高校
NOHEBI
戸美学園
ITACHIYAMA
井闥山学院
1ST REPRESENTATIVE: ITACHIYAMA
2ND REPRESENTATIVE: FUKURODANI
VENUE SPONSOR REP: NEKOMA

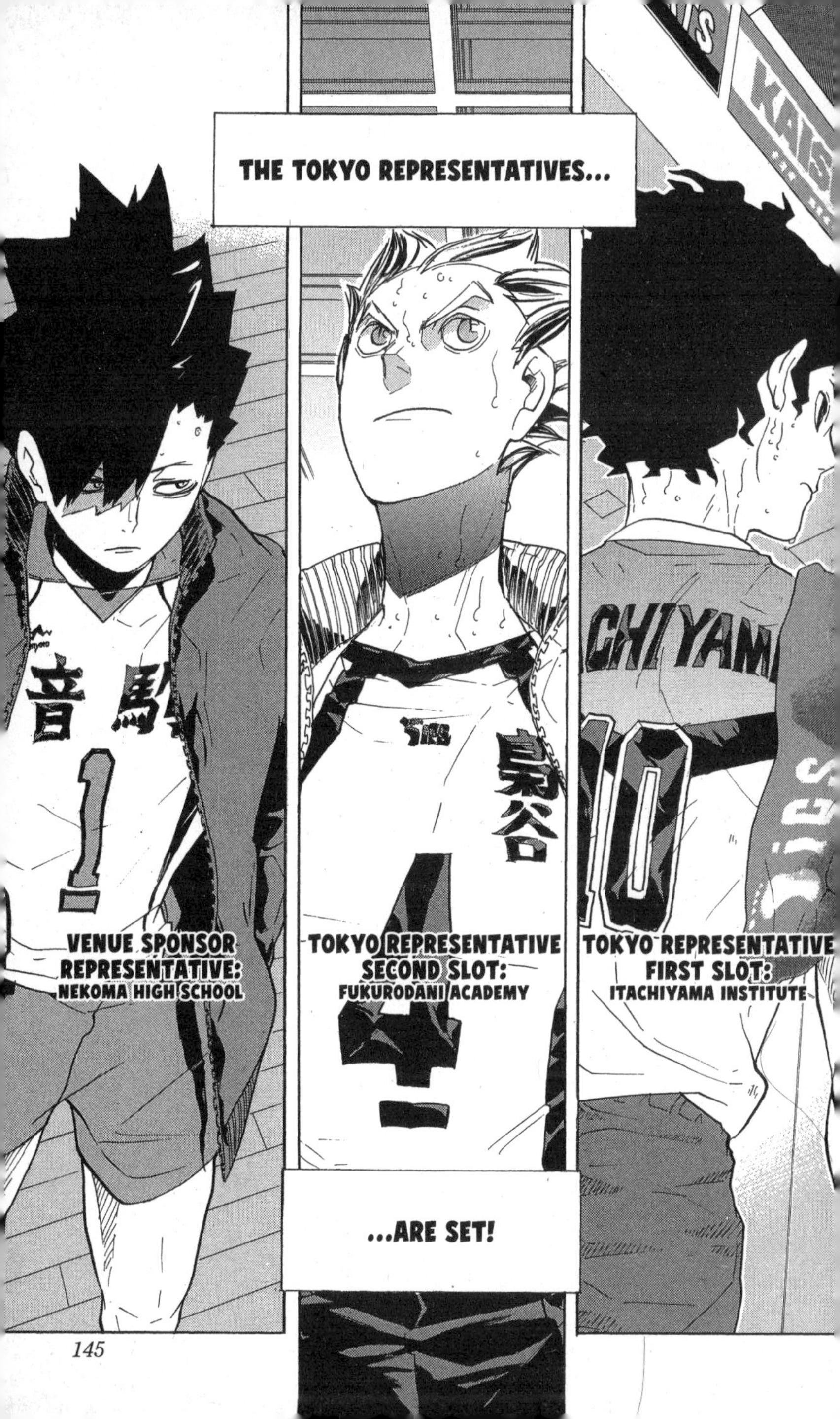
THE TOKYO REPRESENTATIVES...
TOKYO REPRESENTATIVE FIRST SLOT:
ITACHIYAMA INSTITUTE
TOKYO REPRESENTATIVE SECOND SLOT:
FUKURODANI ACADEMY
VENUE SPONSOR REPRESENTATIVE:
NEKOMA HIGH SCHOOL
...ARE SET!

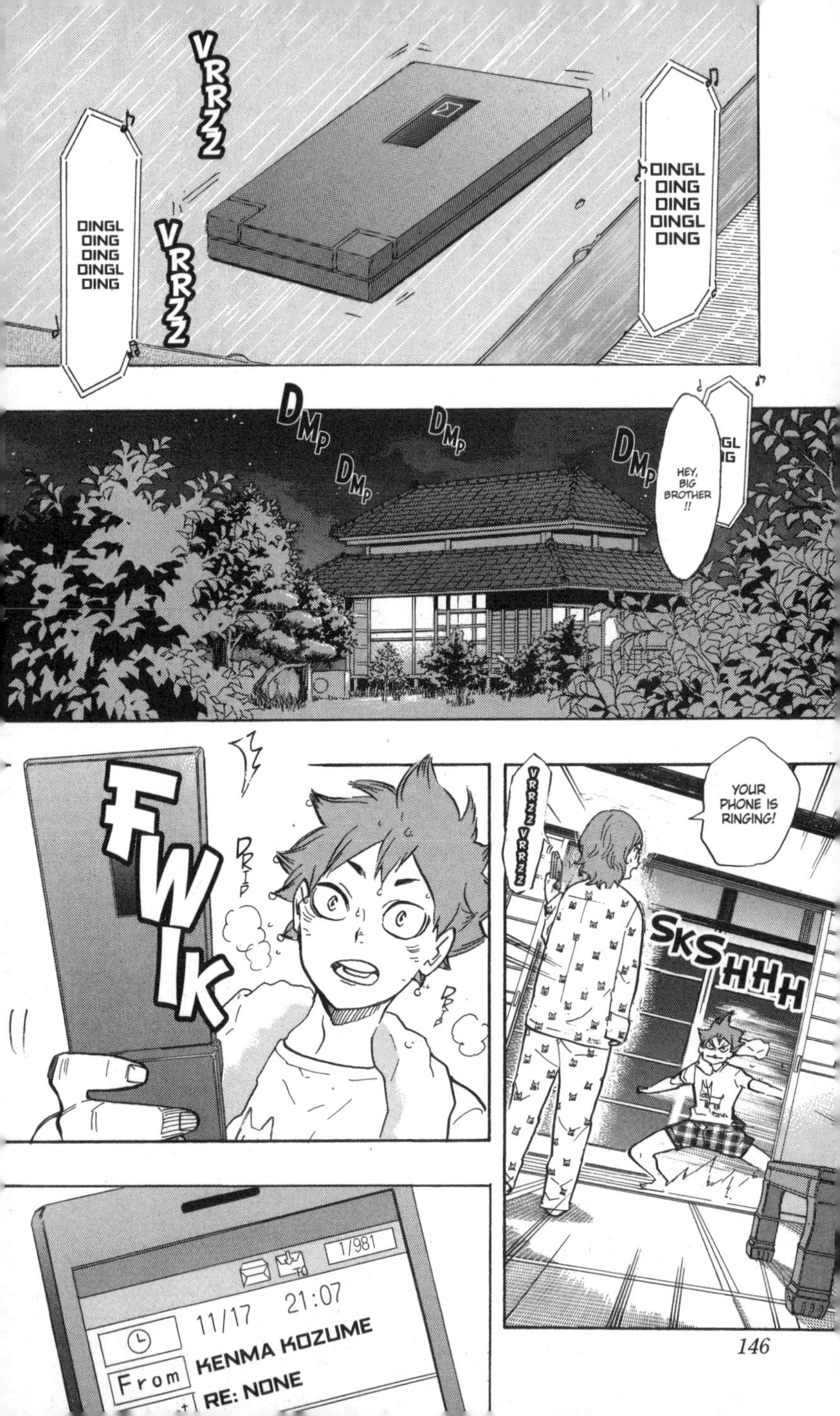

DINGL DING DING DINGL DING
VRRZZ
VRRZZ
DINGL DING DING DINGL DING
HEY, BIG BROTHER !!
DMP
DMP
DMP
DMP
YOUR PHONE IS RINGING!
SKSHHH
VRRZZ VRRZZ
DRIP
FWIK
DRIP
1/981
TO
11/17 21:07
From
KENMA KOZUME
RE: NONE

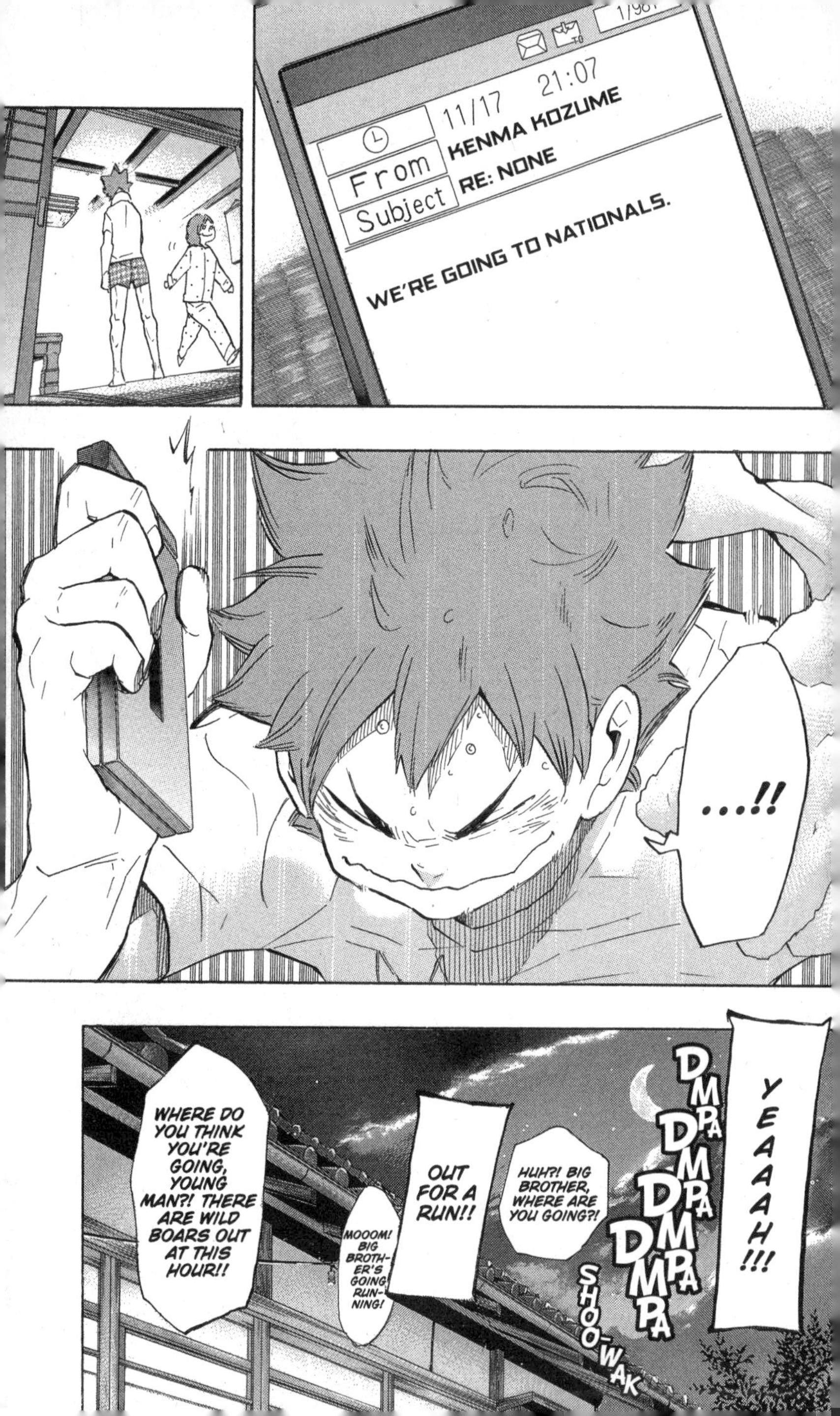
11/17 21:07
From KENMA KOZUME
Subject RE: NONE
WE'RE GOING TO NATIONALS.
...!!
YEAAAAH!!!
DMPA DMPA DMPA DMPA DMPA
SHOO-WAK
HUH?! BIG BROTHER, WHERE ARE YOU GOING?!
OUT FOR A RUN!!
MOOOM! BIG BROTHER'S GOING RUNNING!
WHERE DO YOU THINK YOU'RE GOING, YOUNG MAN?! THERE ARE WILD BOARS OUT AT THIS HOUR!!

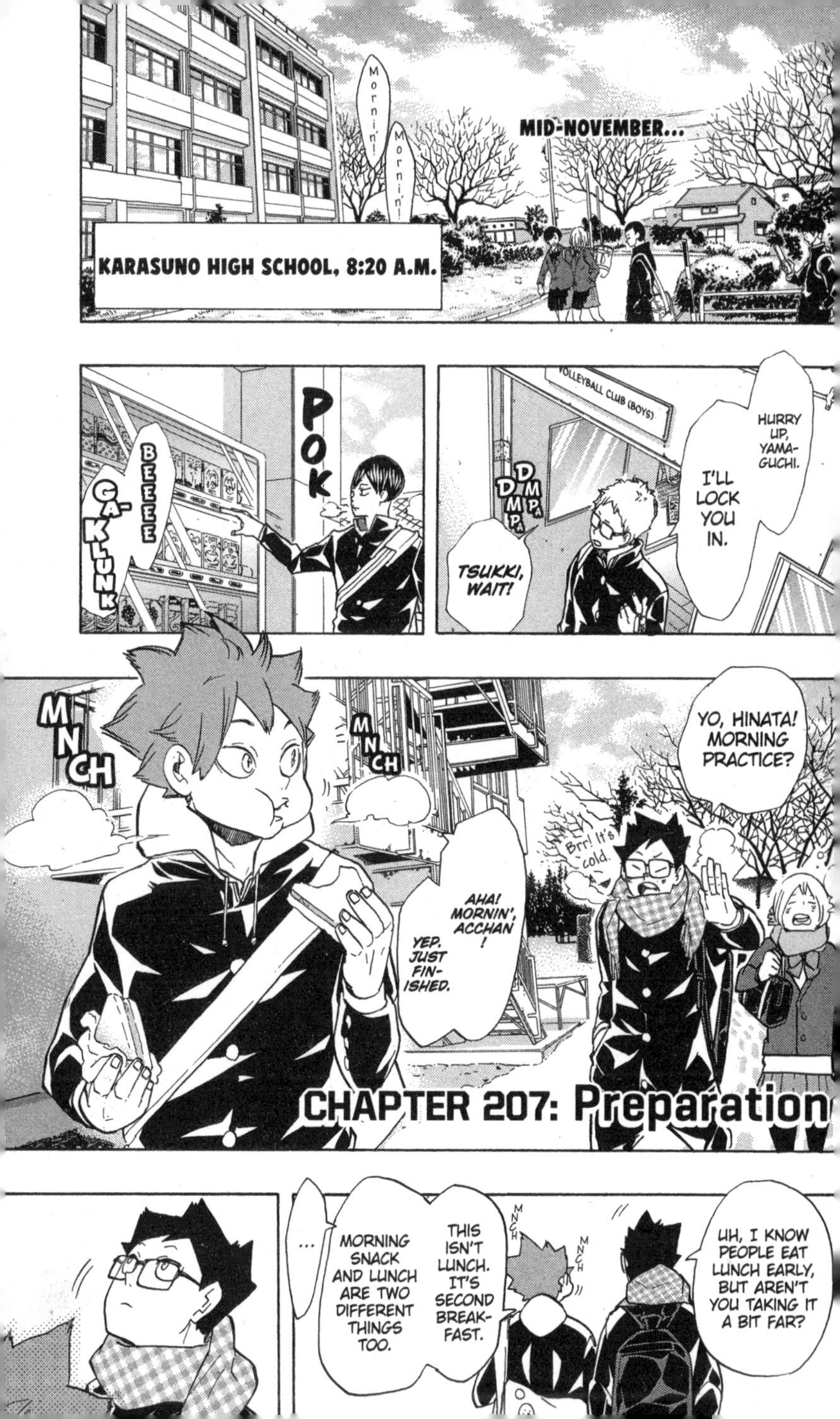
MID-NOVEMBER...
Morni'n!
Morni'n!
KARASUNO HIGH SCHOOL, 8:20 A.M.
VOLLEYBALL CLUB (BOYS)
HURRY UP, YAMAGUCHI.
I'LL LOCK YOU IN.
DMPA DMPA
TSUKKI, WAIT!
POK
BEEEE
GA-KLUNK
YO, HINATA! MORNING PRACTICE?
Brr! It's cold.
AHA! MORNIN', ACCHAN!
YEP. JUST FIN-ISHED.
MNCH
MNCH
CHAPTER 207: Preparation
UH, I KNOW PEOPLE EAT LUNCH EARLY, BUT AREN'T YOU TAKING IT A BIT FAR?
MNCH
MNCH
THIS ISN'T LUNCH. IT'S SECOND BREAK-FAST.
MORNING SNACK AND LUNCH ARE TWO DIFFERENT THINGS TOO.
...

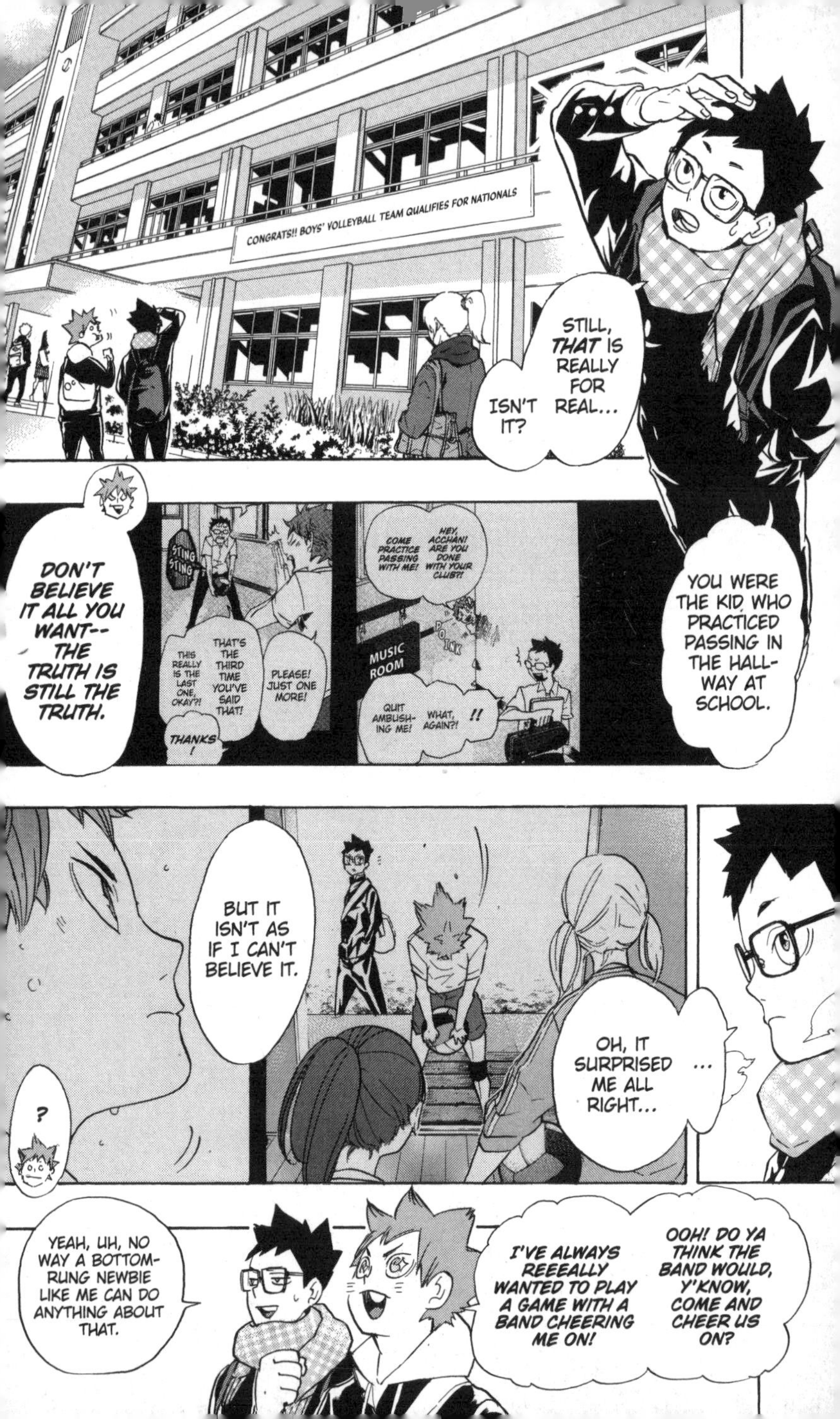
STILL, THAT IS REALLY FOR REAL... ISN'T IT?
CONGRATS!! BOYS' VOLLEYBALL TEAM QUALIFIES FOR NATIONALS
YOU WERE THE KID WHO PRACTICED PASSING IN THE HALLWAY AT SCHOOL.
HEY, ACCHAN! ARE YOU DONE WITH YOUR CLUB?!
COME PRACTICE PASSING WITH ME!
POINK
MUSIC ROOM
!!
WHAT, AGAIN?!
QUIT AMBUSHING ME!
STING STING
PLEASE! JUST ONE MORE!
THAT'S THE THIRD TIME YOU'VE SAID THAT!
THIS REALLY IS THE LAST ONE, OKAY?!
THANKS!
DON'T BELIEVE IT ALL YOU WANT-- THE TRUTH IS STILL THE TRUTH.
...
OH, IT SURPRISED ME ALL RIGHT...
BUT IT ISN'T AS IF I CAN'T BELIEVE IT.
?
OOH! DO YA THINK THE BAND WOULD, Y'KNOW, COME AND CHEER US ON?
I'VE ALWAYS REEEALLY WANTED TO PLAY A GAME WITH A BAND CHEERING ME ON!
YEAH, UH, NO WAY A BOTTOM-RUNG NEWBIE LIKE ME CAN DO ANYTHING ABOUT THAT.

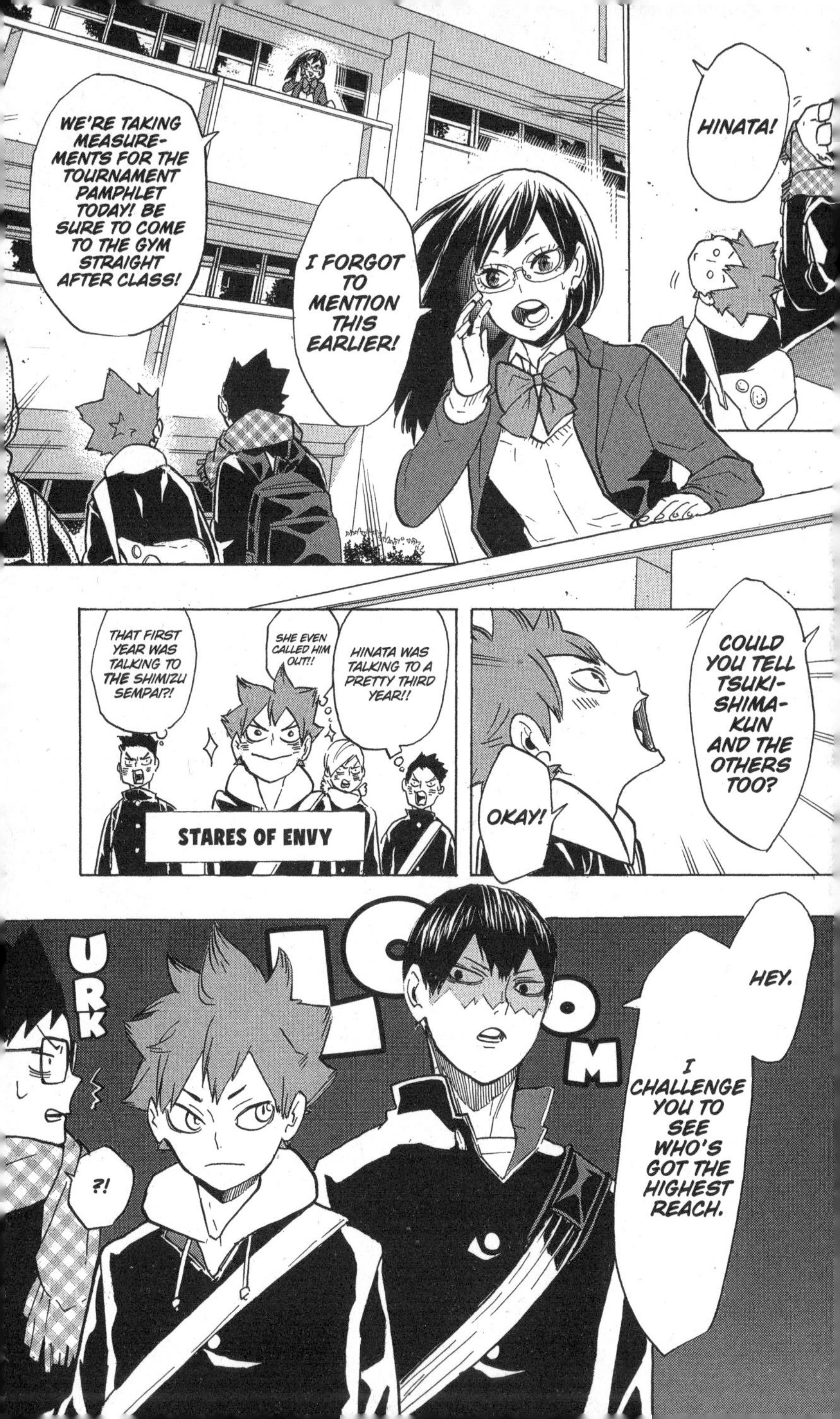
HINATA!
I FORGOT TO MENTION THIS EARLIER!
WE'RE TAKING MEASUREMENTS FOR THE TOURNAMENT PAMPHLET TODAY! BE SURE TO COME TO THE GYM STRAIGHT AFTER CLASS!
COULD YOU TELL TSUKISHIMA-KUN AND THE OTHERS TOO?
OKAY!
HINATA WAS TALKING TO A PRETTY THIRD YEAR!!
SHE EVEN CALLED HIM OUT!!
THAT FIRST YEAR WAS TALKING TO THE SHIMIZU SEMPAI?!
STARES OF ENVY
HEY.
I CHALLENGE YOU TO SEE WHO'S GOT THE HIGHEST REACH.
LOOM
URK
?!

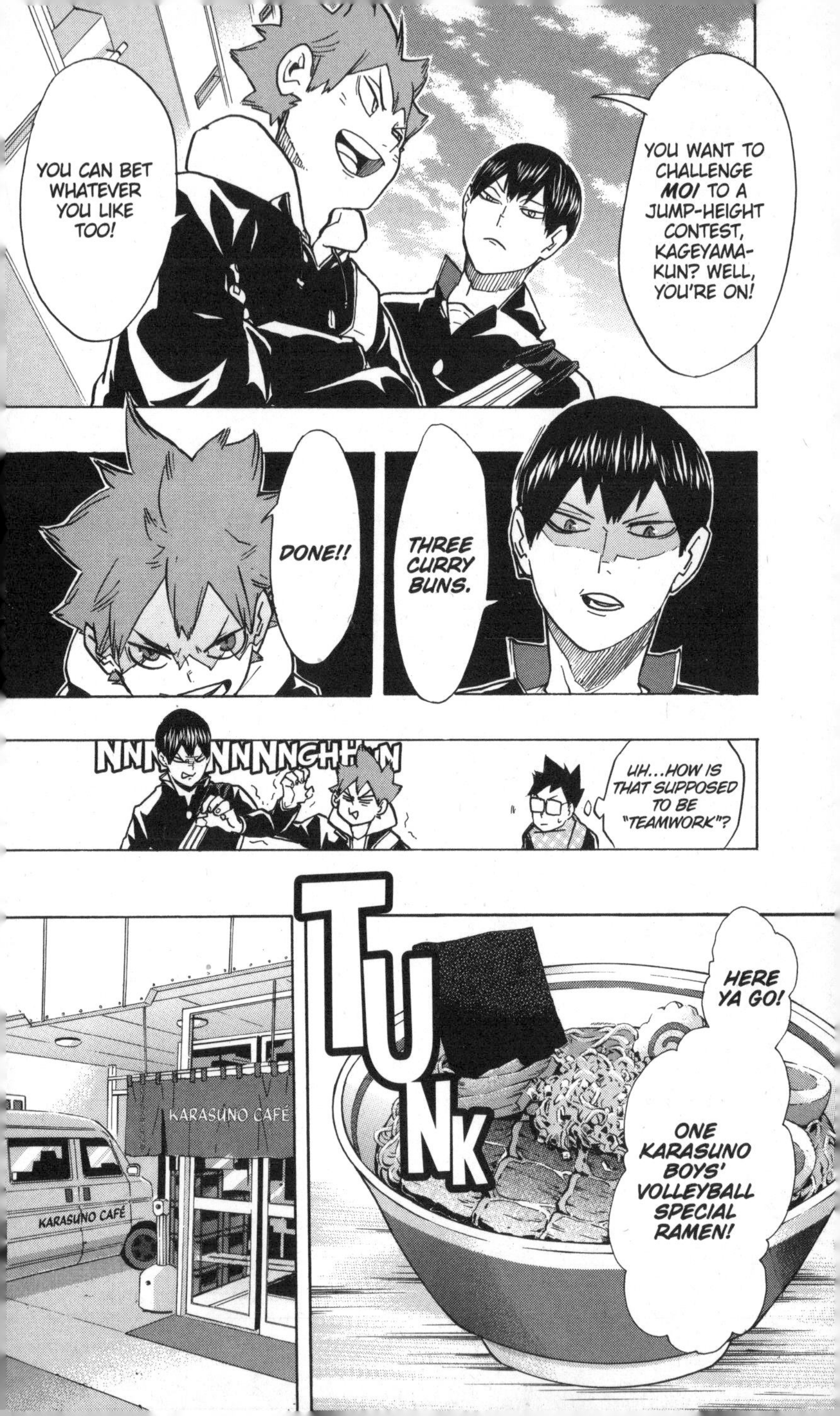

YOU WANT TO CHALLENGE *MOI* TO A JUMP-HEIGHT CONTEST, KAGEYAMA-KUN? WELL, YOU'RE ON!
YOU CAN BET WHATEVER YOU LIKE TOO!
THREE CURRY BUNS.
DONE!!
UH...HOW IS THAT SUPPOSED TO BE "TEAMWORK"?
HERE YA GO!
ONE KARASUNO BOYS' VOLLEYBALL SPECIAL RAMEN!
TUNK
KARASUNO CAFÉ
KARASUNO CAFÉ

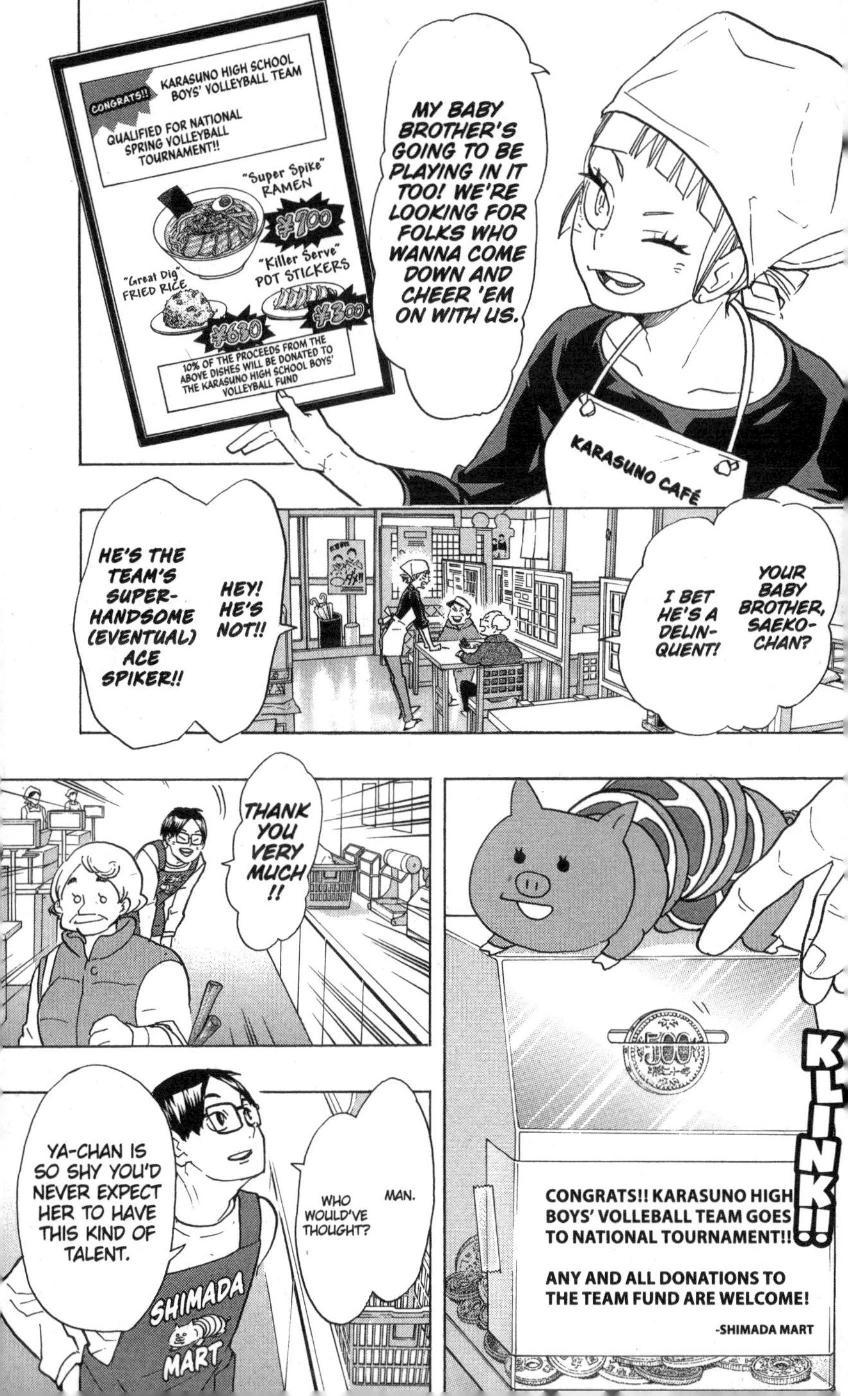
MY BABY BROTHER'S GOING TO BE PLAYING IN IT TOO! WE'RE LOOKING FOR FOLKS WHO WANNA COME DOWN AND CHEER 'EM ON WITH US.
CONGRATS!!
KARASUNO HIGH SCHOOL BOYS' VOLLEYBALL TEAM
QUALIFIED FOR NATIONAL SPRING VOLLEYBALL TOURNAMENT!!
"Super Spike" RAMEN
¥700
"Killer Serve" POT STICKERS
¥300
"Great Dig" FRIED RICE
¥680
10% OF THE PROCEEDS FROM THE ABOVE DISHES WILL BE DONATED TO THE KARASUNO HIGH SCHOOL BOYS' VOLLEYBALL FUND
KARASUNO CAFÉ
YOUR BABY BROTHER, SAEKO-CHAN?
I BET HE'S A DELIN-QUENT!
HEY! HE'S NOT!!
HE'S THE TEAM'S SUPER-HANDSOME (EVENTUAL) ACE SPIKER!!
KLINK!!
CONGRATS!! KARASUNO HIGH BOYS' VOLLEBALL TEAM GOES TO NATIONAL TOURNAMENT!!
ANY AND ALL DONATIONS TO THE TEAM FUND ARE WELCOME!
-SHIMADA MART
THANK YOU VERY MUCH!!
MAN.
WHO WOULD'VE THOUGHT?
YA-CHAN IS SO SHY YOU'D NEVER EXPECT HER TO HAVE THIS KIND OF TALENT.
SHIMADA MART

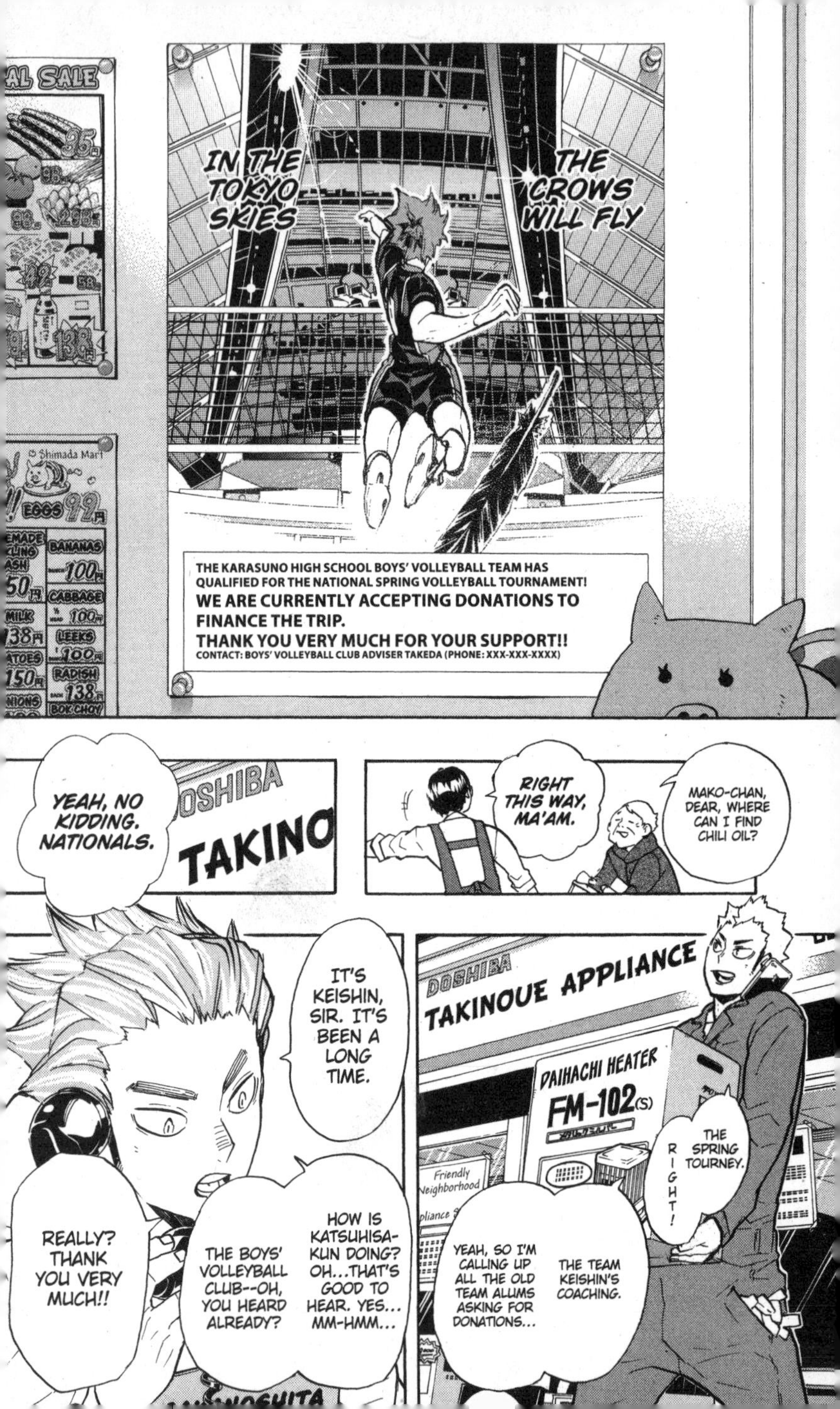

AL SALE
Shimada Mart
EGGS 99円
BANANAS 100円
CABBAGE 100円
MILK 138円
LEEKS 100円
RADISH 138円
BOK CHOY
IN THE TOKYO SKIES
THE CROWS WILL FLY
THE KARASUNO HIGH SCHOOL BOYS' VOLLEYBALL TEAM HAS QUALIFIED FOR THE NATIONAL SPRING VOLLEYBALL TOURNAMENT!
WE ARE CURRENTLY ACCEPTING DONATIONS TO FINANCE THE TRIP.
THANK YOU VERY MUCH FOR YOUR SUPPORT!!
CONTACT: BOYS' VOLLEYBALL CLUB ADVISER TAKEDA (PHONE: XXX-XXX-XXXX)
MAKO-CHAN, DEAR, WHERE CAN I FIND CHILI OIL?
RIGHT THIS WAY, MA'AM.
YEAH, NO KIDDING. NATIONALS.
OSHIBA
TAKINO
DOSHIBA
TAKINOUE APPLIANCE
DAIHACHI HEATER
FM-102(S)
Friendly Neighborhood
THE SPRING TOURNEY.
RIGHT!
THE TEAM KEISHIN'S COACHING.
YEAH, SO I'M CALLING UP ALL THE OLD TEAM ALUMS ASKING FOR DONATIONS...
IT'S KEISHIN, SIR. IT'S BEEN A LONG TIME.
HOW IS KATSUHISA-KUN DOING? OH...THAT'S GOOD TO HEAR. YES... MM-HMM...
THE BOYS' VOLLEYBALL CLUB--OH, YOU HEARD ALREADY?
REALLY? THANK YOU VERY MUCH!!

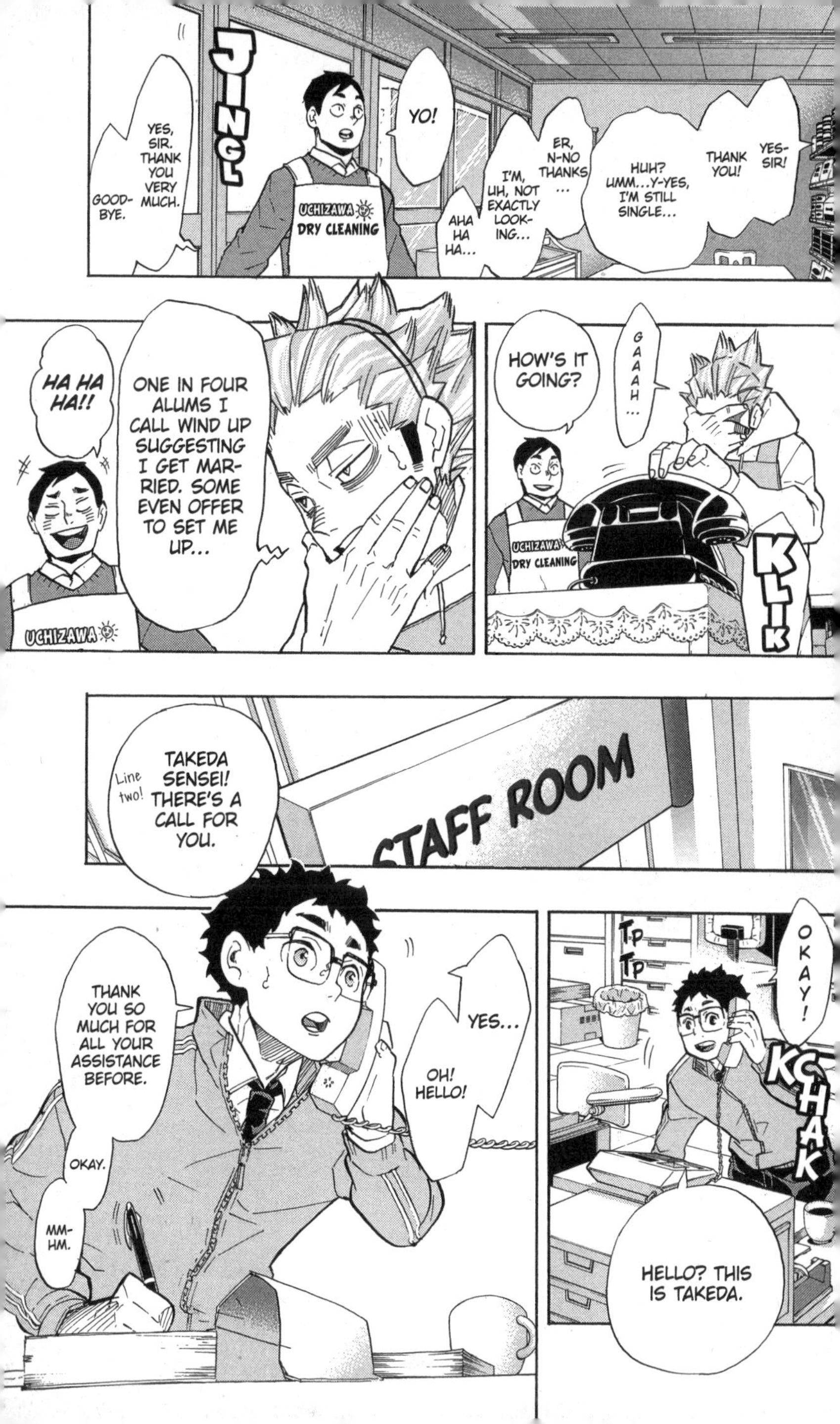
YES-SIR!
THANK YOU!
HUH? UMM...Y-YES, I'M STILL SINGLE...
ER, N-NO THANKS...
I'M, UH, NOT EXACTLY LOOKING...
AHA HA HA...
YO!
JINGL
YES, SIR. THANK YOU VERY MUCH.
GOOD-BYE.
UCHIZAWA DRY CLEANING
GAAAH...
HOW'S IT GOING?
KLIK
UCHIZAWA DRY CLEANING
ONE IN FOUR ALUMS I CALL WIND UP SUGGESTING I GET MARRIED. SOME EVEN OFFER TO SET ME UP...
HA HA HA!!
UCHIZAWA
TAKEDA SENSEI! THERE'S A CALL FOR YOU.
Line two!
STAFF ROOM
OKAY!
Tp Tp
KCHAK
HELLO? THIS IS TAKEDA.
YES...
OH! HELLO!
THANK YOU SO MUCH FOR ALL YOUR ASSISTANCE BEFORE.
OKAY.
MM-HM.

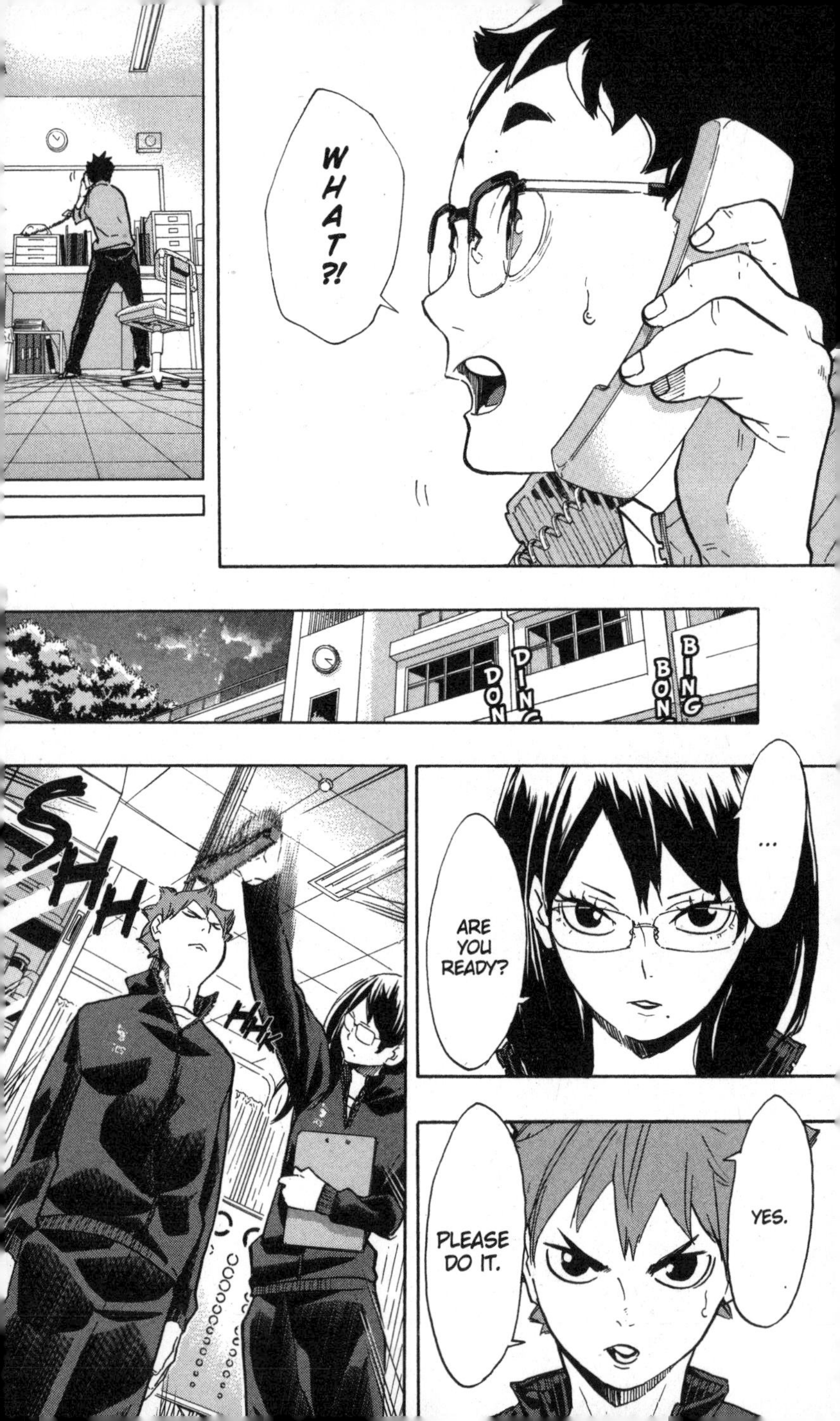

WHAT?!
BING
BON
DING
DON
...
ARE YOU READY?
YES.
PLEASE DO IT.
SHH
HHK

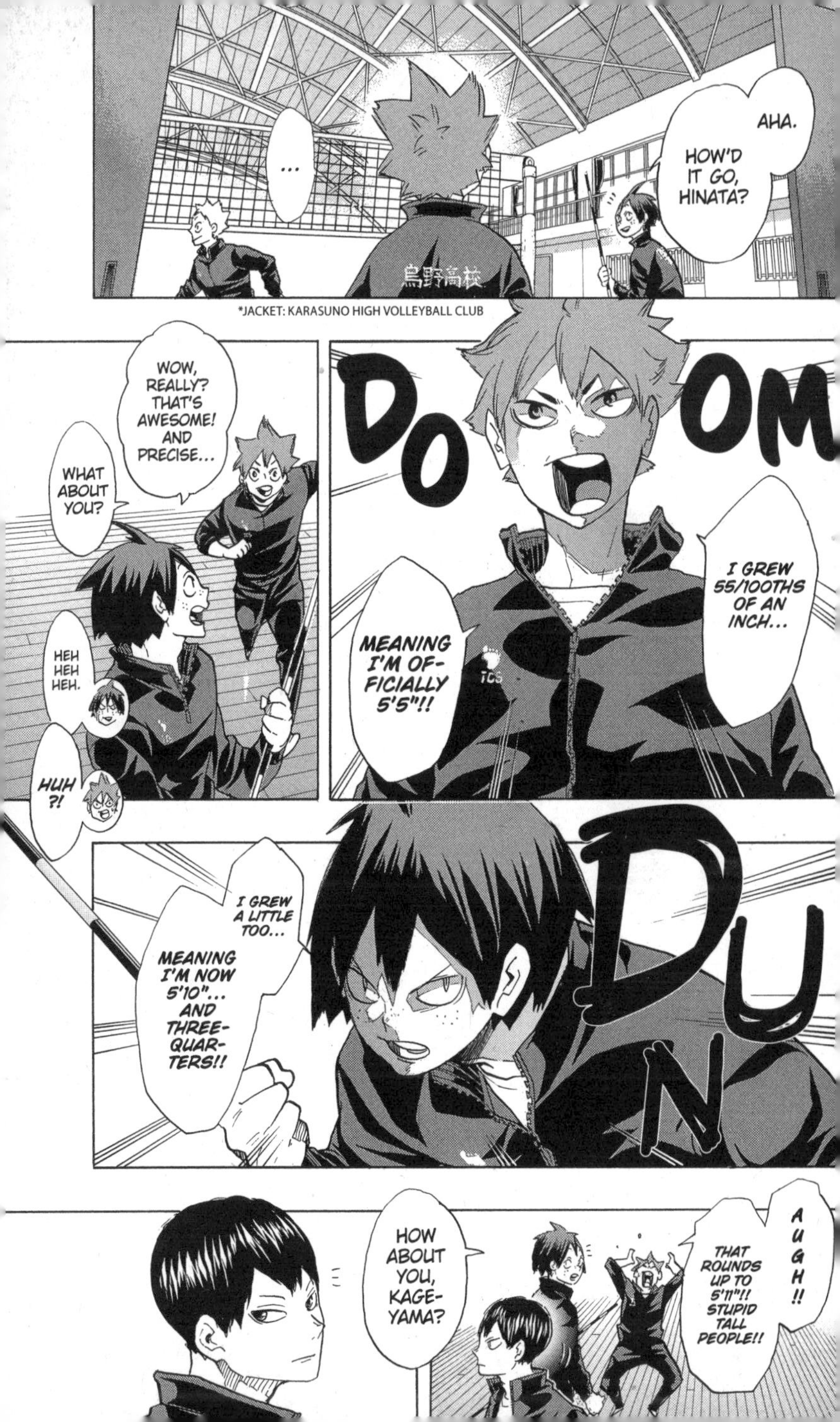
AHA.
HOW'D IT GO, HINATA?
...
鳥野高校
DOOM
I GREW 55/100THS OF AN INCH...
MEANING I'M OFFICIALLY 5'5"!!
WOW, REALLY? THAT'S AWESOME! AND PRECISE...
WHAT ABOUT YOU?
HEH HEH HEH.
HUH?!
DUN
I GREW A LITTLE TOO...
MEANING I'M NOW 5'10"... AND THREE-QUARTERS!!
AUGH!!
THAT ROUNDS UP TO 5'11"!! STUPID TALL PEOPLE!!
HOW ABOUT YOU, KAGEYAMA?
*JACKET: KARASUNO HIGH VOLLEYBALL CLUB

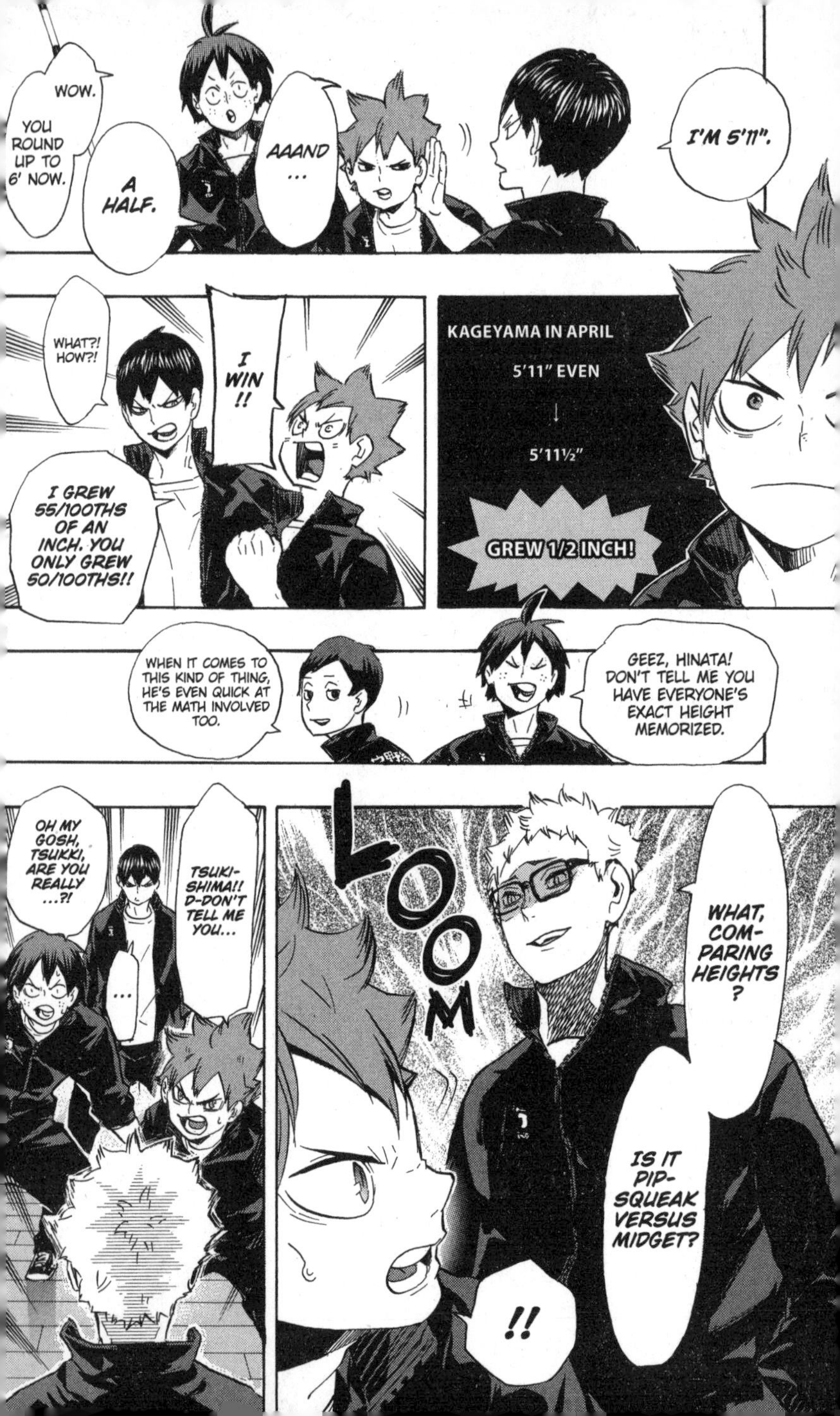

I'M 5'11".
AAAND ...
A HALF.
WOW.
YOU ROUND UP TO 6' NOW.
KAGEYAMA IN APRIL
5'11" EVEN
↓
5'11½"
GREW 1/2 INCH!
I WIN!!
WHAT?! HOW?!
I GREW 55/100THS OF AN INCH. YOU ONLY GREW 50/100THS!!
GEEZ, HINATA! DON'T TELL ME YOU HAVE EVERYONE'S EXACT HEIGHT MEMORIZED.
WHEN IT COMES TO THIS KIND OF THING, HE'S EVEN QUICK AT THE MATH INVOLVED TOO.
WHAT, COM-PARING HEIGHTS?
IS IT PIP-SQUEAK VERSUS MIDGET?
LOOOM
!!
TSUKI-SHIMA!! D-DON'T TELL ME YOU...
OH MY GOSH, TSUKKI, ARE YOU REALLY ...?!
...

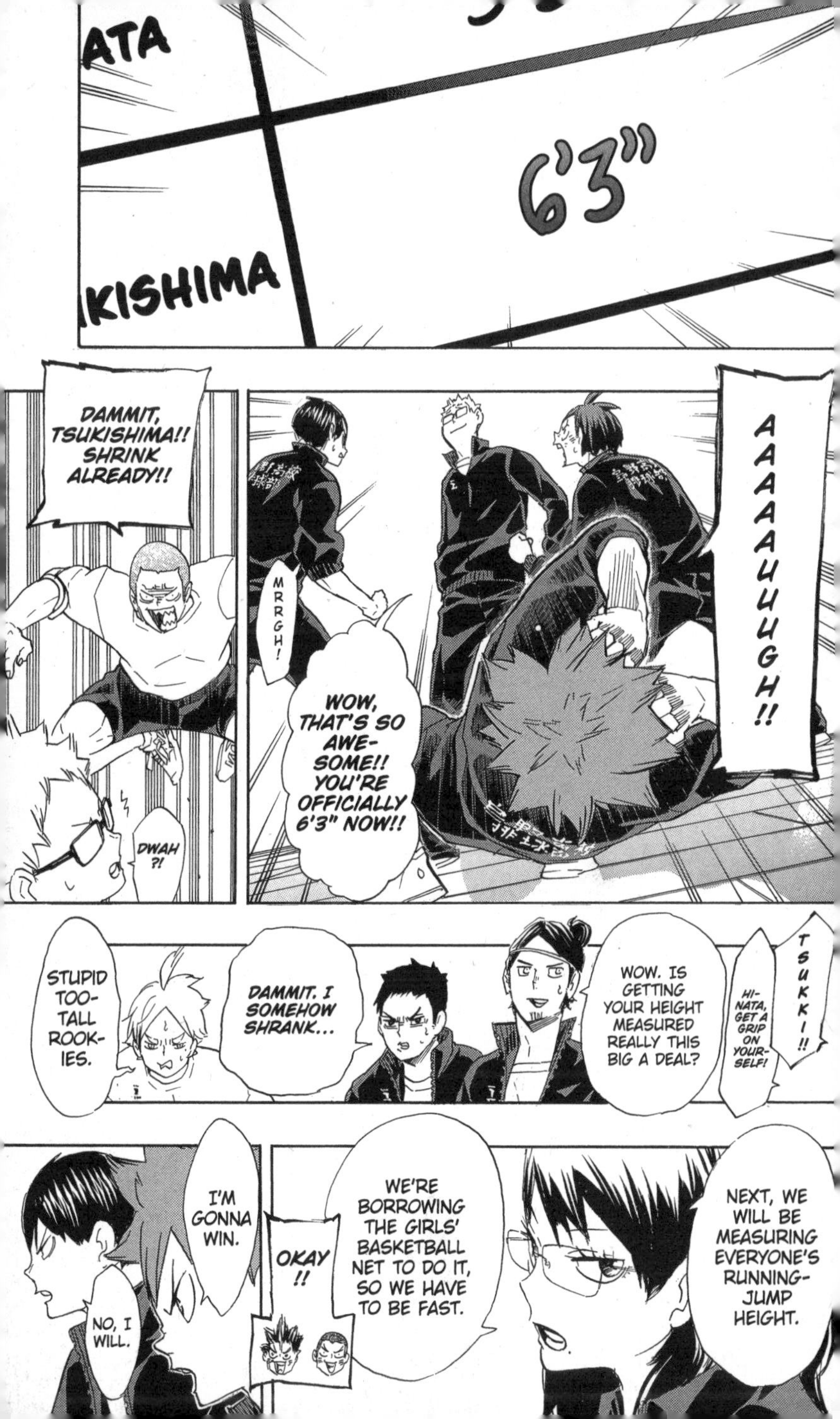
ATA
6'3"
KISHIMA
AAAAAUUUGH!!
MRRGH!
WOW, THAT'S SO AWE-SOME!! YOU'RE OFFICIALLY 6'3" NOW!!
DAMMIT, TSUKISHIMA!! SHRINK ALREADY!!
DWAH?!
TSUKKI!!
HI-NATA, GET A GRIP ON YOUR-SELF!
WOW. IS GETTING YOUR HEIGHT MEASURED REALLY THIS BIG A DEAL?
DAMMIT. I SOMEHOW SHRANK...
STUPID TOO-TALL ROOK-IES.
NEXT, WE WILL BE MEASURING EVERYONE'S RUNNING-JUMP HEIGHT.
WE'RE BORROWING THE GIRLS' BASKETBALL NET TO DO IT, SO WE HAVE TO BE FAST.
OKAY!!
I'M GONNA WIN.
NO, I WILL.

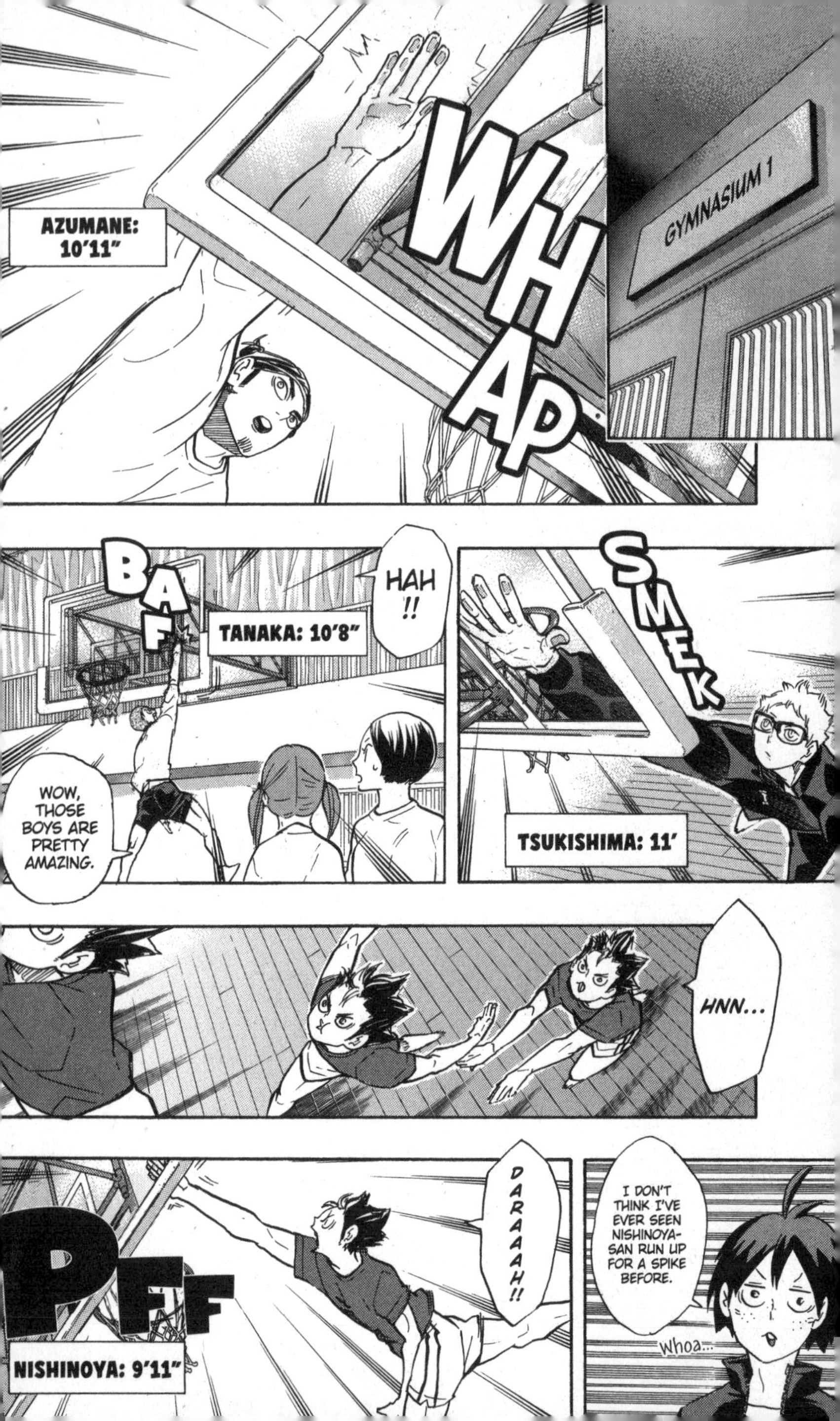
GYMNASIUM 1
WHAP
AZUMANE: 10'11"
SMEK
TSUKISHIMA: 11'
HAH!!
BAF
TANAKA: 10'8"
WOW, THOSE BOYS ARE PRETTY AMAZING.
HNN...
I DON'T THINK I'VE EVER SEEN NISHINOYA-SAN RUN UP FOR A SPIKE BEFORE.
whoa...
DARAAAAH!!
PFF
NISHINOYA: 9'11"

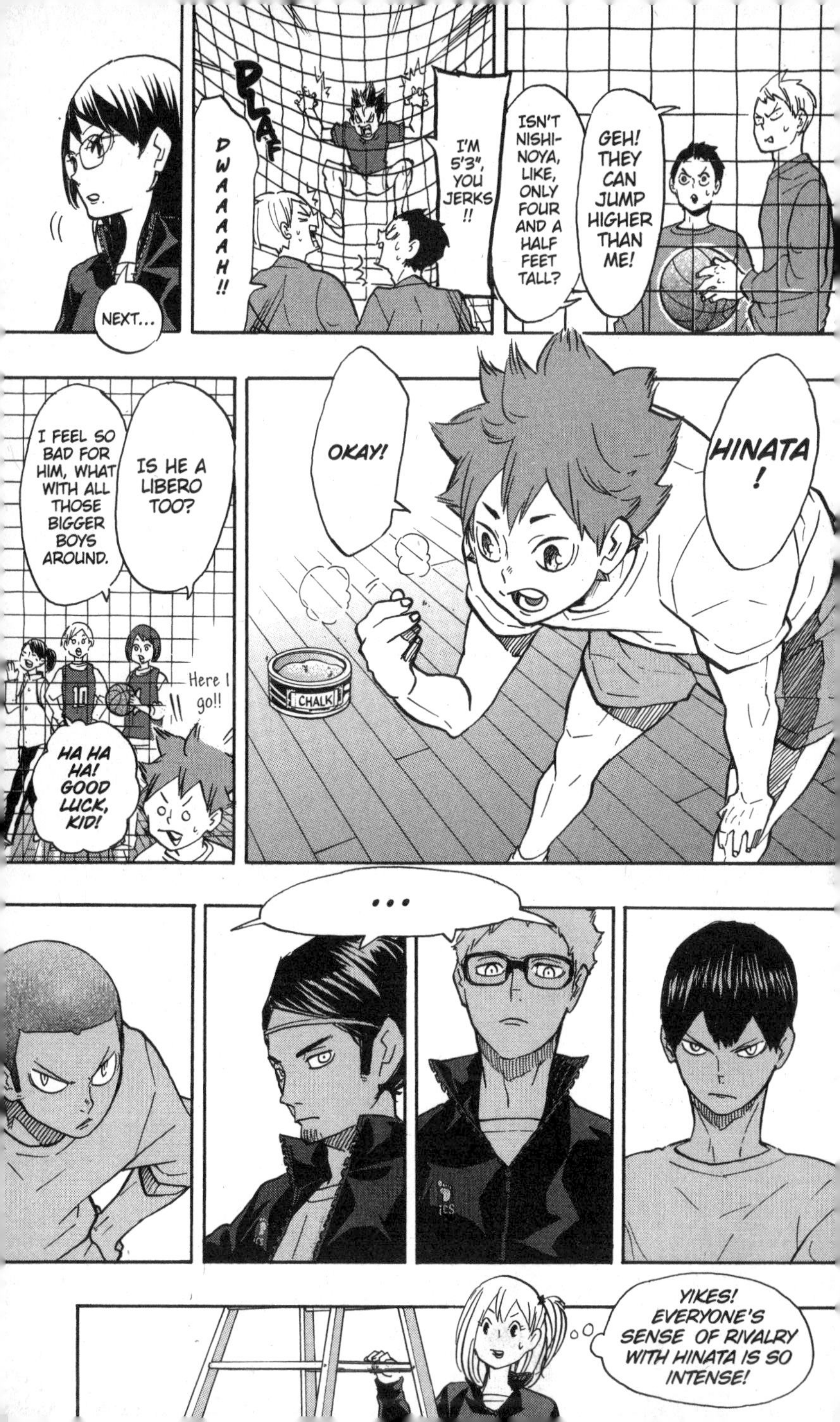
GEH! THEY CAN JUMP HIGHER THAN ME!
ISN'T NISHI-NOYA, LIKE, ONLY FOUR AND A HALF FEET TALL?
I'M 5'3", YOU JERKS!!
PLAF
DWAAAAAAH!!
NEXT...
HINATA!
OKAY!
CHALK
IS HE A LIBERO TOO?
I FEEL SO BAD FOR HIM, WHAT WITH ALL THOSE BIGGER BOYS AROUND.
Here I go!!
HA HA HA! GOOD LUCK, KID!
...
YIKES! EVERYONE'S SENSE OF RIVALRY WITH HINATA IS SO INTENSE!

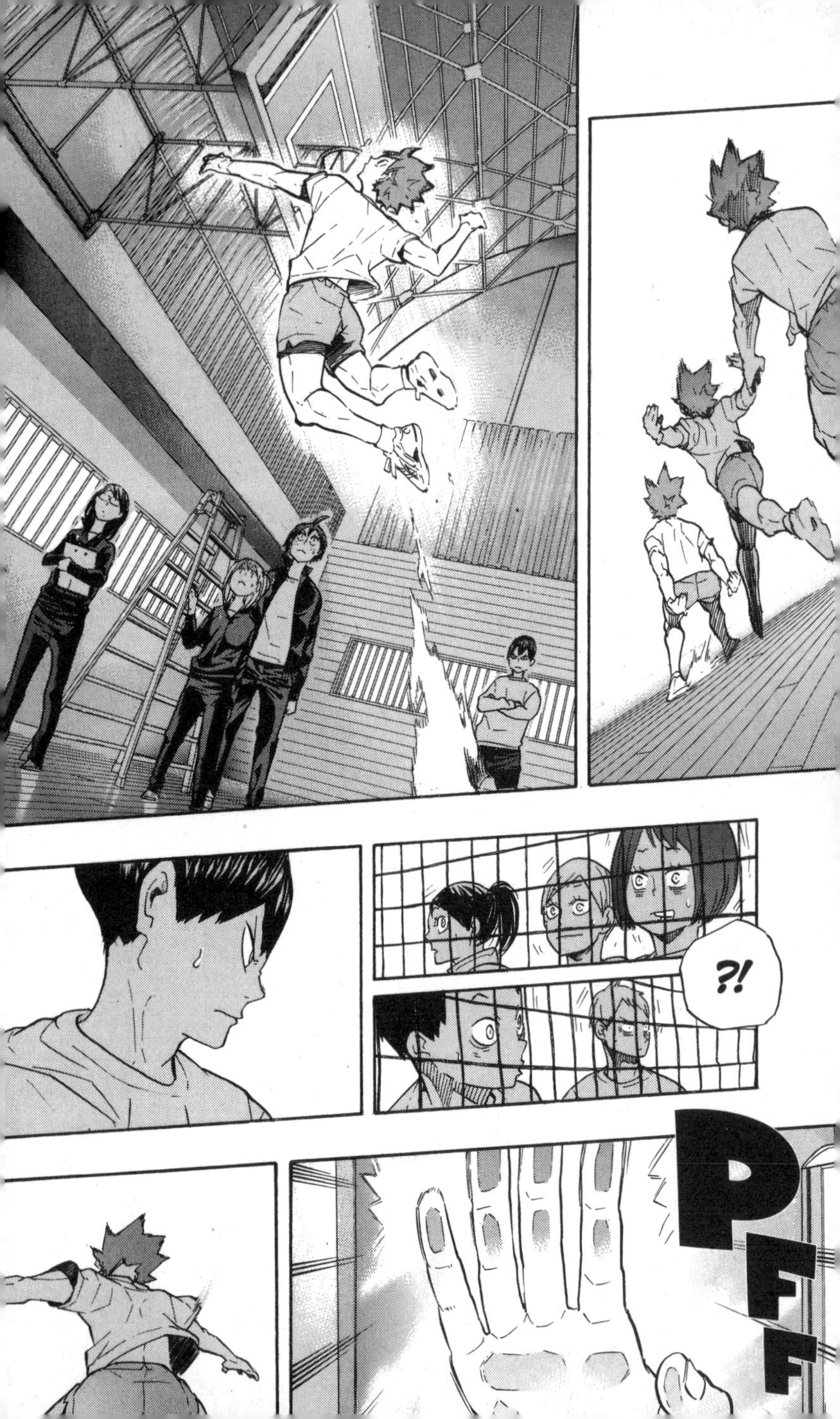
?!
PFF

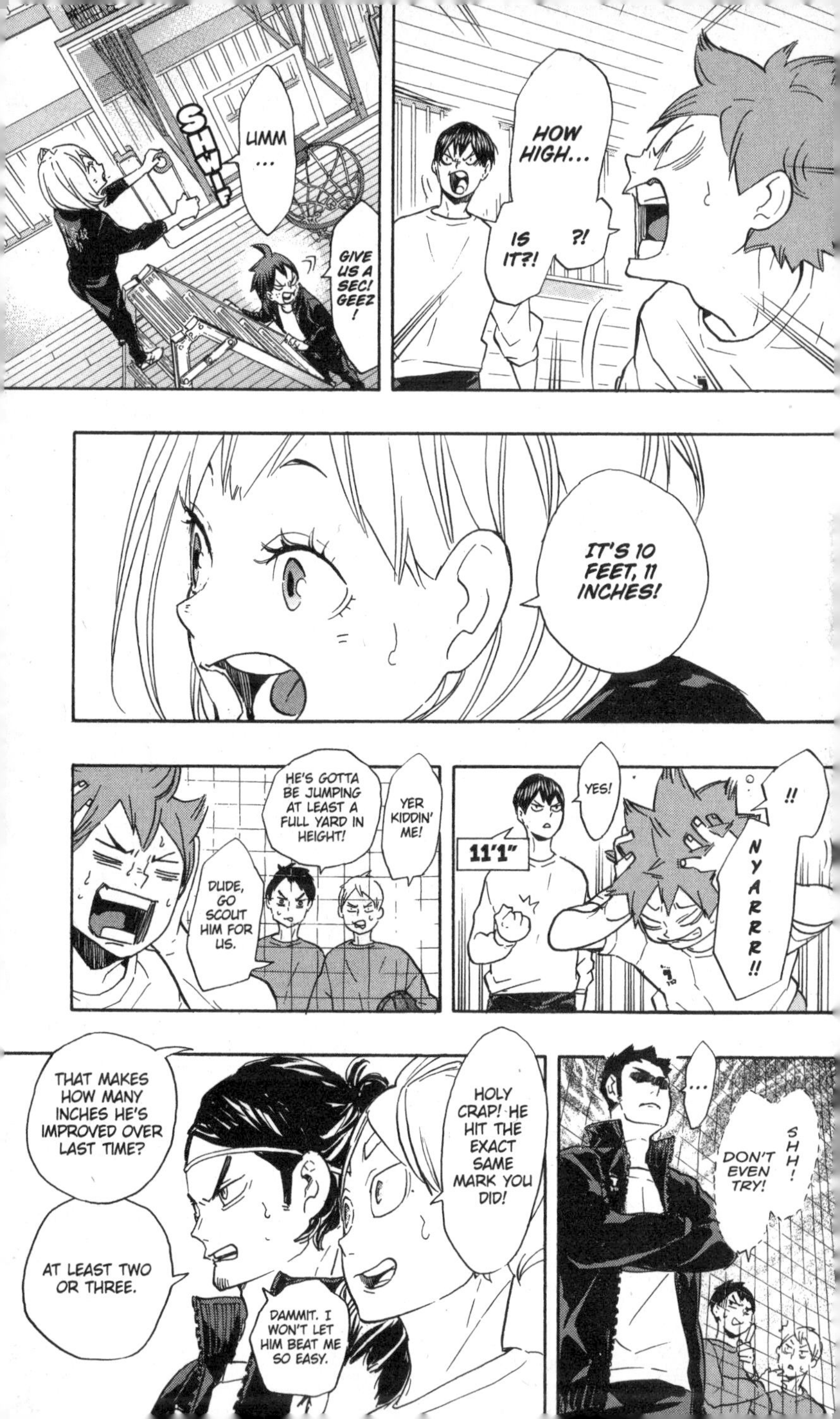
HOW HIGH... IS IT?!
?!
UMM ...
SHWIF
GIVE US A SEC! GEEZ!
IT'S 10 FEET, 11 INCHES!
!!
NYARRR!!
YES!
11'1"
YER KIDDIN' ME!
HE'S GOTTA BE JUMPING AT LEAST A FULL YARD IN HEIGHT!
DUDE, GO SCOUT HIM FOR US.
SHH!
DON'T EVEN TRY!
...
HOLY CRAP! HE HIT THE EXACT SAME MARK YOU DID!
THAT MAKES HOW MANY INCHES HE'S IMPROVED OVER LAST TIME?
AT LEAST TWO OR THREE.
DAMMIT. I WON'T LET HIM BEAT ME SO EASY.

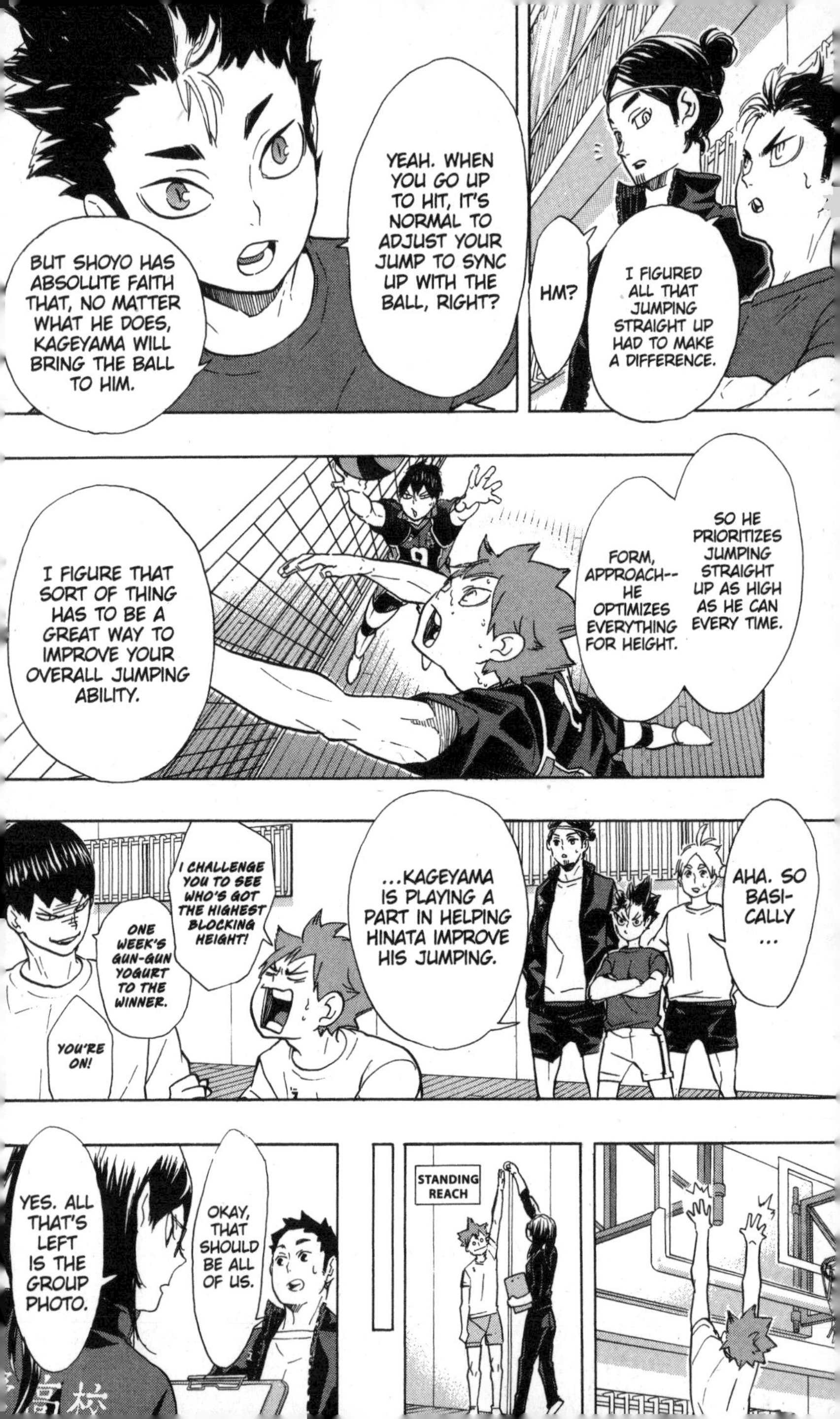
I FIGURED ALL THAT JUMPING STRAIGHT UP HAD TO MAKE A DIFFERENCE.
HM?
YEAH. WHEN YOU GO UP TO HIT, IT'S NORMAL TO ADJUST YOUR JUMP TO SYNC UP WITH THE BALL, RIGHT?
BUT SHOYO HAS ABSOLUTE FAITH THAT, NO MATTER WHAT HE DOES, KAGEYAMA WILL BRING THE BALL TO HIM.
SO HE PRIORITIZES JUMPING STRAIGHT UP AS HIGH AS HE CAN EVERY TIME.
FORM, APPROACH-- HE OPTIMIZES EVERYTHING FOR HEIGHT.
I FIGURE THAT SORT OF THING HAS TO BE A GREAT WAY TO IMPROVE YOUR OVERALL JUMPING ABILITY.
AHA. SO BASI-CALLY ...
...KAGEYAMA IS PLAYING A PART IN HELPING HINATA IMPROVE HIS JUMPING.
I CHALLENGE YOU TO SEE WHO'S GOT THE HIGHEST BLOCKING HEIGHT!
ONE WEEK'S GUN-GUN YOGURT TO THE WINNER.
YOU'RE ON!
STANDING REACH
OKAY, THAT SHOULD BE ALL OF US.
YES. ALL THAT'S LEFT IS THE GROUP PHOTO.

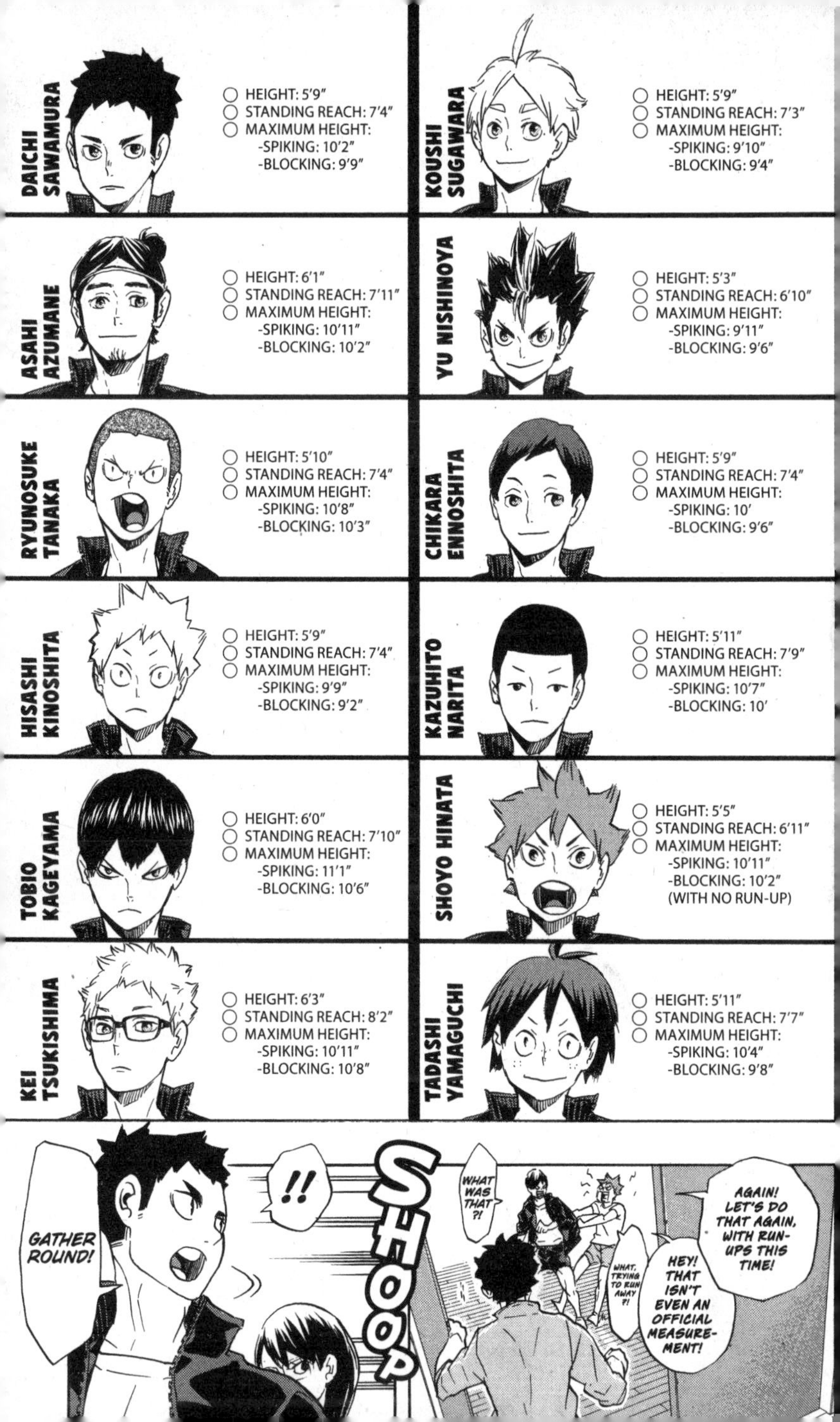
KOUSHI SUGAWARA
HEIGHT: 5'9"
STANDING REACH: 7'3"
MAXIMUM HEIGHT:
-SPIKING: 9'10"
-BLOCKING: 9'4"
DAICHI SAWAMURA
HEIGHT: 5'9"
STANDING REACH: 7'4"
MAXIMUM HEIGHT:
-SPIKING: 10'2"
-BLOCKING: 9'9"
YU NISHINOYA
HEIGHT: 5'3"
STANDING REACH: 6'10"
MAXIMUM HEIGHT:
-SPIKING: 9'11"
-BLOCKING: 9'6"
ASAHI AZUMANE
HEIGHT: 6'1"
STANDING REACH: 7'11"
MAXIMUM HEIGHT:
-SPIKING: 10'11"
-BLOCKING: 10'2"
CHIKARA ENNOSHITA
HEIGHT: 5'9"
STANDING REACH: 7'4"
MAXIMUM HEIGHT:
-SPIKING: 10'
-BLOCKING: 9'6"
RYUNOSUKE TANAKA
HEIGHT: 5'10"
STANDING REACH: 7'4"
MAXIMUM HEIGHT:
-SPIKING: 10'8"
-BLOCKING: 10'3"
KAZUHITO NARITA
HEIGHT: 5'11"
STANDING REACH: 7'9"
MAXIMUM HEIGHT:
-SPIKING: 10'7"
-BLOCKING: 10'
HISASHI KINOSHITA
HEIGHT: 5'9"
STANDING REACH: 7'4"
MAXIMUM HEIGHT:
-SPIKING: 9'9"
-BLOCKING: 9'2"
SHOYO HINATA
HEIGHT: 5'5"
STANDING REACH: 6'11"
MAXIMUM HEIGHT:
-SPIKING: 10'11"
-BLOCKING: 10'2"
(WITH NO RUN-UP)
TOBIO KAGEYAMA
HEIGHT: 6'0"
STANDING REACH: 7'10"
MAXIMUM HEIGHT:
-SPIKING: 11'1"
-BLOCKING: 10'6"
TADASHI YAMAGUCHI
HEIGHT: 5'11"
STANDING REACH: 7'7"
MAXIMUM HEIGHT:
-SPIKING: 10'4"
-BLOCKING: 9'8"
KEI TSUKISHIMA
HEIGHT: 6'3"
STANDING REACH: 8'2"
MAXIMUM HEIGHT:
-SPIKING: 10'11"
-BLOCKING: 10'8"
AGAIN! LET'S DO THAT AGAIN, WITH RUN-UPS THIS TIME!
HEY! THAT ISN'T EVEN AN OFFICIAL MEASUREMENT!
WHAT, TRYING TO RUN AWAY?!
WHAT WAS THAT?!
SHOOP
!!
GATHER ROUND!

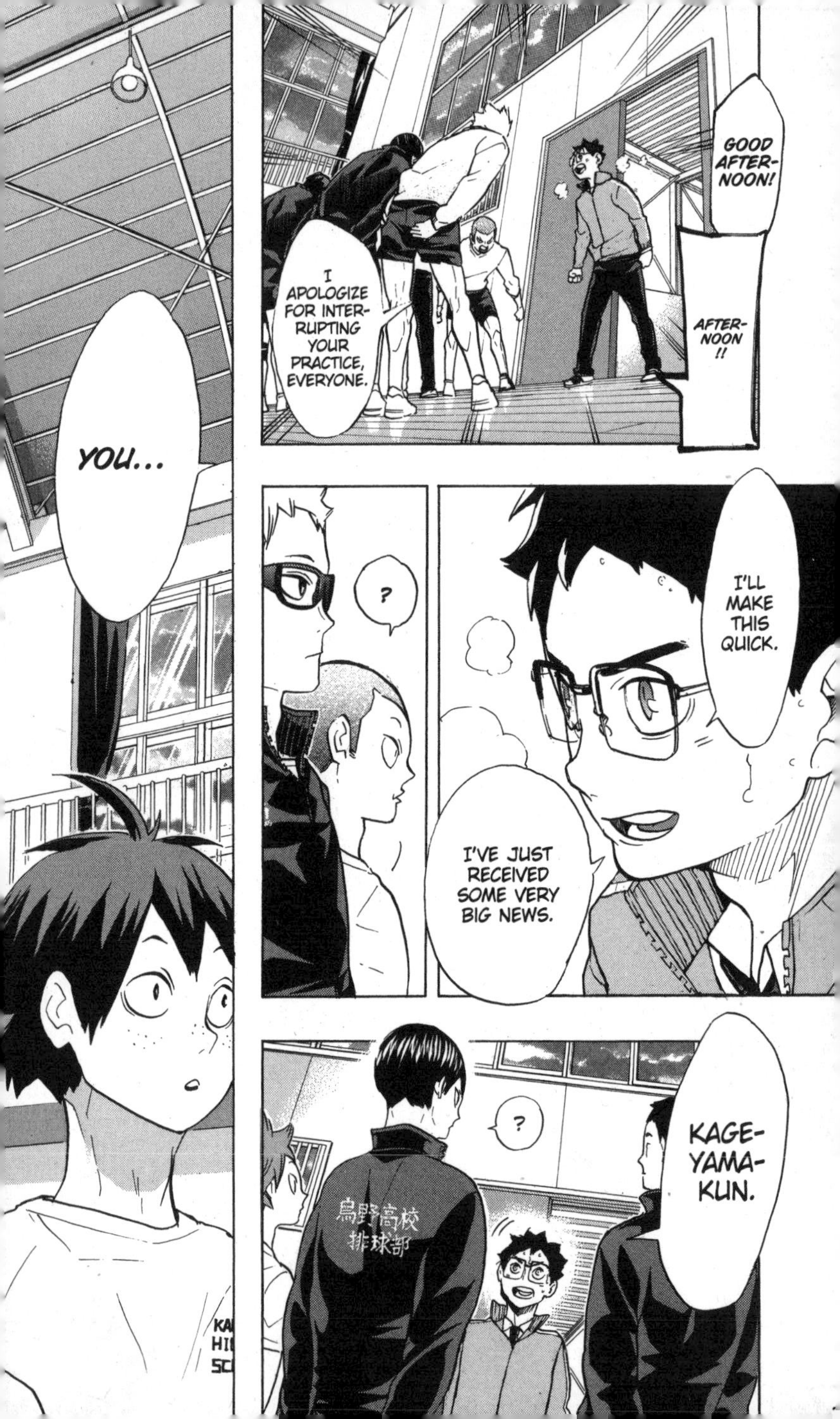
GOOD AFTER-NOON!
AFTER-NOON !!
I APOLOGIZE FOR INTER-RUPTING YOUR PRACTICE, EVERYONE.
I'LL MAKE THIS QUICK.
I'VE JUST RECEIVED SOME VERY BIG NEWS.
?
KAGE-YAMA-KUN.
?
烏野高校
排球部
YOU...

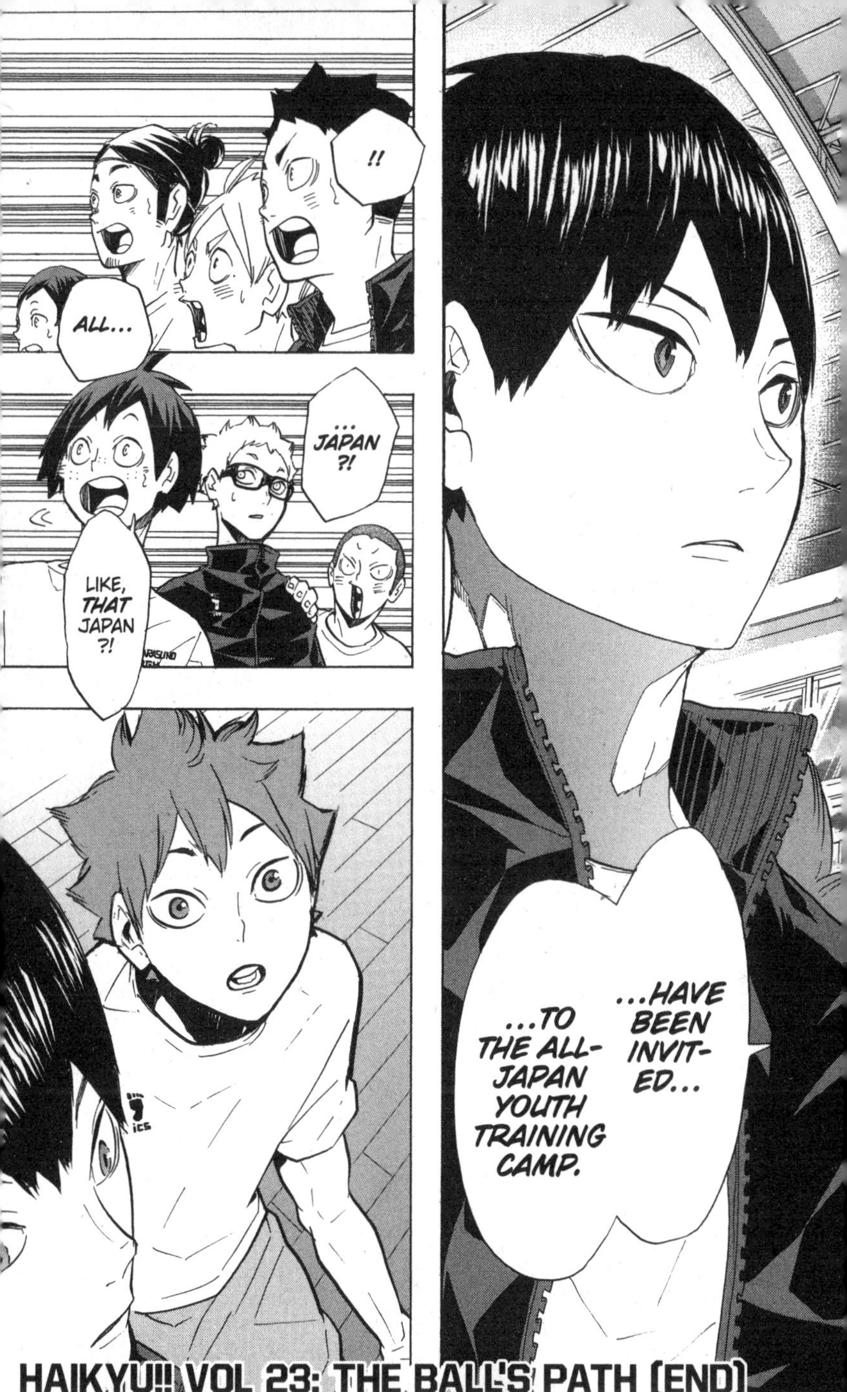
...HAVE BEEN INVIT-ED...
...TO THE ALL-JAPAN YOUTH TRAINING CAMP.
!!
ALL...
...JAPAN?!
LIKE, THAT JAPAN?!

HAIKYU!! VOL 23: THE BALL'S PATH (END)

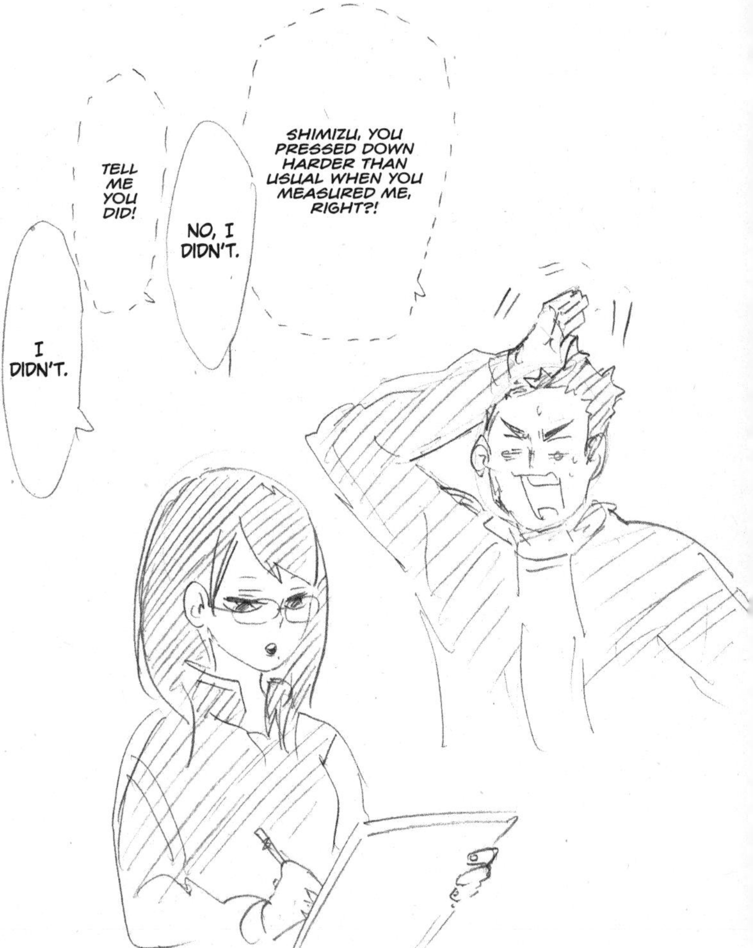
SHIMIZU, YOU PRESSED DOWN HARDER THAN USUAL WHEN YOU MEASURED ME, RIGHT?!
NO, I DIDN'T.
TELL ME YOU DID!
I DIDN'T.

IN THIS VOLUME, WE HAVE NOT ONE, BUT ***TWO*** BONUS STORIES AHEAD! ONE IS A LITTLE TEAM INTRODUCTION THING I DID WAY BACK WHEN FOR *JUMP SQ* THAT I FIGURED I SHOULD INCLUDE IN A VOLUME AT SOME POINT. THE OTHER IS A SPORTS FESTIVAL SIDE STORY I DID FOR *WEEKLY SHONEN JUMP* WHILE I WAS WORKING ON THE TOKYO QUALIFIERS PART OF THE MAIN STORY LINE. IT'D BEEN A WHILE SINCE I'D LAST DRAWN THE KARASUNO TEAM, SO I REMEMBER HAVING A WHOLE LOT OF FUN DOING IT.

ENJOY!!

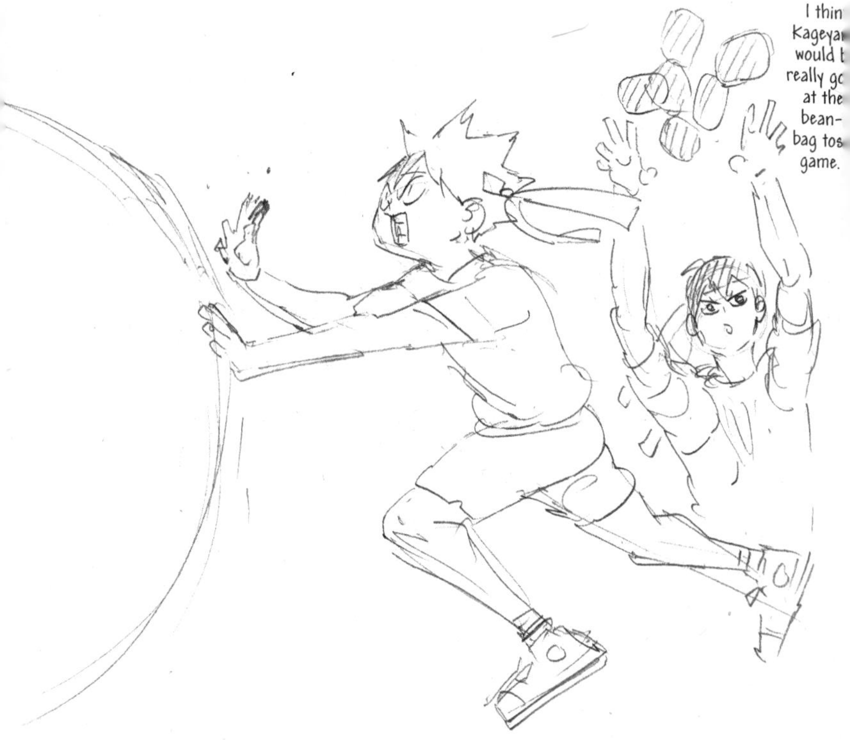

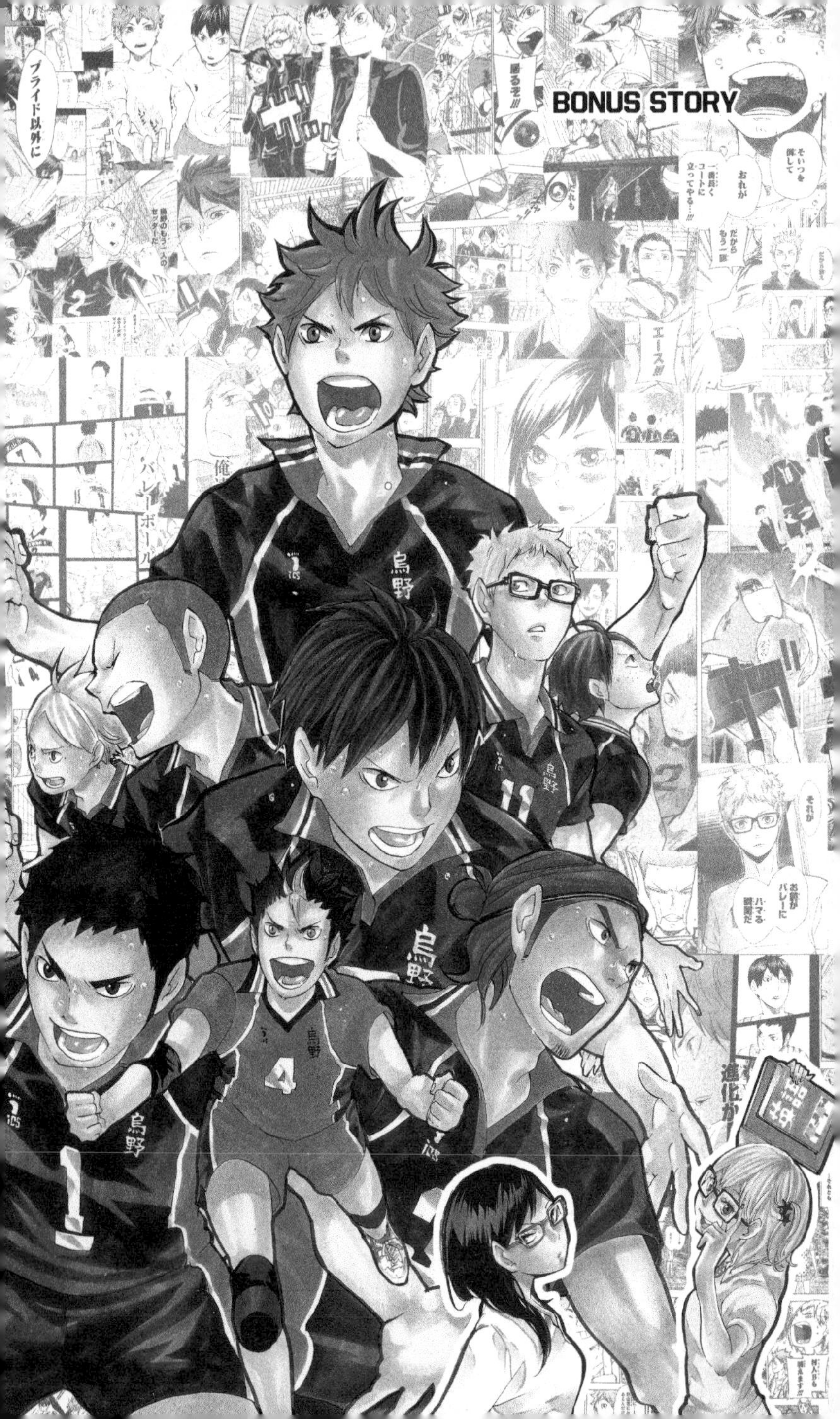
BONUS STORY
プライド以外に
エース!!

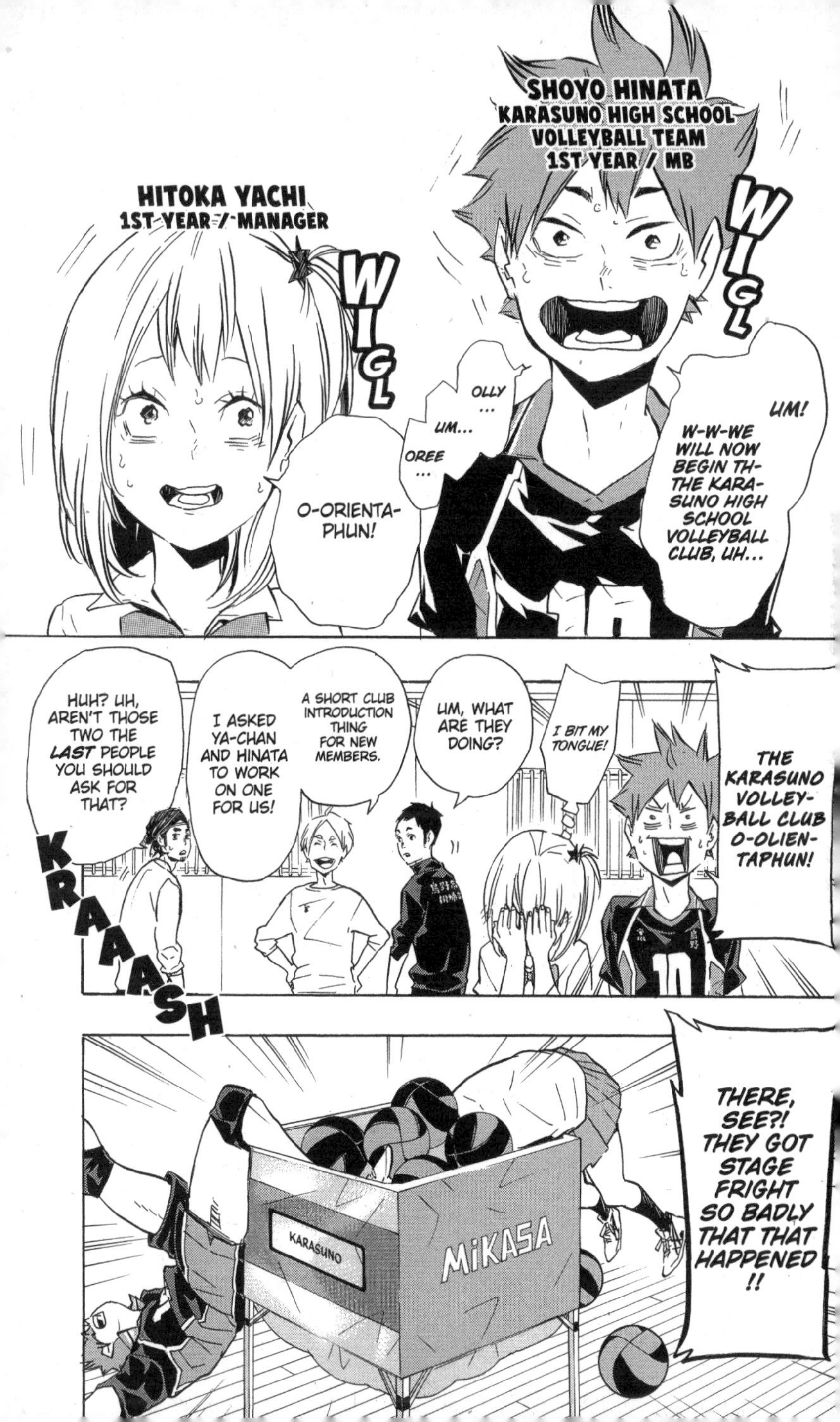
SHOYO HINATA
KARASUNO HIGH SCHOOL VOLLEYBALL TEAM
1ST YEAR / MB
WIGL
UM!
W-W-WE WILL NOW BEGIN TH- THE KARA-SUNO HIGH SCHOOL VOLLEYBALL CLUB, UH...
OLLY...
UM...
OREE...
HITOKA YACHI
1ST YEAR / MANAGER
WIGL
O-ORIENTA-PHUN!
THE KARASUNO VOLLEY-BALL CLUB O-OLIEN-TAPHUN!
I BIT MY TONGUE!
UM, WHAT ARE THEY DOING?
A SHORT CLUB INTRODUCTION THING FOR NEW MEMBERS.
I ASKED YA-CHAN AND HINATA TO WORK ON ONE FOR US!
HUH? UH, AREN'T THOSE TWO THE LAST PEOPLE YOU SHOULD ASK FOR THAT?
KRAAAASH
THERE, SEE?! THEY GOT STAGE FRIGHT SO BADLY THAT THAT HAPPENED!!
KARASUNO
MIKASA

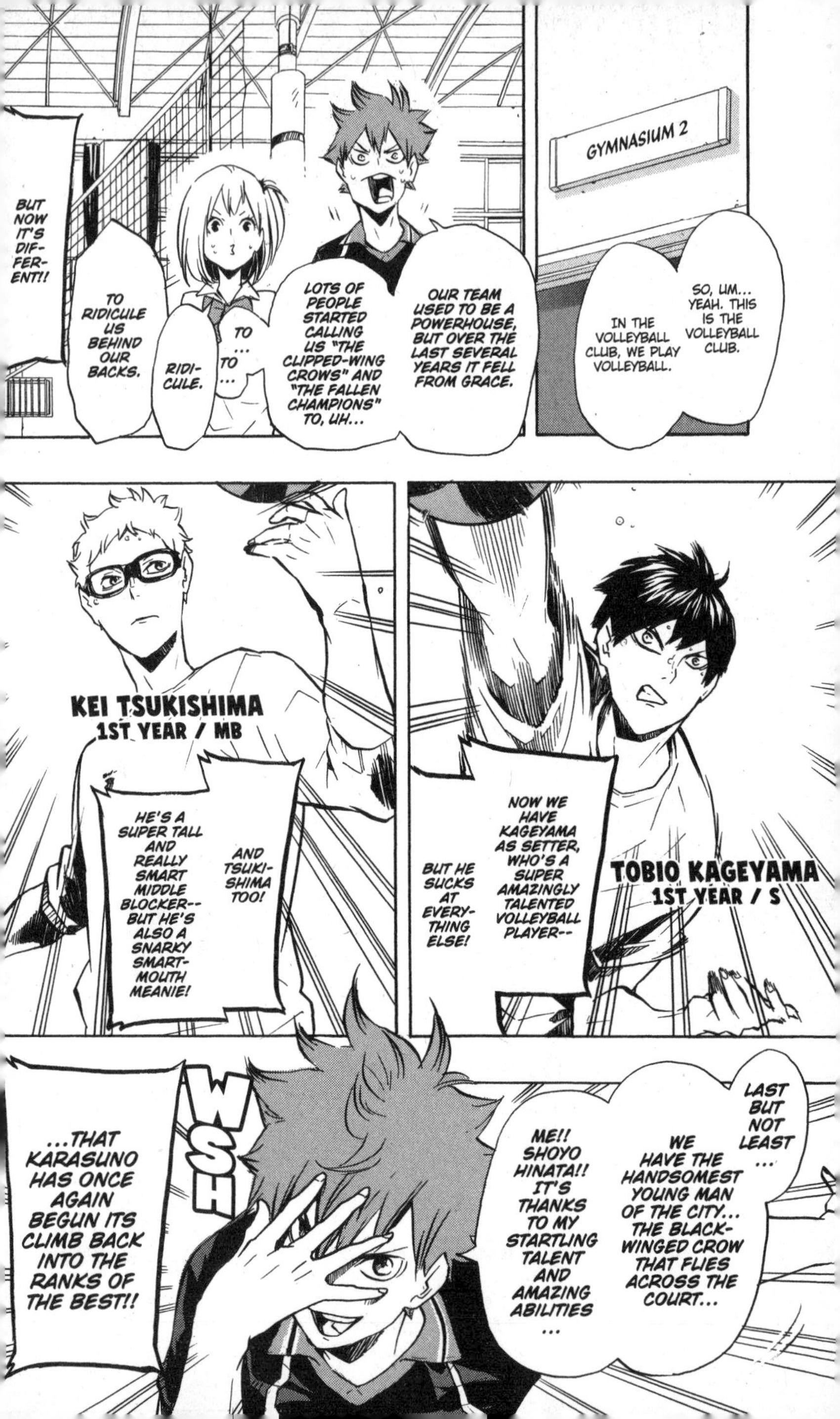
GYMNASIUM 2
SO, UM... YEAH. THIS IS THE VOLLEYBALL CLUB.
IN THE VOLLEYBALL CLUB, WE PLAY VOLLEYBALL.
OUR TEAM USED TO BE A POWERHOUSE, BUT OVER THE LAST SEVERAL YEARS IT FELL FROM GRACE.
LOTS OF PEOPLE STARTED CALLING US "THE CLIPPED-WING CROWS" AND "THE FALLEN CHAMPIONS" TO, UH...
TO... TO...
RIDICULE.
TO RIDICULE US BEHIND OUR BACKS.
BUT NOW IT'S DIFFERENT!!
TOBIO KAGEYAMA
1ST YEAR / S
NOW WE HAVE KAGEYAMA AS SETTER, WHO'S A SUPER AMAZINGLY TALENTED VOLLEYBALL PLAYER--
BUT HE SUCKS AT EVERYTHING ELSE!
KEI TSUKISHIMA
1ST YEAR / MB
AND TSUKISHIMA TOO!
HE'S A SUPER TALL AND REALLY SMART MIDDLE BLOCKER--BUT HE'S ALSO A SNARKY SMART-MOUTH MEANIE!
LAST BUT NOT LEAST...
WE HAVE THE HANDSOMEST YOUNG MAN OF THE CITY... THE BLACK-WINGED CROW THAT FLIES ACROSS THE COURT...
ME!! SHOYO HINATA!! IT'S THANKS TO MY STARTLING TALENT AND AMAZING ABILITIES...
WSH
...THAT KARASUNO HAS ONCE AGAIN BEGUN ITS CLIMB BACK INTO THE RANKS OF THE BEST!!

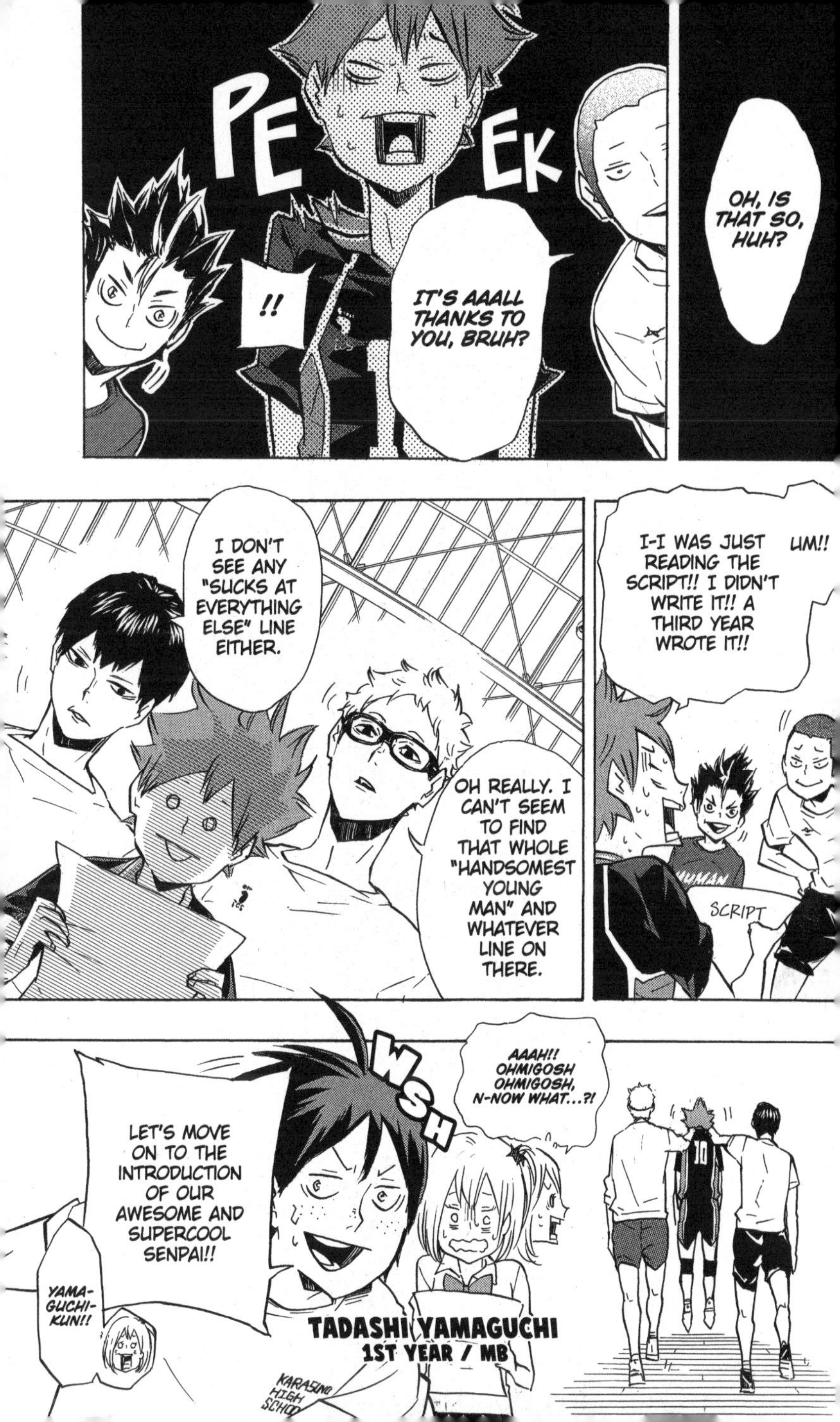
OH, IS THAT SO, HUH?
PEEK
IT'S AAALL THANKS TO YOU, BRUH?
!!
UM!!
I-I WAS JUST READING THE SCRIPT!! I DIDN'T WRITE IT!! A THIRD YEAR WROTE IT!!
SCRIPT
OH REALLY. I CAN'T SEEM TO FIND THAT WHOLE "HANDSOMEST YOUNG MAN" AND WHATEVER LINE ON THERE.
I DON'T SEE ANY "SUCKS AT EVERYTHING ELSE" LINE EITHER.
AAAH!! OHMIGOSH OHMIGOSH, N-NOW WHAT...?!
WSH
LET'S MOVE ON TO THE INTRODUCTION OF OUR AWESOME AND SUPERCOOL SENPAI!!
YAMA-GUCHI-KUN!!
TADASHI YAMAGUCHI
1ST YEAR / MB
KARASUNO HIGH SCHO

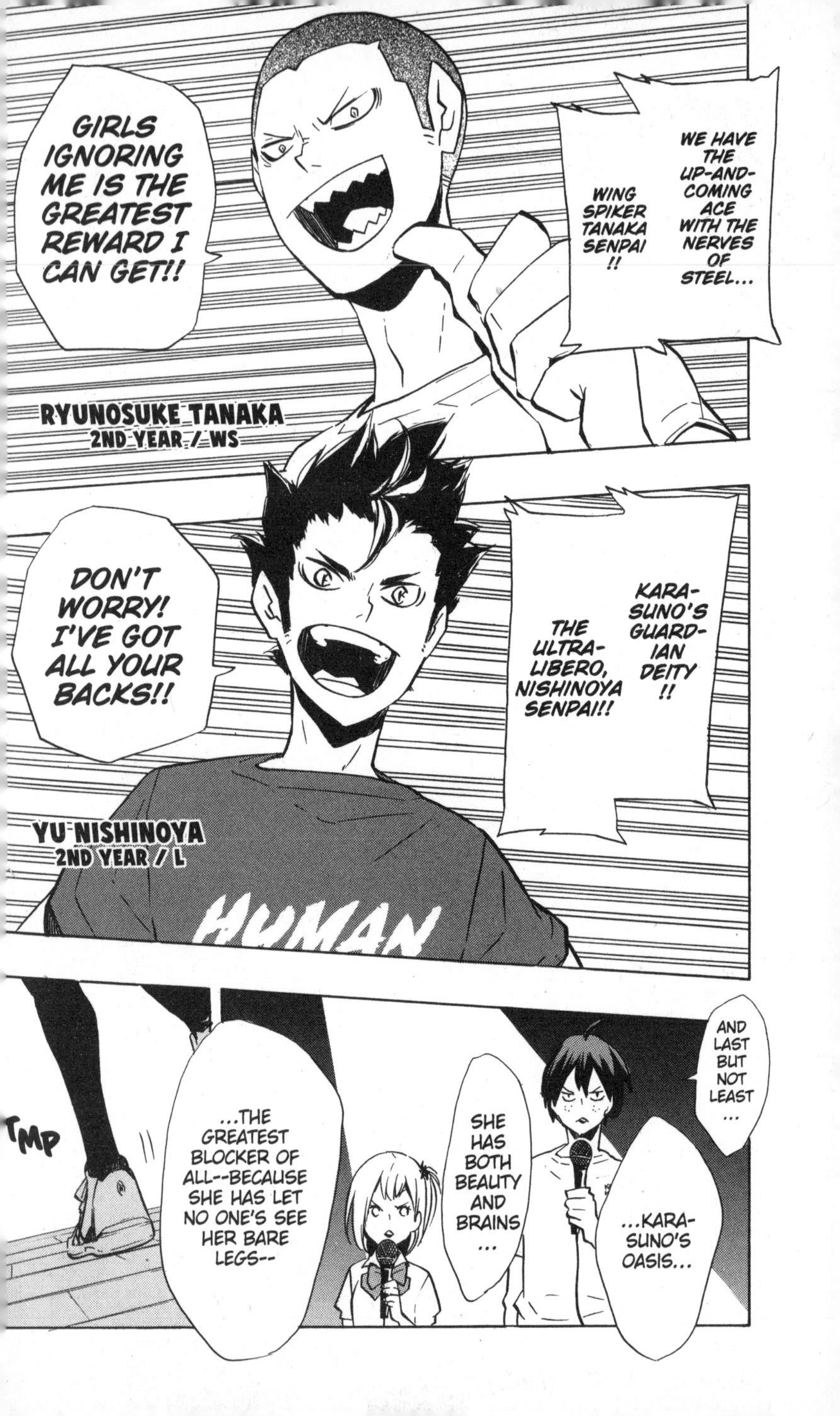
WE HAVE THE UP-AND-COMING ACE WITH THE NERVES OF STEEL...
WING SPIKER TANAKA SENPAI!!
GIRLS IGNORING ME IS THE GREATEST REWARD I CAN GET!!
RYUNOSUKE TANAKA 2ND YEAR / WS
KARA-SUNO'S GUARD-IAN DEITY!!
THE ULTRA-LIBERO, NISHINOYA SENPAI!!
DON'T WORRY! I'VE GOT ALL YOUR BACKS!!
YU NISHINOYA 2ND YEAR / L
HUMAN
AND LAST BUT NOT LEAST...
...KARA-SUNO'S OASIS...
SHE HAS BOTH BEAUTY AND BRAINS...
...THE GREATEST BLOCKER OF ALL--BECAUSE SHE HAS LET NO ONE'S SEE HER BARE LEGS--
TMP

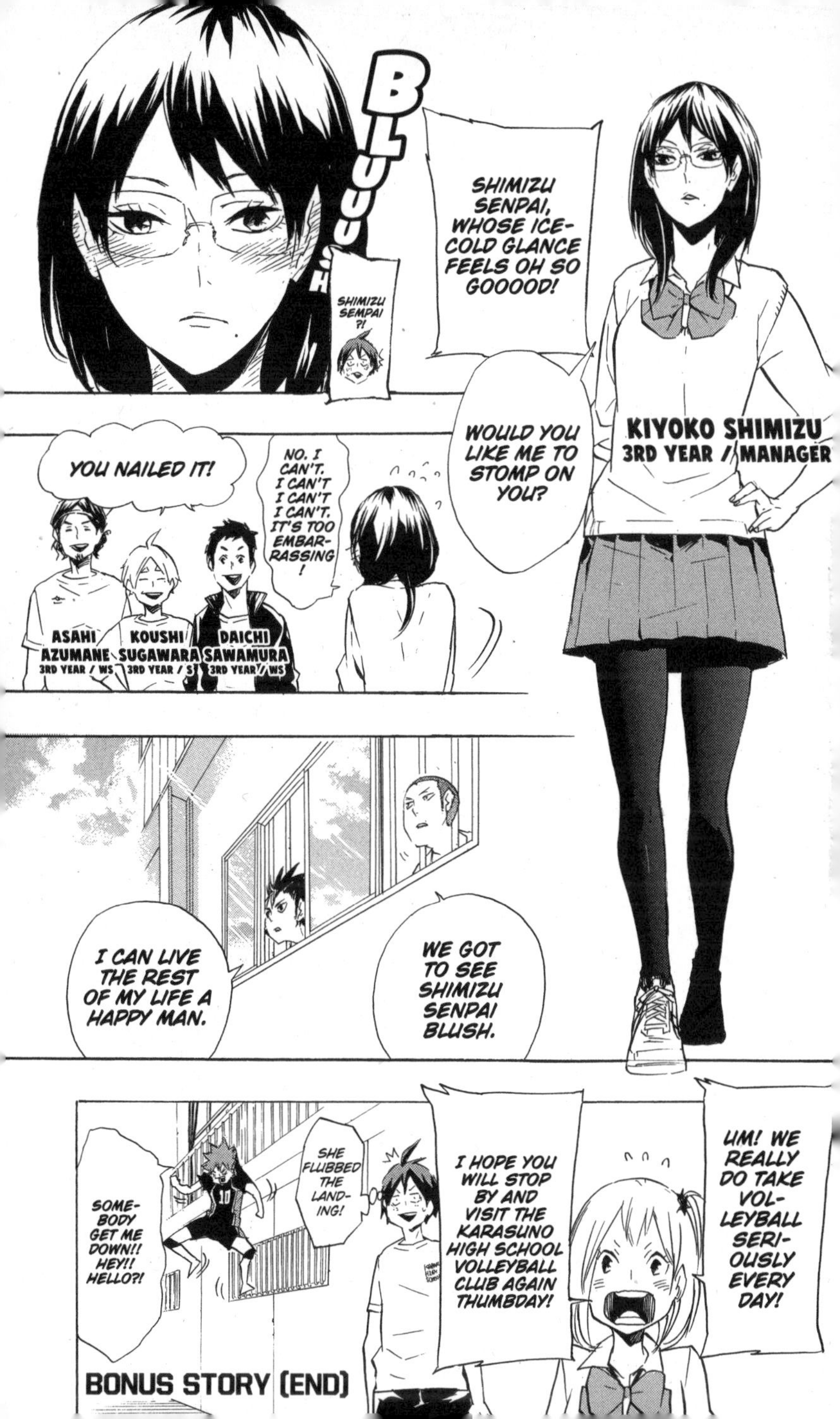
SHIMIZU SENPAI, WHOSE ICE-COLD GLANCE FEELS OH SO GOOOOD!
WOULD YOU LIKE ME TO STOMP ON YOU?
KIYOKO SHIMIZU
3RD YEAR / MANAGER
BLUUUSH
SHIMIZU SEMPAI ?!
NO. I CAN'T. I CAN'T I CAN'T. IT'S TOO EMBARRASSING!
YOU NAILED IT!
DAICHI SAWAMURA 3RD YEAR / WS
KOUSHI SUGAWARA 3RD YEAR / S
ASAHI AZUMANE 3RD YEAR / WS
WE GOT TO SEE SHIMIZU SENPAI BLUSH.
I CAN LIVE THE REST OF MY LIFE A HAPPY MAN.
UM! WE REALLY DO TAKE VOLLEYBALL SERIOUSLY EVERY DAY!
I HOPE YOU WILL STOP BY AND VISIT THE KARASUNO HIGH SCHOOL VOLLEYBALL CLUB AGAIN THUMBDAY!
SHE FLUBBED THE LANDING!
SOMEBODY GET ME DOWN!! HEY!! HELLO?!
BONUS STORY (END)

HAIKYU!!

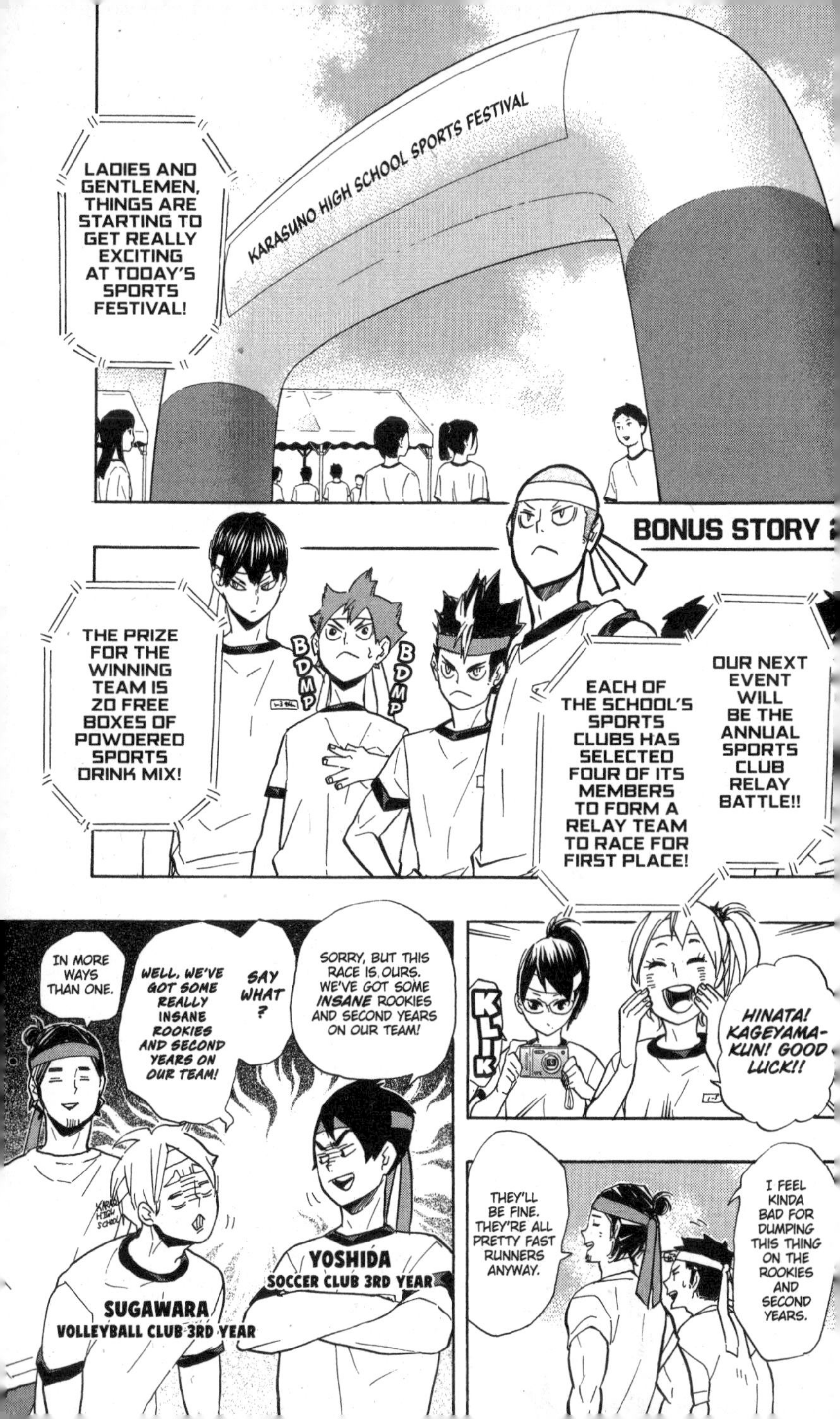
KARASUNO HIGH SCHOOL SPORTS FESTIVAL
LADIES AND GENTLEMEN, THINGS ARE STARTING TO GET REALLY EXCITING AT TODAY'S SPORTS FESTIVAL!
BONUS STORY 2
OUR NEXT EVENT WILL BE THE ANNUAL SPORTS CLUB RELAY BATTLE!!
EACH OF THE SCHOOL'S SPORTS CLUBS HAS SELECTED FOUR OF ITS MEMBERS TO FORM A RELAY TEAM TO RACE FOR FIRST PLACE!
BDMP
BDMP
THE PRIZE FOR THE WINNING TEAM IS 20 FREE BOXES OF POWDERED SPORTS DRINK MIX!
HINATA! KAGEYAMA-KUN! GOOD LUCK!!
KLIK
I FEEL KINDA BAD FOR DUMPING THIS THING ON THE ROOKIES AND SECOND YEARS.
THEY'LL BE FINE. THEY'RE ALL PRETTY FAST RUNNERS ANYWAY.
SORRY, BUT THIS RACE IS OURS. WE'VE GOT SOME INSANE ROOKIES AND SECOND YEARS ON OUR TEAM!
SAY WHAT?
WELL, WE'VE GOT SOME REALLY INSANE ROOKIES AND SECOND YEARS ON OUR TEAM!
IN MORE WAYS THAN ONE.
YOSHIDA
SOCCER CLUB 3RD YEAR
SUGAWARA
VOLLEYBALL CLUB 3RD YEAR

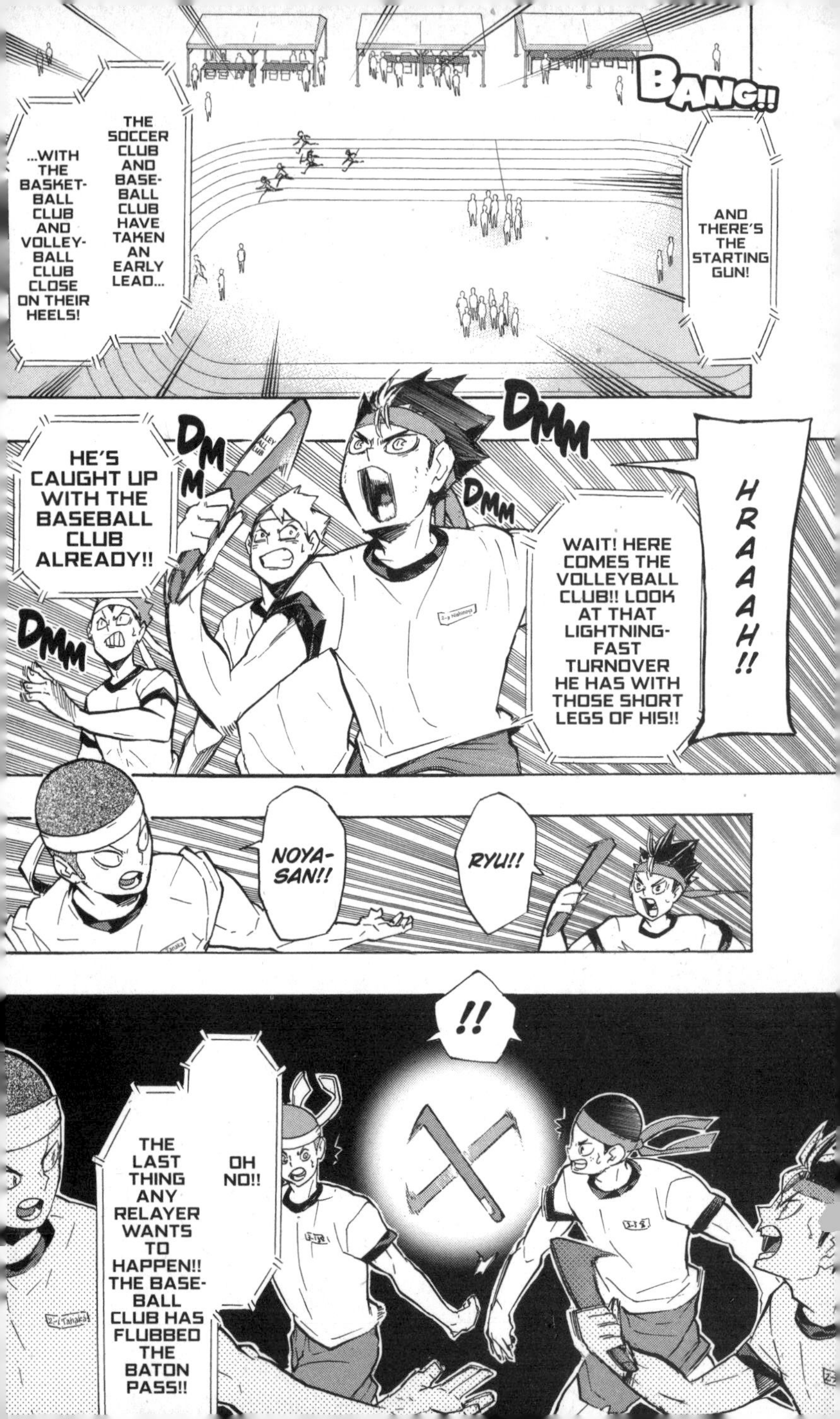
BANG!!
AND THERE'S THE STARTING GUN!
THE SOCCER CLUB AND BASEBALL CLUB HAVE TAKEN AN EARLY LEAD...
...WITH THE BASKETBALL CLUB AND VOLLEYBALL CLUB CLOSE ON THEIR HEELS!
HRAAAAH!!
DMM
WAIT! HERE COMES THE VOLLEYBALL CLUB!! LOOK AT THAT LIGHTNING-FAST TURNOVER HE HAS WITH THOSE SHORT LEGS OF HIS!!
DMM
DMM M
HE'S CAUGHT UP WITH THE BASEBALL CLUB ALREADY!!
DMM
RYU!!
NOYA-SAN!!
!!
OH NO!!
THE LAST THING ANY RELAYER WANTS TO HAPPEN!! THE BASEBALL CLUB HAS FLUBBED THE BATON PASS!!

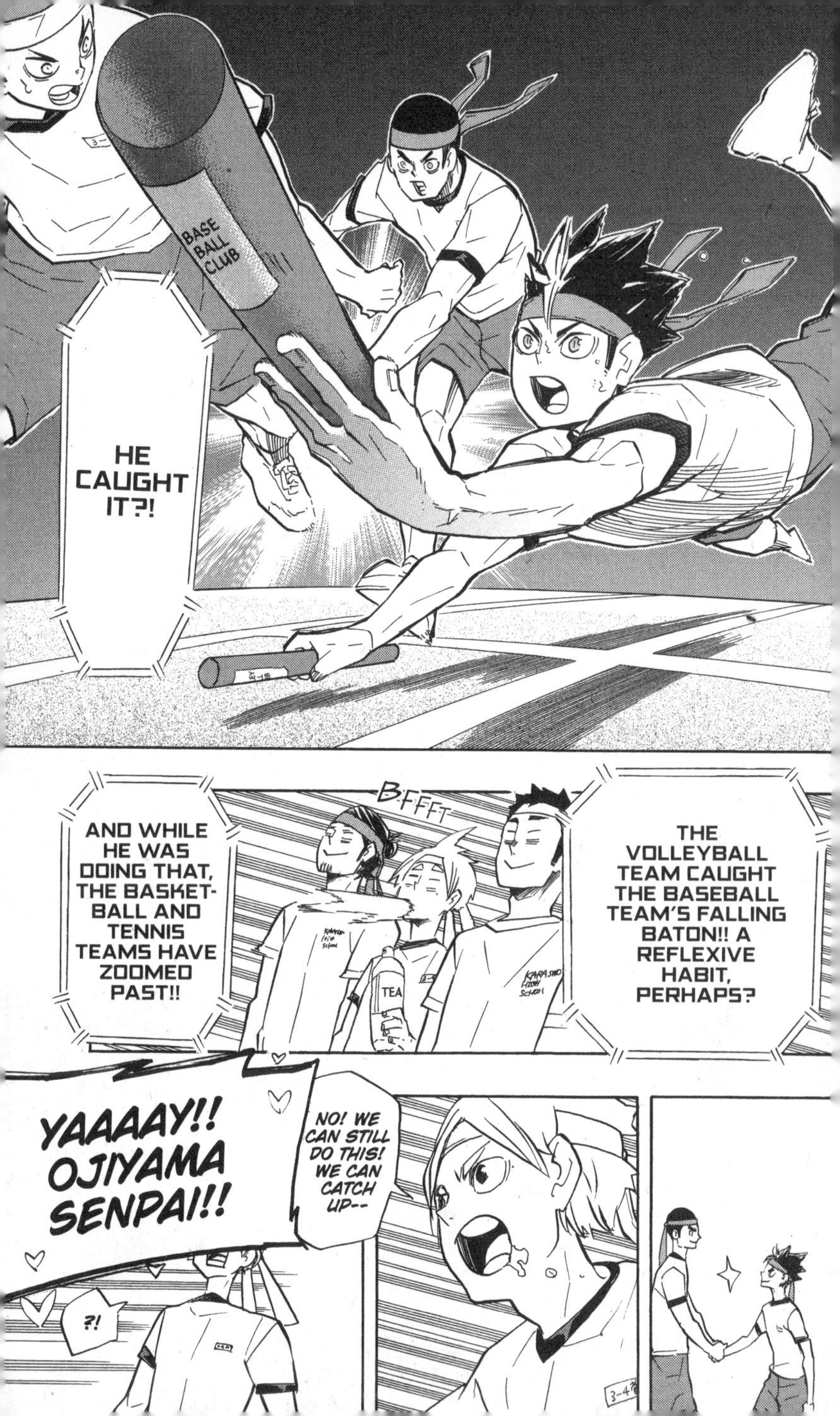
BASE BALL CLUB
HE CAUGHT IT?!
THE VOLLEYBALL TEAM CAUGHT THE BASEBALL TEAM'S FALLING BATON!! A REFLEXIVE HABIT, PERHAPS?
BFFFT
AND WHILE HE WAS DOING THAT, THE BASKET-BALL AND TENNIS TEAMS HAVE ZOOMED PAST!!
TEA
NO! WE CAN STILL DO THIS! WE CAN CATCH UP--
YAAAAY!! OJIYAMA SENPAI!!
?!

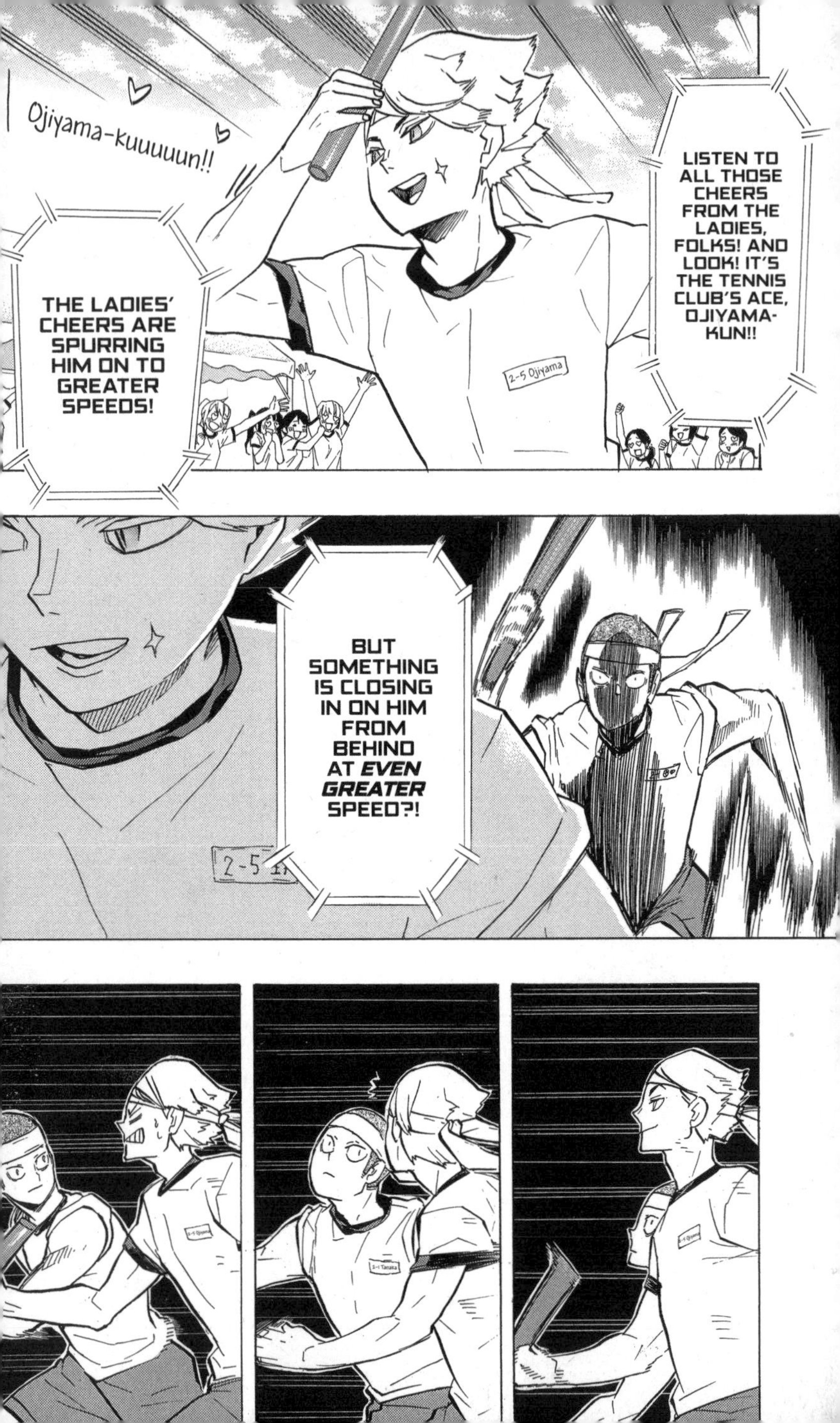
LISTEN TO ALL THOSE CHEERS FROM THE LADIES, FOLKS! AND LOOK! IT'S THE TENNIS CLUB'S ACE, OJIYAMA-KUN!!
2-5 Ojiyama
Ojiyama-kuuuuun!!
THE LADIES' CHEERS ARE SPURRING HIM ON TO GREATER SPEEDS!
BUT SOMETHING IS CLOSING IN ON HIM FROM BEHIND AT *EVEN GREATER* SPEED?!

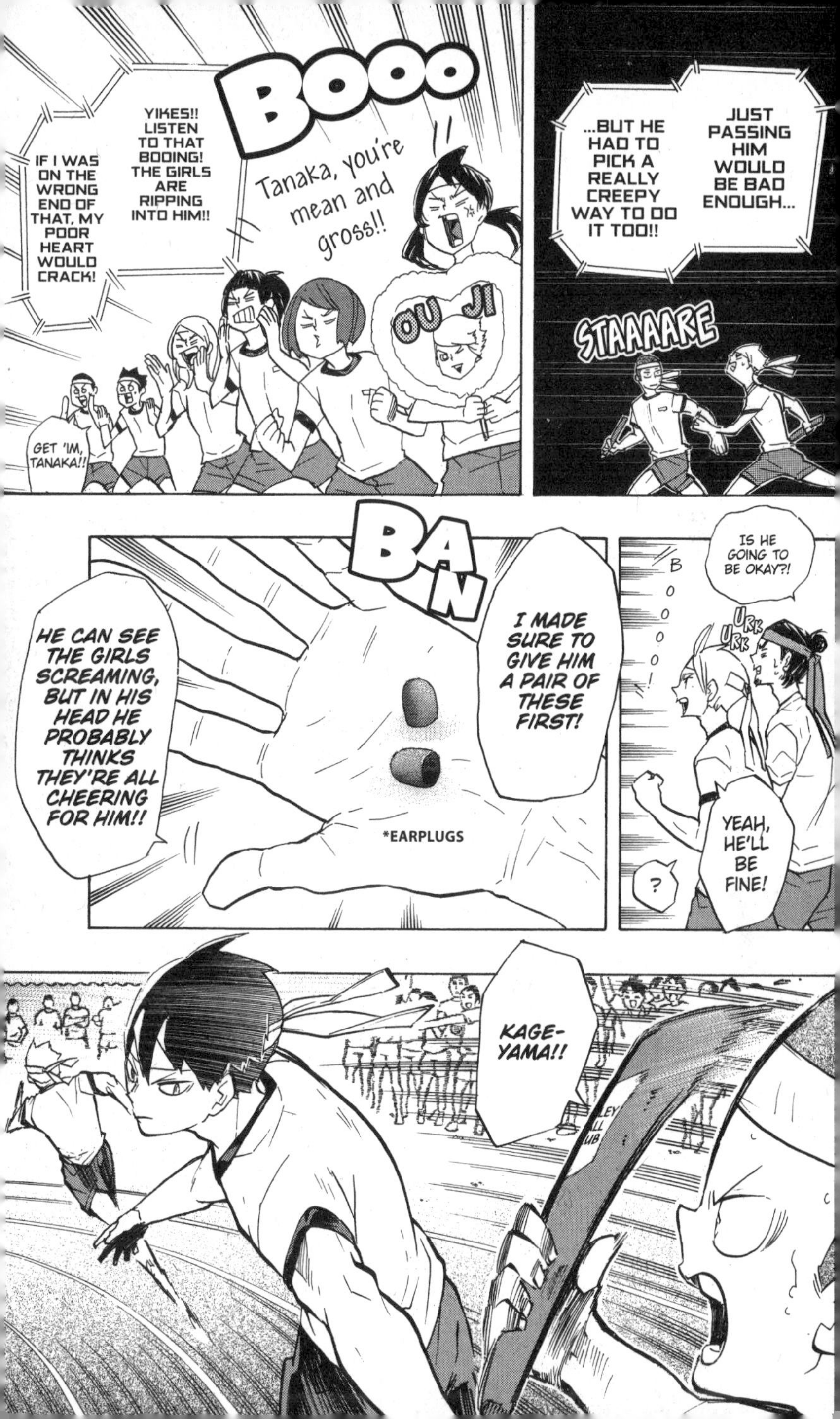
JUST PASSING HIM WOULD BE BAD ENOUGH...
...BUT HE HAD TO PICK A REALLY CREEPY WAY TO DO IT TOO!!
STAAAARE
BOOO
Tanaka, you're mean and gross!!
OU JI
YIKES!! LISTEN TO THAT BOOING! THE GIRLS ARE RIPPING INTO HIM!!
IF I WAS ON THE WRONG END OF THAT, MY POOR HEART WOULD CRACK!
GET 'IM, TANAKA!!
IS HE GOING TO BE OKAY?!
BOOOOO!
URK URK
?
YEAH, HE'LL BE FINE!
BAN
I MADE SURE TO GIVE HIM A PAIR OF THESE FIRST!
HE CAN SEE THE GIRLS SCREAMING, BUT IN HIS HEAD HE PROBABLY THINKS THEY'RE ALL CHEERING FOR HIM!!
*EARPLUGS
KAGE-YAMA!!

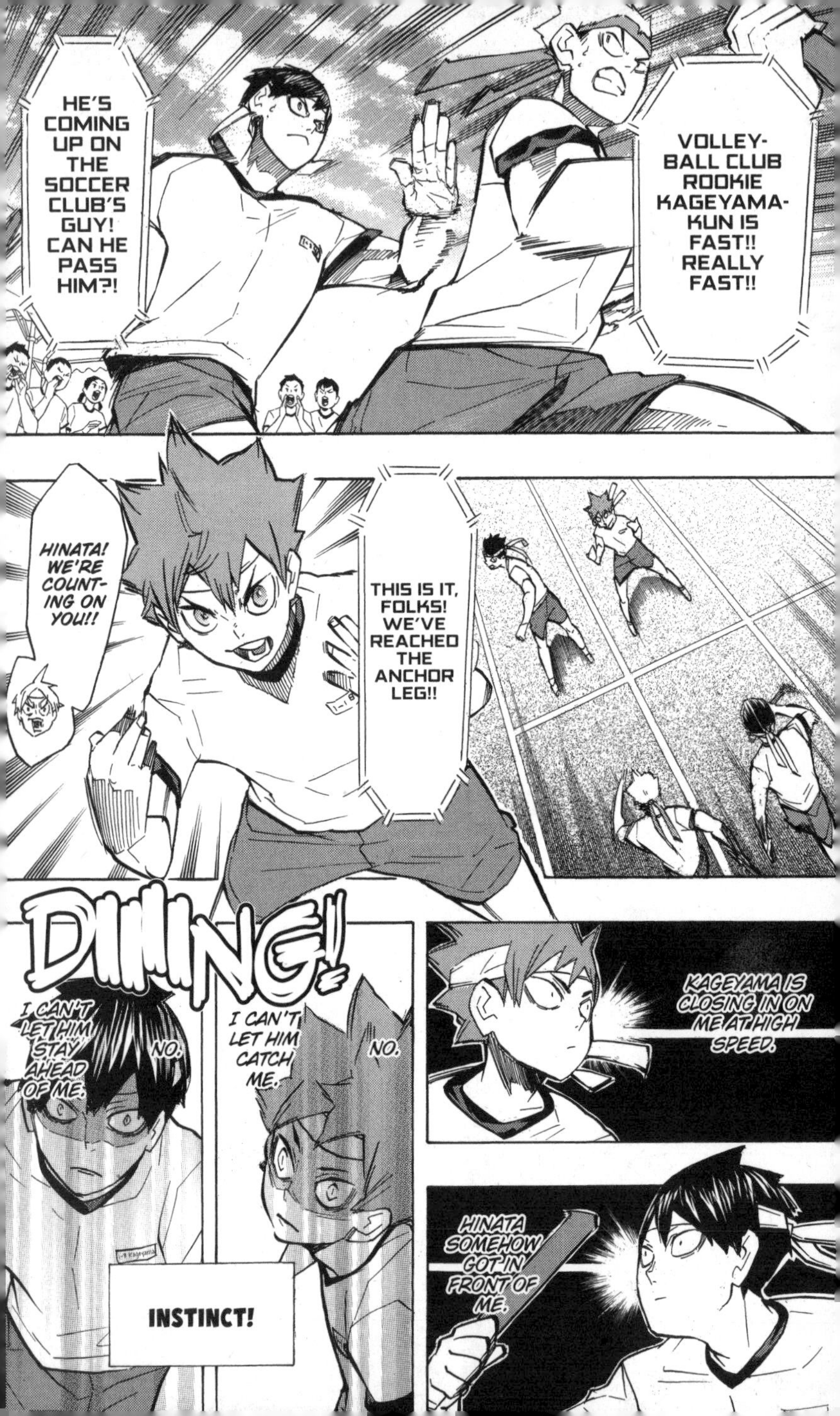
VOLLEY-BALL CLUB ROOKIE KAGEYAMA-KUN IS FAST!! REALLY FAST!!
HE'S COMING UP ON THE SOCCER CLUB'S GUY! CAN HE PASS HIM?!
THIS IS IT, FOLKS! WE'VE REACHED THE ANCHOR LEG!!
HINATA! WE'RE COUNTING ON YOU!!
KAGEYAMA IS CLOSING IN ON ME AT HIGH SPEED.
HINATA SOMEHOW GOT IN FRONT OF ME.
DIIING!
NO.
I CAN'T LET HIM CATCH ME.
NO.
I CAN'T LET HIM STAY AHEAD OF ME.
INSTINCT!

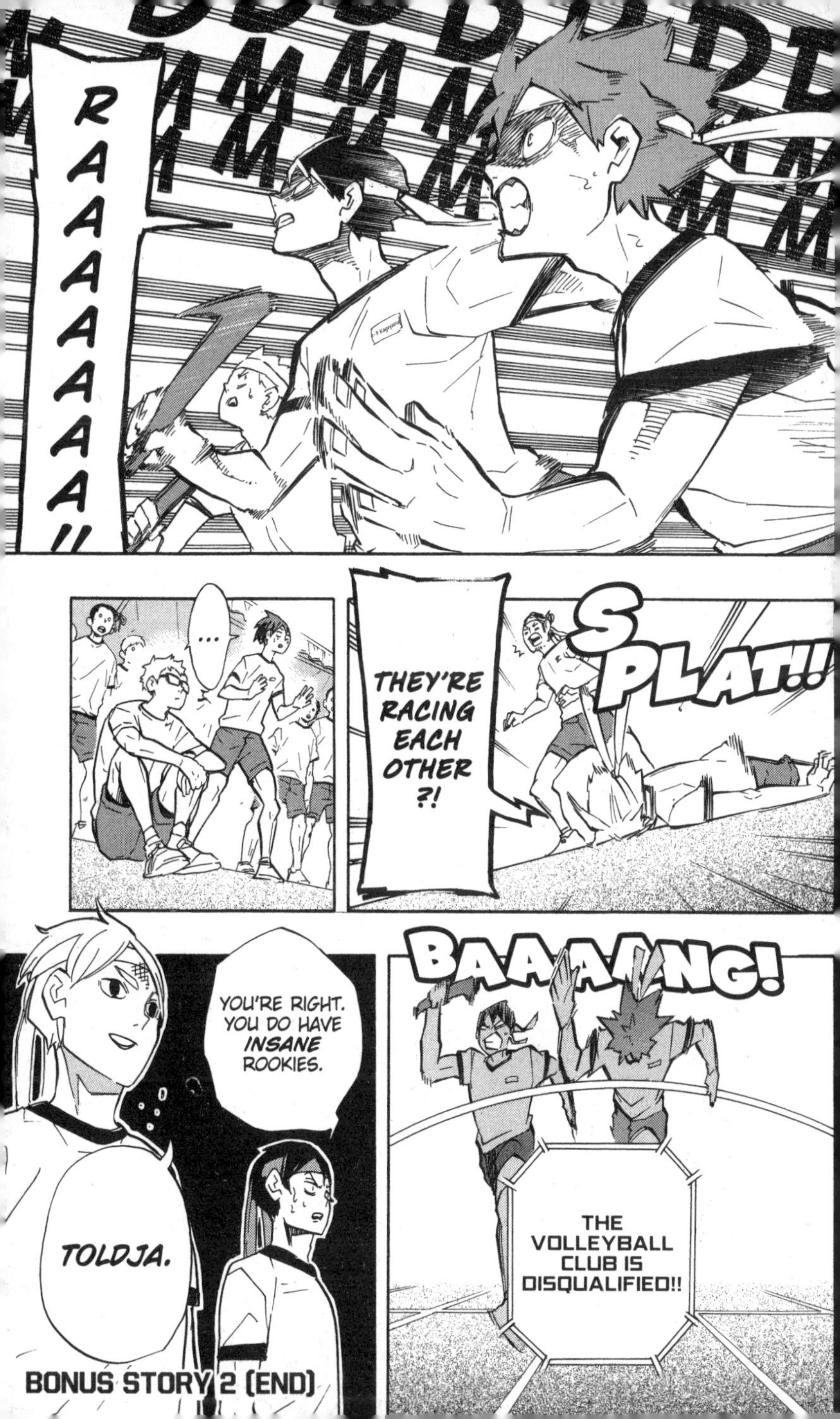
RAAAAAAAA!!
SPLAT!!
THEY'RE RACING EACH OTHER?!
...
BAAAANG!
THE VOLLEYBALL CLUB IS DISQUALIFIED!!
YOU'RE RIGHT. YOU DO HAVE *INSANE* ROOKIES.
TOLDJA.

BONUS STORY 2 (END)

EDITOR'S NOTES

The English edition of Haikyu!! maintains the honorifics used in the original Japanese version. For those of you who are new to these terms, here's a brief explanation to help with your reading experience!

When saying someone's name in Japanese, a suffix is often attached to indicate how familiar the speaker is with the person. Some are more polite and respectful, while others are endearing.

1 *-kun* is often used for young men or boys, usually someone you are familiar with.

2 *-chan* is used for young children and can be used as a term of endearment.

3 *-san* is used for someone you respect or are not close to, or to be polite.

4 *Senpai* is used for someone who is older than you or in a higher position or grade in school.

5 *Kohai* is used for someone who is younger than you or in a lower position or grade in school.

6 *Sensei* means teacher.

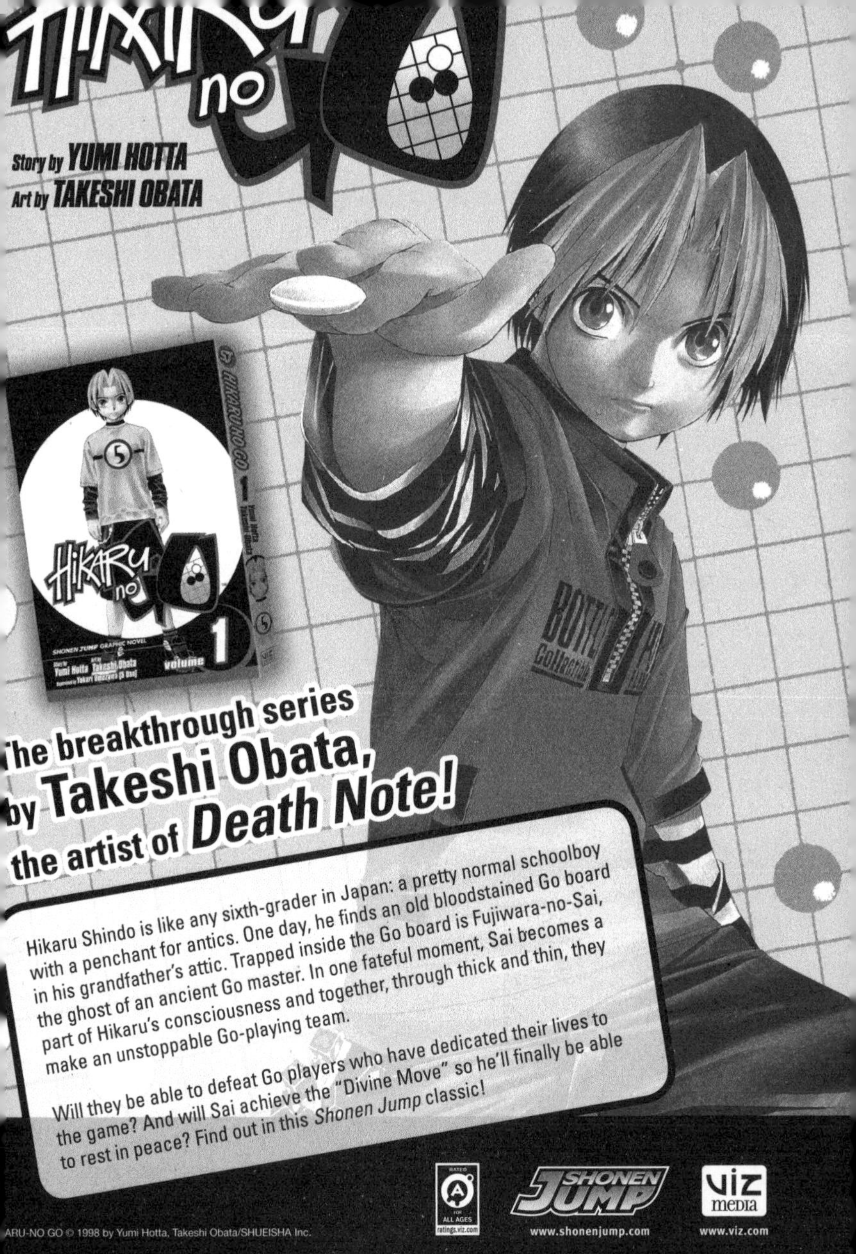
no
Story by YUMI HOTTA
Art by TAKESHI OBATA
HIKARU no
SHONEN JUMP GRAPHIC NOVEL
Story by Yumi Hotta Art by Takeshi Obata
volume 1
The breakthrough series by Takeshi Obata, the artist of Death Note!
Hikaru Shindo is like any sixth-grader in Japan: a pretty normal schoolboy with a penchant for antics. One day, he finds an old bloodstained Go board in his grandfather's attic. Trapped inside the Go board is Fujiwara-no-Sai, the ghost of an ancient Go master. In one fateful moment, Sai becomes a part of Hikaru's consciousness and together, through thick and thin, they make an unstoppable Go-playing team.
Will they be able to defeat Go players who have dedicated their lives to the game? And will Sai achieve the "Divine Move" so he'll finally be able to rest in peace? Find out in this Shonen Jump classic!
RATED A FOR ALL AGES ratings.viz.com
SHONEN JUMP
www.shonenjump.com
VIZ media
www.viz.com
ARU-NO GO © 1998 by Yumi Hotta, Takeshi Obata/SHUEISHA Inc.

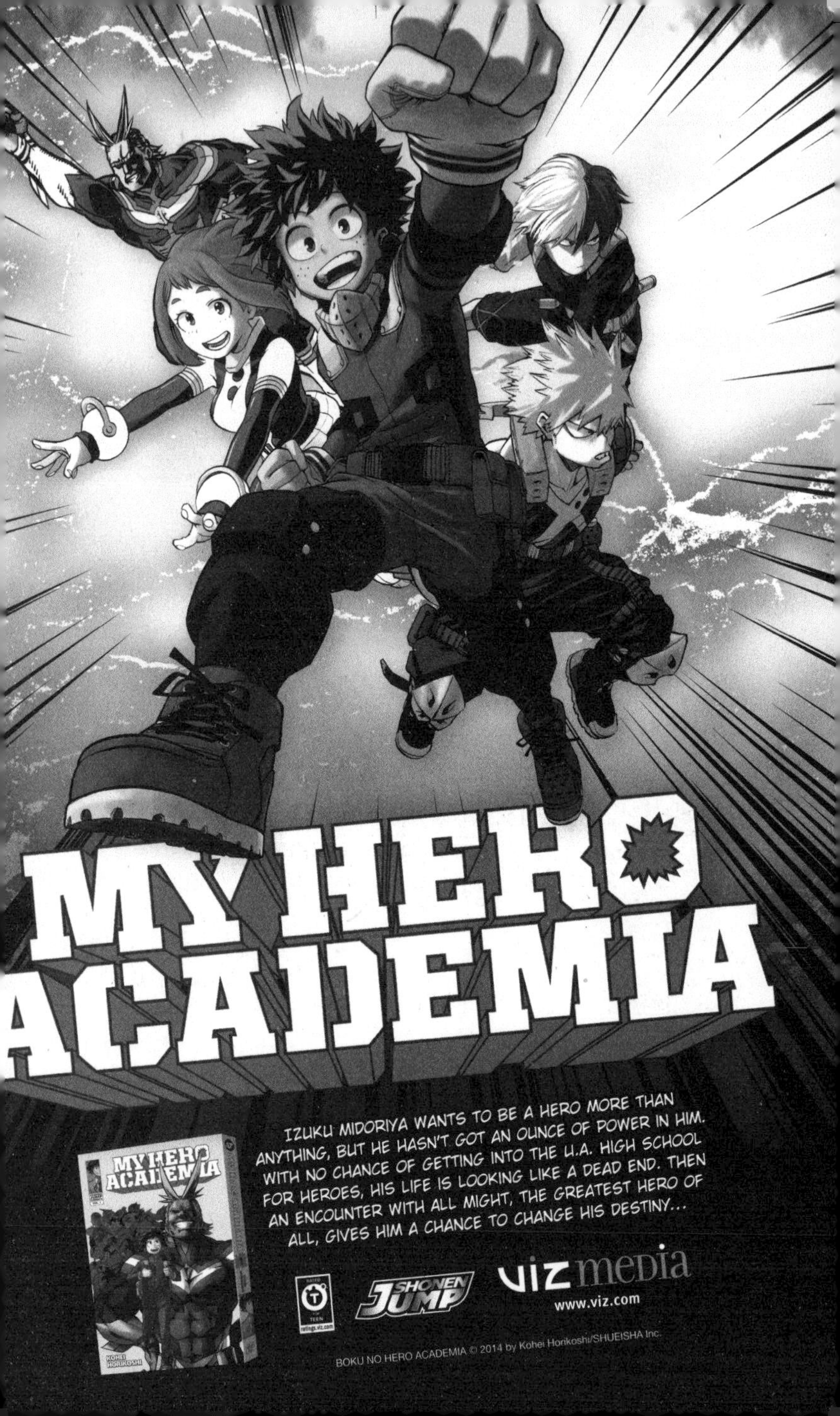
MY HERO ACADEMIA
IZUKU MIDORIYA WANTS TO BE A HERO MORE THAN ANYTHING, BUT HE HASN'T GOT AN OUNCE OF POWER IN HIM. WITH NO CHANCE OF GETTING INTO THE U.A. HIGH SCHOOL FOR HEROES, HIS LIFE IS LOOKING LIKE A DEAD END. THEN AN ENCOUNTER WITH ALL MIGHT, THE GREATEST HERO OF ALL, GIVES HIM A CHANCE TO CHANGE HIS DESTINY...
MY HERO ACADEMIA
KOHEI HORIKOSHI
RATED T TEEN
ratings.viz.com
SHONEN JUMP
viz media
www.viz.com
BOKU NO HERO ACADEMIA © 2014 by Kohei Horikoshi/SHUEISHA Inc.

A PREMIUM BOX SET OF THE FIRST TWO STORY ARCS OF ONE PIECE!

A PIRATE'S TREASURE FOR ANY MANGA FAN!

STORY AND ART BY EIICHIRO ODA

Comes with EXCLUSIVE POSTER and the ROMANCE DAWN mini-comic!

As a child, Monkey D. Luffy dreamed of becoming King of the Pirates. But his life changed when he accidentally gained the power to stretch like rubber...at the cost of never being able to swim again! Years later, Luffy sets off in search of the "One Piece," said to be the greatest treasure in the world...

This box set includes VOLUMES 1-23, which comprise the EAST BLUE and BAROQUE WORKS story arcs.

EXCLUSIVE PREMIUMS and GREAT SAVINGS
over buying the individual volumes!

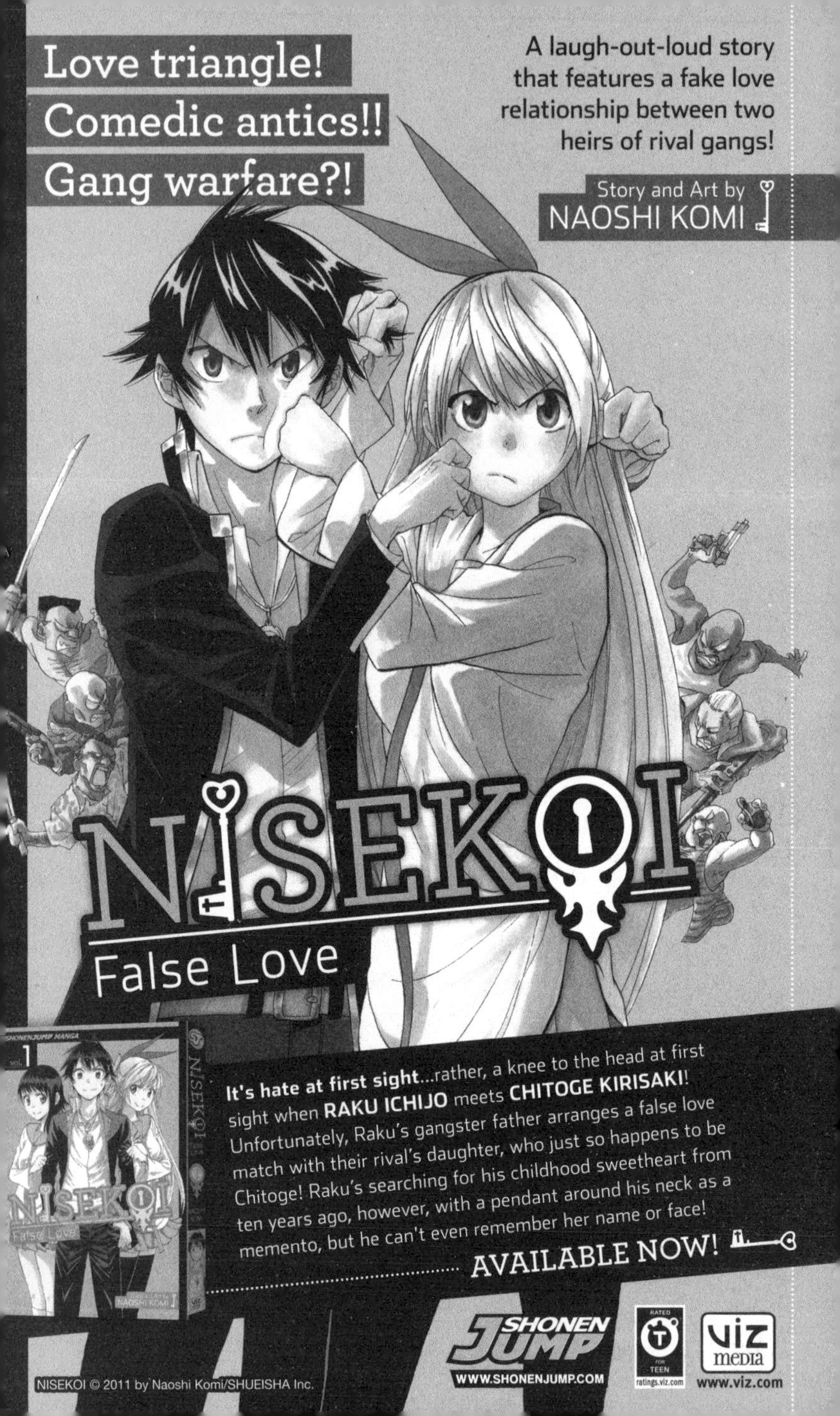

Love triangle!
Comedic antics!!
Gang warfare?!
A laugh-out-loud story that features a fake love relationship between two heirs of rival gangs!
Story and Art by NAOSHI KOMI
NISEKOI
False Love
It's hate at first sight...rather, a knee to the head at first sight when RAKU ICHIJO meets CHITOGE KIRISAKI! Unfortunately, Raku's gangster father arranges a false love match with their rival's daughter, who just so happens to be Chitoge! Raku's searching for his childhood sweetheart from ten years ago, however, with a pendant around his neck as a memento, but he can't even remember her name or face!
AVAILABLE NOW!
SHONEN JUMP
WWW.SHONENJUMP.COM
RATED T FOR TEEN
ratings.viz.com
VIZ media
www.viz.com
NISEKOI © 2011 by Naoshi Komi/SHUEISHA Inc.

You're Reading the
WRONG WAY!

HAIKYU!! reads from right to left, starting in the upper-right corner. Japanese is read from right to left, meaning that action, sound effects and word-balloon order are completely reversed from English order.

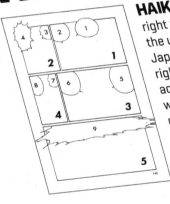